"**The new face of the environment.** This is a personal story about activism and [Manos'] road home is a long and tortuous one. Idealistic young men and women should take heed of the price one must pay to live according to high principles. **Manos' writing style is poetic and flowing,** especially when he writes about plains animals and their landscape. Although the language of the street often makes its way into his prose, there's no denying his writing glows when he writes about the environment. **The reader may come away filled with a certain sadness** that the author suffered from bad decisions and even worse behavior. **But an abiding love for a special part of the world has helped him rise above his flaws and become a better man. This is a story not often told.**" — Yvonne Marcotte, *Epoch Times*, New York staff

———————

"**If you haven't joined the movement after reading *Ghetto Plainsman*, then you haven't read the book.**" — Judge Maryellen Hicks, and host of KKDA "Speakout"

———————

What they're saying about Great Plains Restoration Council

(www.gprc.org):

"GPRC's ecological perspective has been an invaluable help in giving our youth opportunity to learn about nature, to connect with the environment, to enjoy it, love it, develop a sense of ownership of it, responsibility to protect it and to keep it clean and healthy for future generations." — Ana Colin-Hernandez, Peer Advocate Coordinator, AIDS Outreach Center

———————

"GPRC's goal of building a national movement of young people taking care of their own health through taking care of the special places on Earth is one we at Patagonia wholeheartedly believe in. GPRC combines hands-on work, community building, and action. Their leadership in the communities they work in is a vital inspiration for both growth and change." — Yvon Chouinard, Founder and Owner, Patagonia, Inc.

———————

"**In his fascinating new book, *Ghetto Plainsman*, Jarid Manos fashions peace, beauty and hope from the unlikely raw materials** of his own personal biography and his observations of the grave dangers facing our shared environment. Part detailed memoir, part sophisticated manifesto and call to action, *Ghetto Plainsman* is one jolting, shocking read, but a ride well worth taking." — Bill Nevins, *FIVE Magazine*

GHETTO PLAINSMAN

by Jarid Manos

Illustrations by Adrián Torres

Cover photograph by Jarriel Jones

Design by Brian Blankenship

Library of Congress Cataloging-in-Publication Data

Manos, Jarid.
Ghetto Plainsman/Jarid Manos
[Biography]
p.cm.

ISBN13: 978-1-60414-760-5

www.jaridmanos.com

Originally published by Temba House Press.

Manufactured in the United States of America

"Silence is the absolute poise or balance of body, mind and spirit. The man who preserves his selfhood is ever calm and unshaken by the storms of existence — not a leaf, as it were, astir on a tree: not a ripple upon the surface of the shining pool... his, in the mind of the unlettered sage, is the ideal attitude and conduct of life."

— Ohiyesa, 1911, [Santee Dakota Sioux]

"...unmistakably identifiable by a crudely-emblazoned clenched-fist "Earth First!" and other prison graffiti-style cult tattoos on his arm and shoulder."

— *Varmint Hunter Magazine*

"Peace is not this utopian idea of dashing through a field of dandelions, you know; it's hard work."

— Aqeela Sherrills, who brokered the historic peace treaty between the Crips and Bloods in South-Central Los Angeles

Foreword

HOUSEKEEPING

This book took me eight years to write.

Many people have wanted to know how I got into my work of protecting our endangered Prairie Earth and creating Ecological Health programs that serve our threatened youth. I'm very aware that the last thing people think when they see me walking down the street is, "Oh that dude saves prairie dogs and helps kids help themselves get healthy!" I know I'm an odd mix to most people, a streetsmart dude who's also in love with America's flyover country, the Great Plains. My path to this work can't be summed up in a sound bite. When I mentioned to a few people that I wanted to write a book about the violence that was really going on in the American West, it was suggested to show it through my own experiences, how I changed, and how and why I got involved. It's taken several years to let go of this story, a painful reminder of an angry, reactionary, and undeveloped young man unconsciously seeking more than just immediate survival. But my work is ultimately not about me.

Here in this crucible-like first decade of the new millennium, I am so focused, so driven toward the practical implementation of visionary ideas, so interested in bringing people together from all walks of life, of all colors, cultures and communities, that it's hard to imagine the angry, radical militant I once was. My former backlash hatred against my enemies, against a whole slate of planetary destroyers and those who tried to smash, consume or keep me down, quite honestly, made me little different than the Hate People themselves. Hate and anger are so unproductive. I am uninterested in blame or politics.

So much of modern life is immature and profane. My work with Great Plains Restoration Council (GPRC) is focused on building a new path of maturity, sustainability, health and wellness for our tenancy here on Earth. As I look over this book before it goes to print, I think, "It's funny the distances we must go to learn something and get somewhere." I haven't arrived by any means, but I can say I've come a long way. I've found something worth keeping, worth living and dying for. And that is our incredible living blue and green Earth, and our children's health and long, *long*-term future.

In this book, in order to keep the flow concise and protect the innocent and not so innocent, I've made minor adjustments or combinations of some names, places and events. A small portion of this book has been fictionalized in this way. This was done for thematic efficiency, to protect identities, and also to allow me as a writer a little literary license. I wanted to stretch my wings here, rather than write an encyclopedia.

Any possible likenesses real or imagined are not intended to disparage any person. There is also a bit player named "Martin" who is a composite of two people. Dialogue has been painstakingly reconstructed in order to provide the reader with the most precise essence of a person's character. Outside of these minor adjustments you have a straight-shot non-fiction parable.

Parable because when I finished the manuscript and had editors go over it, they continued to tell me that what I had, among other things, was an ongoing analogy between the problems of the Earth and those of the body. Body and Earth, Soul and Soil, all are inseparable to me, and the health or disease of any of these affects the other. "Body" ultimately comes to represent all of us, our civilization.

Some of what follows is ugly and embarrassing. When I consider the editors' comments, I see how I decided to keep some things and omit others. Some omitted events are more outlandish than those recorded here, some boring as hell, but they are not integral to the theme of the book. In any case, I wrote a book that made me take risks.

My business is now 'in the street' and of course it bothers me because I'm an extremely private person. Hell, my dream job used to be an anonymous baggage handler at the airport.

I have always regarded the human world as mostly a war zone. This war zone outlook colors the story, the journey, and my whole life even today. But compared to so many others, people and animals, I've still had an incredibly blessed, easy life. I thank God for how lucky I am to be healthy, vital, and alive.

CONTENTS

SECTION SEVEN

SECTION EIGHT

Prologue

'80s Reel

Sitting in my drawers beneath the Harbor Bridge, drinking a $1.79 six-pack of Schaefer beer and jug of Gallo Chablis, one right after the other, taking in the world around me. Our seedy old North Beach side of downtown Corpus Christi is sweltering... This hot Texas sun... The bridge keeps me in shadow.

The weight of the traffic pushes down on the bridge seams overhead. Wonder what'd happen if the bridge just smashed down on top of me. Maybe it'd block out all the thinking. Too much thinking.

Head hurts too much. I wanna give in, pass out. Can't stop this low panic inside... Shit, I'm still a teenager and I can't shake this fucked-up feeling I've already used up my life and ain't nothing else to rebuild like I thought. I'm supposed to be starting a new life.

There's a giant abyss up ahead but I can't see it, just sense it. Approaching, and getting closer. And at any moment I'm gonna step into it without knowing —

And if I did?

* * *

Dear Reader,

In this life, there have been moments when I suddenly asked myself:
Where the hell are you? Right now? Right this minute?

All I'm gonna say is, if you've ever had zero confidence or struggled or suffered in any way, maybe you will endeavor to *cause less pain.*

Because you understand.

SECTION ONE

"Violence is just another form of communication."

— overheard on Ludlow Street, Lower East Side, NYC

CHAPTER ONE

If You Were Missing

"This is how you kill a wounded duck," my father said, thrusting the hen mallard up so I could see. "You can do it two ways. Grab the neck in both fists like a rope and pull in opposite directions and you can tear the inside apart without breaking the skin. That's how we used to do it in the slaughterhouse. That's how we had to make blood sausage for those Polish people. The blood fills up the gap and hardens, and they slice it, cook it, and eat it."

I saw the duck's stiff tongue sticking out, like she was gagging on something. She struggled again in his grip, her bright orange feet trying to kick at his hand. A drop of blood, bright red lung blood, rolled off her tongue and fell into the water.

"But this way is better. You only need one hand." He grabbed her by the head in his right fist and spun her around, wringing her neck multiple times. Feathers puffed off and wafted away. Her wings fluttered and died down. "You don't want to shoot them again because you'll ruin the meat with all that shot."

I learned all about duck hunting as a kid, hauling decoys and paddling the canoe off the marshy shores of Lake Erie for my father. He and I rarely spoke unless it had something to do with work or a job he needed me to do. I didn't mind. I already liked the silence. And getting to go to Lake Erie took my mind off things in the same way hard work did, off problems that otherwise weighed me down like an anvil. My father was the standard yellow-brown-skinned immigrant who saw the world's value only in how much hard work, especially physical labor, was accomplished and how much farther ahead he could get that day. He hated personal expression. And he liked to hunt and fish, but not for the outdoor experience of it. What mattered was getting the kill, the landing, the final acquisition of things that were not things. Meat in the freezer, or sometimes just the kill if it wasn't edible.

Back in the blind, he snored as the Sun rose higher, blazing light across the marsh.

There wasn't a cloud in the sky. It was going to be what he called a bluebird day, when ducks stayed put and enjoyed the sunshine, or flew sky-high. For good hunting, you needed a blustery, cold, stormy day with heavy clouds that stirred the ducks up, kept them low and kept them moving.

My mind drifted back to earlier this morning. Me rowing out here in the silence, setting the decoys in the pre-dawn blackness, leaving him behind in the blind, the Moon wobbling on the water. Sweet-wet-muck smelling fresh lake water. The canoe paddle dipping in. The open black horizon of the lake had pulled at me.

My legs began to cramp from sitting still. Hate to sit. I checked his watch. It was only 9:30. We were supposed to stay here till 12, or at least that's how long the permit was for. I checked the safeties on the guns.

His sleeping head was slumped sideways against the flimsy wooden panels of the blind. Some powdered donut sugar had fallen on his hard black stubble beard. His hunter-green baseball cap was pulled down over his face, but I could still see the three hairs poking out of one of his fleshy nostrils. He had a stern look on his face, a scowl, even while sleeping.

That look never seemed to go away. As far back as I could remember, it was always there. It flowed down between his thick black eyebrows, down his big sloping nose and onto his lips, which seemed to have a natural outline to them, though they were creased and dry. He had strands of white in the short curls of his inky black hair that stuck out the back of his cap.

I glanced at his wader boots, then my wader boots. I looked at the two thermoses, one filled with coffee, the other hot chocolate. Hate coffee. I picked up a donut and slowly ate it, making sure I wiped off any powdered sugar left on my face.

The sun would be warm on our faces, I thought, if it weren't for the thatched cover over our heads. I wanted to feel that sunlight. When I thought of God I automatically thought of the Sun. I looked up through the rectangular gap of the blind, out at the blue sky. The gap was only wide enough to stand up in and shoot from. There was a viewing slit through the wood in front of our faces, or if you wanted, you could peek over the rim, while scanning for ducks to be ambushed.

I wanted to talk to him.

I looked down at my boots. Involuntarily shivering from the chill and tiredness and lack of movement, I sat on my hands.

Looking over at him again, I took one hand from under my legs and made as if to poke him awake. I stopped. My eyes strayed to the imprint of the wood grain bench on the back of my hand. Then focused back on him.

I let my hand fall to my lap. He always looked so mad. His snore, a steady rise and fall sub-rhythm, had begun to sound almost soothing and peaceful. I heard two shotgun blasts in the distance, muted punches of sound reverberating across the flat marsh.

I knew very little about my father. The main thing discussed was what work I had to do, couched in his ever-present disapproval and disgust with me, and that was it. As a child I certainly never felt man enough, period, even though I tried to prove myself through the constant hard labor I hated at the time, but would greatly appreciate much later for the physical fortitude it did instill in me.

I knew hard labor could refute his sneering insinuations that I wanted to be "body-beautiful." I couldn't help how I looked and I refused to even consider what he was accusing (that was I gay); I just knew that hard work would beat out of me any traces of being one of "those" kinds of people. He was simply and always an unreachable man. His scowl, his specter, and the belt, along with the assignments of endless physical labor, summed him up for me. The only time I saw him smile was for pictures. A mongrel from far Southern Italy who came over on a boat inside his mother's belly, it seemed to me he carried a certain level of shame or self-consciousness for being a short yellow-brown immigrant man in American society, especially in the era he grew up in, perhaps overcompensating with his stiffness, perpetual scowl and baseball cap worn too high. He'd never spoken about it, so it was only much later, after I asked him during an unannounced end-all visit I made, after many years of absence, that he revealed our ancestors were not just from Southern Italy but traced to North Africa and the Moors. He seemed embarrassed to admit it.

By then he was an old man; he looked like a short Osama bin Laden. He shook his head and said, "They were called the Moors."

That was all I got out of him. But it was interesting to me, and answered many questions of not only why the world reacted to me like it did, especially as I got older, but also my very strong genetic impulses toward Open Country. I had to do my own research, with the help of a genealogist librarian in Colorado. I'm intensely desert. My nomadic blood traces across the entire desert trade routes of the Mediterranean, North Africa, the Middle East, and Western Asia.

I learned that Saracens was another word for Moors, which is another word for African Arabs. Saracens was additionally more broadly applied to include desert people from the Middle East. Pre-Islamic and Islamic, Pagan, Animist, pre-Christian and Christian, the entire region was a fascinating upheaval of blood mixtures written in thousands of years of great journeys, personal turmoil, tribalism, conquests, horrid slaughters, wholesale ecological devastation and climate change, and reverse conquests. Berber/Tuareg, Bedouin, Arab, African, Turk, Asiatic, Phoenician, Southern Coastal Spanish, Italian and French all became tied together by the Mediterranean Sea and the dry lands beyond. Countries have always been artificial political boundaries. Through this story I garnered a deeper sense of time and connections. The dark blue Mediterranean, ringed by aqua shallows, at one time filled with wild dolphins, untouched underwater caves, and teeming shoals of fish (all diminished or degraded now) and bordered by African grassland steppes that became European empire granaries that became desertified, was equally a fertile combustion place for the mixing of peoples on its African, European and Asiatic coasts. Often, this occurred through wars and their aftermath, sometimes just through the nomadic impulse and trade that the region embedded. Like the mixing of its legendary spices, anything could come up.

But despite strong ancestral impulses, the long avid agility of nomadic people of dry Open Country, I really have no identity. My culture has been the street. And when you have to constantly face being seen for whatever ethnic identity a person thinks you are, or the irritating, intrusive question "What are you?" thousands of times from people of all races and colors, you don't want to be anything except left alone. I'm proud of my desert heritage, but ultimately, as an Old World plainsman more interested in the times before the Qu'ran and the Bible, I will never really belong to any race or within any boundaries. I'll always just be the stray dog, the plainsman, the nomad traveler through life and across lines, fitting in nowhere even if able to blend into many streets around the world. When my work is done here (in this longest of commitments ever), I'm sure I will have moved on again, disappeared. Live simple and quiet.

As a kid, I couldn't hate my father. I would try, it would flicker up, then fall flat, dissipate. I just felt nothing. I sensed, or wanted to believe, that somehow he was different, even though the belt, and especially my universal sense of suffocation, was attached to him too. But I hated other people, including my paper route customers who smiled in my face and said insane bad things under their breath thinking I didn't hear them, and the big Polish kid, and especially all the old men who followed me around in the park and the street and tried to do things to me. I wanted to kill them. I knew where the guns were. I knew that would ruin my whole life. I knew, even then, that I was trapped, with no way out.

CHAPTER TWO

Who Would You Be?

I still dream about the silent flash of fireflies in the welling darkness, the Ohio-humid slickness of bare underarms in the summer dusk, dip of a paddle in sweet water…

In moments of quiet, when I allow myself to think back to my earliest years, I again feel that internal flushed heat that stays in your body when the air is nearly 100% humidity and there is nowhere for it to escape.

Separate from all the bad feelings, I think there lies in me a small, private grieving for what was once there in the Ohio country, even though I only knew its last, dying breaths.

The Ohio I remember was such a physically hard place to live in. Damp no matter what season, frigid in winter and boiling hot in the summer. But over the course of my youngest years, before I finally made my breakout, a personal relationship formed with my natural surroundings, built on mutual resilience.

Daddy long-legs, I thought. From up above I used to watch the high-stepping spiders, and I wondered if they were now crawling over me. Having tried to balance on the aluminum guard of the window well, I lay crumpled upside down at the bottom, my sneakers pushing into the sky. The glass shards sticking into my head and the backs of my arms made me feel prickly, crinkly. Hot. Sticky. When I rolled my head, I felt — *heard* — the crunching of glass inside my skull. Like I had a big red grin munching on something it wasn't supposed to back there. I had finally succeeded in balancing upright with no hands on the window well guard.

When I fell backwards, around the age of three, my head cracked wide open on the basement window brick ledge. Hot blood flowed out. I lost a lot of it and they had to give me a transfusion. Lying upside down, I worried if I was going to be in trouble again on this perfect cloudless day.

They never got the blood removed from the brick ledge, and over the years the stain grew darker and forgotten.

Since then I've been prone to what I call my "passouts." At certain times, I just start to lose consciousness. My head begins to feel very heavy, or squeezed, while behind my eyes I sense a fizzy gray lightness approaching. A strong yearning to fall into that lightness wells up inside me. That yearning is my definition of pure desire.

Over time, I became able to mostly hold my passouts at bay, at least for a little while, since they start suddenly, but approach gradually. I've managed my passouts for so long that I hide them well. As long as I can get someplace to put my head down, or even close my eyes for a few minutes, I can control them. A lack of being able to do so, or stress or anxiety, or people talking too much, seems to trigger attacks.

In my passouts, especially as I began to grow older, I'd often go into a wild, shimmering, whispering world, into a wilderness so deep it transcended comprehension.

It was like falling into a living painting that folded up and around me, swallowing me whole. Slanted animal eyes that glinted from the edge of darkness, the dip of my palm into warm river water, or the sense of suddenly turning around, seeing my own trail stretching back through an infinity of open grassland beneath a blue and pink, rose-hued horizon at twilight, gave me promises.

Sometimes, in the background of all this, even though I couldn't actually see her, and everything was so unformed, I would sense a very dark-skinned woman wrapped in wind-blown white robes and veil, blue-black arm extended, beckoning. Her original feet were planted in the Earth, and for some reason I always knew her back was leaning into the West, even at night when the Sun was down. I knew she was wedded to the Great Sun, who (*kneel down, press your forehead into the ground*) I knew was my Overwhelming True Father.

The Shadow World was my secret sharer. For the longest time, I didn't get what that meant to me.

My little low-rider banana bike, painted a sparkling bronze, served early on as my main mentor of freedom. I loved to hang out in the park, near the pond, where I could catch catfish and bluegills and hope for a bass, or at the playground on the other side where I could just kick around in the dirt or make myself dizzy on the self-propelled merry-go-round.

But sometimes, bad people hung out there, even in the daytime. I quickly learned to spot them before they saw me. Sometimes this big teenager would appear and always cause problems. One time he stole my wire basket of bluegills and, after dumping them on the grass, stuck firecrackers into their gasping mouths and blew them up. I'd heard he also did it to cats and dogs, the ones he could catch, only instead of in their mouths he'd jam the firecrackers up their butts, after tying their legs.

The public bathrooms were by the playground. White middle-aged men with hanging faces and rabid eyes would often hang out there, always with these looks like they were crazy or had forgotten something. They would stare at me, especially at my ass, or follow me with these sick-looking grins. I wanted to shout: "Leave me alone! I ain't one of you!" It wasn't only in the park that I sensed or noticed these threatening men. By the school, by the ARCO gas station, the corner store… really they might show up anywhere, and leer, or start following. I had to always be on guard.

Under an overcast sky, I glided on my bike toward the restrooms, scanning the area from side to side. Why did they have to set the bathrooms so close to the woods? Approaching, I tensed and hesitated for a moment, even though I could barely hold my pee any longer.

There was a car parked down there. I couldn't tell if somebody was inside. I didn't see anybody hanging out, either. Making one more pass just to be sure, I directed my radar into the woods behind the low brick building. They were the only woods I would never go into.

I swung off the bike, trying not to let my tennis shoes make any noise in the gravel path. Leaning the bike against the warm brick on the WOMEN's side, I walked silently around to the gaping entrance of the MEN's. Pressed up against the brick wall, feeling its soaked-up warmth in my palms, I leaned in, listening.

I whipped around the corner and went in, trying to avoid the puddles on the discolored concrete floor. Partially afraid, but bladder bursting, I decided to just get it all over with. I rushed to the stall, ready for reverse flight if somebody happened to be in there. The gray cinderblock stall only came up halfway from the floor. I peeked around. It was empty. Somebody had pooped on the metal seatless toilet and the toilet paper roll had fallen in, with a long sheet leading up and over and onto the floor, the brown soak gradually spreading. There was some piss on the floor in front, and large wet foot tracks across the restroom. But at least there was nobody in here.

I hurried to the urinal and tried to calm down so I could pee.

I stood up on my toes a little so when the stream came out it'd hit higher up and not splash on me. Trying too hard to relax, worrying about my exposed back, I closed my eyes, counting numbers. Counting backwards and forwards. I kept my ears open, listening. All I could hear was my heart beating. Good.

My bladder finally relaxed and a hot pitch of urine forced out, then flowed, hitting the back of the urinal, splashing. I didn't care. I rolled my head back with relief, willing it to flow all out and hurry up too.

Gravel crunched beneath footsteps outside. I jolted. I shut my pee off the best I could and quickly tried to jam myself back into my drawers. I whipped around and rushed for the door, zipping up, just as the big hairy pink-faced man came bearing down on me through the entranceway. He was grinning with that same crazy look they always have.

Eyes wide, wires inside buzzing and hot I kept my head down and tried to rush through to the side, wincing in the last moment before contact. I hit the side of his belly and he spread his arms out wide to snag me like a gill net. He rotated and tried to flatten me against the wall, humping, hairy arms and breath and everything stinking like lunchmeat, trying to hold me in, grabbing for my dick and balls, and I squirmed out and bolted. I flung myself to my bike, hearing his shoes squishing backward in the puddles of liquid on the floor. Hot and jerking like I wanted murder, I grabbed the bike and hopped onto it in one motion, pedaling as fast and hard as I could out of there.

I was horrible in school. Didn't give a shit about my lessons; what did anything in the books have to do with me? Didn't get along with anybody there either and I avoided them. I always felt dirty, second class, out of place, constantly embarrassed, secretly scared, and never tough enough. I was not big yet, but all the kids still wanted to fight me or beat me down, especially the big Polish kid whose grandfather lived on the same street. People thought because of my sour, silent face that I was always ready to fight, which was crazy. The teachers were just as bad; after all, they wanted to fit in and be cool too. And people bugged me about my "alien" or "devil" eyes which have this desert slant and very light yellow-green tint that's indigenous to nomadic Tuareg people of the Sahara Desert, and which I later learned to cover with the bill of a baseball cap or shades or both.

Earlier, by the time I was seven or so, I got my first paid job pedaling two different newspapers every morning and afternoon. I kept my prized low-rider bicycle wiped clean and shiny, but I'm sure the wire newspaper baskets I'd bolted to its rear wheel compromised some of its thunder.

Two things stand out from that time. From the drugstore I'd bought a notebook that had a cover painting of a grinning, skull-faced, hard-hatted man driving a bulldozer forward, his blade smashing the living jungle of life, tossing magnificent animals, bald eagles, lions, everything, to the side. Some were upside down in mid-air. All the animals' eyes looked blankly at me, as if they couldn't see anymore, and their tongues were hanging out. And, second, as I rode my bike, my recent attention to telephone pole after telephone pole made out of killed tree after killed tree. As I looked around, and saw telephone poles endlessly everywhere, and bulldozers approaching some of my favorite places, a great worry began to creep in, like a hand reaching for my throat. I would touch some of the telephone poles, dead trees stuck into concrete, seeing how they were stripped of all their tree parts, imagining their tops filled with branches.

In winter, every morning at 4 a.m., I forced myself out of my warm bed to get dressed in many layers of heavy clothing. When I was finished, only my eyes were open to the subzero temperatures. So I wouldn't dilute my sharp night vision, I never turned on any lights while getting dressed, nor did I look directly into any streetlights outside. Using natural and honed stealth, I'd slip out unheard. In my snowsuit, facemask and big boots I was a little abominable snowman, sweating beneath all those layers. My hooded wool facemask was crusty with frozen exhale and probably a little snot. It only had two holes for my eyes.

With the whole town sleeping, those early mornings cast me out into a pitch-black world of silence. The crunch of my tires on the hard crust of frozen sidewalk snow and ice, and the uneven humming of the pedal-generator that juiced light into my feeble bike headlamp depending on how hard and steadily I pedaled, were the only sounds.

At one of my last stops, at the top of Plum Street, with the wooded valley below, I stopped at the driveway and laid my bike down like I always did. Folding up the paper in my mittens, I walked up and dropped it on the porch, always careful not to make any sound.

A large American elm, rare in its life and age, hovered above me. Its gnarled branches twisted up into the pitch-black universe. As I got back to my bike I stopped, and just let my arms fall to my sides.

I became fixated on the old elm's upper branches, where they met against the starless, pre-dawn sky.

The frigid air had been still the entire route, which I was glad for because then the only windchill I had to deal with was human-powered.

I pulled off my facemask. A small cloud of steam puffed out of my wet hair and face as sweat instantly evaporated. I could see my shadow on the sidewalk created by the fluorescent streetlight behind. A wind was rising. The handful of desiccated leaves still attached to the top branches began to twitch back and forth. Then the branches themselves moved slightly, stiffly. I felt the tree might suddenly bend over in one sweeping arc, as if to scoop me up. My legs were loose, and I thought I might just fall back into the puffy snow, maybe sleep for a long time. I quickly glanced at my feet. Rocky, frozen, broken pavement.

The wind grew, but its edge softened. Around me, although my face and scalp had started to freeze, a gradual reversal of that cold air... The air passed over me in a silent whispering stream, moving three or four remaining leaves high above my head; seemed to have a current of warmth — almost balm — inside it. How could it be? This was the middle of frozen deep winter.

Standing with the tropical breeze evaporating the last of my head's moisture, I began to sense I was shrinking, getting smaller and smaller, and warmer and warmer inside. The leaves rattled, the wind blew in my ears, I felt drowsy, shrinking, comforted... intoxicated... like I could just fall into (her arms?)

The giant elm tree, the rough wooded valley below, the twitching leaves, the punched-down field, the silence and pitch-black sky... Sky so black and open it even swallowed the stars, stretching further and further away from me, up into the heavens now, pulling me with it. And I wanted to go. Somewhere. I knew wherever would be so much better than here.

Take me right now, I croaked in a small voice. Lord, how I wanted to go.

Out of my clouded, childhood haze, if I'd thought about the future at all, I could only ever dream of one place — Texas. It radiated in blue and yellow daylight, barely but always visible, a distant, promised land. From the first time I'd been brought to the state on a trip as a young child, somehow I knew it was home. It sparked ferociously in me, this great wide-open land of red-arching sunsets over grassy, spiked horizons that stretched from the wild blue sea coast inland toward some distance unknown. It carried with it intimations of ancestral land, of standing on an edge between worlds, where the prairie met the sea. When I had to leave Texas I'd secretly vowed I'd come back and live there, some day, somehow.

Aside from Texas, and more distantly, I occasionally saw myself older, raising a daughter on the beach of some tropical island, swimming, always swimming in the light blue sea, untangling her wet black hair, grains of sand glistening on her brown skin and coarse in the crevices of my sun-blackened hands, never cold. I don't know where this image came from.

A thought came: *You should just run away.*

I squeezed my eyes shut. But how? I don't know nothing! How'm I gonna get to Texas when I don't have any money? And there's no bus or anything. Shoot, I don't even know how to get to the next town!

You'll have to stick it out then; wait 'til you get a little older. Then take advantage of whatever you can get.

The thought of being trapped for that much longer sunk me like black muck.

The harassment only got worse each year that I got older, but I was way too ashamed and embarrassed to tell anybody, even if there had been somebody I felt I could've trusted. I was aware that my body was drawing attention, even if I didn't understand exactly why. Old men stalked me, drove alongside me, stopped me, followed me, taunted me. And they all made comments about my butt, which I couldn't quite figure out. I couldn't look at any of them, in my mind they were all monsters from stinking caves, and as they came for me and as I fled from one place to another to another, over and over and over again, I just knew that inside their small, squirming mouths all their teeth would be rotting. By nine, "Pretty Boy" was fighting words at school or on the street corners or out by the gas station where I picked up my bundle of papers. More than once, other kids tried unsuccessfully to make me stand on my head so it would force my ass to melt back into my body and go down. Although I was still small-bodied and more afraid than I would ever admit, I could fight my way out like a rat if cornered. One bleached-blonde woman in the town would taunt that I had a "colored girl's ass." She was the same woman who in the hot steaming summertime would suddenly go into fits at the mere sight of me, especially if I had my shirt off, and start chasing me, trying to hit me, screaming hysterically as I fled from her that I'd "turn into a Negro!" because, like the flip of a light switch, I instantly turned dark in the sun.

I only wanted to disappear more. My stealth came in handy when I needed to vanish. I was good everywhere, but especially in the woods, even in the fall when the ground was covered thick in dry leaves and twigs. I was most definitely proud when I read in a book that the same dry-woods stealth techniques I'd taught myself were what the Shawnee Indians had used to melt through the forests back when they'd lived here. Before they'd been slaughtered or forced out.

The big Polish kid at school was a constant problem. He was always trying to start shit. I wanted to hurt him, kill him. I did everything I could to bottle that anger up inside because I was scared I might go too far. And who knew what the consequences might be?

Raking leaves furiously one gray October afternoon, my face raw, I saw only red as I made large piles at the edge of the woodlot. That lurking lady down there had caught me by surprise and slapped me so hard I'd thought for a second I could see out my ear hole. As I used the inverted rake like a pitchfork to haul the leaves into the woodlot and scatter them, I noticed that the big Polish kid was banging around his grandparents' place. I could see him diagonally through the woodlot, cleaning up some things out by the street. He sure was ugly, I thought to myself as I raked harder. I thought about how I hated him. He was much bigger than me. A few grades older, too.

I took the longest construction nail I could find out of the coffee can by the porch and slipped it into the pocket of my second-hand corduroy jacket. I picked up the big leaf rake again and entered the woodlot, stalking across the brittle woods floor without cracking a twig or crunching a leaf.

He never noticed me until, just a few yards away, I leapt across the shallow marshy ditch and charged. In my mind I let out a bloodcurdling Haiiii-YAH!! But of course no sound came out of my silent throat.

I whapped that big Polish kid so hard with the leaf rake that he stumbled backwards.

Barely able to hold onto the huge rake, and shaking with anger and adrenaline, I hit him again. The long rake flew out of my grip.

He came at me. I grabbed his garbage can with both hands and hurled it at him. With a bang, that bounced off him too.

In the last second before he was on me with his fists, I took the nail out of my pocket and stabbed him in the shoulder. I don't know how much damage I did because his forward lunge made it rip back rather than go deep, but I squeezed out a prayer that I hurt him bad.

He beat the shit out of me. The whole left side of my face swelled up to twice its normal size, closing my eye and turning the mess as black and blue and bloody looking as day-old summer road kill.

In school, everybody wanted to touch my blood-bloated shiny purple face. I got a week of in-school suspension because they knew it wouldn't be punishment for me to be out. I argued that they had nothing to do with my life outside the school. Fell on deaf ears.

Stewing, I put together my own survival kit, consisting of the only three things I knew for sure in this world: 1) Everybody is a threat and filled with hate, 2) There is danger everywhere, and 3) Things are guaranteed to shift for the worse at any moment without warning.

CHAPTER THREE

Passage in Flight

There were parts of town where I could be alone. I hung out in the abandoned open-pit ore mine, or walked along the railroad tracks. I sometimes stopped and tried to imagine that wolves and elks and even buffaloes had once lived here, northern pikes had swum in every lake and stream, and billions of wild blue passenger pigeons had convulsed the sky before heading down to the Texas Gulf Coast prairie each autumn. Those giant flocks of big, sleek, native blue doves with the apple red breasts were extinct; people had killed them all off. Every last one.

I just couldn't picture how all those animals and birds, all that life, could've lived right here and now there was nothing. There was no real forest or prairie anymore, mostly just scraggly woodlots and rangy, old degraded fields growing back up into meadows. And in the house, alone in the bathroom or kitchen, I would stare at the metal sink faucet, and wonder: How did people make such a thing out of the woods? Or how about a tv? How did we get from there to here? Nothing even closely resembling those things existed out in the fields or in the ground. And further, water really did not come from the faucet, but again, from *out there*. My tightly closed perspective of the world became malleable.

I looked for black walnut, persimmon and white oak trees because I'd read of a giant green luminescent silk moth, called a luna moth, who used to live in the forest. I knew the trees they liked, especially the black walnuts, but couldn't find any.

Seeing a luna moth became an obsession. The big moths were not extinct, just very rare. In fact, this long-tailed, green silk moth became an unreachable apparition, a heart of the lost wilderness, an otherworldly green ghost sailing through the night woods of the past. Lunas were said to be a perfect ghostly-bright green, and 6 or 7 inches in length from tip to tip, with long tendrilled tails, a yellow and blue decoy eye on each hind wing, and giant feathery antennas. I studied everything I could find in the library about them.

I was mystified that, once they hatched from the cocoon, the giant luna moth did not eat for the rest of her or his life. After spending the whole winter cramped up, changing from caterpillar to such perfection, they only lived about four days, and if they didn't find a mate, they died alone, without ever connecting, without passing on their genes. Their entire life seemed geared toward just those few days of freedom — and a chance of momentary physical contact with a soulmate.

I had to see one. I had to see a luna moth alive, in the wild. I had to know that some were left, silently flying through the night.

Funny how I never even knew how close I lived to snowy cold Canada, whose border was just a short distance up into the swirling bowels of Lake Erie. I read and read. I liked the library. Ohio's forests and prairies had been America's first West. The Old Northwest. I found old books telling me about the land before colonists and settlers arrived. I wanted to know about my world, and what had happened here on land that I stood on. I'd read of the great Hinckley kill, where all the settlers of a newly-marked township had gotten together and, armed with long rifles, surrounded the primeval forest in a giant circle. They beat the bush as they all walked in, closing the noose, pushing every living wild animal into the center. Any that tried to break through were shot. At the end of the day there was a pandemonium of animals trapped in front of them, surrounded on all sides, and the people shot and killed them all, buffalo, elk, deer, wolves, bears, eagles, owls, lynx, wolverines, otters, martens, rabbits, foxes, birds, everything. Again, I was awestruck that all those animals had lived right here, right where my feet walked. I imagined the panic, the flames as the forest was cut down and set afire, the end-of-the-world flapping of crazed wild birds attempting to escape through the smoke and realizing they had nowhere else to go, everything, their entire world, crashing down.

The pile of death was so large it refused the settlers' attempts to burn it, and for weeks its rotting stench attracted so many vultures that they began returning every year. A legend arose and remains to this day that the "buzzards" come back each year to this spot and, in fact, the township has made a local holiday with festivities out of it.

One afternoon, ten, eleven years old, in the library I found a book with some very old sketches or etchings. As I remember it, flat, stiff line drawings showed colonists or conquistadors mingling with Indian people on the Atlantic coast or maybe in the islands. Some Indians were in canoes off the shore, frozen in motion. The Indian women were bare-breasted. One man in armor was effortlessly and bloodlessly cutting off the breast of a half-naked Indian woman with a big scissors. She was just staring face forward. The flat drawing, the idyllic setting, and the flat faces on everybody including the woman made it look like it was a simple, normal everyday act. Other pictures had Indian people tied up flat on their backs, side by side like sticks of cordwood, being held or shipped for slavery, a lot like those drawings I'd seen of African slaves stacked on ships of the Middle Passage.

My fluid motion and natural ability to move, sight unseen, in the woods and tallgrass prairie meadows increased with my need to retreat from people. I chewed on sassafras leaves, swallowing the juice. I ate sun-bursting blackberries, raspberries, gooseberries where I found them. In the grass meadows, bees, butterflies, all kinds of other insects, and hummingbirds buzzed around me as sun or rain soaked into thick waxy stalks of long grass. There was a large old garden, now an overgrown field, bordered by a gnarled apple tree that had a rusted, handmade iron tool hanging from it. My father said he'd once shot a possum in that field with nine babies clinging to her back. Her breasts were swollen pink with milk, and he had to hit each baby over the head with a hammer. That was the way it was. Nature was to be cleared. He had become a good American.

From Canada to Texas, our Midwestern thunderstorms are unlike any other on Earth. That heavy, pea-green afternoon darkness lowers as clouds condense, giant thunder rolls, pressure builds with the first few warning tongues of white-purple lightning, and then finally the deluge, the pounding, the roaring of the rain and the thunder, the shaking of the Earth herself…

I shuddered, thinking again about the men at school, or behind the gas station, or … trying to force them from my mind. They weren't people; they were *its*. I shook myself, trying to get even the thought of the "its" off me, out of me, as the skies above thankfully opened and raked cleansing rain down hard on me.

Too much pressure, I thought to myself. Another spring was coming on, but I only felt gray. Just don't want this stupid life anymore. Twelve years old and everything is shit. I am not one of *those* people. I'd rather be dead than be one of… one of *them*. What is it that makes them single me out?! I usually managed to avoid them getting too close or touching me, but they were always lurking somewhere, and they were always choosing me to come after. I wished I could kill them.

Need to be more of a man.

Thunderstorms drenched and shook the afternoon. No one was home. On impulse, I pulled off my windbreaker and shirt and ran around in the steady rain, ramming myself into trees, bouncing off them, bloodying my chest and face and arms. After a couple good tries I knocked the wind out of myself and fell to the grass, gasping.

I picked up my clothes and walked to the house, scraped flesh smarting.

I went into the bathroom, trying not to leave footprints on the floor from my wet socks. I turned on the lights, then shut them off. Gray afternoon light filtered in through the small opaque window, the old mustard wallpaper making the bathroom feel cramped. I stood in front of the mirror, dripping, skin scraped, breathing hard. I partially opened the window. I could hear rain pelting the rhododendron leaves outside.

I reached into the cabinet and picked up this old barbershop razor, the kind that folds like a jackknife.

Shivering and soaking wet, I drew the blade along the inside of my arm, staring at it with wide eyes. I tried to calm my breathing down. My belly jerked in and out. Slowly I pressed the blade into my skin, trying to gauge at what point it would cut me. I desperately needed to push it all the way in.

From out of nowhere, a thought came: *You should take care of yourself.*

A door slammed, and I jumped, cutting myself. Not much, but enough to draw blood. I heard keys clatter on the kitchen table. Panicking, I quickly shut the bathroom door and locked it.

Hurrying, I washed off the razor and put it back. I paced back and forth inside the tiny bathroom, unable to think, trapped. The window was small. I whirled around and caught the reflection of my small yellow body in the mirror. A tiny trickle of blood trailed down my arm. In the dull light it looked almost black, like a perfect little snake slipping out of my arm. I pulled on my clothes; listened intently for the moment to escape. When I was sure, I slipped out and bolted back into the rain, down across the creek, across the overgrown field that used to be a garden, and into the woods.

Around 13, after another trip to Texas (and vowing that I would return permanently, when I could just find a way to get there) we moved to another house. This was further south in a different county, way out in the country with a three-acre lake that had been earthen-dammed decades ago from a creek. My father had moved his way up the economic ladder, had suddenly made some money (so I figured out) in investments — a far cry from the early days. Though there was no communication, I could tell there was more money, mostly by the appearance of new work machines like 4WD trucks, tractors, hoists, snowplows, chainsaws, and all kinds of others signifying more labor for me. There was also the bigger house. And in the last few years I lived there, around Christmas there were airplane trips to someplace warm, like Mexico, where he could go ocean fishing, and/or hunt for ducks and doves. Aside from that, little changed. He still wore the same brown suit to work everyday.

Needing to be a man more than ever, I took up trapping for a year. I got a pellet gun. I fished. I tried to hunt squirrels and rabbits, and like other rural boys, trapped raccoons and possums. I wasn't very successful and soon quit, but when I was, it was brutal and bloody. I didn't understand. It was your normal, everyday country work, unthinking, unconscionable and grisly. You had to club the animals to death so you didn't ruin their fur. Sometimes, before they died, their eyes would hemorrhage and fill with blood.

The fur buyer's shed reeked of buckets of liquefying hide-scraped winter fat and that raw meat smell of dead naked bodies piled on cold, half-frozen ground in the corner. Above his head, hanging from the rafters and partially obscuring the lightbulb, was a long row of skinned pelts, mostly coons and a few foxes, each one stretched inside-out to dry on wire frames, their luxurious winter thick fur glistening through where the animal had been slit open across the rectum, peeled and inverted.

He rarely gave more than a few dollars for the furs of young raccoons or possums I brought in.

I went to work for a greenhouse.

I began buying my own clothes, to avoid having to wear the embarrassing second-hand or homemade or out-of-style things. Sometimes I wore the same outfit two days in a row, because I liked how fresh I thought I looked, and wanted to make it last, not realizing that I was just further emphasizing how out of touch I appeared.

Up in the east corral, although there were new machines for other work, I still had to split firewood the old-fashioned way, with a sledge and iron wedge or, if they were smaller logs, I could use an eight-pound maul and a good, strong overhead blow. But with my head so clouded these days, wanting to shut down all the time now, buckling under the pressure of holding so much in, I didn't really mind. I went on autopilot, and built up the cords of wood. It was during one of those afternoons that I became aware I'd been visualizing the stash of liquor bottles in the back room cabinet in the house. If I thought about it, the liquid inside all those shiny glass bottles beneath the sink might almost be magical. Bottles of liquor standing down there below the sink, in that silent back room, in the dark of the cabinet, all alone, liquid that might even be warm, hot. I thought about how good that might feel in my insides. Who would know if I took a bottle?

The woods on the other side of the lake were the closest I'd ever come to wilderness. They stretched up and over creased hills thick with hickory, oak, sassafras, beech and even a few black walnuts. How I sought out those black walnuts. I knew luna moths especially loved them.

The hills went down into creek bottomlands, and back up and down more wooded hills. Except for the occasional jet airline high over head, those woods stretched into silence. To the side of the house, there was a long-grass prairie meadow filled with Indiangrass, switchgrass, big bluestem and other wild grasses. Wildflowers reached up to the Sun, filling the green prairie with colors. Goldenrods, milkweeds, sunflowers, compass plants, prairie docks, blazing stars, spiderworts, orchids and lilies buzzed with tiger swallowtails, monarchs, red-spotted purples and other butterflies. Grasshoppers, dragonflies, and hummingbirds whirred. For me, it was like disappearing into a hidden pool. It was bigger than me. I knew it ended — I could walk to its end in half an hour — but it was my Prairie Earth. And by the corner of the east corral, there was an immense white oak, easily 400 years old, whose crown spread across the sky, who had already been an old tree when the first settlers arrived. Sometimes the oldest tree had been used to mark a boundary or survey corner. It had certainly known passenger pigeons, buffaloes and wolves, and I wondered if Tecumseh's Shawnee warriors had ever camped near its massive trunk.

I still spent all my free time outside. I had the sense that the constant pressure from people, the hate from all sides, could make me break, slip, cross a threshold. It was a simple equation: my hatred of them because of their hatred of me. I think as I got into my teens I was in a state of underlying panic, possibly even frozen, terrified of what I could become if I didn't ratchet myself down with self-control. I knew my anger made me capable of murder. That I could take these specific people out, and be glad to do it. That potential for loss of self-control was my biggest fear and biggest threat. My second biggest fear, as looming and impossible to deal with as the first, was that somebody might find out that I was having these… these feelings, this private attraction to… to… other guys. Ugh. These feelings came from nowhere; I was terrified of them. I hated myself because I couldn't help it. If only I could kill myself, kill that out of me. But I was too much a punk to even do that. My only consolation was that I could not imagine kissing another guy, and was still attracted to girls, if not that much. So there was still hope. I might be safe. As long as I never kissed no dude, there might be hope. Otherwise…

I put it out of my head. That would be the end of the world. I could not bear the thought of being… one of… couldn't even say it… one of them. *Those* people. That would be the worst life sentence. Hopeless, ugly, without light, without end. I'd rather be dead.

I focused on getting through each day. All I needed to do was make it through high school, and my escape plan would succeed and I wouldn't have to live on the street, likely fall into homelessness. I'd been more or less grasping onto this plan since I was ten years old.

I tried very hard to not think about the liquor bottles, but they were always in my thoughts now. Taunting me.

In school, I started passing out a lot. Right onto the desktop. I got in-school suspension again.

In the overheated History class one afternoon, with the lunch-stuffed students dozing off as the heavy teacher's face got redder and redder like an over-ripe tomato, I listlessly turned the pages in my textbook, ignoring the drone of his voice. I came across a small black and white photo in the bottom corner of the page that made me sit upright. It was the battle site at Little Bighorn, in Montana, where Crazy Horse and his crew wiped out Custer. The photo mainly showed the cavalry cemetery, just some white crosses stuck in the side of a small hill. But at the far right edge of the photo, you could see the grassland stretching out into a horizon that seemed infinite. Unlike my long-grass prairie, you could walk forever into those Great Plains, disappear to less than a speck. *And find what? What you think you might find over that horizon?* I stared through the little corner portal. Something familiar tingled in my belly. I promised right then that I would go.

Halfway through 9th grade, the vice-principal discovered me and began a sexual pursuit that lasted the rest of my years there. He was an old, leering, sharp-dressed faggot with dyed black hair that was a shock against his white cadaver skin and gray temples. He wouldn't leave me alone. I couldn't go to the urinal without him following me into the bathroom. He'd scurry up behind me and grab my shoulders, in hopes of pulling me backwards so he could see my dick, or brush up against my ass. He'd corner me in a stall or call me into his office...

The vice-principal wielded decades of power at the school and in the town. I knew I would be the one who lost if I said or did anything about it. He could do worse to me than I could ever do to him. And anyhow, I was brought up by my father not to complain. A man is supposed to be able to handle anything. Buck yourself up and quit whining.

I imagined killing the old faggot. Normally I carried a knife. Though I could easily have gotten guns if I'd wanted.

I broke from school whenever I could slip out undetected or with some excuse. But the VP knew. He even came out to the parking lot one day as I was bolting, just to let me know with his big Halloween grin that he was letting me get away with it. I still made no friends in this new school; I was too preoccupied. Each day was my challenge, and I was now robotically determined to make it through. It's weird how you can be both conscious and clouded at the same time.

I grew numb to the VP. Anyway, he wasn't the only one. They were everywhere; I was growing used to it, and I just had to be constantly on guard, wherever I went. On autopilot, I even began to butter up the old faggot with false shreds of friendliness so he'd write me passes out of there. He'd try to hold my hand momentarily as he handed me the slip of paper, a big, sick grin on his face like he was insane. I thought my knife would look good stuck in that face.

Sitting on the floor of the silent back room in the house, I swallowed my first gulps of stolen liquor. I began to feel warmer, comforted. Like an hourglass emptying of sand, the cloudy gray afternoon began to brighten. I pulled the hood of my sweatshirt up over my head, and drank the whole bottle, though I didn't even know what "vermouth" was. All I knew was that it was liquor. I became an alcoholic instantly, loving and needing that warmed-up/everything-not-so-bad feeling, and built my life around it, getting anything, beer mostly, wherever I could.

But I was a functional drunk, and did a pretty good job of hiding it. I took a job at a roadside diner out by a freeway exit/entrance ramp, a place where everybody was always going someplace else. I washed dishes, cleaned toilets, mopped floors, bussed tables, and did everything that was lowly enough that nobody else would do it. I worked full time hours, filling my afternoons and nights and Saturdays and Sundays, $2.50 an hour. I picked up dirty tampons and scrubbed off bathroom stall graffiti. Daily, I changed the highway 'Specials' sign out front with the help of an uneven aluminum extension ladder that more than once hurled me to the weather-broken asphalt. I scalded my hands raw washing egg-filthy plates and lipstick-smeared water glasses that still had ice cubes in them. I hauled buckets of grease and overstuffed, sliming, black Hefty bags of waste; I unclogged hair- and grease-snarled drains.

I wore a paper hat and a polyester uniform shirt. I didn't talk much. Time marched on. If I got too drunk, too hung over, I'd just puke till it was all out in one of the toilets I was cleaning, mints, guts, liquid heaves, and all. As effortlessly as high-class people holding a cocktail in one hand and a cigarette in the other, my left hand clutched the can of Comet and my right the heavy-duty plastic scrub brush.

One night as I was on my hands and knees under the kitchen's fluorescent lights struggling to get some stubborn hair and grease out of a floor drain, the manager lady stalked up to me in high heels and sheer panty hose, shins stopping at my face.

I looked up expectantly.

Her lips were closed and she twitched them. "You're the Spanish version of a dumb blonde," she said.

With only one more year left in high school, I struggled as hard as I could not to drop out. I was determined to at least do that. I knew from my father that no real man was a quitter. I truly hated school, but was sharp enough (which is not the same as "educated") to scam my way through with the minimum of effort and passing Cs.

The last time I put a heartfelt effort into anything school-related was in English class that year. For the final exam we had to write a composition paper. I did mine on the extinct passenger pigeon — the beautiful, sleek, sky-blue dove with an apple-red breast, long pointed tail, and perfectly-shaped hourglass-neck — that was native from the Gulf Coastal and Fort Worth Prairies of Texas all the way up to the original giant hardwood forests and tallgrass prairies of Ohio. In my library books, having learned about the land around my feet, I'd long ago found one of my totems who, like the luna moth and the buffalo, mythically represented the lost fertility and abundance of the North American continent.

But the passenger pigeons were completely lost, dead, killed. Not even a possibility of a single one left alive. The wild blue doves, once numbering in the billions, had literally thundered from Texas to Ohio, booming across these woods and open long-grass prairies in flocks so large that a single flock could block out the Sun for three days in passing. Some say these migrations helped create the legendary Cross Timbers of Texas, narrow north-south strips of live oak forest in the prairie that may have been started by the birds' seed-filled droppings. More wild passenger pigeons lived at one time then the total number of all other birds alive on the continent combined. The passenger pigeon was to the Shawnee what the buffalo was to the Lakota.

Market hunters staged contests where a minimum of 30,000 birds had to be killed just to be eligible for a prize. In 1896, in a single day hunters killed nearly all of the last quarter million birds, even though they knew they were killing the last wild flock of passenger pigeons.

The story of their extinction resonated deep within me. I closed my composition paper with a quiet little description — using entirely my own words — of the last moments of Martha, the very last passenger pigeon on Earth, as she died and fell to the floor of the cold concrete cage in the Cincinnati zoo at 1 p.m. on September 1, 1914.

The teacher gave me a D-, along with a sharply inked accusation of plagiarizing the ending. I protested that I'd written the whole thing; she sneered and said I "should be a writer then." She said it with a contemptuous laugh.

After that, I realized that cheating paid off as much as honest intellect. Only physical labor held unmistakable value.

I rarely came home before dark anymore, but one late afternoon found me way out in the woods, catching up with old territory. It was my last October there. I had managed to stay alive and stay in high school, and my planned spring escape was now just around the corner of one last Ohio winter. I began working my way back to the house as the afternoon slipped from the sky.

Much of the woods were second-growth, half-a-century old, thick and brushy, tangled, blended with tatters of original old growth. Traces of two abandoned farmsteads were back there, sinking into the woods, left behind since before the Depression. Trees had grown up right through the rusty handbuilt machines and implements, swallowing them. In many places it was hard to walk through these woods. It was ok, though. I'd spent a lot of my youth crawling slowly. Deep inside there, it was silent.

I crested a hill, and stopped. In a small open patch of dried blackberry brambles, I stood up, thorns dragging at my sweatshirt. Breathing quiet, like the woods themselves.

The valley bellied down to the creek bottoms, hills rolling off on all sides.

The bare October woods were the color of deerhide, and the approaching clear-sky twilight blushed the thick growth with colors of crimson and cool rust. I could hear the distant rushing of the blood through my veins, up into my arms. A wind with the promise of a months-long coldness lifted from the North and blew over those hills, passing through the tops of bare trees that shadowed against a draining sky. A crescent Moon and the Evening Star shined in the deepening blue. And there came one moment when I knew phantom wings and hourglass-neck silhouettes, flitting through other silhouettes, up there.

Before the snows came, I found a silk moth cocoon, spun tightly and wrapped smooth with dried pieces of caterpillar mouth-incised black walnut leaves. I had a feeling that it might be Luna, but I couldn't be sure. I even debated leaving it where I found it, but I knew I had to know.

I carefully placed the cocoon on a bed of leaves and wild grass in a wide-mouthed gallon jar, and added a long twig, though spring and emergence were on the other side of another long and brutal winter. I covered the top with a screen.

I wanted so much to see one just once, to be able to watch such green living luminescence fly off into the darkness.

When spring finally came, I was restless over my approaching escape, working hard every day at my diner job. So close. Ready to die. Ready to start my real life. All within reach.

Warmth was in the air, birds were back north, the woods a brilliant, buzzing fresh green. Butterflies flew about. But day after day nothing emerged from the cocoon in the jar. I checked. I waited. I gradually gave up. I had lost my last chance to see alive a luna moth.

Time passed as I squeezed money out of my hours, and beer and cheap wine out of my bottles. So busy I hadn't been out to the prairie or the woods in a couple months.

On the day before my strategically planned escape, I made it back out into the woods again, maybe needing the release, maybe simply to say goodbye.

Immediately though, I felt something was off. I kept walking.

I went over the first hill and down into the bottomlands. I crossed the creek on well-known stones, and headed up the next hill. I thought I noticed a clearing up ahead where there shouldn't have been one, and puzzled my eyebrows. I knew these woods too well to have gotten turned around. I pushed forward.

I stepped out into it and saw that the rest of the woods was cut down and bulldozed. Hot glaring sun in what once was a cool, fragrant, green-shaded woodland. I knelt down in some broken ferns where a bulldozer had crushed across a fragile stream as if it wasn't even there. Between the tank-like tread marks I noticed the hurried tiny footprints of a mink.

I knew mink tracks, but had never — still haven't — seen a live wild one.

They put up a bunch of expensive houses. Streets, concrete, sewers, mailboxes — where silence and secrets, a hidden wilderness, had once thrived. They called it "The Preserve." I wonder if anybody living there has any inkling of what lies beneath.

When I left what was left of those woods for the last time, and went back to the house, I thought to check the jar.

It was a Luna Moth. Throughout my youth, Luna had been an animal of totem mythical significance, never seen, only whispered and dreamed about.

But I couldn't release the giant green silk moth as I'd planned, couldn't watch him disappear across the long-grass prairie into the gathering dusk of black tree trunks, through streaming fireflies and thick humidity.

Seven inches long from wingtip to tail, the Luna Moth was dead at the bottom of the jar, lying there stiff in the dried leaves and faded wild grass, his four days passed. He lay in perfect condition except that his mythical luminescent green, the color that I had yearned for, had lit the darkness of my dreams, had faded to colorless white.

CHAPTER FOUR

Cuerpo y Mar

Where the hell are you? Right now?

"I am sorry for you," the East Indian woman said, looking at me through the bulletproof glass. She had a small dark red stone glued to her forehead. "There is only the night rates available after 2 a.m. Right now you must pay by the hour." I smelled incense and beans. It wasn't even dark out yet.

I just stared at her, my teenaged head hanging, not comprehending. Hot, dirty and exhausted, I was somewhere in Memphis, Tennessee, having finally escaped Ohio well before dawn, finally heading to my fabled Texas after waiting and planning for so many years. A young clueless dude on the road starting life over. Somewhere, in the darkness before this first dawn, it had occurred to me that I was dead, had died years ago. Too much pressure, until I'd burst, died, withered on my vine.

But as I would keep finding out, there was always something that dragged me back to my feet, driving me crazy, when all I wanted to do was check out and rest forever.

Everything now would be a new life, I told myself in Memphis. I tried to focus on that thought, but it fell away beneath the fragments of too many things, and I went blank.

Having driven through the night, the morning, and the afternoon, I just wanted to rent a room and sleep. I'd pulled off the Interstate in an industrial warehouse district after seeing the motel sign advertising FREE MOVIES!! My head was so tired... shutting down... didn't trust it to drive even a few more miles.

"Well?" the woman asked. "Do you take the room or no?" Behind bulletproof glass, her face was round, slightly oily, but with no expression of any kind, not even impatience. Which I'm sure I heard. The ruby-like stone glinted.

I checked the sky. Still a few hours before dark. I walked out, finally guessing that the hourly rates meant this was some kind of porno place. I was in the middle of some chain-linked, cracked-pavement wasteland with the Interstate elevated and its traffic roaring overhead.

I drove around a few blocks, legs cramped from the trip. I saw more factories and warehouses, all closed for the weekend. The sky was overcast and the air Southern grimy with vehicle soot and humidity.

Parking next to an abandoned lot, its chain-link fence sagging and torn, I got out, grabbed my bottle of warm 7-Up, and sank down onto a concrete parking bump.

I folded my arms over my knees and dropped my head. Dimly, I heard the repeated slap of a basketball on the pavement and the boom of rap music. I looked up and watched three black dudes playing ball, their shirts off, shiny with sweat. One was very big, tall, and dark-skinned. Mindlessly I stared at his feet running and jumping in bright, white, Run-DMC-style high-top sneakers. I was so tired. My mind drifted.

I glanced up at the Interstate that I'd just exited, looking at the rusted fence strung alongside it, tops of speeding vehicles visible behind. I had a sudden image of being a little kid standing on the overpass above the new Interstate in Ohio, my fingers twisting into the links of the already-rusting fence that separated me from that freeway and its weed-overgrown, trash-littered slopes, and all the traffic passing beneath me, going someplace, somewhere else. I closed my eyes, remembering the dirty warm humid air, and how the gasoline-scented highway ruffled my wiry black hair. Sometimes I'd thought my head was like one of them blackbirds, just wanting to lift off and fly away, my whole head flying away, clutched beneath wiry black wings.

When they'd been building that Interstate, they'd had "Dynamite Days." They'd used bombs to open up the Earth for the freeway's passage, and the whole kindergarten class had to gather in those safe areas of the school just in case anything shook loose on our heads. Winter caught up with the construction crews before they could finish, and every day after school I rough-sledded down into that giant unfinished roadbed, bulldozed out of woods and old fields, the taste of snow in my nose.

The basketball players decided to take a water break. After drinking from a gallon jug, the big dark dude came jogging out to where I was.

I stood and leaned against the front of my car. Still a teen, I hadn't reached my full height yet. He ran up. He was maybe in his mid-20s. He glanced at the old maroon-colored Ford and its license plates. "What's up, cousin? Haven't seen you around here before. You lost?" he asked. He was breathing through his nostrils, eyes flashing.

"I wanted to check into the motel, but they say no overnight rates. Not till 2 in the morning."

He bounced the basketball. His bright blue gym shorts shined, so did his white sneakers, white teeth, and whites of his eyes.

He was standing close to me. He bounced the ball again. "Nuthin round here," he said, glancing back at his friends. "This it."

He looked at me for a second longer.

I shrugged.

He made a motion like he was going to put his right hand out, as if to shake, then didn't and turned and jogged back to his friends, bouncing the ball.

I decided to drive some more, but was so tired I only made it to the next exit. I pulled into a parking lot where a few cars were stored, so mine wouldn't look so out of place. I locked the doors, rolled the windows up to about half an inch from the top, and lay down across the old bench-style front seat, stretching my legs the best I could. My feet were swelling inside my shoes, but I was too tired to reach down and take them off. I threw a jacket over my face. Sweaty, sticky, and needing a shower, I passed out, thinking about bright white teeth, bright whites of eyes.

The royal blue Gulf of Mexico heaved with a strong, gentle swell. The Texas sunlight rimmed and fractured off each rolling wave. I thought: I'm finally home here.

Living for good in Texas. At last I'd made it. I never really expected to make it, still be alive. It was too long a stretch of time. I'd only been able to deal with the moment and day I was in, and thoughts as they came to me. I could never focus on any one thing for too long. Now here I was, in Texas, only a few years away from 20, and still alive.

Every customer seemed to be calling for me or for another deckhand, having tangled their lines in somebody else's, or hooked themselves, or needed more bait, or had begun vomiting from the heat and motion, or even because he or she had hooked a fish. A hooked fish often added to the bedlam as it swept through the mess of lines and hooks streaming overboard into the sea.

First trial day — to see if they'd give me a job. We were drift fishing for amber-jack, dorado, jack crevalle, possibly barracuda and blacktip shark, or the occasional real surprise like a mako or sailfish, using heavy-duty baitcasting reels. All these fish fought like underwater bulldogs. Even the more "experienced" customers could barely control their lines, or themselves.

I wiped my knife on my jeans and stuck it into its belted sheath. I was always enthralled by the momentary, impossibly brilliant colors of an adrenaline-rushed ocean fish just gaffed and hauled and splashing furiously out of the water. It was our job to club them, and their colors rapidly shot down toward death after the first blow.

Marking the passage of a successful run, a few dozen bloodied, 20-to-30 pound fish, some still faintly gasping, hung from ropes, their long bullet bodies and strong tails sloping onto the deck. Other fish were tagged and hauled into the big iced fish-box near the entrance to the cabin.

A commotion erupted up the starboard side. A customer's rod was bent nearly in half, and a deckhand was leaning over the railing, positioning a gaff. Shark, I thought, from the way the other customers were milling around, getting in the way.

I pushed my way through the crowd. "Oye, Eddie Berto! What's it — shark?" I cleared my throat. He couldn't hear me. "*Tiburon?*"

Elbowing in, I glanced over the side at the thrashing blacktip shark as Eddie Berto, in one motion, lunged at the fish and yanked, arms and back muscles straining.

"Wait *para mi*," I grunted.

The crowd shouted as the gaffed shark cleared the water, splashing and slapping its tail. Not that big; I guessed this blacktip was maybe 60 - 70 pounds, but these little sharks fought like hell. Eddie strained to pull him up over the railing. Before I got to Eddie Berto's side, the shark swung his head through the railing and bit into the fisherman's knee, locking his jaws.

The crowd gasped and fell back. Eddie Berto's eyes widened as he struggled to hold on. The fish's tail slapped back and forth. The old, thin fisherman just stood there holding onto his rod with the still-hooked shark now clamped into his leg.

"*Ayudame*," Eddie Berto said through gritted teeth, looking at me like he was completely in a fix.

"*Cabron*," I said, calling him a goat and rolling my eyes at him. I yanked out my knife. Dropping to my knees, I grabbed the shark's head. The shark tussled, but didn't let go of the old man's knee. His teeth seemed to be mostly embedded in the man's jeans.

I poked him in the gums with my razor-sharp knife. The old man's leg was strangely dry.

Shark's teeth fall out relatively easily. Carefully, I jabbed and pried, trying not to slip and stab the customer in his leg.

The shark suddenly let go and began thrashing again. I rushed to Eddie Berto's side and we pulled the fish up over the guardrail, where it fell off the gaff, hit the deck, and slid down into the crowd. The shark bit into a different customer's foot. He screamed even though the shark's small mouth didn't even bite through his shoe. I looked up at the captain, who was watching us from the flying bridge.

So much for that job, I told myself later that night. Captain just a hick anyway. Edilberto, who everybody called Eddie Berto, was the only deckhand on the boat who didn't speak good English, or acted like he didn't. He pleaded for his job back, though I doubt the captain bothered to understand a word he said. I just walked. A $1.79 six-pack was waiting for me, ice cold in the nearest 7-Eleven's glass-doored cooler, and that was better than anything.

After dark, drunk and still out at Port Aransas, I returned to the docks where all the fishing boats were. I was starting to figure I'd be sleeping in the car tonight, though my North Beach apartment, on this side of the bridge from downtown Corpus, was only about 40 minutes away.

The night air coming in off the sea was warm and fragrant in a salty, ripe kind of way; it mingled with the faint smell of cleaned fish and hosed-down wood and concrete. The floating wooden docks lay tethered to pilings, aligning the boats that hung like chess pieces on the marina's dead calm surface. A fluorescent streetlight dimly illuminated the ten or twelve feet of green water below the boats. I could see the bottom.

I leaned on the railing and checked how my head felt. I'd lived with my passouts for so long it was an automatic thing, even when drunk. Head not hurting yet. No passout coming. Yet.

I settled in Corpus Christi, Texas, which they say is the real 'windiest city' in America. North Beach was a seedy isthmus of dirt and sand, existing in the shadow of the arching Harbor Bridge just past the oil refineries that lined the shipping channel mouth of the Nueces River flowing into Corpus Christi Bay. I guess it's been redeveloped since, but back then North Beach was its own forgotten sand and grit-blown beach barrio. The winds would start blowing off the Gulf and, as I walked down through the dirt alleys in between flapping clotheslines, yowling cats, and shawled Mexican grandmothers ducking like Arab women, I would begin to feel that the winds and sand were all there was in the world. Or were the world itself, one long sand-blasted wind tunnel between shabby single-room 'hood houses and stick-stilted apartments that, no matter how many twists and turns, always led back out into the mouth of the giant, growling Gulf. Warm weather and the chance to live where the open ocean met the open West. My place was part of a small, pre-fab studio apartment complex up on stilts, with only a weedy vacant lot between it and the bay. I was trying to take some community college classes, but already was barely showing up anymore.

The window faced a cluster of old one-room cottages that served as the eroding edges of the wind-tunneled alleys. The *abuelas* hung their *ropas* out to dry, and had to shake off the sand coating from each shirt or skirt or pair of work jeans or *Cloro*-brightened sheet, revealing a snapping strength inherent in their small, wiry bodies. They set food out in weighted pie tins for the hundreds of tailless alley cats that stalked and seethed over North Beach. In my little apartment, I killed the cucarachas with liquid Dove dish soap, a trick I learned from the old grandmothers across my alley. A 7-Eleven was within walking distance for my $1.79 six-packs of Schaefer beer and half-gallon jugs of cheap Gallo wine.

The winds seemed strongest from late evening through the night. They would blow and creak and whistle and groan through the screens, coating my humid, naked, sleeping body with fine dust and grit. This grit was something you could never fully shake or wash out of your sheets; there was always more, and it rasped against my nerve-endings as I ground deeper into sleep.

There was something toothy about North Beach, with its coarse, broiling sand and murky water, dead jellyfishes and broken glass, stingrays, incoming oil freighters, near-constant winds, washed up trash, fluttering clotheslines, tailless cats and shawled abuelas. Something about the changeable weather's sticky humidity, blazing sun, or damp gray, or open and dry Coastal Prairie-blue skies and howling grit-laden night winds. In fact, most of the South Texas Gulf Coast feels like this — toothy, peeled raw, like sand and salt rubbed into a sunburn. Not really a paradise or a vacation. But still, always, beckoning.

And sometimes the winds would suddenly stop, completely pull back out to sea, and Corpus Christi Bay became flat as glass. I would dive into it, swimming far enough out to get naked. The Texas sun heated the top layer of water and made me perspire. Broiled by the sun, sweat piercing my shoulder blades as the cleaved water folded back in and over me like wings, I made sure my broad strokes broke only the slightest disturbance. Far enough out, I switched to breaststroke through the water's underpulse, and I was a sea snake, eyes and mouth barely breaking the surface, sky meeting sea and me at water level, puffy clouds in the hot blue sky above providing oasis pools on the water's surface. As I swam further, the nutrient-rich brown water deepened to blue-black, trailing out my breathing mouth. Down below, I knew there were things, big things roiling in the cooling layers of water, that underpulse, rolling their eyes up at me as I passed overhead, sometimes bumping into my legs. I could see none of them; I was sure some came right beneath my belly before diving down again, and I might only feel them as a tendril of cooler water brought up with their momentum, or a swirl, or nothing at all. If I thought about it, it would scare me, and I quickly pressed the thought from my mind, let the water pulse everything away but arm strokes and sea and sky. I could see straight out the mouth of the bay to the Gulf, all the way to forever; and that great plain of water pulled always. I swam more, floating if I got tired, silent gasps for air, bubbles... I stopped and let my legs fall below me. Treaded water.

Civilization... back there beyond the beach. Should I even go back?

On the other side of the Harbor Bridge, the bayfront marina was the centerpiece of Corpus Christi's freshly skyscrapered downtown, filled with pleasure boats and bordered by a long concrete boardwalk. Seagulls and pelicans careened overhead. On calm bright days kids rollerskated, couples walked, fishermen cut up squid for bait and cast out with spinning reels, hoping for some croakers or grunts or maybe a little bay-wretched flounder or speckled trout for dinner. And at its edges, as in many public places, men with motives prowled.

Shirt off, sitting on the T-head docks, I stared at the gentle rise and fall of the water. The hot afternoon sun was intoxicating, gripping me so deep inside my bones seemed to be expanding. I'd been resisting the urge to go for beer. I'd decided I would wait until it got dark.

My mind lulled. The thought crossed again that I had to get another job soon but for now I pushed it away.

I knew I was partially hidden by the rows of boats. My eyelids began to fall, breath slowing. Subconsciously, I became aware a passout could be coming in. But… so relaxed and loose and blood-warm from the sun… Don't care.

Still, out of the corners of my eyes, I kept track of my surroundings, of cars looking for parking spaces — bright sun glinting off glass windshields, chrome, mirrors, of people coming and going. Legs and bodies moving as peripheral shapes.

Urban seagulls wheeled in the blue air, *cree*ing at each other.

The same little red car passed a third time, slowing each time. I began to tighten up and pull out of my swoon. I watched from the corners of my eyes.

The red car parked. A burly white man probably in his late 40s with brown hair, mustache and sunglasses started walking in my direction, head down as if looking for something.

He walked a few steps past me, slowed, then leaned down, messing with his shoe. He stood up.

"Excuse me, do you have a cigarette?" he asked, adjusting his voice.

"No," I said, turning away slightly, narrowing my eyebrows to look mean.

I looked back at the dirty water between the boats.

He walked a few steps closer, leaning on a wooden piling.

"Nice day," he said, taking off his sunglasses.

I said nothing.

"Lots of horny women in this town, huh?"

I nodded and shrugged.

"I know this woman — she's really horny right now. She's my best friend. She lives upstairs from me. She really would like to… you know, have a young boy like you…"

"Oh," I said.

"Well, I saw you here, and I just thought you might want to go for a ride…"

I looked around. Nobody was in the immediate vicinity. I could feel his eyes all over me.

I stood up, casually holding my t-shirt in front of my basketball shorts.

I walked with him to his car. He popped a tape into the cassette player as we drove out of the city's marina, crossed Ocean Drive, turned south, and drove a short distance inland to some nicer apartment buildings, not far from downtown. A different version of that song *Holiday*, by that new singer Madonna, came out of the speakers. It had faster, deeper beats, like a dance mix or something.

"Madonna says next year will be her year," he said.

"She probably just a one-hit wonder," was all I said.

As I followed him in, I realized that I was shivering a little. I forced myself to stop it.

He went to the back stairwell and yelled "Shirley!"

He came back. "I guess she's not home. Now that's fucked up," he said. In the same moment he put his hand on my still sun-warmed bare chest and pushed me toward the couch. "Why don't you sit down and relax for a minute? I'll get you some water."

I sat down. The couch was white canvas, the walls were freshly painted white, and the window looked up and out at the bluest of blue skies. The Sun was on the other side of the building, so the light coming through the window was the softest light reflecting off the bluest atmosphere, filling my eyes. So much refracted light made me feel like I was being washed out of existence. I felt I could just... pass out. I tried to pay attention to what was happening, but—

He returned with a glass of water, and a towel, setting both down on the glass coffee table.

I closed my eyes.

I heard him move the coffee table and kneel down in front of me. His hands started grabbing all over my chest, then he plunged his face into my crotch, reaching for my waistband and pulling down my shorts. Inwardly, I resisted for a moment longer, then dropped my head back. Crossing that bridge.

I felt his mouth slide down onto me, wet and lukewarm, slowly moving up and down and around, then faster. With his hand he grabbed and squeezed the base of my balls. I clenched my fists, suddenly wanting to punch him, smash his head open like a cantaloupe. I kept my eyes closed. The feeling that all my insides were tingling and piling up in my groin was overwhelming. I knew I wasn't going to be able to hold on for long. I rocked my hips, not caring about anything. In another minute, I gulped some air, bucked, he backed off a little and I shot on his face and shoulder and on myself too.

I kept my head back, eyes closed, instantly feeling different. Like something sinking.

I heard him wiping his face off, then felt him lifting me up with his hands, wiping me off, working the towel in and around thoroughly. I clenched my fists harder.

He stood up, leaving me with my shorts down, my legs still spread. He went to the kitchen.

I opened my eyes. He came back with his own glass of water and sat next to me. I pulled my shorts up. The whiteness of the room and the blue sky through the open window filled my head.

"I gotta go," I said.

He took my brown nipple between his rough fingers and held it, squeezing it a little hard, looking me over, head to toe. I turned my head away.

"You look really beautiful," he said. "You might not know it now, but you should consider yourself very lucky. You're blessed with your youth and good looks. I know many people who would love to have you… mmmm… all this." He rubbed his hand down my chest to my stomach. I curled my fist. His voice got thick. "I would've liked to have done a lot more to you."

My head was still turned away, staring out the window up at the blue sky, hands clenched.

"You're just a boy," he said. "But if you take care of yourself, you could have a charmed life."

I took a job as a busboy in the top-floor restaurant of a downtown hotel. Wearing a starched white shirt, black bowtie and black tuxedo vest, I buttered up the woman bartender like all the rest of us busboys did so she would splash rum in our cherry cokes.

The same lounge act performed the same songs every night, complete with big hair, tambourine, sequined dress and red-cellophaned spotlight. The zenith of the evening was always "*Gloria.*" Nightly, like clockwork, when the plump singer began to sing "GLORIA — YOU THINK YOU'RE ON THE RUN NOW!" building up to a tonsil-busting, lounge-belting crescendo, Rey, Huberto, Lupe, Rodney and myself knew we had made it through another night and could start putting up some of the bread baskets and doing our closing chores. In our starched, food-stained shirts we all smelled like Kmart cologne, hair gel, roast beef, butter and bread rolls and a faint underaroma of sweat. "BUT YOU REALLY DON'T REMEMBER……CALLING GLORIA… *GLORIAAA!...*"

I allowed a woman customer twice my age to pick me up, and in her bed, my face between her thighs, I made her orgasm three times in a row, acting purely on instinct. At the school, I met this sexy, kinky-haired, married woman and we dated for awhile, on free evenings taking the tops off her blue Datsun 280ZX and sizzling at high speeds down the straight-line barrier island roads out on Padre Island, smoking joints. Her husband was always out in the Gulf working on the oil rigs. She pierced my ear lobe with a sewing needle and put a small silver hoop through it. I dated her until I got bored, or more honestly, felt not right about it. The underlying urgency that I needed to *do something* grew stronger. There was something that I was missing. *Missing out* on. Sometimes I thought about going to a bigger city. I started thinking hard about this. If I was gonna go someplace else, why waste time? Just go straight to the heart of everything. A flash of excitement went through me.

New York City, I thought. I tried that thought on for size, and nodded, as I drifted around the dusty downtown.

Drunk at night, I prowled the alleys outside the bail bond and porno shops on Chaparral. Hookers and drug dealers hissed offers from dark doorways and alleys.

Days and nights got hotter as summer approached. I continued to sit under the Harbor Bridge in my drawers, soaking drunk. Or stood in my bathroom, face under the faucet, water running for a long time, washing my mouth out, washing my face off. And up in the hotel restaurant, my serving tray balanced with glasses of ice water with lemon slices and baskets of warm bread wrapped in red cloth napkins, I'd occasionally catch myself staring past my reflection in the plate glass windows out at the bayfront marina and the blue Gulf beyond. "Where the hell are you, right now?" was what I said to myself. I began scheming to find a way to get to NYC.

I drifted more, down to the border, thinking, trying to focus.

As the jail cell door clanged shut, I sat on the cot, glad at least that the handcuffs were off. The obese Mexican store manager of the Port Isabel supermarket, near the Mexico border, had been following me around, wearing his big pink apron, and to spite him, I'd stolen a fifty-five cent block of foil-wrapped cream cheese.

The two jail cells were little more than a cage split in half by bars, a few paces from the deputy's office. The other prisoner and I stared each other down through the bars. *Pinche mi culo!* was written on the wall behind his head, with big scrawls written over that by somebody who had come later. On my side there was a love song to "Marisa," complete with music notes drawn into the orange paint that had long ago been stained by Gulf air and the grime of inmates.

Driving back to Corpus a day later, scruffy and unwashed, halfway up I pulled onto the road shoulder and shut the car off. The whole western sky was lit up in a massive red-orange flatland twilight. I could not believe that sky.

I got out and walked across the empty road, stepping a few feet into the sparse, grassy brush. I heard a distant, piercing sound — laughing or crying; tingled my spine. I cocked my head, concentrating, hoping. The coyote howled again.

I became conscious of the sea, the Gulf of Mexico, at my back, even though it was a couple dozen miles east. And again I knew I was at the edge of another world; it was *my world*, a spiky, grassy terrain, filled with animals that crawled and whispered, who pawed at the Earth and flashed in the Western sun, rolled their eyes, flicked their tongues, snorted, rumbled, or heaved their sides at twilight. Here I was, and out there, *there* was. It was my eternity. If I just stepped in, crossed into the other side…

I knew I couldn't be sure of coming back.

The setting red Sun was about face level to me across the South Texas plain now, and the round ball of my face looked straight back into it. And the Sun paid no attention to me at all and sank, pulling the blue sky down with it.

Last days in Corpus….

I sped up the Harbor Bridge. The wind blew through the open windows of my car and the high cables of the bridge flashed by as I sped. I reached its summit and looked out both ways like I always did, out to the June-blue Gulf, and inland up the

ship channel with all its oil refineries and tanks. No refineries were on fire and belching black smoke today.

I reached the top of the bridge and floored the gas with my bare foot, surveying
the narrow island as I came down. The intersection down where the bridge ended was
dangerous because people never stopped. Having the right of way, I raced on ahead
as a 4-door sedan rolled through the stop sign to the right. I could see the little Avis
sticker in the windshield and the gray heads of two tourists as they plowed broadside
into my car.

The old Ford careened across the road, spinning around. Glass from the back
window flew in a kaleidoscopic twirl of quarter-sized chunks and I bounced through
that. In slow motion a couple little blood scratches magically appeared in my arm and
bare chest. The big fish I'd caught earlier off the Island thumped in the trunk. The
flapping, clanking seat belt mocked me. Something yanked in my lower back. I held
onto the steering wheel and fell back down into the driver's seat. One of my sneakers
flew out the window.

The car came to a halt about 50 feet away on the other side of the street, facing
back toward the Harbor Bridge. I looked out through the intact front windshield
at the tourists' car. Their car was not badly bashed up. They got out, and instead of
coming over to me, went to a nearby house. They moved with ease. They were fine.
The old man's tourist-pastel sport coat hung squarely on his shoulders, which seemed
permanently stiff from either a lifetime of privilege or resignation. I couldn't see his
face. His wife stalked behind him. It would take a stiffer wind to move her helmet of
iron-gray curls.

Dazed, and suddenly sleepy, I got out, carefully picking up my sneaker. I lowered
myself onto the grassy curb. Least they were calling somebody.

A police officer arrived and stopped on the other side of the road. The tourists
who'd hit me reappeared and talked to him as he filled out paperwork. They pointed
at their car but wouldn't look my way.

Realizing that time was passing and my side of the story was still not being heard,
I jumped up and started to walk across the street. "Hey!" I said. "What about over
here? THEY hit me!"

Before I made it halfway across, the cop sternly shouted at me to get back to my
car. From the sound of his voice, I knew he meant business. I turned around. My
lower back was beginning to hurt.

I opened the trunk, pulled out the 25 lb. jack crevalle by his sharply forked yellow tail, and laid him down in the tropical grass. This car wasn't going anywhere. The
whole right rear was smashed. I reached into the car for my duffel bag, t-shirt and
other sneaker.

I sat back on the grass curb. When a tow truck came, followed by a new rental car
for the couple, the cop got in his car and left. The couple got in the new Avis, the tow
truck driver hitched up the tourists' busted rental car, and all left.

I stood. Wait a second. What about me?

Not having a clue as to any rights I might have, or even what to do in such a situation, I stood there waiting. There was no insurance on the old vehicle. I rubbed my back.

Another tow truck came down the Harbor Bridge. The scrawny hippie driver began hitching up my car. He handed me a piece of paper telling me where the car would be. He walked to the tow truck and jumped in.

Realizing he was about to drive off, I rushed to get my apartment keys. "Wait a second," I said. "What am I supposed to do?"

"You need to leave the car key in the ignition, but take everything else," he said, as if I was stupid.

"That's not what I meant. I mean, what am — "

He closed the driver's side door and pulled out. The tow truck and my messed-up car rolled back up the Harbor Bridge and out of sight.

I put my keys in the duffel bag and waited for my rental car to come. I stood next to the fish in the stiff grass, with its big, dead, silver dollar eyes. Stiffly, I sat down again.

Two short, older Mexican dudes came out of the apartment complex behind. One had a bottle of aspirin.

"I give you for the fish," he said, pointing and smiling, pulling at his waxed mustache with his other hand. He poured out two aspirin.

I looked up at the bridge. Lots of cars and trucks were flying over the bypass, but no rental car, or any car, was heading down the North Beach exit.

I motioned my head at the dead fish. "Don't worry 'bout it. Go ahead." Most people didn't consider jack crevalles good to eat. But then I wasn't exposed to high standards, and I guess they weren't either, because they grinned broadly as they reached for the fish and lugged it back to their patio grill.

I put my sneakers on and tied them. With my t-shirt I wiped the little bits of drying blood off the scratches in my chest and arms. I threw my shirt over my shoulder, hiked up my big shorts, stuck my baseball cap onto my head sideways, and grabbed the duffel bag. My back was starting to kill me. All the injuries, bumps, bruises, cuts, strains and sprains I'd already had in life flashed through my mind and I wondered: what if they start to become cumulative and I have to live with constant pain? Bull in a china shop, people had always said about me.

Slowly, I humped my way back to the apartment along Gulfbreeze Road.

CHAPTER FIVE

I Might Be Cold

"Baby, you need to watch yourself. Sit up. Now look at that — you bout set yourself on fire."

Dimly, through the fog of my other world, I heard her voice, and felt her weight bear down on the bench as she sat beside me. I raised my head up off my knees and looked at her, blinking into the hazy afternoon sunlight streaming across wide Houston Street. The Marlboro butt, burned down to the filter, fell forgotten out of my fingertips. It rolled past her thick old woman's feet, which were stuffed into too small shoes on the old gum-spotted concrete bricks, and stopped next to a partially-eaten chocolate chip cookie. The cookie looked still good. Probably not been there too long. They'd just taken a little bite out of it, and accidentally dropped it. Yeah. In the background, a voice was talking on somebody's radio — passing cab or boombox — about the new drug crack cocaine and how this one was gonna be real different; its addiction was so intense and overwhelming it made people act like rabid dogs, and the city needed to be prepared for a whole new wave of violence and crime.

"Huh?" I said, more of an exhale. The thin afternoon NYC sunlight was irritating me. It gave no real warmth; just sort of poked into my head.

She looked me in the eyes and twitched. She cracked a smile, flashing a gold tooth. I remembered about my eyes and shielded them with my hand, trying to recall where I'd put my sunglasses, or if they'd fallen off.

Her hands clasped her purse in her lap. She was wearing a flowery dress and light sweater that was probably not enough for the East Coast-clammy, cool, late September air.

"What's wrong, baby?" she asked.

Putting my elbows on my knees, I stared down at the concrete bricks making up the surface of the little wedge "park" we were sitting in, between Houston and First, and Avenues A and B. I looked again at my smoldering cigarette butt, next to the choco chip cookie. I rubbed my face, wondering why she was bothering me. I didn't want to talk to nobody.

"I can't seem to stay awake," I mumbled, glancing at her and quickly turning my eyes away again. The Houston St. traffic seemed to roar and be distant at the same time. "I mean, I was gonna take these classes, I mean I'm trying, I even got this schol-arship… I know, believe it or not, but—"

"It's okay, baby. I understand. Maybe you just need some time. All right. Everybody gotta find themselves."

I stiffened my shoulders. What the hell that supposed to mean? People were always making hints or some shit, trying to tell me about me. I reached down for the cookie and took a bite. It was crisp and airy, like it had been manufactured instead of baked. A few crumbs fell off my lip onto my chin. I wiped them away with my sleeve.

She shook her head, not saying a word.

"What!" I said, preparing for motion, ready to leave.

Some English city pigeons flew in to peck at the buckets of fatty glop that workers from Katz's meat deli across the street had dumped to the side of the bench. The bloated birds gurgled in their throats as they puffed their chests and bobbed and strutted into the yellow, clumpy mess, sounding like they were having some kind of obscene sex. It made my stomach queasy. I glanced across the street into Katz's Deli, where through the windows I could see men in white uniforms and paper hats bustling between hanging columns of meats and sausages and rows of frying hot dogs. I could smell the place from here.

"Child, last time I ate a hot dog was back in the '60s when I bit into it and a hairy bone was inside and it got in my mouth." She put her hand to her lips.

I squinted at her. She cracked a smile at me again. I got up and walked away.

"All black people are related, no matter what," she said back there. "Remember that."

I walked up First Avenue, thinking it was hard to believe I'd been in New York for well over a year. I tried to remember coming here from Texas. Or why. I really had no answer. I just vaguely remember thinking that if I was going to go somewhere, I should go to the heart of everything so I wouldn't have to go anyplace else. Unlike the couple other times I'd been to Texas and had to leave, this time I didn't even look back. Now I sensed I was on a one-way ride, for better or worse. Momentarily a sharp pang of panic hit me, that I'd made a serious mistake. *Maybe you shoulda stayed in Texas.* Pushed it all out of my mind.

My little $340 dollar a month room was in a 3rd floor East Village apartment overlooking First Ave. and St. Mark's Place. My room was the size of a Volkswagen, and you couldn't walk around in it if the bedroll was open.

I crossed St. Mark's, passing my apartment building with the graffiti murals, the overturned trash cans and the small-time drug dealers on the corner. I couldn't bring myself to go up to my room just yet. I rented from a 300-pound woman who gave phone sex for a living. The walls were old and thin. She had candida, left nasty messes of yeast and blood on the toilet seat, and douched with warm vinegar; the whole apartment smelled like that. It was impossible to use the bathroom in peace if she was home, because it was her throne and she would come banging in, terrorizing me. I was afraid I was starting to have a complex about bathrooms, which could not be healthy for my intestines and bladder.

I'd discovered the roof of the six-floor walkup. It would be an excellent ledge to jump off. I'd watched the upstairs neighbor drop a full-size TV out his window. When it hit the sidewalk, it exploded with a big BOOM, shattering into so many pieces that, as far as a block away, the small-time drug dealers scattered.

I turned down 9ᵗʰ, picked up a pint of cheap gin, a 12-oz. Rolling Rock, and a pack of cigarettes, and headed into Tompkins Square Park. Settling onto a bench, huddling into my jacket, I drank and smoked and gazed at the Tent City of homeless people that had gradually formed in the park over the last year. It was a vague worry of mine — that I could become like that. My head hurt all the time. I'd already spent a few nights in the bandshell, drunk and sleeping on top of newspapers that had been somebody else's bed. I told myself I had enough of a survival instinct to avoid falling down that far. I hoped I was a little different — stronger or sharper in some way than the homeless all around me. But...

I flicked my ashes, thinking of my Independent Study classes. On a whim, feeling a little worthless, I'd written out the application for a new scholarship, and gotten surprised with a partial acceptance. I'd re-contacted my father who, with his recent financial means, agreed to help cover the rest, as long as I didn't come back. Which of course I had no desire to do. Once gone, I was to stay gone. And that suited everybody. I'd only used the school as a scheme to get here. Even stayed in university housing at first, because it was cheapest and easiest, until it drove me crazy. And I'd even, for a deluded moment, thought that this small town backwoods mongrel in the big city could become like "one of the golden people" that I saw around — have a beautiful girlfriend, wear new clothes, go to hip clubs, snort good coke, all that 80's shit. But I could never shake the feeling that I was fronting, that I was out of place, dirty, second class. And I couldn't control my drinking. Some nights found me crawled up behind a Dumpster — for safety, comfort and to be alone — or once (or twice) even passing out on a subway grating huddled into the stream of warm air shooting up from the city's underground. Snapping out of it from time to time, I'd shower, shave, chameleon myself upright, and nobody would know a thing.

Going to New York City was supposed to have been about changing my life for the better.

Grimacing, I realized I was losing — wasting — what likely was my best opportunity to save myself, lead a "normal" life. *Don't lie. You had no real interest in going to school. You just hustled your way here; took the easy route. You're only here because you couldn't think of anything else to do. And now, what?*

I closed my eyes, feeling out this sense of foreboding inside that was increasingly spreading. This nothingness, this empty, wasted worthlessness, pall of blackness, blotting out everything.

I was slipping, losing control... not getting anything out of the study program... didn't care... barely able to keep from getting kicked out. *Your problem is you can't concentrate.*

I had cheated or written my way through, always at the last minute. I truly did not care. My head hurt. I missed most of the few actual classes, or passed out onto the desktop as the radiators hummed and buzzed, or showed up so drunk I had to leave, feeling everybody's eyes hot on my back, visualizing my head suddenly exploding in a big BOOM of brains and blood. But still I continued, as if it was even too much of an effort to quit. Not a quitter.

I drank from my bottle of Bombay, then from the Rolling Rock, eyeing the people preparing for the night in Tent City. I wondered if I should have gotten me some Jim Beam instead. I loved both. And 40s of Colt or O.E., or big Budweiser too. And of course my most favorite, Rolling Rock, which wasn't malt liqua', but still…

Why didn't they make 40s of Rolling Rock? I snorted, beer almost coming out my nose as I laughed at the thought of me swigging a giant green bottle of Rolling Rock. Yeah, such nice green bottles. Clear dark green glass, with a horse's head stenciled in white. Shaking some clarity into my head I reminded myself that I had to go to an actual class tomorrow afternoon. And oh shit, yeah, I had to go work for that old faggot photo-collector in the West Village in the morning, too. Always gotta keep the j-o-b, boy, whatever it is. Otherwise…

I got up and walked away from Tent City quickly. *As long as you never let yourself become like that…*

"You alone?" I asked Constantina as she let me into her apartment. I hadn't seen her in months, but the big-hipped Hungarian girl was one of three girls I thought I liked. I'd given up on Babette, the beautiful, black, pretentious girl from Barbados. Babette considered herself — with good reason — just too worldly and cultured for me. Babette's mother was a well-traveled foreign diplomat who wore black lace underwear she'd leave hanging in the bathroom smelling of perfume, smoke, and womanly scent. Thiona, the voluptuous Greek girl, high society all the way, she just strung me along, giving me just enough attention to keep me around in case she needed something.

"Do you know what time it is?" Constantina shut the door behind me. The room was dark, illuminated only from the orange streetlights outside. "You're drunk," she said, waking up fully now. "I haven't seen you in so long. Where have you been?"

I found my way through the room shadows and sat on her bed, pulling her with me. She didn't resist too much. "Sorry to wake you," I slurred, fake pouting. "Want a cigarette?"

She reached into my jacket pocket and pulled out my pack of Camel Lights. Two hollow-point bullets also fell out and clattered to the floor.

"What was that?" she asked as she lit two cigarettes and handed one to me.

"I don't know. Come here." I lay back on the bed. "Want a drink?" I pulled out my second pint and upended a swallow.

"No, silly," she said in her thick, luscious accent. She took both cigarettes and crushed them in the ashtray and laid on top me. She started kissing me, smearing me with lipstick, sort of grossing me out. My head was spinning from all the drink. I focused on her body. I rolled on top of her as we took off our clothes. I began rubbing against her, making myself hard. I used my hands along her body, listening to how each movement made her respond.

"Wait," she murmured, her accent making her sound pouty herself. She paused.

I rested on top of her for a second. "What's up?" I asked as if getting sleepy.

"Do you remember when we were in Central Park last summer, and we were hanging out in Sheep Meadow on that big towel? And everything was so hot and sticky, and it began to pour rain?"

"Umm. Yeah, I guess."

"And I suddenly had to pee so bad. And how I finally just squatted behind that tree, and you held the towel up?"

"Oak tree. White oak."

"And we walked downtown, down 5th Ave. in the rain…"

There was a pause.

"Hey!" She hit me. "You're not listening!"

"Yeah," I said, groggy. "I'm listening. What about it?" I was not feeling drunk anymore.

She was quiet for a few minutes, and I began to drift off again.

"You're not the person I thought you were."

It took me a minute to actually hear what she had said. "What the hell that supposed to mean?" I asked, and tried to roll off. She immediately dug her fingers into my back, holding me on top of her.

"What," I said. "Lemme just get outta here."

"No. Don't go!" she whispered in my ear. "Please don't go."

I heard something in her voice that made me lift my head and look at her pale face in the dark.

"I'm still a virgin," she pleaded, and pushed up into my groin. "I'm sorry. I really want you to. Come on. Let's do this."

I shook my head as I looked her in the face. "Don't," I said and acted again like I was going to pull away.

She drew a finger down the middle of my spine, lingering. She flashed a small smile and raised her eyebrows.

I reached down behind her and grabbed her ass in my hands, and pulled her against me. I moved my hips, slowly making myself hard again. "You sure?" I said. "I can get out of here. Not a problem."

"*Noo*," she whispered thickly, and grabbed me with both her hands, guiding me inside her.

I pushed gently, then stopped, waiting for her to relax and open up.

"Oh, shit," she cried softly. "It hurts. Shit. O.K. Push a little harder." She reached around and gripped my ass, pulling me in deeper.

"You sure?" I asked one last time. As I pushed in, I thought I felt something give a little, something different from the normal wet. I was afraid it was blood. Maybe I was just imagining things.

She raised her head and bit into my ear. "Come on!" she said.

We began screwing. I started to work up a nice salty sweat. She was crying, maybe laughing too. It was bugging me out. Concentrating on what felt good down there, I glanced back at our hips slapping together, and closed my eyes.

An image of two men flashed into my mind, men grinding like that, hip muscles clenching, and I quickly opened my eyes, shoving the image away. I hurried up my rhythm, hitting it hard now, working her body with my hands, gritting my teeth into her neck.

She finally started gasping, and I hit it a little more past the point I knew she would be satisfied, and then started to pull out. She tried to stop me. I arched my back, slipping out, and grabbed myself and finished it off on her soft stomach.

I hesitated for a second, catching my breath, then rolled over and flopped onto my back, grabbing the sheet. I glanced down and saw a small smear of something dark on the white sheet.

"I'm so glad we did this," she said, rolling her head around on the pillow.

I got up and began pulling on my jeans and boots, automatically checking to make sure my wallet, knife and keys were in the pockets.

Put a bullet through my head, I thought to myself.

The smell of water, the Hudson River meeting seawater as it flowed down the lower west coast of Manhattan, calmed my abraded nerves as I walked out to the end of the dilapidated pier. Open space, fresh air, room to breathe.

My shoes crunched on broken glass. The rusty, sagging chain link fences didn't keep anybody off these piers. Halfway out on this pier, in a strange little jungle of giant green weeds sprouting from old concrete and wood, a homeless man had homesteaded his own shack out of tar paper, cardboard boxes, and plastic buckets.

I climbed through a hole in the chain link fence, walked farther out, hopped over the concrete barrier, and stepped onto the last jagged slab of concrete, which was cracked and slanting down almost into the water, just a few feet above the smooth flowing surface. I often sat there, feet dangling. I could tap the water with the soles of my shoes. My stomach was all acidy. I sat down.

Below the wide-open blue twilight, New Jersey buildings across the river in the distance began lighting up on the other side. Tiny flashing police sirens raced up or down what I assumed was New Jersey's version of Manhattan's West Side Highway. I had a new sense of the curve of the Earth westward, a horizon out over those New Jersey cliffs and buildings.

I thought the river was some 30 or 40 feet deep, but I couldn't remember if somebody had told me that, or if I'd read it somewhere or just assumed it. Thiona had been the first one to tell me about the piers, and how you could get a sense of space and, turning around, view the city as a backdrop, as if separated from it. Under the milky green water, a used condom, ghostly latex white, swam by, along with some bottles, plastic grocery bags, and other unidentified crap. A cheap plastic baby stroller followed, hanging in a current a few feet below the surface. I watched it leave, heading south to the harbor, and eventually the ocean. I wondered if it'd pass the Statue of Liberty and all them tourists with their green foam liberty crowns on their heads, and if any of them would see it.

Like the welling of the water, my inconsistent urges to be at the bottom of that current, with the whole river on top of me, came and went. Me down there, rolling in the strong moving water, bumping silently against the bottom, my shoulder or back or whatever stirring little slow-motion bursts of silt and muck…

I turned and faced the city. The Empire State Building off to the northeast always looked so sudden and looming from this standpoint, even though it was all the way in the middle of the city at 34th and 5th. No special city events were going on; tonight its spire lights were just plain old regular white instead of lit in some representative color. At the south end of the city, the World Trade Center stood stark and silver, sleek twin pillars in the sky.

I slitted my eyes to survey the waterfront. Across the West Side Highway, at the corner of Christopher, was the Badlands Bar; south of Christopher was all-black Kellar's — tiny hole-in-the-wall crammed with sweating people and an out-of-date disco juke box — and both up and down for blocks further were camouflaged places with non-descript doors and no names. In my head I heard that Bronski Beat dance track again, *I Feel Love,* that summed up those places. With drink up in me, fueling late night forays, hidden bar dance beats contrasting the boom beat Public Enemy street, I'd follow. Pulsing hot rhythms, dim red smoky lighting, back rooms with curtains; anonymous men cast in angle and shadow, the smell of fresh cool cologne, light sweat and something like sex or heat. And the simultaneous sense of both threat and desire. Which might have been the same thing.

Wearing baggy clothes and a baseball cap for anonymity, I stepped off the graffiti-tagged 2 train and hopped up the stairs into the blinking, flashing, false-daylight brilliance of Times Square. The Deuce was still lively, though quieting down a bit. I checked the Newsday building to see if its circling, neon, screaming headline flasher would tell me what time it was. Had to be after midnight. I stopped in the middle of the sidewalk flow of worn-out hookers, drug dealers, and shifting, unknown men, and checked my balance, inwardly trying to shake the drink from my head. Taking a deep breath, I began walking down 42nd St. towards 8th.

Abandoned old theaters loomed above on either side. Others promised SUPER TRIPLE XXX PORNO KINKY TOTAL SEX DOUBLE FEATURE — SERENA'S SUCKING SINS and THE BEST OF VANESSA DEL RIO.

With my baseball cap pulled far down over my eyes, I tried to imagine a straight line for me to follow down the sidewalk so I wouldn't wobble, appear out of control. That would show weakness. Hands in pockets, a little dizzy, I parted through the sea of people.

Jangled music and hard rap beats from a hundred different radios blasted through the street. Black, brown, Asian, white expressionless faces with complex intentions shined, reflecting the false daylight and crazy blinking lights — eyes lowered or head-on direct, darting, casing, challenging, looking for openings.

In nearly every alley or abandoned doorway, glass pipes flared as somebody fired a rock of crack. Impromptu 3-Card Monty games were still springing up on overturned cardboard boxes twenty bucks a bet. Bits and pieces of the continuously moving throng of people were lost or gained as somebody slipped into a peep show or out of a blazing porn emporium. Hookers still on shift stood their ground on every corner, splitting the crowd. I concentrated hard on my imaginary line. I realized I probably reeked of alcohol. This can't be me, I thought. I quickly stopped thinking about anything.

I felt some people looking at me.

Head spinning, I rounded the corner onto 8th Ave. I leaned up against the wall and tried to act casual, eyeing men for a split second from beneath the ball cap as they walked down the sidewalk between 42nd and 43rd. Waiting for something.

From across the street, this guy was watching me, standing silhouetted in front of the blinking neon lights of Show World, the biggest "emporium" of them all. Nearly twenty women dressed in short skirts and high-heeled boots milled on the block, hoping to sponge off the place's popularity. As soon as I noticed him, he crossed diagonally and walked right up to me, hands in his jacket pockets. A cigarette was in his mouth; he was unshaven, about 15 years older than me, medium-skinned, mixed with something.

"What's up?" he said.

"Nothin'." I stuck my hands in my pockets.

He narrowed his eyes and tilted his head as he checked me out.

"You want to check my teeth too?" I asked.

"You don't have to be like that," he said. He reached over and lifted my ball cap to see my face.

Instinctively I moved away from his reach, but the brick wall was behind me, so I stepped to the side and almost fell. I steadied myself and stood my ground. I shook my head to clear it.

He smiled, puffing smoke.

"Come on," he said. "You're drunk." He began walking up towards 43rd. I followed, my head foggy. Still had this urge to get into something. Couldn't concentrate. Way too drunk.

We rounded 43rd and halfway down the street he pulled me into a space between two parked cars, where there was a gap in the street lighting and we were cast in shadow.

He looked around, then pulled me down with him onto our knees. The hard pavement dug into my kneecaps. He unzipped his jeans and then mine. His dick stuck up at an angle, hard, and I could smell it, like a day without a shower.

I wobbled and caught my balance, shook my head to again try to clear my thoughts. With one hand he turned my cap backwards and grabbed the back of my head and yanked my face down, using his other hand to start jacking on my dick. Mind all drunk and hazy… He shoved his dick into my mouth and began slamming his hips back and forth, fucking my mouth, his hairy belly hitting my face and the stiff head of his dick hitting the back of my throat, gagging me. I tried to breathe through my nose.

He forgot about jerking me off and grabbed the back of my head with both hands, using them to make my face smack in harder. I'm about to black out, I thought dimly, trying to keep my balance. In the distance I heard him say "Yeah... Yeah." The cigarette fell out of his mouth and rolled on the oily asphalt. Suddenly feeling helpless, I didn't know what else to do but keep going. Didn't know nothing bout this shit — what you were supposed to do to have sex. My eyes zeroed in on the burning orange embers of the cigarette. Again I felt my eyes closing. If they did, I'd black out for real. I forced them to stay open. With my head snapping back, his hands clasped around it, I heard him cough "Oh YEAH."

"You didn't even come," he said as if from somewhere far away as we stood up, my head spinning. I spat on the ground, then again. My stomach felt sick.

What just happened? I wondered dimly. Did I really just let him...? Spitting again, I blinked and tried to steady my balance.

A nicely dressed theater couple walked by, noticed us, and looked away. I quickly pushed myself in and zipped up.

"You know, you really should be more careful," he said.

"This my first time." It came out slurred. I wobbled again for balance.

He laughed. "Yeah, right. You wouldn't be out here like this. But you really should be more careful, unless you don't care. That's probably the case already though, I bet." He shook his head.

I turned my cap back around to the front and pulled it way down over my face.

He took off, walking backwards for a second. "There's something new going around," he said. "That's why you can blow me, but I would never do you. Anyway, I gotta go." He walked to the corner, crossed 8th again, and disappeared into Show World.

I spat again, and tried to pull my cap down even lower over my eyes. I stuck my hands into my pockets and began walking slowly, wobbly, shaking my head repeatedly to clear it, get my balance back into my legs. Head really spinning. Need a drink.

Halfway back to 8th, and hoping the dude wouldn't come back out before I passed, I decided to turn around and walk away through the quiet shadows of 43rd.

I imagined an ax swinging down into my face. Hard. With my hands on the handle.

My head began squeezing. I knew what that meant.

I needed to just make it back to the N or R train and sit down for a minute. Then I'd be alright, at least as far as the passout.

I walked and stumbled until finally, through sheer will, stabilized my balance enough to get me to the train before somebody could jump my drunk ass.

Back downtown on 1st Ave., cold and strung out, steadier, I made it to the all-night wholesale bakery. Its door inside the gate was tied open to release some of the heat from the baking ovens, creating a cocoon of warmth and aroma pillowing out onto the sidewalk. I twined my fingers into the gate and called to one of the workers baking fresh bread. He brought me my usual, a loaf of hot whole wheat just minutes out of the industrial-sized ovens.

Through the gate I handed him 70 cents. Sticking the football-shaped loaf inside my jacket, zipping it tightly all the way up to the neck, I made it to a bench in Tompkins Square Park. Had seen my big roommate's lights on; she was working the phones.

I sat on a park bench in a corner below some bare, arching trees, hidden in late night darkness. Rats squirmed in the overflowing trashcan a few feet away. I huddled into the loaf of bread as it soaked its shivering warmth into my chest. I bent over till my face rested on my knees. I rocked slightly from side to side. Until I passed out.

The crescent Moon shone cold white in the blue-black sky, palely illuminating the desert plain. A night wind hustled across the landscape, as if it had traveled thousands of miles or thousands of years, scratching bits of sand, dry grasses, or oasis palm fronds as it passed. For a moment I thought I heard or saw flapping robes and a woman's outstretched arm so black it shone blue. I watched and breathed, and soon the horizon seemed to shimmer, and then it was an ocean, and the Moon was a bright orange Sahara Sun lowering into that ocean, reflecting off the waves. At that point I knew I had always looked west. And followed. Followed the Sun west.

Advián 2006

SECTION TWO

"Crazy Horse dreamed and went into the world where there is nothing but the spirits of all things. That is the real world beyond this one, and everything we see here is something like a shadow from that world."

— Black Elk, 1931

CHAPTER SIX

Shadow World

"Shit, the real niggas is the one who don't get caught. Only Stupid keep going back. The smart nigga learn real quick and stay out of the joint 75% the time. The other 25% — well, that's your excuse, what you can't help. You in this business, they come looking for you. It's just a game of numbers and chance. How you run your game. Most too stupid to learn. So they keep goin on lockdown. And with these new "Three Strikes" laws, shit gon get hectic, people doin' some extended stay. The numbers gotta just be bout the dollars you take home. Nothing else. Not like all them fools out here. The chance is you fit the descrip, you slip, you do the trip." He sniffled and looked agitated.

"Rikers or Upstate," I said.

A car raced through the changing-to-red light that stopped the rest of the 1st Avenue traffic northbound at the St. Mark's intersection. Sitting there on the step, I imagined it swerving through the bunching-up mass of slower cars heading uptown. All those red taillights flaring sharply, clear and seemingly brighter at this time of evening when the sky is still light but the day ending, the shadows like canyons up the avenue. Slick Rick bass beats pumped back through our ears. I sat my brown-bagged 40 down onto the step next to me and retied my shoe.

Bossman, dark-skinned, thin, wiry body, sharp cheekbones, could be 50 or 35; he leaned against the brick wall, lighting a cigarette. Noticing a regular approaching, without missing a beat he strolled down St. Mark's towards the park and intercepted the customer halfway. As they passed, their hands touched for a split second, butter-flying close between bodies. Money and drugs exchanged. Both continued walking in opposite directions.

Across from me, against the wall of my apartment building, the home crowd of homeless sat drunk and loud between a row of chained-down, bashed-in trashcans. A mural was painted on the red bricks immediately behind them, depicting a crew of homeless people sitting against another wall with a big broken hole gaping onto a rubbled cityscape of graffitied subway cars, spilled trash, and hordes of urban desperate. The live drunks seemed to emerge from the mural.

This pretty blonde female I knew walked past the drunks, and they made all kinds of noise, her leggy presence causing them to momentarily come out of their stupor. She wore a sexy red dress. I lowered my head slightly, watching her from beneath my brows. She rang my apartment doorbell. I held the beer bottle in front of my lowered face. Her name was Apple, at least to me. I knew her, but she didn't know me like this.

Flipping her mane with impatience, she turned around and strode past the howling drunks again, ignoring them, heading back to her apartment over on 10th and 3rd.

Bossman returned. My buzz was coming on good. I wondered if Bossman was a user. He'd said, "Dealers can't be users." He looked like a user. Tall, thin, constantly fidgeting or moving, he reminded me of a crackhead, wearing that XXL green and white nylon Adidas sweatsuit. But I didn't think he smoked crack. Bossman mostly only sold trees, small time, on the corner. But then, that never meant nothing.

"You know, you be aksin' lot a questions like you wanna get your own game. But you need to step if you do. This whole area taken. I got two kids to feed."

"You make bank," I muttered. "I seen it. Even off these little dime bags people smoking."

"Sometimes. But I need all of it. My white-to-five job don't cut it. What I really need is somethin' like *that*." With his elbow he pointed to the Twin Towers of the World Trade Center and the other Wall St. buildings looming in the distance over lower downtown. "What I really need is do like them white folks down there — they do most of the drug dealin' in this city anyways. Right inside they offices, behind closed doors. Shit, many them in button down shirts, briefcases and Brooks Brothers ties! They don't pay *nuthin*! Out here I gotta pay the fucking cops almost half what I make just so I can go home to my kids every night. Shit, that's the way to do it, behind closed doors, or at least in a controlled situation. This constant shit out here make you jumpy."

"But you still make bank. I can't even save up $300 for this car I seen for sale on Staten Island."

His hand slipped discreetly back into his pants as he spotted another customer approaching. Walking off he said, "You talk too much. What you need a car for anyways? In a few years, your drunk ass gon' be right up in between the garbage cans like the rest them," he said, nodding across the street. He met up with his customer and they disappeared around the corner onto 1st.

Yeah, you think, I thought, smirking, a little lightheaded.

The urge was coming on, to feel something more… to get drunk, high… something more. I upended my 40 and drank the last swallow, wondering how much change I had in my pockets that I could add to what I'd saved upstairs. I suddenly thought seriously about getting high tonight. Rarely did drugs. Usually just drank. As I swallowed, my eyes inadvertently glanced up into the blue-deepening twilight sky over the city. The Sun had set, at least for everybody down here, but higher up, a jet's metal skin flashed a split-second, blood-orange-sunset reflection.

I drank again, any last drop, and lobbed the big beer bottle at the nearest trashcan. The bottle ejected out of its brown-bag condom, failed to grip the mound of overflowing trash and bounced onto the sidewalk, making a thick-glass clunk, but not breaking. It rolled into the gutter.

I opened my eyes, filmy, head spinning, throat cracked and dry. The 1st Ave. soot-stained ceiling of my room came into focus. I wondered what time it was. A regurgitating lump slimed around inside my stomach, looking for an upward way out. Way too much drink and cigarettes.

Lying there on my back, stomach surging with a life of its own, I bore down again, trying to keep it still.

My eyes anchored on all the anti-smoking propaganda I had taped to the wall, gruesome, graphic info on how smoking would turn your insides into a mucous-green cancer lump. None of that had helped me quit smoking, just made me hate myself more for being so weak.

The shakes were going to make me puke. It was definitely coming. I couldn't stop spinning. Drool slipped out of my mouth as I groaned quietly, afraid to even move.

I closed my eyes, willing an ax to come swinging out of the wall down into my face, splitting my head in half. Put an ax through my head, I said. Just stop all this thinking.

I rolled off the floor mattress and crawled to the toilet, hanging my head down into the bowl and vomiting, water and puke splashing up onto my cheeks and eyelashes. The cold porcelain rim pressed into my throat. Sour, stinky chunks. I didn't even care about the bloody yeast messes and pubic hairs and piss stains that were usually left on the toilet rim by my 300 pound phone sex roommate, which my convulsing throat was surely resting on.

Still seeing green and black spots, but finally empty, I took a shower. Drying off, I walked to the window, looking down at the East Village scene.

Prana Health Foods was just across the street on 1st Avenue, with its books on self-healing and vegetarianism, nutritional supplements, fresh organic produce, good home cooking, vegan fresh baked goods like tahini cornbread or blueberry muffins...

Especially the books. Staring at me right in the face. Again the thought: *You should take care of yourself. Ain't nobody gon do it but you...*

The cavernous brownstone apartment off West 11th Street had a mausoleum feel to it. With Jean Harlow's porcelain doll face smiling through the framed glass behind him (smiling so hard and falsely into the camera it looked like her face was going to break like pottery), the old homosexual 7-foot tall photo collector squeezed my shoulder and smiled himself, squinting through the smoke from his ridiculously thin Virginia Slims cigarette. Very hung over, I had to take a shit, and I needed for him to just finally leave. I shifted on my feet. A month ago, after answering an ad in the Village Voice, I'd gotten the job as his all-around assistant.

In his inflated British accent he told me where the list of things to do was, and who I should deliver things to, and what else I needed to do to hold the fort down while he was gone. He smelled like bad coffee breath, even from three feet away. With a bigger smile he told me I could stay here and sleep in his bed if I wanted. Or just come and check in. It was up to me, he winked, with full confidence in my abilities.

It was an easy job. Walking out of the building with him, holding my guts in, I helped him carry his crap to the corner of 7th Ave and got him a taxi. Closing the cab door, I walked back to the West Village brownstone, glad to have the keys and this whole big place to myself.

I reached into the petty cash folder inside his file cabinet. I had expenses. He would understand, or likely, not even notice. Not too much.

The phone rang, and I picked it up. A stuttering movie star voice; I rolled my eyes. I looked up at the fine-art black-and-white photograph of Katherine Hepburn next to all the other Silver Screen stars on the wall — Jean Harlow, Greta Garbo, Mary Pickford, Merle Oberon and others, most of whom I'd never heard of before I'd taken this job. I tried to understand what she was saying, hoping she'd hurry up. I was going to have to use the bathroom real soon. Stepping from side to side, I reached for the notepad and wrote down that she'd called. "Yes, Ms. Hepburn," I said. "Will do, Ms. Hepburn. Yes he will, Ms. Hepburn, as soon as he get back." I glanced at the wall mirror over the fireplace and saw how green I looked.

Functional, I insisted to myself.

I hung up the phone and ran to the bathroom and with a giant relief took care of my business. I opened the window and washed up, suddenly feeling very empty but good and clean for a moment. Returning to the living room, I sat in the plump easy chair. The afternoon was clouded and gray. Through the closed windows, I could hear it raining outside. Very quiet inside the apartment. I rested my head back, staring at the impeccable, smooth white ceiling.

Before I noticed it, my breathing and heart rate dropped a notch. Diaphragm rose and fell, free now, bloodstream surging, rushing, repairing, cleansing.

The ceiling began to come apart, dissolve into bright gray, fizzy particles as a slight steady pressure, like fingers, not painful, pushed into my temples. My eyelids sagged as I tried to sit upright. I took a deep breath. The fingers pressed deeper into my head, more pointedly, squeezing. But still not painful... almost, but not. Just steady pressure.

My eyes began to roll back. My head nodded. I pushed myself up out of the chair and reached for my sweatshirt, snagging it in my fingers just as I slumped down onto the shiny hardwood floor. I fell over onto my stomach, my hands spreading the shirt feebly beneath my face and chest. Face down, breathing very shallow, with a last shudder I straightened out, hands flattening between my thighs and the floor.

Dimly, I heard tires slicking against wet pavement, a distant car horn. I thought I felt a breeze on the back of my neck. Was a window open?

The rain. But it sounded hollow, echoing, like it was inside instead of outside. Lying there I... walked toward the sound, toward the middle of an empty gray room. I realized I could see through the falling mist of rain that cut the room in half. Somebody was standing on the other side, staring at me.

Hanging my head, averting my eyes, I rubbed my bare arms and looked down at what I was wearing. Hanes white t-shirt, rumpled blue jeans, yellow buck work boots.

Tentatively, I lifted my head to check again through the falling wall of water, embarrassed, shy. I folded my arms, protectively, over my chest.

The dude on the other side was wearing exactly what I was. And he had the same black hair, same skin color, same eyes, same package, same everything. Same, but different. His skin looked more alive, more lifeblood color; buff and built, he stood straight up with confidence. And half his lip was curled in a sneer at me. His hands hung confidently at his sides.

The phone... I got up from my sleeping position on the concrete floor by the back wall in Gare du Nord, Paris' central train station, and hauled the army surplus backpack up onto my shoulder. Rubbing the sleep out of my eyes, I zeroed in on one of those yellow public payphones on the other side. I pulled out the francs I had in my pocket. Bought them at the Cambio place in New York.

The big clock on the wall said it was after 7 a.m. Been here since I'd gotten in last night. Thiona had said over and over how beautiful the South of France was. "Just fly to Paris; we'll go to the South from there. You have to come; you can do it. All you need is your ticket." I'd listened to her, and she'd made me sure. Thiona was the woman for me. The voluptuous dream of paradise, a life of beaches, high class, wealth and no problems, where you could forget everything, leave everything behind, and not be touched by anything bad. The best life I could reach for.

Flipping back her long black hair, she'd turned me on with stories about how bathed in sunlight and moonlight the Mediterranean and the South of France were. She was always telling me I had to meet her in France, and how we'd have the best time of our lives in such exotic beach places as Nice and St. Tropez. She told me how the Moon shines over the water. She told me how everything — the people, the beaches, the clubs — was so different. Life was just better there.

My head felt like it was shutting down, but I tried to think harder, clearer. That dark pit inside of me was opening wider. Hadn't she said she'd meet me here?

I suddenly wasn't sure. I thought harder.

Yeah she did. I'd brought some weed up to that Pakistani travel agent on W. 34th St. He got me a cheap ticket. But it was all I had, that and some food money. We were going to stay at her friend's place.

I looked at the phone again, jangling the francs in my palm.

What the fuck you doin' here? Hardly any money...

Then on top of that I remembered that my ticket was non-changeable. I was stuck here for almost two months?

If you beg her, you'll just make yourself look worse. What's she gonna do, at one or two in the morning or whatever the fuck time it is over there, jump on a plane now? Face it; she didn't come. Stood you up.

I looked around the station. I looked at the phone.

Don't waste any more of your money.

Hanging my head, I began to walk out of the city. Following a map I got at a kiosk, I searched for the road leading south. The heavy gray sky began to mist. In a couple miles my shoulders were already killing me. This old army backpack I'd bought down at the surplus store in Chinatown had heavy canvas straps, no padding, and was digging into my flesh. Another mistake. You keep fucking up.

My heart rate increased with my pace and I briefly focused on it. Over the last year, since the fall anyway, something was changing in me. I'd begun to become conscious of my body. Last November, I'd caught bronchitis, and after that, I just never had the desire to smoke a cigarette again. I couldn't imagine dragging smoke into my lungs. After all the fighting and misery and self-hatred over my weakness, the smoking had gone away on its own. And the drinking — that iron burden of alcohol that had ruled my life for so long — it soon began changing too. The burning desire, the vicious grip, the helplessness to it had begun to loosen, slip away on its own. As I walked out of Paris, I realized this was an amazing thing. My old self had been such a messed-up, powerless, hung-over, alcoholic basket case. For years. And now, it was just gone. No big bang, no major breaking point. While I still very much loved a good buzz, it was different. It wasn't about anything. It was just a couple drinks. I could and would stop before it got out of hand. It was as if all that alcoholism had been pushed out of me on its own, like a deep infection finally being forced up to the skin and passing out of the body. Inside me, things were changing. I was passing out a lot more. I felt sleepy a lot.

I had a new sense of the human body, something I couldn't put my finger on — that it knew things, was intelligent, capable, in some ways miraculous. I had the sense that my body was gearing up in sleep, especially during passouts, and cranking up the temperature, repairing things, getting to work.

In my passouts, I was so healthy and vital. I went places that vibrated with health. When I came back to this side, some of that lingered for a while. I withdrew further from society. Wanted to be alone like never before. Read lots and lots of books about health, and how the body works. Decided to become a vegetarian. Read labels fanatically. And the passouts came on narcoleptically warm and beckoning, took me to places I didn't want to come back from.

Walking through outlying industrial warehouse areas, I made it to the traffic circle and stood there for hours trying to thumb a ride, holding up my little piece of cardboard saying *SUD*. (South.) Cars whizzed and whizzed past. No one stopped.

After dark I crawled down the hill and passed out. The next morning, waking up damp and sticky, I tried hitchhiking some more, and when one of the first cars stopped for me, I thought maybe I would start getting lucky. Maybe hitching was going to be easier than I thought.

The car was filled with smoke, and a big white cloud of it puffed out as I opened the door. Cold air-conditioning blew hard on me non-stop. The driver, maybe in her 30s, wore plastic-framed glasses and red short shorts, her plump but not fat legs flattening out on the vinyl seat. She chewed gum, wrapped it, threw it in the ashtray, lit a cigarette, finished that one, lit another one with the end of that one, then chewed some more gum. I was so glad I had been able to quit smoking. Had I been as bad as her? No, you only smoked a pack a day. Stopping at a rest area halfway down and catching my reflection in the mirror, I saw that my face was covered in little bloody welts. There was a slimy gray slug behind my ear. Slugs had sucked on my face all night. Why hadn't the lady said anything?

She dropped me off in Marseilles, in the south of France. I roamed the rundown dockside neighborhoods of the *Quartier Nord Africain* where all the young African-

Arab dudes hung out. Everybody spoke French; many also spoke Arabic, Spanish and English. I used my street knowledge of Spanish to help me try to understand French and I picked up the Southern dialect quick. I made a few friends; they began to call me "Jihad." I thought it was because I never laughed. I liked the nickname. Coming up to me and throwing play-punches into my chest they'd say, "It's not that serious," to my angry sullen face. I soon got bored, restless, and headed west out of town. I guess I could have stayed; in a way it felt like home, rang a distant memory — the dry air, the rugged ancient coastline, the village life, the sea, the strong sun. Without me opening my mouth, strangers already assumed I was a local and addressed me in Arabic. In a couple years I would have been fluent, everything else would've been forgotten, and it could've been as if I'd been born there and lived my whole life there.

But I felt like I had something else I needed to do.

I tried to hitchhike, but nobody would give me a ride. So I walked and walked west. And walked some more. Searching. Heading west.

Needed some place of quiet. Any place to disappear into. I'd take fields, vineyards, orchards, anything, just to get away from people. It didn't matter; just somewhere I could be alone. My head hurt. I couldn't find a place to be totally alone. The country was crowded.

The summer sun seared into me. Day after day I tried to thumb a ride, standing by the side of the road, growing increasingly desperate as car after car, hour upon hour, passed, ignoring me. Each day I walked more, then stopped to try again, hot glass and chrome flashes and the constant roar of cars burning into my brain. The asphalt was melting, popping thickly beneath my feet and sticking to the soles of my Converse sneakers that were already wearing out. The straps of the old army backpack cut blistering arroyos into my shoulders. I concentrated on trying to spread the pain through my shoulders and back so it wouldn't stay bunched up at those two contact points. I cut strips off my blue foam sleeping pad and duct-taped them on as padding. It didn't work well. I taped up my disintegrating sneakers. I made signs on torn out pieces of paper from my journal pleading for a ride, for mercy, taped them all over my chest and back, and the signs got increasingly desperate and erratic. *JE SUIS ICI!* said one. I am here.

I began counting how many cars passed me — rejected me, ignored me — over the course of an hour, two hours, three hours, then averaged that out to where it soon became apparent to me that I was being rejected 10,000 times a day. I threw most of my stuff away, to lighten my load.

I grew mute. When I'd run into people, I'd find I couldn't talk anyway. I'd open my mouth and swear I heard my voice, but people looked at me blankly, or worse, looked right through me as if I wasn't even there. I used pen and scraps of paper when I absolutely had to communicate.

Finally, with more than a month still left to go, the States a distant memory now, I crawled up under a highway overpass and in the shade, panting, mouth too dry to even drool, I closed my eyes, seeking blankness. The green spots gave way to a memory of riding in the back of a truck as a kid. As the truck sped under an overpass, I caught a glimpse of a buck crawled up in the wedge of the concrete embankment. The deer was lying on his stomach like a dog, head and neck still upright, legs tucked beneath him except for his right front leg, which was stretched out front, sticking straight up in the air and bent in the wrong direction, shiny black hoof in front of his face like an exclamation point. A gleam of white bone at the joint shone through velvety smooth fur. The deer's head was staring forward, his mouth open, long shoe-flap tongue hanging, and blood was smeared on the his teeth.

I decided to give up hitchhiking, give up people for good, just walk. Don't need no fucking body. As far as their world was concerned, I had ceased to exist, and them for me. The whole countryside felt crowded and developed. What other people saw as pretty green vineyards and rolling farmscapes I saw as conquered, lifeless and constricting. I would stay invisible.

Hair napped up, facial stubble grown thick, I got skinnier and skinnier. I lived off fresh loaves of bread and raisins bought with my few dollars, and ate large peaches and fresh figs from orchards along the roads.

I drank lots of water. If you drink so much water till your stomach sticks out, you don't feel hungry, at least for a while.

I continued westward, pulled by the Sun, and by — what? The air got dryer, the countryside more parched. I veered onto a quieter route. Found passages where only a handful of cars might pass all day. I walked and walked, often at night, slept in ditches and leafy vineyards, got repeatedly routed and chased by roaming packs of feral dogs, their yellow-white fangs dripping saliva. I kept on the move. At night, after I bedded down in the ditches, soft-bristly little hedgehogs began waddling up to me, checking me out, plying my face with their little fleshy paws and fingers, climbing onto my chest, sniffing, staring as my shallow breathing gently pushed them up and down. I held still so as not to startle them, my throat choking up.

Further on, in southwestern France I found one little pocket of wildness, a hidden place I could disappear into. It was an area of rough, mountainous desert, more arid, less green. The closest town was St. Guilhem de le Desert. I slept on the side of a mountain, beneath a lone fir tree. This was as far as I could go. My first full day out there, I climbed a sheer cliff face, the sun beating down into my bare neck and back. The joints of my fingers strained under the pressure of pulling myself up as I wedged the toes of my shoes into whatever crevice I could find. I could smell the clean dry rocks as the sun heated and expanded them.

Seeing a path over and up, I inched my way sideways across the wall like a spider, only to stick my hand into a yellow-jacket nest at eye level. An angry cloud of buzzing wasps erupted. They blew up in my face, stinging me all over, puncturing my neck face chest back arms head and ears repeatedly with their hot poison stingers. I swooned with the rush; my head fell back, I gasped "Aaah." I focused on the hot sun burning into the top and back of my head, not the hordes of insects crawling and buzzing all over me, stinging me, even as I eyed the nest in front of my face. I couldn't swipe or do anything, because if I did, I'd likely fall 40 feet and shatter on the broken boulders jutting out of the tangle of rough brush. I went into action, squirming laterally away, back in the direction I'd come from. Still, the stinging blasts continued in wallops. Forty, fifty times they stung me. But there were only two choices: The jagged rocks below, or this. I hung on, and willed myself to spread the hot needle shocks of pain throughout my body and out through the top of my head and bottoms of my feet.

The yellow-jackets began calming down and dispersing. Some clung to my body, some to the sand-colored rock wall a few inches away from my face and hands, as if staring at me. Their black eyes glistened back the Sun in twin refracted white points, their short stern antennaes arched, yellow and black barred abdomens breathing in and out. I got a better grip on the rock face and chanced one arm free, carefully swiping most of them off me, then scrambled up to a ledge where I brushed the rest off, my belly popping in and out with rapid little shocks. I shivered, feeling cold, even though it was hot.

Swollen and puffy, my skinny grimy body made it back to my hard rock mountain with its single tree and little scurrying scorpions. The scorpions loved my shoes at night; and each morning I made sure to shake them out and they'd flip their tails in full defensive posture as they hit the ground running.

Each night I collapsed into a heavy leaden sleep beneath the lone fir tree.

Each night, while in the deepest grip of sleep, something strange and transfixing began to pull at my unconsciousness. Each night I found myself slowly forced awake to the very odd sight of the dark sky in the valley below turning light, a hazy gray lightness in the middle of the night. Thick with sleep and incomprehension, I asked, "How could it be getting lighter? How come I can see all the bushes and rocks down the valley, in the darkest part of the night? How can it be?"

These questions tormented me. I was struck with angst and desire, this shimmering low particle light, deep in the most secret part of the night.

And then, always at the point I couldn't keep my head up any longer, so thick with sleep, I'd think I might see something. But my head would be forced back down onto the bed of soft pine needles and old blanket.

Eventually, the remaining weeks passed and it came time for me to head back. I had to walk all the way to Montpelier to catch the high-speed TGV train to Paris. The last leg was 40 miles, and I decided to do it overnight. I pushed and pushed myself, hauling up the miles, dirt and peach juices stuck to my face. As I allowed myself a short rest in the middle of the night, flat on my back in a ditch, a rubbery little hedgehog waddled up, crawled onto me, made an exploratory circle on top of my chest and face, twitching his nose, then climbed down and snuggled in my armpit and went to sleep against my side. I held still, not wanting to disturb him, taking in the sounds of the crickets, the silence of the old land's night and then, out of the blue, for the first time in years and years one or two tears squeezed out like a momentary fissuring of an underground spring, cutting through the dirt and sticky peach juices and grime that caked my face. I had become just another roadside animal. My chest swelled with pride.

I arrived in Montpelier feral, blistered, swollen and stung, hair woolly and beard a wiry snarl, beyond recognition or redemption, a different man. My trip was over. I boarded the uncomfortably air-conditioned train that would take me back to Paris and my plane ride home. I fidgeted and squirmed in my seat at the back of the train, pressing my forehead against the window which wouldn't open, smearing it with face grease, staring helplessly out at the open-air world where plants grew and animals crept. The woman in front of me kept pulling the shade down and I kept letting it flap back up. After the third time she whipped her head around at me, then got up and stormed up the aisle into another car.

As the train picked up speed, I watched what was just "scenery" to most people flash by. I was the child of my youth, silent and alone in the backwoods and accidental prairies and abandoned ore pits, merged with the private man I had become. My secret shared experience with the Other, the hidden soul of the natural world, had — instead of bolstering me — cut a tiny slit through which my strength and remaining hope would escape over the next few years.

In a rugged scrub desert in southwestern France, as in the American West for years to come, I envisioned — no, craved, no, struggled for — my pristine place in Nature. The only place where I could be real, where I was home, was inside my private compact with the Shadow World, with the ancient personal spirit of Nature. And I knew that consummation of that, like I'd experienced in my passouts, would despairingly be always just out of reach.

CHAPTER SEVEN

Lost Angeles

The subway train shook, shifted to one side, rumbling around the bend, heading down the dark underground tracks into Astor Place/8th St. Station. I glanced at the backs of my hands, noticing the skin was once again changing to its fall yellow with the fading year. The wheels screeched; long fluorescent bulbs overhead flickered off for a split second as the electrified third rail connection was briefly lost; people dozed. I sat on the hard orange plastic seats squished between two strangers, a dozing Palestinian man in a rumpled business suit and a heavy-set Russian woman with lots of bags who stared straight forward, hunched over as if she had a hump in her back.

The scratches and cuts on my arms, legs, and face had faded as the weeks passed and I became a New York City person again. I'd managed to put a little bit of weight back on, but thought I was still pretty thin. I closed my eyes, pulling the bill of my ball cap down, taking thirty or so seconds to myself before the train lurched to a complete stop. *¡No se apoye contra la puerta!* said the little sign above, with a red slash through a stick man leaning against the doors. Doors jerked open and the crush of downtown people spilled out.

I let myself get pulled out with the crowd, flowing up the grimy, gum-spotted concrete stairs. Inside my head, I listened to the people breathing hard around me as they climbed up into the overcast New York afternoon.

Heading into the East Village, I passed the big cube sculpture balanced on one of its corners in the middle of the intersection. Some teenagers were trying to spin the cube; it budged and they got it turning. A man was sitting beneath it with a brown-bagged bottle at his feet. He made a drunken brushing motion at the kids, as if to swat them away. I headed down towards St. Mark's Place.

The days were getting a lot shorter now. Dark soon. A punk rocker kid walked in front of me wearing a leather jacket; on the back he had painted WRATH NEVER DIES in slashing red and white letters.

I paused before I hit 1st Ave, stepped over to the side, glancing around me. I pulled out a pint of Bombay gin from my jacket pocket. A hollow-point bullet fell out onto the sidewalk with a ~clink~ and rolled down into a restaurant stairwell. I didn't look down, quickly uncapping the flat bottle and sneaking a drink, then capped it and put it back, wiping my lips. The alcohol's warmth rushed through me. I reached for another quick swig, then capped it. Just wasn't the same anymore.

Again my mind flashed to the old black-and-white photo I'd seen in the whaling book at the Strand Bookstore. The whalers had shot the mother polar bear and her bloodied rumpled body had been hauled up with a crane and dumped on the ship's deck. She was laid out on her side, legs together, mouth open, eyes very dead. Her live-captured cub was standing next to her, a thick iron chain around his neck, his face immobilized with shock. He was staring directly into the camera. His thick white coat was soaked with icy seawater, his face caked with his mother's freezing blood from trying to nuzzle her to get back up.

I jammed the pint back into my pocket and went around the corner into Prana Health Foods. I spent another hour in the book section, learning more about vegetarianism and different things you could do to have a healthy body. Now about the drink… I could probably give it up completely. What I needed to do was leave the city soon.

Restless… Can't stay put. The little car, only $326 in Staten Island, a little white Datsun B210…

City just wasn't right. Needed someplace to go to ground, be outside, be away from people. Dry… West. Open land calling. Can't stay put. Gone.

The inside of the car felt like a womb to me, holding me as it hummed across the southern end of the nation, dash lights glowing green. I kept the heater on; the vents blew warm air that smelled a little like burnt oil.

Least I was on the "southern route." On the way out of New York, straight down 95, sleeping overnight in the car, I had woke up frozen, and my toes and fingertips didn't feel the same for a few days.

Money not that much left, I thought to myself. If you sleep in the car till you find a place in LA, and get a job as soon as you get there… should be able to swing it. Then you can figure it out from there.

Crossing the low belly of the Deep South, swampy forests arched overhead, not completely distinguishable from the dark, seeming to form the roof of a mossy tunnel as I pushed down Interstate 10. The inner sanctuary of my car was repeatedly pierced from behind by the headlights of giant trucks roaring up from behind, overtaking me, at the last minute swinging out to the left to pass before crushing me or pushing me into the ditch. I couldn't see the truck drivers because my little car was so low but I imagined each one's head thrown back like a laughing skull, Confederate flag cap tilted back, dashboard lights gleaming off gleeful, rotting teeth. I passed through the sleeping cities of Mobile and New Orleans, crossing the bridge over Lake Ponchartrain in a driving rainstorm lit by fluorescent streetlights and flashes of lightning, the rain coming down so hard cars hydroplaned, and some pulled over.

"The sun is riz
the sun is set
and here we is
in Texas yet"

Said the graffiti on the toilet wall of the roadside rest area in Far West Texas, next to some death threats in Spanish and misspelled racial slurs. Hours and a couple hundred miles ago, I had driven through the Hill Country, dodging exploded bodies of deer every quarter mile or less, hit by semi's at such high speed that they had burst in a gush of blood and organs sprayed more than 20 feet across the blacktop. A yellow highway department truck with a blinking light was slowly traveling along, scraping up each remains. It appeared to be a full-time job, repeated daily after dawn. Coming over a small rise I had accidentally bumped over one very fresh death, a deer's shoulder, neck and head rolled in torn skin. My car's underside and rear panel were flecked with blood and stiff deer hair.

Periodically, with my head shutting down, about to pass out, I pulled over, locked the doors, covered my face with my jacket and curled up into oblivion. I had a complex about some stranger looking through the window or windshield at my face while I was sleeping.

As I went under, I thought about Texas out there, outside the car windows. I almost remembered something from my past, the childhood, why I'd first wanted to get to Texas so bad, but my mind drifted, pushed it away. And it was gone. The only thing that mattered was living now. Funny how once my mind had gotten over something, moved on, it shut all memory of that off and threw it out. The childhood, the past, and anybody and anything associated with that were so long gone. None of it had anything to do with me. I had died, had been rebirthed, I was over 20 years old and deep into this new life now. This was my time, my life. I didn't know where I was going, but I was free of anybody's chains.

Facing the potholed gravel parking lot, I sat on the back steps of the apartment building on Wilcox between Sunset and Hollywood and thought for a moment about the Hollywood sign. Those dirty white letters up on the dull scrub hills had wavered in the warm, grainy air as I'd driven into the belly of the Los Angeles basin, afternoon smog burning into my eyes and throat. Now they hung overhead just a short distance back.

The winter morning sun was strengthening and I rubbed my arms. The back steps just outside the window of my ground floor room were my new hangout. The little white Datsun B210 was parked there. It looked patient. It had driven me all across the country. No problems at all.

Hadn't shaved in over a week. Last time I'd let it go this long was in France. I rubbed my hand over the hard stubble and yawned, glad for the sunlight sinking into my body and warming me up.

My head began to nod. I blinked my eyes to keep them open, glancing around, listening too. No one was here or coming.

Good, I thought. Looks like I'll be able to have this whole back area to myself. My own private porch. Just outside my apartment door.

I folded my arms across my knees. The sun warmed up the blue-and-white twill of my engineers overalls; that warmth spread into my forearms. I dropped my head to my knees, releasing my mind to go wherever it wanted. I began to doze, but my ears kept watch, like a sleeping cat, still aware of the sounds around me. Cars. Horns. The clank of some tool on the concrete floor of the auto shop past the razor wire fence with the old jackets thrown over it for easier climb-over. Spanish radio through an open window somewhere. This ability to rest on the inside, and be alert on my outer layer was my Watchman. I would like to sleep for twenty years.

I rocked myself slightly, to some beat I was making up or caught from some passing car.

I heard footsteps coming down the alley to my left. I held on to my space for a second longer, then as they approached the corner I lifted my head.

This guy in a light gray jacket and clean blue jeans and dark ashy skin turned the corner, walked over, passed around me, and sat down to my right, next to me.

"I see somebody's new here. You beat me to my spot," he said, putting the end of the straw into his mouth. His tallboy can of Colt 45 was neatly covered inside a crisp paper brown bag.

I didn't say anything. He had a yellowish-white patch of hair in his tight, short haircut. His lips were very dry and cracked, almost white. His dark, bluish-black hands were ashy as if dusted in the creases with white chalk. I glanced sideways at his clothes; they were clean and pressed. His black leather walking shoes were shined, at first masking the fact that they were old and worn.

He saw me looking and said, "It'll always be the shoes. People will always tell about you by your shoes. Or try to, anyway."

I shrugged.

"How long you been here?" he asked. He cracked a friendly smile. I winced. His lips were so dry and peeling I thought they might split and start to bleed.

"Just got here." I looked out at the dirt parking lot where my car was standing by itself. Most people in my apartment building didn't have a car.

"Well, you found the spot. This is the Grand Central of downtown Hollywood, that's for sure. At least for us homeless cats. Though I wouldn't stay here at night. You found it on I bet was probably your first day, huh. Congratulations. Wilcox has always been the spot, especially this block, between Sunset and Hollywood." He laughed.

"What you mean. I'm going to stay here tonight."

"You're crazy, when there are so many other places. This is only a place to come to during the day. At night you don't even have to go to a nasty shelter, this is L.A., where it's endless summer. But I can't give away all my secrets. But nobody stays here at night. Too many gangs and drugs, and the PO-lice in they ghetto birds, son." He stuck his finger straight up at the sky.

I wrinkled my eyebrows at him and curled my lip. "I live here. I just moved in. In this apartment building."

He made a small laugh, like a cough. "Ooop! Oh. Cough. Sorry. Oh, ok. Well, better you than me, I guess. What they charging you — one-fifty?"

"One seventy five."

He put out his hand. "I'm Bones. They call this Bones' Alley," he said, nodding at the alley to our left.

I thought about it for a second. "Jihad," I said, slitting my eyes.

We shook hands.

He looked over at the Datsun.

"Oh, okay. I get it. Then that's your car, then. New York plates, huh. The city, huh."

"Yeah. It's a good car. Made it all the way out here in one piece too. And you see I got it locked down with that Club thing, too, on the steering wheel."

"I see that. What apartment you live in?"

"One of them back here. Why?"

"Which one?"

"Why you gotta know?"

"Hey, man, relax." He held up his hands, one of them holding his brown-bagged beer can between his thumb and forefinger. "I'm just asking cause I know about all of them. The one right here, the apartment right behind us" — he pointed to mine, right through the wall — "is notorious for cockroaches, no matter what they do. Man, I done hung out here 20 years. They all got something up with them. Back in the day, I stayed in a couple of them. But never for long."

We heard voices coming down the far alley on the other side of the brick building, arguing, loud. We both turned our heads, expectantly.

"I bet that's Susan and her big Indian dude, what's his name."

"Hey Bones!" the curly-red-haired woman slurred, shouting, as she came around the corner, hauling a large blue hiking backpack, followed by a big thick Indian guy wearing navy coveralls and shouldering a heavy backpack too. She threw her pack down against the wall and plopped down, leaning against it. "Hey, man," she yelled at Bones. "Give me some of your beer! You always never share!"

Bones ignored her.

She pulled out a dirty cigarette butt that looked like she'd picked it up off the street. She lit it, trying to get a few drags. Talking through pursed lips sucking on the butt, she yelled at the Indian dude, who was still holding his backpack over his shoulder. His dark eyes looked angry in their pockets of bloodshot white ovals.

"Sit your ass down!" the red-haired lady yelled at him. Her mouth stretched wide in all directions as she talked. Her white skin was freckled and blotched.

"Fuck the fuck off, you fucking ugly drunk red-headed white bitch," he said through gritted teeth, his Native accent slurried with alcohol, hard to understand. He threw his pack down, hitting her with it. He was unsteady on his feet, seeming to think for a moment about what she'd said to him. He reached down and grabbed her by the throat with one big hand. "Bitch, you don't talk to me like that." She tossed the cigarette butt and kicked and pummeled at him. "OWWW! You FUCKER!" she screamed in a grating, scratchy voice, loud even through the constricting grip. "YOU FUCKER!" She kicked and twisted and tried to spit at him. He let her go and plopped down beside her, elbowing her hard in the side. Her face got bright purple with rage which, beneath the flame of red hair, didn't make her exactly attractive, and she scratched at him with her gray, chunky fingernails. He reached for a drink of Purple Rose.

She started crying and sobbing, big streaks of tears dragging down her purple unwashed face. I could smell both of them from where I sat. Stale alcohol. Stale sweat.

A Mexican dude with a buzz cut, wearing an old gas station work shirt and pants and tore-up boots, climbed through the gap in the plank-and-chain-link fence, He got himself caught on one of the wires and almost fell down trying to pull his sleeve loose. He leaned back against the fence, pulled out his dick and let loose a kidney-damaged reddish yellow stream that sprayed down his leg and splashed into the dirt, creating a muddy gray puddle.

The redhead lady and the Indian dude started fighting again. Bones drank from his straw and asked me more about my car.

The black iron grate door behind Bones and me opened and a girl in a tight top, loose skirt, and fringed, knee-high turquoise boots came out. She smiled widely, and her teeth were big, with spaces between them. She was carrying a full case of Budweiser in cans.

"Hi guys," she said in a throaty, self-assured voice. "Well, somebody help me already!"

Bones held the door for her. She set the case down and sat on the steps. She had her hair cut in a cropped bob and dyed in a shade which in NYC would be called Puerto Rican blonde, meaning black hair turned a sort-of rusty orange. She had slanted eyes.

She smiled at me as she passed out the beers. I accepted one and cracked it open.

"You can tip me later, honey," she said, smiling big. "Who are you?"

"He's new on the block," Bones said. "He just moved in."

"Well, welcome. My name is Pia. I'm half Chinese, half Mexican, and half Italian. I'm just getting off a work. I did really well last night. It's going to be a fun day!" She popped open a can of beer and tossed her head back as she drank.

"Hey! Give us one," screamed the redhead in her scratchy voice. Leonard, the big hulking Indian, got up and came to get two cans of beer.

"Well just ask," Pia said, turning her head to wink at me and crack that sex grin again. "How bout you, Bones? Hahahahahaha. You about finished nursing that tall-boy yet?"

"Hey," she said, talking to me. "Is that your car? Great. You can take me to work. I work downtown."

"She's a stripper," Bones said, not missing a beat. He carefully took out the Colt 45 tallboy from the brown paper bag, removed the straw, made sure the last drops were emptied out of the can, crushed it, and put the folded up can in his pocket. He placed a Budweiser inside the still-crisp brown bag, popped it open, and inserted the straw.

"Five cents," Bones said over the screeching of the loud lady, meaning the can in his pocket.

A thundering, thumping sound approached overhead. Helicopter.

"Ghetto birds starting late today," Bones said, looking at his watch. I looked too, checking the sky and saw it was noon.

The rapid whirring booms got louder and louder till the police copter came right over our heads, real low, hovering. Dust and gravel whirled up in the parking lot, stinging everything. Bones and Pia shielded their eyes. I squinted, then shielded my eyes with my hands as my head got pelted in the mini dust storm. The redhead spat up at the copter, only to have the spit slapped back into her face. "FUCK YOU!" she screeched. The Indian guy covered his face with his arm, spilling his beer onto his leg. The Mexican dude at the back fence with his dick still poking out finally fell down and rolled to a stop in his puddle of piss and gray mud. The helicopter pulled up and began making wide circles over the neighborhood, tilting to its side on each loop around.

Don't get too comfortable, came a thought inside my head.

Through my hands, I peered out at everybody and everything around me. I got up and went inside to my apartment, closing the iron grated screen door behind me.

"See you later, Jihad," Bones said.

The refrigerator was in the living room because it wouldn't fit in the kitchen. It stood next to the old couch. There was nothing else in the apartment. I'd taken the cushions off and laid them end-to-end on the floor. They smelled a little musty so I wrapped them in pages of the LA Times, then thought I could have more padding if I stuffed whole sections of newspaper under the cushions. I put my sheets and blanket over all that.

I undressed, aware that I was starting to smell and needed a shower. I went into the cracked tile stall, glancing in the mirror. I shivered. Needed to go look for a job. Needed to first take this shower. I turned the water on and it came out cold. A bunch of little cockroaches began streaming up out of the drain. I shut the water off and looked for something to smash them with. I ran into the kitchen dripping water on the dirty carpet and got my liquid Dove dish soap and ran back, squeezing out a line around them, trapping them, then dropping the lethal liquid in big criss-crossing X's on top of them. They ran in panicked circles, twitching and dodging, jerking, and finally slowing, then flipping over, little legs quivering as their bodies convulsed into death.

I turned the water back on, this time using the handle marked cold. The water quickly warmed up to scalding hot. I guided the nozzle to wash all the little cockroaches down the big hole in the floor drain and stepped in, glad for the heat soaking into my body, steaming up the small bathroom.

Toweling off, I got dressed and decided to shave. It took me two razors to cut through that thick, wiry black growth on my face. I looked like a totally different person, clean, fresh, just a boy. I pulled on some jeans, a white t-shirt, black suspenders, and my black sneakers. I grabbed some toilet paper and tried to wipe the shoe leather down a little, thinking about what that dude Bones had said about keeping yourself clean, keeping appearances up. Squeezing out some gel in my hand, I ran it through my hair and tried to comb and slick it back the best I could.

Bones was the only one still out on the stoop by the time I headed out to my car. Him, not counting the guy passed out along the back fence.

"Whoa. Mr. Chameleon. I almost didn't recognize you."

I unlocked my car door, stopping for a second before I ducked in. "Getting me a job," I said.

He grinned, nodding his head as if to say 'Sure. Don't worry. Soon you'll be back with us.' His beer had to be empty, but he sat there, calmly, with the can in the bag, the straw sticking out.

I bristled a little then let it go. "Where the others go?" I asked, out of curiosity.

"They'll be back. They just went to get something to drink. Good luck on that job search of yours."

"Yeah," I said.

I rolled my window down part way, pulled out through Bones' Alley, made a right onto Wilcox, then another right onto Sunset. I drove west down Sunset, passing old neon-lit motels, a few spindly palm trees, and people walking, some who looked like hookers or pimps.

At a stoplight, I jumped, noticing a cop car behind me. Seconds and minutes ticked. Things crawled inside me. I tried not to look in the rearview mirror.

The light changed. I pulled up into the next intersection to make a left turn, and when the cars cleared I gently pushed the gas. The cop car suddenly came up right behind me and turned its flashing lights and siren on WHOOP WHOOP!

I gritted my teeth, throat tense, trying not to let my hands shake. I pulled to the side and shut the car off.

Watching them in the rearview mirror I began to duck, try to shrink, as the cops got out and crept up both sides, guns drawn.

"Get out of the car!" shouted the cop on my side. "With your hands up where I can see them!" As I got out, slowly, he came up to me and grabbed my left arm, pulled me to the front of the car and turned me around, against the hood.

I shifted and he thumped me with the heel of his hand. "I said, DON'T MOVE! You got any weapons or drugs or needles on you?"

"No!"

He began searching me, feeling me with his palm and patting me down. He ran his hands up inside my legs, tapping my balls. He checked inside each of my pockets.

"Where'd you get this car!"

"I bought it on Staten Island. New York. I bought it for $326 dollars!"

He grabbed my t-shirt by the neck and twisted it in his hand, choking me, at the same time pushing me over the hood, bending me over.

Involuntarily, I jerked. The other cop across the hood of the car pointed his gun at my throat and said, "If you so much as move one more muscle, I won't even have to come over there to show you I mean business." I noticed a small crowd of Mexican grandmothers and white trash and black b-ballers gathering.

"I said, 'WHERE'd you get this car!'" said the cop wringing my neck.

"Bought it! In Staten Island," I gurgled. "Just going to look...for... a... *job*." Air was being cut off.

"Where's the registration then? And your license!"

"It's in the car."

"What gang are you in! Haven't seen you around here before."

"What?"

"He doesn't have anything on him," the cop said to his partner, letting go my shirt from around my throat. The crew neck of my t-shirt was all stretched out and hung loosely. "Don't move," he said to me.

The other cop came around and pulled me to the front end of the hood. "Sit right here, and look away." I turned my head.

"Don't look at me!" he yelled. "Can we search your car? If it is your car."

"I don't have anything. I'm going to look for a job."

"I'm going to ask you one more time, can we search your car!"

"Yeah, go ahead."

"Where's your registration and license?"

"It's in that little green duffel bag on the floor," I started to point.

They both jerked to attention. "If you move one more time…" said the second cop. "Where do you live?"

As if blessed with a sudden clarity, I remembered a street I'd passed in Silver Lake a couple days ago while looking for an affordable apartment, and the lie came out perfect without missing a beat. I wasn't going to tell them where I lived so they could come later and do much worse to me.

With the first cop keeping me under control, the other began searching my car. He finally found my papers, and went back to call in a check. Unable to find anything, he searched the whole vehicle, pulling out the stuff I hadn't yet unpacked from the trunk.

"What's this!" he yelled, having discovered buried deep my old fishing knife, pulling it out of its old black sheath and turning the blade over.

I'd forgotten all about that. "It's just a fishing knife," I muttered. I suddenly remembered my butterfly knife. And was relieved to remember I'd left it at the apartment in my other clothes.

They finally let me go. The crowd had lost interest in the spectacle and drifted away. The cops kept the knife, and gave me a ticket for having it. The first cop said, "You need to screw your license plates on tighter. A police officer's gonna think you just stole this car. And you need to switch your plates and license to California. There's a lot of gang activity here. We'll be watching you."

"You're not wearing any underwear, are you," said the white businessman with the gut straining at his starched shirt as I brought him and his friend their cocktails. I shook my head, disgusted, but he thought I meant that no, I wasn't wearing any underwear and he grinned broadly.

A little glassed candle sat in the middle of each table, and people were talking and eating and being loud and drunk. Pennyfeather's was filled to capacity, as the bars were closing and people rushed in to the little 24-hour La Cienega spot to get a last drink and some early breakfast. I tried to keep all my tables straight in my head. Big black women stuffed into way too small dresses, showing belly rolls of fat, sucked on egg-and-syrup-sticky long-painted fingernails and batted their eyelashes as I came near, flipping their big blond braided weaves and smiling drunkenly. Prima donna white actresses with pertly cut hair settled in and demanded service *right now*. Joking, drinking, higher-end Mexican or Salvadoran gangs came in and took whole corners, forcing people to move, flashing jewelry and taunting the black actors and singers and gangsters and wannabes across the way. Asian mafias with their super-slicked women in shiny, thousand-dollar leather jackets said nothing in English except their orders, which they gave with earnest seriousness. Ken-doll white boys, actor wannabes too, came in looking like they thought they were the stars of the whole show.

A lot of the customers ate most of their meals and then complained loudly, demanding that they not have to pay because the food sucked. The rednecked cook in the white hat made a racist comment about each large order, correctly guessing the ethnicity of each customer by what they ordered.

Few customers left even 10% as tips. L.A. is trash, I thought. Traffic, smog and shallow people.

I tuned the whole thing out and just shuttled orders. It was a job. Each morning I had my first after-work drink, back in my apartment kitchen at 8 a.m., swigging Rolling Rock beer from the familiar green glass bottle. After much looking, I'd found a little tienda (they would've called it a bodega in New York) that sold Rolling Rock, not far from where I bought the newspaper. The Sikh in the 7-Eleven a few blocks away, where I got my 40s of malt liquor, had given me the crucial info. Tiny little cockroaches seethed up the corners and walls of my kitchen, and over and around my growing pile of newspapers. I was glad they didn't seem to go into the other room. I made it into my makeshift bed on the floor by 9 a.m.

"Glad I got the day off," I said out loud to myself, shivering with wired exhaustion and the damp winter chill as I curled up under my covers, thinking ahead to the whole day and night ahead of me. No heat in the apartment. All to myself. Don't have to talk to a single person.

I thought about the woman I met last night. Lahumba, she'd said her name was, after we got to talking. Probably quite older than me, but ageless, beautiful. She gave me one of the photo cards she used to promote herself as an actress. She seemed both very L.A. and different — her own person. She was very beautiful, exotic, sleek and polished, and had good, real hair that was long, coarse and brushed to a shine. She said she'd be comfortable with leopards and wild men in African jungles and beaches. That was an odd thing to tell me. She and that dude friend of hers were sitting at the corner table near the door, and she'd looked up into my eyes as I brought the water glasses over. In the candlelight her black eyes seemed like liquid pools.

I thought about her some more. She'd given me her home number. Her friend had acted like just another pretentious asshole. I could tell she had gotten a little annoyed with him. Right in front of him she had told me he was gay and that he was jealous of her. I double-taked, and hoped she didn't see it. She'd leaned forward almost confidentially as she'd said it, as if to say her friend would never understand the attraction between a woman and man who'd just met.

Lying there, I thought some more about her, checking my body response and how I felt. I didn't really feel anything for her, physically. Yet she was sexy and beautiful.

I jumped awake to screams upstairs, thinking the Spanish *novelas* had begun. My ceiling and the Salvadoreña's floor were not very thick. Either she or the police helicopters made sure I got up by noon every day.

It sounded like real screams, though. And banging on her door. Bones had said her boyfriend would do this.

She screamed again. A long curdling Bloody-Mary-to-the-Mother-of-Jesus scream. She'd kicked him out a couple days ago. I heard the door break in. I lay there, listening.

She stopped screaming. I heard something else, a new sound, like sobbing, but then just the sounds of the Spanish soap opera on her TV. I never once saw her face though I imagined it discolored and puffy, like the faces I imagined on her *novelas*. I went up to check on her once, also thinking it would be a good time to let her know how loud her soaps were, but she never opened the door.

January got cold and rainy. With no heat, I learned to use the ghetto fireplace — the stovetop burners — to keep the apartment somewhat warm. I fought my battle with the cockroaches. I walked my neighborhood, feeling an increasing urge to walk and walk. Cars would follow me, especially on the main boulevards like Hollywood and Sunset, pulling up ahead, stopping and idling, waiting. I would ignore them, trying not to get mad, and keep walking, as they would pull up ahead again and stop, idling, again and again.

I'd also tried going at night, and staying on the side streets. The ghetto birds came and hovered and thundered day and night over downtown Hollywood. At night I soon learned to do my best to avoid getting caught in that shock of white spotlight as they radioed for ground forces, where I could get stopped, thrown and searched.

I drank water till my kidneys hurt. But still, nothing made me feel clean. I tried to find something, anything I could do to take care of myself. Needed some control. If I could just get anchored, get balanced, I could get healthy. In February, as it began to warm up, I started jogging again, but was unable to find anyplace to go that was free of cars and machines and trucks and helicopter noise and the glare of metal and glass.

Pia kept asking until I gave in, and gave her rides to her job downtown. She tipped me, and bought me some blue bandanas and a pack each of XL Hanes t-shirts and tank tops. On my days off, I'd roll up and tie one of the blue rags around my head, to complement the tank top and hanging jeans and boots, without my stupid ass realizing I was now sporting Crip-wear. Thought I just looked good. Most nights rang or popped with gunshots, and shook with the thundering of the ghetto birds. I got to know all of the homeless who congregated in my back lot and Bones' Alley.

Twice, sensing a pending problem with cops, I beat out the LAPD. I eluded them by acting slow behind my wheel, then suddenly turning through oncoming traffic and losing them in the Hollywood side streets, parking quickly in an anonymous line of cars and getting out to walk. I pulled on a ball cap I kept in the car, and stayed in the alleys, walking like I had a job to do, like I was an apartment super or something, till I came out on a main street as a pedestrian.

In my apartment, I moved the two couch cushions I used for my bed into the narrow walk-in closet, along with their sections of newspaper padding, so I wouldn't be directly beneath the Salvadoreña's main area of activity.

Lahumba and I went to Venice Beach and we sat at an outdoor café on the board-walk. She wore a mini skirt showing her strong womanly legs and sat on my lap as we watched the ocean, the sunset, and people going by. She drank a glass of wine, holding it with her fine fingers, clearly cultured and cosmopolitan. She smiled and tossed her coarse black mane in the breeze.

Dennis Hopper passed by, the whites of his eyes grayed like he needed some drugs real bad. A rollerskater dude came along, pulling his dog on a leash. The dog was struggling to hop forward with his two front legs, his eyes sparkling and tongue lolling as he enjoyed his beach walk I mean drag. The dog didn't have any hind legs and was strapped to something with training wheels. A light-skinned black woman stopped right in front of us, grinned, bugged out her face at us, then tore off her clothes to reveal three small tits across her chest. She decided to streak and took off running. "Oh My God," Lahumba laughed, tilting her head, showing her polished smile. She reached for her glass of wine.

As we left the beach, she asked if she could come over, saying she wanted to talk with me about something. I groaned, guessing what she wanted to ask.

We went into the living room, and I sat on the edge of my "bed" in the closet because there was nowhere else to sit, our legs sticking out the closet door.

"Oh, never mind," she said, sitting down next to me, seeing where I had her sit. She had scored a local commercial, and seemed on the verge of some real success. "Don't you want something more?" she asked.

At that moment the husband of the woman upstairs came back again, but this time he was in the lot right outside my window, and he began firing his handgun into the woman's window. Glass exploded in pops. He had a small boombox radio with him. I crept up to the window to watch. He hurled it and I could hear the salsa beats flying up into the air before it hit the brick wall and shattered, raining parts down. He ran as the ghetto birds came thundering, sweeping their giant spotlights, though it was just coincidence and they were oblivious to him. We heard sobbing through the ceiling from the woman upstairs.

Lahumba had just moved into a brand new pink palace of an apartment complex maybe half a mile away, south of Sunset. The complex was a first attempt to gentrify the neighborhood. The builders had promised the new tenants that the neighborhood was changing, and they'd be getting in on a good deal.

In another week, responding to her call of distress, I found Lahumba trapped on her brand new pink stucco balcony like a black Rapunzel, with cops, a Mexican gang and a Salvadoran gang having a three-way gun battle in the hallways of her building, police copters booming overhead. The entire parking lot was barricaded by police cars. I walked to the edge, among the bushes.

"Help me get down!" she yelled to me on the sidewalk, her hair whipping in the machine wind.

"What do you want me to do!" I yelled back. "Jump up there?"

I stayed with her out on the sidewalk. Nothing else I could do. In a few hours they let her back in.

On the floor of my apartment, next to the door of the closet bedroom, I lay on my back, reading some of my bedding material — LA Times, LA Weekly, those freebie Thrifty Nickel papers, the West Coast edition of the New York Times. The cockroaches had gotten so bad that they not only swarmed the whole kitchen, especially where I had piled all my newspapers, but my bed. Was it the cushions? I didn't understand. I had covered them with newspapers, and then placed a bed sheet folded in half over that. But still, they came for me, crawling up into my crotch or running in panic down my bare leg as I woke and swiped at them. Sometimes my hand or fingers accidentally mashed them against my body in a hurry to get them off me, and their guts squirted onto my skin, and I'd have to take a shower and soap that shit off.

Lying there, I pulled out another section of my bed and began reading, mindlessly turning the pages, listening to the telenovela upstairs. I came across a story about this place, this "Arctic National Wildlife Refuge" way up in Alaska 150 miles north of the Arctic Circle. It was 19 million acres, huge, and open, and the northern 1.5 million acre swath of it was called the Coastal Plain and buffeted the Arctic Ocean. They said it was one of the wildest places left in the world, filled with immense herds of wild caribou migrating across this great plain up there, like they said the buffalo used to do down in the Great Plains. It was a summertime birthing place, and everywhere you looked the grassland by the sea was buzzing with life, all kinds of incredibly beautiful wild animals, birds and plants. Three kinds of bears, caribou, moose, Dall sheep, wolves, wolverines, swans, ptarmigans, millions of visiting birds from every continent on Earth including Antarctica. Wild flowers and grass tussocks grew and, off the beach, the waters teemed with fish and whales. Gwich'in Indian people lived up there too, and had lived with all of that life and abundance as part of their culture for 20,000 years. It was a complete, healthy circle of life.

The article said the caribou came down out of the mountains in the summertime to give birth, so they could be cooled by Arctic Ocean breezes, which helped keep away mosquitoes. They'd been doing this same thing for a million years.

Can't believe such a quiet, pristine place still exists, I thought. I remembered the stories in my library books about the buffalo and the birds and the prairie dogs on the Great Plains, how the image of those teeming multitudes in the grass had haunted me. Here was something — a culture of life in perfect health and balance. It absolutely needs to stay just the way it is, I thought.

The article said the oil companies and the president, George H.W. Bush, wanted to drill for oil, bring in their trucks, bulldozers, pipelines, smokestacks. The fragile balance of life in this birthing ground would be torn to shreds and replaced with a roaring, belching industrial complex.

I closed my eyes, imagining that great place up there. Imagining how it must be to come out of the mountains and see such a great grassy sweep of pristine, living land below, filled with such quiet. It seemed like another planet. I just couldn't believe that something like that still existed in this world. I felt worried, but thrilled. They wouldn't let something like this be destroyed. Who is "they?" I asked myself. The groups in the article, I assured myself. It will still be ok. I know I won't ever go up there. I don't care; I just need to know something like this exists. God I need to know it. Please, God, protect it, I found myself praying.

My eyelids gradually closed and soon, it seemed, I was walking down the last mountains up there at the top of the world, and spread out below me was this great plain filled with all these snorting, slowly migrating caribou, and beyond them the breezy icy Ocean.

As I climbed down, suddenly my feet were no longer touching the ground, and I was soaring out over this Refuge, with whirls of wild birds whizzing by me in the air, banking and rising, some squawking at me or giving me a side glance with a yellow-bright eye. As I swooped lower, I saw that the whole plain was indeed alive with wild birds and animals, not just the big ones, but the little ones too, and the place was bursting with berries and tussocks of grass and wild flowers. Breezes off the blue ocean were so pure they felt like the cleanest water soothing the most thirst-scarred throat.

I walked west down Santa Monica Boulevard into the sun, rolling my gait, passing old warehouses, warping telephone poles, and nondescript buildings with no windows. It was warm for an early March day, in the mid 80s. I had peeled down to a tank top, the bottom pulled out over my jeans, my t-shirt thrown over my shoulder.

Santa Monica Boulevard always gave me the impression of being both deserted and having something going on — but just under the surface — at the same time.

Boys and men hung in clusters near nondescript warehouses, or came in and out of other buildings, which I guessed were film production places. Cars passed, some going slow on purpose, coming back down Santa Monica a second and third time. Women went into some of the buildings too, holding clipboards and briefcases and things like that, and always seemed to be dressed professionally, with skirts showing L.A. legs that looked like they'd been to the gym. Some of these women stepped out of shiny new vans with deeply tinted windows, followed by camera crews hauling equipment and a couple of nice-looking buff-built guys. And then there were spaces of a whole block or more where there was nobody.

"What's up Papi?" said one guy as I passed, nodding his head at me once. I turned to look at him like he was crazy for speaking. He was standing in a doorway entrance, below a sign in script that said something-Productions, smoking a cigarette.

"I know you ain't talking to me." I started to say it mean, but let my voice relax.

His dark eyes burned. Then his pouty lips broke into a smile. He looked like he was Mexican and black. He was wearing a black tank top and jeans, and obviously worked out. "Alright, alright," he said. "But they need some new trade upstairs."

I walked for a couple miles westward, just following the Sun, thinking as it blazed into me how it was stretching that warm light over this whole side of the Earth, and just ten more miles further west or so, once and for all past this wasteland city, there'd only be the open Pacific. Soon it became just me and that Sun. Walking into that sun, I peeled my second shirt off. I didn't care. I stuck the ends of both shirts into a belt loop. I let my hands hang open at my sides, fingers together, palms discreetly turned up into the Sun. I tuned out the occasional people passing me, or saying something, or the cars pulling up to the curb and tapping their horns.

At some point I sat down at a bus stop, my arms stretched out along the top of the bench, still facing into the Sun. My head grew heavy, fell backwards. It may have even been a few hours before the cops came and pulled me off, searching me, but all they had in their hands was a sun-blackened scarecrow. I simply said "Yes, sir" or "No, sir" or "I really don't know, sir" to whatever question they asked — I hardly heard them. I pulled my tank and t-shirt back on. "Get moving, boy!" one of them said.

Still partially in my own world, I drifted up to Sunset and, with the setting Sun now gripping into the back of my neck and head and through my t-shirt into my shoulderblades, I made my way east to deep Hollywood. Sun sparked off the chrome of the jammed up traffic, the bright metal making my head hurt, the hazy polluted air wavering above the lurching vehicles. Metal screeches and gasoline-roars filled my ears. I looked north to the mountains, if only to connect my eyes to something natural. I saw the grayish-green scrub hills where civilization crawled up and began to peter out. I had a momentary sight of myself trapped down here in a maze of choked streets and traffic, police helicopters hovering overhead, everything concrete and steel and bad air, without a blade of grass anywhere.

I remembered the thrill of getting on the road, of movement, of just shutting another place off and leaving it completely behind.

You should just go back to New York, I thought to myself.

The thought of spontaneous action quickened my step. Leaving something behind, discarding it into the forgotten and irrevocable past, and heading into something new and unknown was the most exciting thing.

From beneath my car, hands stained with automotive grease, I said to Bones: "Lahumba says you can't and never will win with the cops. She say they can and will do to you whatever they want to. I think they can also sense when something is up with you, like if you think they're shit. They got an extra street sense too, only on the opposite side. They can sense it just the way we can sense them, and what is up with them. So she says the best thing to do is just play their game."

Bones, squatting down by the edge of my car, was listening, smoking a rare cigarette as he sipped at his straw stuck in his brown-bagged tallboy can of Colt 45.

"Well, yeah, now, if she put it like that, I guess she's right. How would she know, though? I know they don't bother her. Looking like she does, I'm sure she gets away with everything."

"I think from her brothers. Brothers back in Pennsylvania." I pulled off some dried deer hide stuck to the bottom of the car.

"I hate to say it," he said, "But I've got less problems now with the cops, now that they all know me, and also because I've been homeless for so long, too. I'm not saying it's a bowl of cherries. But less problems too because I'm not worth anything financially to people anymore."

"You never said how it happened," I said. "I always wonder what it's like at that last moment. Is there a line you suddenly cross, and boom, you homeless?" I finished checking the struts and chassis, looking for potential leaks, then squirmed out from under the car and wiped my hands on a rag. I went to the trunk and pulled out my lug wrench and jack.

"Nothing big. It was really pretty simple. Twenty years ago I was walking across the street down in Santa Monica a few blocks from the beach and a guy ran me over. He had no insurance. I had nothing. And $20,000 in hospital bills."

There was momentary silence as we both contemplated such an enormous sum.

I went to the back tire. It had a slow leak.

Bones stood up and bent down at the waist, rolling up his pant legs, first one then the other.

I noticed the motion and turned to watch. His legs from the knees down were tore up and keloided with scars, big ugly, discolored scars. He lifted up his shirt. He had a gash-like scar across his belly, too. He pointed to the one on his neck that I'd seen. "It's the combination that always gets you. I wouldn't be here if all the things hadn't come down at the same time. But it was all them together. I lost my job, I was unable to work, I couldn't walk for six weeks. I had all those hospital bills. Then my girlfriend left me. Right at the wrong moment. That one ingredient changed the whole recipe. Shit, I could've handled all the rest, I think. I could've found a way."

I yanked at a lug nut, squeaking it loose. It was the first time I'd ever heard Bones curse. I loosened the other three, straining momentarily on each before it gave.

"That just changes everything," he said. "And everything just unraveled out of my control, boom. I fell past the point of no return."

I began jacking up the rear left wheel.

"Funny thing is, I don't think I could go back, now," he said. "Even if I could. I've gotten too used to this. I got a place to wash up and brush my teeth each morning, a place to eat, and I make enough on cans and other stuff to get by. And get me a little drink," he said, cracking a lip-splintering smile.

I shook my head with awful fascination as I pulled the wheel off. I grabbed it in both hands, and he walked with me down Bones Alley to the gas station across Sunset. While they plugged the tire, he showed me the bathroom where they let him wash up. He kept a towel in there, and kept the place spotless.

As we walked back, I said, "The lady at the restaurant called and told me I just was not conforming. I asked her, 'Am I being fired?'" She said, "Yes."

Susan and Leonard were in back, drinking. The Mexican dude was nowhere to be seen.

I put the wheel back on, lowered the jack and, wielding that lug wrench, its iron heft good in my hands, locked the nuts on tight. That done, I flopped on my back and slid under the car, inhaling dust, and checked one last time for God knows what. "I'm glad, anyway," I said. "I hated that place, servant to all those people. I've decided to go back to New York. Too many cockroaches here, anyway. I can't get them out my bed. I even got my bed covered in newspapers, and they still seem to crawl all over me."

"I knew you'd go back," he said. "I can bet you don't stay long enough in any one place to build lasting relationships with folks. Easier that way, huh?"

Staring up at the underbelly of the car, I sneered and thought "whatever." He might as well been talking to the man on the moon. He had me all wrong. That shit didn't have nothing to do with me.

"But didn't anybody tell you?" he continued. "Cockroaches *love* newspapers. They eat the ink. The newsprint. They eat it right off the damn page."

CHAPTER EIGHT

Game Crossing

Speeding up the blacktop strip of Interstate 5 splitting Cali's Central Valley behind a semi stuffed to its gills with cut broccoli...

A head of broccoli flew out, hitting me in the windshield, hard enough that I was lucky the glass didn't crack. I kept an eye on the back of the big truck as I watched the broccoli tumble behind me in the side view mirror. The truck seemed to gun it every time I began to pull up alongside.

The agricultural fields on either side stretched for miles, and seemed artificially bright green. Mexican workers hunched in the rows, strung out in a long line. They wore long-sleeve shirts, and baseball caps with bandanas hanging out the back to cover their necks. I passed a group of pickers close to the road, and caught the gaze of one man as he stood up. His eyes seemed to be watering and so red my first thought was they were bleeding. Pesticides. Wonder how many gonna get cancer, I thought. Just from your damn job.

Another broccoli popped out and flew back to hit my car. "What the fuck is that!" I said to the truck, raising my arms out to the side. I eased up on the gas pedal, letting my car slip back.

Like this the two vehicles sped toward northern California, one behind the other. After a couple hours, we came under giant gray storm clouds that gradually blocked out the sky.

In Sacramento I got onto I-80, starting my long trek east. The road became a gradual ascent into the forested mountains of the Sierra Nevadas. STORM WATCH. CHAINS RECOMMENDED, the electronic highway sign said. I pressed the gas pedal. The air grew colder and colder as I climbed, but stayed dry. It was after dark by the time I made the summit at Donner's Pass, parked at the rest area and pulled my blanket over my head. Hah, I thought. Storm my ass.

I awoke the next morning to the muffled sound of a thunking blade scraping against the pavement and the roar of a blinking, beeping truck. I couldn't see out my windshield or windows. My first thought was somebody had left a thick white wool blanket on the windshield, not knowing I was in here. Snow covered the car.

I unlocked the door and pushed it open. A foot of snow fell in, dumping down the back of my neck. I jumped out, stepping into wet fluffy snow up to my mid-shins, and shook as much off me as I could. I cleared the car with my hands and arms, the wet cold stiffening up my fingers, hands and wrists. In the dry cold air, the storm's moisture had opened up the scent of the pine tree forests that cloaked the mountains, the clean pine scent buffeted by bursts of diesel fumes from passing trucks. I got in and followed the slushy, rock-salted swath left by a big plow truck down the mountain.

The morning sun came out and the snow world began to melt and trickle as I descended toward Reno, into the Nevada desert country.

After Reno, something changed. The traffic quickly died down. The land opened into sagebrush flats wrenched up in sporadic stretches of hard, rock-raw mountains. For miles at a time I drove alone, the only car on either side of the Interstate. An occasional long-haul 18-wheeler or other vehicle would pass going the opposite way. As I headed deeper into this freshly storm-scrubbed basin of emptiness, I saw no human dwelling at all for long stretches, and then I would pass through a tiny town that, with just a couple buildings, seemed overwhelmed by the landscape. Patches of snow held on in little gulleys or north-facing slopes, slowly contracting. I looked from side to side, only casually keeping my eyes on the road. All I had to do was stay between the lines. There was no traffic to worry about.

I felt like I'd entered a different world. The modern world did not seem to have a complete hold over this land, as if the past, even the ancient past, was still alive here. Out in this expanse, there were still secrets in the rocks, crevices, gulleys and in the open plain where a human foot might meet the soil for the first time ever, places not even touched by a native foot, and native people had lived here for millennia.

Speeding through this empty Nevada, I noticed the desert gaining in plant growth, gradually shifting from desert to rangeland as I got closer to Wyoming.

I passed a yellow diamond-shaped sign that said GAME CROSSING.

"What kind of game?" I wondered.

The silence and solitude reached through the windshield, pulling me out there with it. I realized a passout was coming on. I braked and slowed to a stop on the shoulder. There was nobody around. I shut the engine off; even that seemed too loud.

The winter Sun, low in the south, appearing from behind a thin filter of clouds, spiked into my face through the windshield glass. I baked deliciously inside the car, dozing, while the snow patches outside quivered and trickled, shrinking, sending rivulets of icy fresh water down into damp soil holding roots of sagebrush and yellow-brown, winter-worn grasses.

Drove more miles. At sunset, knowing I wasn't far from the Nevada/Utah border, I happened to glance into the sideview mirror at the western sky behind me. "Oh, damn," I said, braking to a stop at the base of a small mountain off to my right. I flung the car door open, grabbed my little camera and ran up the hill, exhilarated by the fresh air in my face. Part way up I couldn't resist any longer and whipped around to look, stopped in my tracks by the glory of western sky spreading out before me in color and light. The Sun was lowering beneath a mass of clouds and sending a blinding flare of orange and red and pink and amber and yellow. Sharp silhouettes of mountains cutting a ragged black line on the western horizon 50 or more miles away were softened by the glow. The top of my car down on the shoulder, and the remaining snowbank — little more than a narrow line of white in a brown-brushed winter rangeland — reflected the sky's light.

At this moment I was here, I was in the wild, I was alone out in the West, the air was cold and sharp on my cheeks, and there was no past or present. Just me here, right now. My car looked so small down there. I took a picture. The tips of the grasses and sagebrushes were painted with the sky's fire.

And just like that, the Sun sank, sucking the colors down with it, bruising the undersides of the clouds black and purple, till there was just an orange pulse, then gathering gloom. I thought of the impossibly brilliant, lit-up fishes I had seen gaffed out of the sea, and how quickly their colors had shot down as they were dragged up into our world and bludgeoned to death. A wind picked up, knocking a little shiver into me.

I looked at the horizon, then at the grasses and stiff bluish-green sagebrush around my legs, and the hard-looking soil. I could smell everything. So clean and alive. This land looked hard, but it was actually so fragile.

I hope this is my last time, was the thought that suddenly came into my head.

Last time what? Last time heading east? Or last time on Earth?

Last time heading east. After this, once I come back West, I will come back to stay.

Full out onto the western Great Plains now... Deep Wyoming... Game crossing signs, wood-latticed snow fences. Silence. Still the only car on the road. Receding patches of snow. Wind, then more silence, then wind again... ceaseless wind. Sun and clouds, pristine air through the half-open window. Pulling over, passing out. A feeling of wilderness just beyond my grasp... And above and below, all this emptiness that pulled and yanked at me, keeping me unsettled and restless. Why did I feel this way, almost desperate; this intense sadness, ache, loneliness, as heavy as that blanket of snow on my car yesterday morning? At last I was in the belly of the continent.

I kept stopping, getting out, pulling over, passing out, driving some more, then stopping again. I woke at dawn just inside the Nebraska line, and stumbled out of my car to take a piss. As I got back in, somebody in a vehicle may have passed and slowed down, and yelled something, before speeding out again. But my head wasn't sure. I didn't care.

By midmorning I took a detour off the freeway and headed up a small road toward the North Platte River west of Lewellen. Brown buttes rose like mythology on the other side. Near an abandoned homestead off a dirt road, I got out. The March prairie sunlight was warm and mellow, strong and concentrated; the air still thin in the elevation. I sensed that without the Sun, if there was cloud cover, the air would be much colder. All around me stretched open plains, tawny grasslands, dry, winter-dead grasses one to three feet high. You 'bout as deep as you can get in the middle of the Plains, I thought to myself. Patches of snow lay in the ravines, dips, and fencerows. As I walked, the occasional wind devil burst out of the grass, making a hissing noise as it spun and scissored away, sounding like tires passing on pavement somewhere, maybe just a couple rises beyond, automatically putting me on my guard and causing me to look around. But it was just me out here. The air was fresh, dry, sweet-smelling.

I climbed over a barbed wire fence. For a long way up the fence line, the posts had old worn-out cowboy boots upended on them. The boots' leather had reverted back to its animal nature as dead skin decaying and hardening in the elements. The grassland here was grazed to the ground. The soil was punched in and trampled by cattle hooves.

Big dried patties of shit were everywhere, poured out like pancakes and hardening on the ground. I accidentally stepped on the edge of one. Inside it was still wet and brown and green.

Something's wrong with the Earth here, I thought, beginning to feel a little anxious and uneasy, not like how I had felt before I crossed the fence.

The land felt sore, bruised. I stopped and looked up at the wide-open morning sky.

I focused back down here, then out to the horizon. I noticed the lines of wire fences, with their bristling points. Everything was boxed in.

What was untouched felt incredible. I tried to think of how I would describe it: Tawny, yellow, wild, free, raw, sensitive, and vital. Imagine it being an endless sea of grass — endless. But when I looked closer, most of it was hammered. Remembering what I'd read in a book, *Lost Wild America*, I began to understand. Right here all around me was land that used to support healthy nations of Indian people, living spiritually and in balance with the land, millions of thundering buffalo, antelope, eagles, coyotes, wolves … Prairie dog towns hundreds or thousands of square miles in size….

"And then came the man and his fences," I said.

And I saw that it was empty. Not empty like the Nevada desert, which had its own kind of quiet, hidden life. The prairie was *emptied*.

I moved over to the abandoned homestead, just a jumble of collapsed junk, and picked around it for a few hours. The main house was gone, flattened, now just a bunch of warped boards, wires, broken stone lying scattered in the weeds and grown up grasses. The house and outbuildings had been placed in a dip in the land that allowed them to be barely out of the main brunt of the wind. Out past the broken windmill ("Chicago Aeromotor" said the faded red writing on one of its blades), I came upon a square hole in the Earth, with concrete steps leading down into some kind of cellar.

Gingerly, I stepped down into it. The air was cooler and old. The floor was packed dirt. A small door hung open. I pulled at it; it creaked open. I ducked inside the little room; on the floor was a pine box child's coffin, maybe three feet long, with the lid partially pulled up on its nails. Keeping one foot in the door so it wouldn't — just for any reason — suddenly close behind me, I leaned in, prying up the lid, the nails making a rust-against-wood yanking sound.

The coffin was empty. I put the lid back. Then I noticed just on the other side a headless cat skeleton lying on the floor, wrapped in webs and dirt and dead moths.

I went back above ground and explored the only standing building, a barn that was shifting off its foundation. It was filled with newspapers from decades past. The pile I started on contained portents of an Islamic Revolution building in Iran. I sat in the musty building, sunlight streaming through cracks in the walls, and found as I read through successive piles that I was able to trace how recent history, in general, went from a little worrisome to bad to out of hand. I wondered if right now somebody somewhere was piling newspapers away, out of sight and out of mind, and somebody else years later would stumble upon them, thinking the same thing about this time.

I drove down through Ogallala, a small Plains town of square red brick and yellow limestone buildings, many vacant and shuttered and others with weathered FOR RENT signs. I saw a blonde lady whose bright pink cheeks matched her bright pink parka. As I stopped and cranked down my window to ask directions I saw her breath catch in her throat and she ran away, mittened hands flapping to either side. Shaking my head, I found my own way back to the Interstate.

Heading east, I decided that history had just recently happened out here on the Plains. The buffalo killing, the Indian wars, the Western settlement had not faded into the obscure past, obliterated by the noise and clamor of the modern world. That was why the West felt different — its emptiness was the vacuum aftermath of a massive change still recent, with a ghost of what had been before still lingering in bits and tatters. In the great silence, not everything was settled.

It was like twilight. Like coming out of a passout. The crack between the worlds.

Driving east on I-80, the country soon began to fill up, and by Grand Island in central Nebraska that sense of being in a different place, a different time, filled with spirits and unknown, was slipping away, falling behind. Before I reached Lincoln it was gone, and the land was just regular America again, *want fries with that?* and I pressed the gas pedal down.

"You can do anything you want as long as you don't become degenerate," brayed Debbie over the music and noisy Happy Hour bar crowd. Dirty-blonde Debbie was the thick-legged, mini-skirted, loud-mouthed hostess from the Vietnamese-owned health food restaurant where I'd gotten a part time job after a bike-messengering gig hadn't worked out. We'd walked over after work for a couple drinks. It's not like I was getting blasted drunk anymore, but I hadn't kicked the drink out the door either.

"What is 'degenerate'?" I asked, taking a big long gulp from my Rolling Rock. Maybe I was drinking a little more than I should but 'oh well,' I thought. The bar she'd taken me to, this spot on West 10th a few blocks up from the river, was filling with people; sunlight hit the mirrors on the bar's walls, bathing us in yellow evening light. A rare, beautiful spring day in New York. The glass doors were open to the sidewalk, and the warming spring air seemed to have everybody in a good mood.

She bumped me in the thigh with her closed fist, and I casually looked down. She bumped me again, and partially opened her hand. A little brown glass vial of coke was in her palm. I reached down and took it.

"Degeneracy is like getting three sixteen year old girls totally blown on a bunch of coke, or drunk, and then giving them some kind of crazy logic why they should have sex with you, because you're not like other guys who just want to have sex, because you *respect* women."

I got off my stool to use the bathroom and looked at her. Debbie smiled like a horse at me. She sipped at her third Seabreeze. I wondered how long Marcia, the head hostess who actually was Vietnamese, would keep her. Debbie was just too rough and loud. Marcia was the polar opposite of Debbie: petite, and refined, with immaculate lipstick and glistening long black hair. Her long, burgundy-polished fingernails and light, smooth skin stood out against her dark mini-skirts. I thought of the way Marcia cast an approving or disapproving eye on everything going on in her restaurant, her hand opening or closing loosely at her side. The motion had made me think of a flower opening.

In the dark I moved over to the window of my third-floor Ludlow Street apartment on the Lower East Side, half a block south of Houston, glad I was at last settled in. $550 a month for the whole apartment — it'd be a tough stretch, but it was the cheapest I could find. Raul, the Dominicano super for the tenement, had helped me get in. I never met Stein the landlord.

Outside, tied to two poles on the building across the street, was a large black banner advertising used pianos. Store had long ago closed. All that remained was the banner now; the fabric was slowly rotting.

At night, the banner cast a streetlight shadow twice its size against the building. The wind-slits that were cut like half-moons in the cloth gave the shadow a face, and when one of the inconsistent Lower East Side breezes billowed the banner out, a grinning black mask of Comedy heaved up the front of Moe's Gifts and Novelties warehouse next door. When the breeze dropped, or changed, so did the banner, so did the shadow, and the big face on the wall grimaced back into Tragedy. Up and down on the building wall.

Somewhere at the bottom of the airshaft in back of my apartment, a stray cat lived. At night he made short yowling sounds, as if filling his mouth with unfortunate vowels that slipped out and up like bubbles in the dark. The cat sounded like a lost, possibly demented, hopeless child.

Below the banner, spray-painted on the metal accordion doors of the shut down building were two large RIPs, one to a kid 19, the other 21. The ballooned letters looped across the metal, festive and colorful, almost childlike, with lots of earnest attention to detail and infill.

Breaking a sweat inside my fresh white t-shirt and pleated black pants, I rushed from the tables to the kitchen and back, running a gauntlet of raised fingers, someone needing more tofu-dill dressing or gomasio or "My sweet potato fries are not cooked right" or "You forgot this; you need to pay more attention" or "How much longer is it going to take?" or —

Eat your own fucking fingers, for all I care, I thought.

My car, the little white Datsun, the perfectly running car and my ticket out of here, had gotten stolen out in Brooklyn. How could I have been so stupid? I hated myself. I had parked it on a no-limit street because I was worried about it in Manhattan, as well as having to constantly move it for alternate side of the street parking every other day. Went to check on it in the morning; it was gone. No trace. Nada.

I only spoke whenever it was absolutely necessary. I couldn't fake a smile. Never could. I just wanted to disappear, close off from people, shut down, get away, be quiet, be left alone. I tried to cover it up, but people reacted to what they thought was rudeness or conceit. "Why do you look so mean?" said one unpleasant customer, reacting to my apparent unpleasantness. But really, I just wanted to be quiet. And why did I have to walk around with a shit-eating grin like all them folks did? If only I'd stayed out West. But I couldn't keep still. I thought of that cellar in the ground, the piles of fallen-down old house junk slowly sinking in blowing yellow grasses way out in the middle of gone-and-disappeared Far West Nebraska.

I didn't even talk to Marcia. She'd recently fired Debbie and was in a good mood. I just did my job, and looked forward to the end of the shift. I was working the lunch/afternoon crowd, and was thankful when the people started tapering off. "Why don't you smile?" asked another customer. I couldn't answer her; and I knew I was close to having the management get complaints about me.

Glowering in the back, near the credit card machine, I drank a glass of water and watched this obviously gay man walk in, with a plaid long sleeve shirt and big bushy mustache.

He sat down at a table not far from the counter and his sleeves momentarily pulled up off his wrists, catching my eye. Stopping with my glass of ice water halfway to my mouth I quickly looked again to be sure what I saw. Before he adjusted himself at his seat and the sleeves slipped back, I saw AIDS sores poking out on his arms, raw, reddish-purple fuzzy flowers.

I turned around, acting like I hadn't seen, wondering if anybody else had noticed, but not looking anyone in the eyes. I suddenly felt flushed. All the stress I had been going through over my lost car suddenly seemed foolish. I felt stupid, while still feeling the after-effects of the car's loss.

Let it go, I thought, drinking from my glass, sucking an ice cube into my mouth.

There but for the grace of God go you, I thought.

But the car had been my ticket to getting the fuck out of this city and going out West once and for all. Now I was stuck. It was a car with no problems. It was free and clear, only $326 dollars, it was … It was gone. Let it go.

An old peace mobile hung from the ceiling light in the front room where I slept on a two-inch thick, six-foot pad of foam on the floor. Probably been there since the 70s. Flies would hang upside down on the it, spinning slowly in any air current, likely drawn to the block by the rotting meat stench coming from the Dumpsters in back of Katz's meat deli across the street. I had lain the foam on top another couple inches of carefully positioned newspapers, all tied tightly inside black Hefty garbage bags. This time I remembered what Bones had said about cockroaches.

Taped to the wall, about a foot above the bed, was a photo of a little white Datsun B210 parked on the shoulder of a deserted Interstate, dwarfed in western sagebrush landscape and glowing sky. "I want to blow my head off," said the graffiti scrawled on the white primer paint next to that. The words looked like they had been written by someone lying down. Looked like my handwriting.

Besides this room, there was the kitchen with a cheap aluminum electric stove, a small backroom, and the toilet in the back closet. The three-and-a-halflegged bathtub was in the kitchen. The floors of the kitchen and back room were bare, rotting, grayed wood stained in spots with liquids past that I didn't want to guess about. In the front room where the bed was, facing the street, the floor was peeling yellowed linoleum. There was one real closet, and I kept my few belongings hanging in that. Behind the walls' primer paint, a coat of cheap green the color of old pea soup was visible.

Sounds of a city unable to sleep, humming to itself in the pre-dawn darkness, occasionally punctured by a distant scream, a cat wailing, and the sounds of chimes — thin glass and metal pipes clanging into each other that hung from the fire escape railing upstairs. The next floor up was the top, then came the roof, then just gray New York sky. From up on the roof I could look out, east and west for blocks, before my view was blocked by higher buildings. On my floor in the apartment behind mine lived this old Puerto Rican grandma, Maria, who liked live chickens from Chinatown. For her soup pot.

Face down on my makeshift bed, still lightly dozing, I felt a cool wind slip into the room over my bare ass. The sticky heat and humidity had briefly lessened with the latest rain; it sounded drier outside. Winds off the Atlantic. Old newspapers and debris scavenging down our side streets. I wasn't leaching sweat like I'd been for the last month, sticking nightly to the sheets. Was the weather starting to change?

It seemed I hadn't slept a full night for a long time. I wondered if I was through sleeping for good. *Maybe you need somebody.*

Somebody down on the street started yelling EDDiiieee! EDDDIIIIEE!!, desperate, pleading. Eddie was the lord of Lucky Seven. Lucky Seven was our block — one of the biggest heroin trade centers in the city. Eddie lived half a block down from me, and his front man came down and fed the pigeons — all the people milling around down there waiting for him — at 4 and 7 in the afternoon. I heard the opening of a window; then the crash of a bottle (I guessed a 40 of Old E, from the sound) on the sidewalk and an AUUGGH! Then running feet. Then quiet again. Somewhere, maybe half a mile away, a car alarm went off. Out on Houston Street, traffic noise rose as the early morning rush began.

I turned over and forced myself to look out at the sky. It was starting to go from black to blue. I saw white spots in front of my eyes. I looked up at the graffiti on my wall and slammed my head back down on the mattress.

Wrapping my arms around myself, I twisted up into a ball. I had a sudden moment where I felt like I was dangling over a huge open pit, and only on the other side — so far away it was invisible — was there ever a chance of connecting with somebody. Somebody who could bridge this gulf, come in this close, take away some of this... this what? And I could do the same for ... (him), I thought. The desire was suddenly overwhelming, bearing down on me like a locomotive. I pulled the sheet up over my face, tried to force it all out of me.

In another half hour, the big semi trucks would arrive at the warehouse next door, roaring and rumbling, ready to load the first of the day's shipments.

Insect legs and waving antennae suddenly raced up my naked leg and I bolted upright, twisting in one motion and slapping my hand down on the big cockroach, swiping it off at the same time. Yellow-white guts squirted out its asshole onto the back of my thigh as it flung off me onto the floor where it fell on its back, legs kicking and twitching and convulsing in the air.

"Ugh," I said, looking for something to wipe off my leg and hand. I reached for a piece of paper from the yellow legal pad by the bed, tore off a sheet and snatched up the still squirming body. I folded the stiff paper around it a few times, then squeezed the cockroach to death between my thumb and fingers, its struggling body hidden from sight as its hard-shell gave way.

I went into the kitchen bathtub to take a shower. The water was lukewarm at its hottest but I was glad for it, soaping up and washing myself down with the unruly hunk of hose, squeezing the cut end to force a harder spray.

The winter turned out to be not that bad; spring gradually came. On my park benches I caught up on the news of the world. I'd been having this increasing sense of foreboding, that things were really starting to go downhill, both for me and for the world. I'd become a fanatical newspaper reader, and had begun clearly seeing that there were connections between what I read and what was happening around me, on many different levels. And I also saw that the official media representation of things often didn't match the reality of what I saw in person. As I understood this, and paid more attention to everything, I began to burn inside.

As for our illustrious oil president, George Herbert Walker Bush, it seemed like he was going all out to kill as much of the environment as possible. Especially my Arctic Refuge. I always kept my eye out for it. I needed to know that this last inviolate grassland wilderness way up at the top of the world was safe and *whole*. Going to sleep at night with the knowledge that there was still one last refuge cushioned everything else. The Refuge was really the last viable thing I could hold on to.

One afternoon during shift change, Marcia asked me, "What's hate to you? What do you hate? Our customers?" She was always coming up with things like this, right out of the blue. Yet she wasn't even a very vocal person.

I shook my head at her in amazement; she was so off track. "Hate is a very strong word. I can define it in two words: George Bush."

She leaned her elbows on each side of the cash register and placed her Viet angular chin in her palm, long shiny burgundy fingernails curling up over her cheekbone. "Why? He's done nothing to you."

I got flustered that she didn't get it. I tried to explain, trying not to choke with indignation. "Yes he has. Whatever he does... whatever he does to the planet he does to me. But I'm not the point! Life ain't — isn't — just about me. He's tryin' to rape and kill and destroy everybody and everything on the planet ... on...on.. Earth. I don't care bout me. What about all those who can't speak, or stand up for themselves, who just want to go about their daily lives? Like the animals who've lived in places for thousands of years. And their entire future is being destroyed for greed!? What about... what about..."

I shut up. She reached her long slender fingers for her wineglass of ice water and lemon and took a sip. The ice cubes clinked against the thin glass. She gave a wan smile, chin still in the palm of her other hand, looking at me.

On March 24, 1989, in another part of Alaska, Prince William Sound, the Exxon Valdez was driven onto a reef and spilled millions of gallons of oil, ruining wilderness shoreline equal in size to that stretching from New York to Miami. Hundreds of thousands of birds and animals died. I watched the catastrophe unfold on successive front pages of the New York Times, and felt myself so helpless, so enraged, so unable to do anything about it that it consumed me. I'd be down at the East River and find myself trying to imagine what all that death would look like, a thousand miles of suffering, dying birds and fish and animals in thick black oil. Last gasps, groaning, blowing bubbles of oil.

Around the same time, Chinese students began massing in Tiananmen Square by the hundreds of thousands, soon more than a million, and were determined to stay until they saw democracy, a free press, and an end to corruption. Again I watched something unfold, with trepidation and anger and a real sense of being just a helpless bystander in the world. It was the Black Spring of 1989.

In another small newspaper article found on one of the park benches, I read about this movement of people out West who called themselves Earth First! Maybe I had dimly heard about them before? They did "direct action." They staged guerilla attacks against the property of those who attacked the Earth and destroyed the environment. They sank whaling ships, spiked trees, burned bulldozers. In my mind I filed the information away. This was something I wanted to learn more about.

The job at the restaurant caused me a lot of stress, but I held on to it. The management wasn't happy with me, except for the owner's partner, named Cheng, who wasn't much older than me. He was always cool to me. They were always telling me to smile, but I just couldn't. I tried and thought I was being nice to the customers. But still the owners complained about my face.

On June 4th, the Chinese government massacred thousands of unarmed students as it took back Tiananmen Square, and I felt that shock ripple all the way around the world. Only days earlier, a single student had faced down four tanks. Now thousands of young people were shot and crushed. The Newsday flasher in Times Square screamed headlines, each brilliant red letter popping around the corner as the message raced around the building: "FOREBODING GRIPS BEIJING, ARMIES CONTINUE TO RUMBLE THROUGH CITY, FOREIGNERS HURRY TO LEAVE....."

And in the restaurant, a pretty brunette customer got up from her seat, turned to walk to the bathroom, and fell face down onto the floor, skidding, her red lipstick slashing a mark across the shiny blonde wood.

I put my tray down and raced to her. I slid my hands under her arms and pulled her up. She was limp. She smelled of fresh flowers. I could feel how damp she was through the thin cotton of her starched white button-down blouse. The restaurant had gone silent, except for the "Soft Hits" playing through the little box speakers up in the ceiling corners.

I carried her back to the bathroom, and she stirred. With my help, she stumbled to the toilet and as I flipped down the lid she sat down on it, putting her elbows on her knees and holding her head up with her hands.

I leaned in, kneeling down. "Would you like some water?" My throat was thick.

She pushed a strand of her shoulder-length hair out of her face and back behind her ear. She looked up at me, her face close to mine; shook her head, eyes filling with tears, and put her head in her hands again. People had crowded in behind me, staring in. I shot them a quick glare and closed the door with my foot.

Without thinking about it, I said quietly, close to her face, "I know it's rough out there. It really is. But we have no choice, we just have to make it, right? What is stronger, jagged glass, or flowing water?"

"Waterrr," she blubbered.

"So we can choose to be whichever, right?"

She shook her head yes, sobbing silently, now. My chest filled with something. My hands felt like they had lives of their own. I reached out and put one hand on her shoulder, held her up gently. That hand tingled and itched, as if something strong, vital, healthy could flow out of it.

"Don't hit the walls!" Stan, the main owner, said, irritated.

I walked out of the restaurant carrying my ten-speed, which I kept in the basement, on my shoulder. I was careful not to hit any of the few customers still here during the shift change.

I rode over to 6th Ave. Swinging in and out of cars that were driving in the bike lane, I raced uptown with cars rushing by inches away, jerking and jamming and flooring it in front of me, coughing out exhaust into my face. I geared down on the pedals; if I didn't keep with the traffic flow, I'd be knocked down, smashed, chewed apart.

Need to release this acidy feeling from work, all those people yelling and clawing for me, Stan always getting on my case…

I entered the Midtown garment district, which was full to the bursting point with honking, screeching, belching cars and trucks trying to get in or out from warehouse loading docks. A dude suddenly stepped out into my path from between two parked cars, walking right towards me, but stupidly looking behind him instead of where he was going. With less than a second to react, I hunched my left shoulder forward over the handlebars, bracing and swerving into traffic the few inches I could go without getting run over. When we hit, dude popped up into the air and fell to the ground as I struggled to keep my balance.

"Look where you going!" I said, breathing hard, looking back at him as I glided wobbly past and straightened up, adrenaline pumping.

He was a big dude, light-skinned black, in Yankees gear; and faster than I expected; he jumped up and ran for me, balling his fists. I dug hard into the pedals and pulled out away from him. "You hit *me*," I said between breaths. "You … right into …traffic! Lucky didn't break my neck. Need to LOOK, stupid!"

A few blocks up, I caught an opening and shot through traffic, deciding to head further east and go up 1st Ave. Always less traffic on 1st, I sizzled up the avenue. The blocks melted beneath me and I felt the pull of uptown. Central Park, the green lungs of this city, was up there. I'd cut back over when I got uptown.

The flat slab of the United Nations building and its low curving wall appeared on the right as I neared 51st St. A cab from behind swung suddenly in front of me, clipping me with its rear left fender and curbing me at the same time. I went sprawling, my leg catching in the bike frame, left hand going out to brace my fall. I hit the ground with a thud that knocked the air out of me, as I instinctively buckled and rolled with the impact. Still, a flare shot up my arm from the wrist to the elbow. I ground down and skidded to a short stop as the cab pulled forward another half a block, disgorging its passenger. I struggled to get to my feet quickly, wary of other cars hungry for roadkill, the burn and thud of pavement throbbing. My body felt as if it had pins sticking in it from all over.

The cab took off. I got on my frail ten-speed bike, fighting the flaring and the shaking after-effects of impact that wanted to set in. As it steadied out, I saw that it wasn't that bad.

The cab passenger came over. He handed me the cab receipt. "I saw what happened. Here's the cab's medallion number and I put my phone number on back."

"Thanks," I grumbled. "What am I supposed to do with this?"

"I said I was a witness. If you need to go to court for reimbursement of medical expenses, you have this information."

"Thanks. I'm all right. I've had worse."

I rode off, but found I was only able to use my right hand. A little further I just decided to turn around and go home. My left hand and wrist hurt more and more. I was going to have to deal with it. I didn't have money to go to no doctor. I didn't trust them anyways. They just wanted to charge you hundreds of dollars, and more often than not they just want to keep you sick so you come back for more.

Otherwise, why would they serve bologna and white bread at a hospital, supposedly a place of healing? It was all lies and bullshit and people terrified of looking beneath the surface. I was so far removed from that world; I needed to find a way to make it through *my* world. Take care of business best I could as it was guaranteed to come at me, rapid fire, unexpected and real. I decided I would ratchet down my drinking even further. *Why give the forces that want your downfall any extra help?* I needed to make sure I controlled the things I could control.

Rode home one-handed. Maybe it was just a sprain, and a few scratches. I could handle it.

"You sure you can work?" Cheng said as I came up the basement stairs with my bike over one shoulder. He laughed, looking wild as he always did with his square teeth and hand-chopped hair, which stood about an inch on his head. His starchy cook's shirt was unbuttoned at the neck and had food stains on the front. "Also, your shirt. You know you have to keep it tucked in. Man, it's not a big deal."

Stan was somewhere in back, though I couldn't see him through the square opening where we picked up our orders.

I rubbed my ACE bandage, pulling at its beige elastic band. I'd wrapped it too tightly around my left arm and wrist. The tips of my fingers were looking a little purple. I noticed Marcia looking at us out of the sides of her eyes from over by the cash register, her fingernails gleaming a reddish shade of purple. The afternoon shift was over. The restaurant was down to a few customers before the dinner shift started up.

"Did all right," I said. "You saw me. I can manage."

"It's OK. But also. Please be careful with your bike when coming up from the basement. We don't want to mark the walls. Your back tire hits it sometimes. OK, man? It's not too big a thing."

I suddenly flared inside, scalp getting hot. "You know what?" I snapped my head at him. "I quit."

The words seemed to hit him. I swung out into the dining room, leaving Cheng standing back there with his mouth open, looking at me like he didn't know what to say.

"Bye, Marcia," I grunted, and headed out past one of our regular customers, the guy with the gray beard and big droopy nose beneath eyeglasses, the one I could never bring enough tofu-parsley-dill dressing to. Marcia's small, slanted eyes had widened a bit, her flower-like hand rising, caught by surprise to flutter a few lacquered fingernails at me. The customer, his mouth full, sat back as I passed. He sniffed, wiping his droopy nose with his napkin, looking up at me through his glasses.

And I was crossing the sea again, the Aegean this time, on the rear deck of a freighter heading toward Turkey, the Greek Islands fading back into the watery horizon.

On impulse I had rented out the Ludlow apartment, took part of that money and more weed up to my Pakistani travel agent friend on 34th St. I had run into Thiona and like a fool I again followed her pleadings. I don't know. She was heading to Mykonos in a couple days, and would be on the island through the middle of August. She said we'd even go to some of the exotic out islands. Paradise offered, again.

Got a cheap ticket to Athens, Greece, a half wealthy, half filthy city. The plan was to take the ferry to Mykonos and meet her there. In Athens at night, I got hit by a Mercedes taxicab right after I'd stepped into the car of somebody who'd offered me a ride. Filthy hospital with hanging bloody blue or white sheets as makeshift walls, and flirting, giggling nurses with mustaches and drippy noses. Had a slight concussion, which made my passouts worse. Stumbled into a filthy hotel off Omonia Square; the room had two or three cots. Don't remember too much. Stayed in my cot. Week, ten days passed? The other cots… strange men in the room… Every time I raised my head, a different person would be there, snoring. Or staring at the ceiling. Or the walls. Or at me.

Don't remember too much… At the front, there seemed to be a dead man, I think. He never moved the whole time, but my head was sort of out of it. I just remember him slumped back in his chair, eyelids baggy and half open, and the little desk light casting upward shadows across his puffy face...

Finally made it down to sun-blessed Mykonos. When I arrived, a small motorboat took me across the sparkling blue-green waters, splashing spray onto my chest and face, to the beach where Thiona lay sunbathing topless with a bunch of her friends. She jumped up and ran to me as if in slow motion, hugged me, then went back to her towel.

And she acted as if I was hardly there, not even acknowledging what'd I'd had to pull off to make the trip. She was down for hanging with her friends, to the café in the morning, to the beaches, to the clubs and afterhours spots at night. She invited me along too. But there was no chemistry at all. I felt like an afterthought. At that point, with my head all cloudy, I really didn't care. While watching her eating a big nasty hot dog, a shiny tube of ground-up red flesh in a bun, putting her feminine lips on that filth, I realized I felt nothing for her, that it was all a lie, a last-grasp lie. Within two days, I was doing my own thing, not joining them.

Mood fouling, I disappeared. Again I was stuck — for more than a whole month. *Unless all along you'd been thinking that you might just... stay?*

I decided to take a boat to Turkey. No plank; had to jump four feet across the water to get on it. On the back deck of the freighter one evening over dark blue water, passing hulking, mythological rocky islands rising out of the swelling sea, and thinking thinking thinking thinking, I finally tried to address what I was afraid might be my sexuality, for real. I tried to imagine it, me being *that*, and the thought repulsed me. I tried to imagine actually coming to terms, having to live with *that*. I tried to come up with any acceptable outcome. I just couldn't deal with any possible scenario! I sensed there was a dangerous pit looming nearby, but I couldn't see exactly where it was, and my steps at any moment might send me tumbling.

The image of my gun barrel emerged before my eyes; I felt the old craving for that trigger. I squeezed my eyes shut hard enough to make my brain hurt, make all images go away. Here I was on the back deck of a freighter, heading to a far off land, under a twilight sky upon the Ancient Aegean, with a toothbrush and one set of clothes. And I might have to actually accept that I was a goddamn punk, and I knew I really had no place to go, no place I could ever rest, no place that was really home, and no place I could escape from myself. Finally, I fell asleep exhausted and hopeless. Thiona was the voluptuous dream of unattainable paradise — yes she embodied beauty, class, wealth, happiness, beaches and leisure, but most importantly she represented the heterosexual me. And I now had to let that die; it was, hopelessly, something I could never be in this lifetime.

In Turkey, for two dollars, I slept on a roof with a donkey who was tied up next to a bed of straw and who stared at me all night. Lots of flies. I walked and bused nearly halfway across the country, heading east, day in and day out toward Iraq... Just drifting through the dusty landscape and ancient civilization, sleeping in ditches or in copses of trees, hardly aware of where I was or what I was doing, gradually changing my clothes to that of the locals, especially after one driver stopped and said he would wash his car with my tattered t-shirt. About halfway to Iraq, I suddenly stopped and realized that this was the farthest East I would likely ever go. *What are you doing here?* I turned around, and headed back West. I returned by way of the Black Sea, walking or hitching with truck drivers on their way to Izmir and Istanbul — the trucks emitting very bad diesel fumes that made me feel even more clouded, unable to stay awake — and one afternoon on a trash-littered Black Sea beach, after taking a swim in strange, buoyant, flat water, I passed out again in the sand and woke up to a giant black bull standing over me, wide nostrils sniffing my face. He had a huge gold ring through his nose. There was a family of gypsies in headscarves with lots of plastic grocery bags filled with worldly possessions standing fifteen feet away, smiling. Smiling so much at the salty green-black water, the trashy beach, the sky, each other, and me. I really didn't know what was going on or where the hell I was, but with my constant passouts I had a hard time figuring anything out, so I didn't try. And nothing seemed really strange or unexpected, just quiet and sort of like, Oh... now there is a big bull with a gold ring through his nose standing right over me, and yes, over here is a family of gypsies smiling, and that water in the sea is sort of buoyant and too warm or something.

SECTION THREE

"The hidden well-spring of your soul must needs rise and run murmuring to the sea;

...But let there be no scales to weigh your unknown treasure;

And seek not the depths of your knowledge with staff or sounding line.

For self is a sea boundless and measureless."

— Khalil Gibran, *The Prophet*

CHAPTER NINE

Mutate and Survive

Damn.

I sat on the Houston Street bench in the little wedge park across from Katz's meat deli, my bike leaned up against me.

Now what did I do? The money I had was all the money I had. That was it. I had lost the part-time bike messenger job. They just weren't feeling me, and I wasn't feeling them. I didn't feel well enough to ride like that all day, anyway.

You shoulda kept your job at the restaurant, instead of flying halfway around the world.

Had I really been in — *Turkey*?

I put my head in my hands and looked down at the cobblestones. Cars shot by; trucks rumbled on the street. City pigeons gurgled in the rancid glop dumped here by Katz employees. On the other benches some of the area homeless sat or slept, their belongings stuffed into shopping carts or strollers kept close by.

What makes you sidetrack your anger onto those few people you don't want to hurt? Cheng and Marcia were the only ones you liked and got along with over there, them and the Mexican dishwashers. That was the first time Cheng was ever in a bad mood, even sounded like a boss. Stan was the one you woulda liked to fuck over. He was the one hard to deal with. I had made it seem to Cheng like he was the problem. As hard as he works. He works so hard, and he was always cool to you. Another case of misplaced aggression.

I hate you, I thought to myself. Why are you such an asshole?

Across Houston, more people began arriving, and turning the corner onto my block. Some were in rags, some in business suits holding newspapers, some just in regular clothes. Some came in wheelchairs, including this woman with a knotted afro-puff who often passed out while waiting, lit cigarette in her hand or mouth, head dropping in notches to her chest. Must be nearing seven, I thought. Lucky 7 was about to open up for a very brief five-minute window of business.

I rubbed my head, pushing my fingertips into my scalp, trying to relieve the pressure that was building up to another passout. I looked up at the sky. Were the days already getting noticeably shorter? It was nearing the end of another summer.

As the daylight began to fade, I moved up Avenue A to Tompkins Square Park and sat on a bench diagonally across from a chubby, middle-aged white woman whose face was frozen in a bottled up look like she was about to scream. I looked up at the canopy of leaves and tree limbs over my head. My brown-bagged 40 of Old E was on the pavement between my feet. I realized that those leaves were the darkest green they would get; soon they would start to change. What was it? September what? Already.

I leaned over, grabbed my beer, and drank. A group of people sitting near the Avenue A entrance to the park were banging on drums, and the repetitive hypnotic drumming reverberated back here.

On another bench across from me an older Puerto Rican man slept, his hands tucked tightly between his legs. I thought about how sleeping homeless people, or drunks losing consciousness, in a last fit of motion before falling asleep automatically retract their hands up between their legs, as if protecting their crotches, their most vulnerable place. I wondered if I did the same thing?

I heard some low arguing and, eyes narrowed, looked to my left. Two guys were walking into the park from Avenue B, oblivious to anything but each other, trying to keep their voices down, their eyes straight ahead. They both had fresh, clean faces, identical short haircuts, nice-fitting white t-shirts, black jackets hanging open, silver hoop earrings, new blue jeans, and yellow buck work boots. I could smell cologne. They both had a look of being so angry yet so emotionally involved with each other that the power of it seemed to scare them. "Man, you're not even listening to me," said the one, trying to hold his voice down.

The other guy stopped. His eyes burned into his friend's face. I drank from my beer and tried to mind my business, but couldn't help looking. "No, it's what you don't understand, is what," he said. "What you don't understand is I love you more than anything, God I do. Just let me go for now. I can't deal with this." He quickly walked away from the other dude, and the other dude tried to catch up. He looked like he was fighting not to cry. They went out of earshot and I stared down into my beer bottle, dumbstruck.

Those guys were gay? It couldn't be. They didn't look like any of the faggots I had seen. I thought they were straight. But they were into each other? I couldn't believe it. The intensity between them had hit me.

"Damn," I said, looking down at my shitty, raggy clothes. I needed to go buy me something fresh. *With what moneys you gon do that, boi?* came a thought I didn't want to hear.

I stood up, just as this brother came walking by, also in from Avenue B.

"Damn what, son?" he said.

"What you mean," I said, taking my beer and about to start walking. But something made me stop.

"Don't front. I saw you looking at those guys."

I didn't say anything and drank from my beer.

"You know, on Thursday nights there's this place right up on St. Mark's between 2nd and 3rd. On the east side of the street, the middle of the block. It's only on Thursday, but you should check it out. They're not all punks in there."

"I don't know what you talking bout. I gotta go." I started walking out of the park towards 7th St., heading back down to my apartment.

"Shit, I ain't worried about you. But the way you was looking, it looked like you wanted to know."

My back to him, I shrugged; kept on walking.

On Thursday, even as I got showered and dressed, I didn't think about where I might be going. I had hung my nicest white t-shirt and pair of jeans inside the shower curtain, hoping the inconsistent steam would smooth them out. I gelled and slicked my hair down, then on second thought pulled a baseball cap down over my face.

Though I'd walked down St. Mark's many times, I'd never known this club was here. I paid my cover and went in, keeping my head down. The club opened up into two long floors, full of young men dressed like the two I had seen earlier, wearing t-shirts and jeans, leather jackets or light windbreakers slipped loosely off one shoulder. Puerto Rican, white, black, Dominican, a few Asian, all mixed together. I saw only a couple women. I went upstairs. Thumping, throbbing music rose up from the downstairs level. The top floor had a pool table and another bar. People hung out and talked. Feeling like everybody was looking at me, I went into the bathroom stall and shut the door.

I tried to relax. Finally, I went back into the club. Somebody nodded at me as I passed. I pushed my way through the crowd, and walked downstairs.

The loud dance beats and bass rhythms vibrated in my bones, hypnotic, warming, exciting. Back in the dark area, the dance floor was filled with people. Men dancing with men. I could smell a mixture of things — cologne, alcohol, hint of warm, clean sweat.

I avoided everybody's eyes. I still didn't believe they were all gay. I had assumed all gays were like circus freaks. Most of the dudes in here looked like normal people. I knew I wanted real bad to talk to somebody, but I didn't have the slightest clue how to start something like that. I slipped through a group of people and went to the corner of the bar. I couldn't look the bartender in the eye. How come people are acting so normal? This is supposed to be a hidden, twisted thing. I ordered something simple, anything — first thing that came to my mind. Vodka and OJ. He filled the clear plastic cup with ice, then with a bottle in each hand poured the vodka and juice in at the same time. He handed me the drink like a regular bartender, as if all this was a perfectly normal thing.

Keeping my head down, face hidden by my ball cap, I handed him the money and left a dollar on the bar. I took a great swallow of that icy, slightly bitter concoction. I drank again, and finished the drink too fast. Shit, I thought, realizing too late I could only afford one drink, after paying the $5 cover.

Holding my cup of ice and precious few drops of remaining liquid, I turned to the front and forced myself to stand casually, like it was a normal bar. From under the bill of my cap, I watched people moving about, talking, coming on and off the dance floor. The throbbing dance music seemed to pulse through my body and into the walls. A tall black woman in a bright dress, model-looking with styled hair piled on top her head, came over next to me and ordered a drink, catching the bartender's attention with a wave of her long arm. In the presence of a woman, I felt myself relax a bit. Standing close to me, she shook her hips a little to the music as she brought the drink to her lips, holding the little straw between the thumb and two fingers of her other hand.

No, wait, I told myself. She's not a girl. Oh shit. She one of them big transvestites. Taller than me, and I'm only a sliver under six feet.

But still, I couldn't bring myself to think of her… him… as a guy. I realized I was glad she… he… whatever, was standing there. Gave me some cover.

I saw a guy I thought was really good looking. Round head, short, buzzed-downto-the-stubble haircut, blatino, white t-shirt, nice arms, jeans, yellow buck Timbs on his feet. I suddenly wanted to talk to him. But he was standing with a few friends. Everybody was with friends. I wondered if one of them was his… if he was with any of them. Or maybe he was straight and just hanging out. How the fuck am I just gonna walk up to some regular dude and start talking to him? I lifted my head up a little so the bill of the ball cap was not completely blocking my face. I sucked the last bit of liquid out of my cup, tilting a couple ice cubes down into my mouth. Thinking hard, I gripped the cup in front of my face as I crunched the ice cubes between my back teeth.

The plastic cup exploded in my hand and I jumped. I quickly dropped the shards and looked around like nothing had happened, my face flushing. Discreetly I wiped my hand on my jeans then stuck it into my pocket. I'm cool. Ain't nuthin' goin' on here. Just chillin.'

The tall drag queen was looking down at me. I had no idea I'd been holding the cup so hard.

"Cup was already broken," I said, finally noticing that some drops of vodka-oj-ice water had sprayed onto my nice white t-shirt.

"Uh huh, cutie. Uh huh" she said, lipsticked lips smiling, still doing her little hip shake to the music.

Turning around to reach for some napkins on the bar, I just decided to press out through the crowd toward the exit. I made it through the open door and burst out into the night air, walking quickly away from the lingering crowd out front.

Miserable the whole night over, the next day I climbed out onto the fire escape and looked out over Lucky 7. Admit it, you fucking homo, I thought. You can't even fucking sleep sometimes, you so fucking desperate for human touch, to meet somebody who is real, somebody you can get with like that.

Well you just need to make it out of here once and for all and then you don't gotta worry no more about that. You know where the real side is. West. The Other Side. Out in the grass.

Climbing back in, I peeled my shirt off and looked down at myself, trying to see how others might see me.

I couldn't. I just saw my normal self. I rubbed my hand down my side, checking out my form, the underlying musculature that sure could use some weights. Body was naturally OK. A little skinny. Swimmer's build, they called it. You need to start working out, I told myself. My hand passed over a little hardened bump or knot in my side underneath the skin, about an inch below the last rib. I stopped. What's that? I twisted to look, feeling and kneading with my fingertips. I felt a little further down on my side, and found another one, but much smaller. I fingered the two small lumps, then checked the rest of my body, finding two more, one on my belly right in the middle and one in my neck beneath the hinge of my right jaw.

I tried to think about what they might be, a little uneasy. I pushed the thoughts out of my mind, got down onto the floor and squeezed off two sets of push-ups, 25 reps each, and went out onto the street.

"I wonder how a bare lightbulb hanging from the ceiling can get so stained," I said into the phone, wondering out loud to Lahumba, lying on my back on the floor, half on and half off the strip of foam that was my bed. My head was turned sideways, flat on the linoleum and looking into the kitchen. I stared at the bulb's brown blotches. My eyes traveled across the decaying, damp plaster ceiling hanging in strips and bulges like in a cave, though somehow none of those clumps ever fell. I didn't tell her about the ceiling or puke-green walls or any of the rest.

"Jihad, I don't want to imagine what kind of place you got, after the one you had here in LA. You need to do better for yourself. I don't know how you do it. You have to claim it! You know, I ask God and Goddess every day for my success. I also burn green candles. Green candles help you bring in money."

"I just don't think I'm supposed to pray for little things. Only really big, basic things — like staying alive and able to walk and things like that. I'm afraid if I did I'd use up what little I might get, period."

"That's nonsense. I ask God and Goddess for whatever I need. We have to claim it!"

I wanted to change the subject..

"So, it's not even been a whole year yet since we met," I said. "God, I can't believe how much has happened. But anyways, I miss you. You're one of the few people I can talk to."

"Is that so," she said in that warm, comforting way of hers, voice soft as fine black silk, laughing. "Well, you know that people meet each other for a reason. Lord, I can't figure out why you and I met," she said. It sounded like she was rolling her eyes.

"Don't roll your eyes at me," I said.

She continued laughing. "I'm only joking. I know there is some reason. But I'm used to champagne and Jags and movie scripts. You bring me over a big ol' bottle of Old English beer and two plastic cups. LORD!"

"Take it or leave it," I said. "Anyway, it's malt liqua', not beer." I sarcastically stressed the word "liqua'" like I was drunk.

"Quit being so serious. You know me better than that. When François had me in his mansion in Haiti, I had everything — my two pet leopards Jume and Jumana, luxury cars, chauffeurs, servants, my own private ocean cove and beach… everything except my freedom. And I will have that level again. But on my own. Before I even get my Oscar. I am claiming it. But just because I am accustomed to having things like that doesn't mean I can't audition to play a street person. I like to have all kinds of people in my life. I mean, I'm living on Los Feliz. And I know *you*, don't I? I can be comfortable wherever."

"Almost wherever," I said. "Remember Hollywood? My place... *and* yours — that new pink monstrosity you thought you were getting such a good deal at. Hah."

"Well we live and we learn, don't we?"

There was a comfortable silence.

"Remember when you came over to my place on Wilcox and were sitting on my cushions, I mean my bed, and you wanted to ask me something?"

"Yessss?"

I pictured her slowly drawing her fingernails up and down the phone cord.

I grimaced, breaking a little sweat.

"Well, when you..." My throat contracted, and I swallowed. My scalp began to feel hot. I closed my eyes. I had to do this. I had to.

"I'm listening, Brotherman... Hello...? Anybody home out there in New York City?"

I swallowed again, gritting my teeth. In a croaky voice, trying hard not to let it sound nervous, I said, "Well, that thing you wanted....to ask me. I knew what it was you were probably going to ask me."

"I'm listening... Hum de dum de dumm... hmmm.... Listening to myself breathe on the phone line is always fun."

"Ughhh," I said, not meaning to say it out loud. "I mean, well, yeah. I think I am... that. With... ugh... that. With guys, I mean." I squeezed my eyes shut and thrust the phone high away from my face, cringing.

"Well that's a big step for you," I heard her voice saying in the phone receiver, sounding tinny from this distance. "I was once in a three-way relationship for about two months."

I slowly brought the phone back down to my ear.

"It was such a trip. She was an actress too, Tania, and his name was MacMillan; he was head of his own construction company. God, we were like panthers in that bed. The first time she went down on me I didn't know what was happening, it was that good. It was always in the afternoon too, when the three of us would meet, and these big white curtains were blowing all around us. It was like a movie by... what's that director's name? Oh anyway. But soon she started getting possessive, and not wanting MacMillan to come around... And I had to move on. It was fun, but I realized I like to be penetrated."

I don't, I thought to myself.

"Lahumba, I'm being serious. I don't think it's... ughh... all the way. I mean it's probably "bi," maybe. I mean, because at first I thought for sure you and I were gonna make love, and I wanted to, but..."

She calmed down and got serious. "I'm listening, Jihad. Go on." Her voice was that soft black silk pillow again.

"This is so hard for me. Ugh. I mean, you probably think it's all about sex. But it's ...I don't know. God this is so hard for me to talk about. It is that, but it's like, something deeper. Like — it's a need from inside that's so intense... I can't explain it.

It's about more than sex. It's so burning and intense it's driving me crazy. I don't know. I can't explain."

I stood up and walked to the window. Across the dark street, the big digital clock in the old guy's apartment window said 3:15. I wondered who else was up this late tonight.

"I'm listening. I understand. When we see each other next, you know what? I'm going to do your tarot cards. Something tells me you need that. I could maybe even do them over the phone next time."

"Hey, I guess we'd better hang up. It's after 3, here. After midnight your time. We've been talking for over an hour. But you're worth it. I don't have enough to pay the rent, so I better watch my coins."

"Jihad, don't tell me that." She sounded like she was acting worried, then I told myself to stop being mean. She was sincere. My head was starting to hurt. It'd been too much talking. I felt myself withdrawing.

"Alright, good night, girl," I said.

"Love and light," she said in a soft voice that she purposely faded out. "*Goddess bless....*"

My hands were cold. Under a low-hung ceiling of gray clouds, I walked down the tar path inside East River Park, against the black iron railing. The river, unrolling in perpetual motion and army camouflage green, puckered with taps of near-freezing rain. As the river met the concrete abutments of the massive Williamsburg Bridge, eddies swirled, mini-whirlpools, sucking and curling, then pulling away.

I looked at my hands. They were yellow and damp. I clenched my fists and the knuckles glared. Any place I put them, they felt bothered, uncomfortable. The rain slanted into me, increasing, as the wind picked up. I kept my head down, water beading off the bill of my baseball cap. I sniffled. Being gay was still a life sentence. I shook my head. How could I accept that? I huddled into myself, walking steadily. Again, a different thought slipped in, for just a moment: What if I just finally did? I mean, just accept it?

Hell no. I shoved the thought away.

But wait, what was that? Right before I pushed that thought away. A split-second sense of flooding relief, that I could actually do it? Not have to hold up this huge weight anymore.

That opening closed. Fuck no. I don't want to be ... *that*. No way. It's the worst thing in the world to have to be. And to be stuck with that for the rest of your life? Hell no. If I admit it, give in, it's a life sentence.

I hadn't called Lahumba in a couple weeks. I was too embarrassed. I couldn't believe I had told her *that*. It must have been the beers. And the fact I was so tired.

I shoved my fists into my pockets. That didn't help either. My jeans were wet and the pockets cut into the backs of my rubbery hands. I tried slipping them inside my pants, pressing them against the smooth flatness of my lower abdomen, just above my groin. I thought about my insides, all that 98.6 degrees heat in there, all those tubes and organs and valves and whatever, all that pumping and surging.

It didn't help. I sniffled again. I dug deeper, sliding my hands down below my balls, which I thought had to be the warmest part of my body. I had envisioned my belly downward as a sort of central point of deep internal heat, radiating from yellow to orange to red hot, like embers of a traveler's campfire. A traveler's campfire was supposed to be salvation and best friend. I remembered how all the sleeping homeless people tucked their hands between their legs.

But my hands were still cold. I pulled them out and kept walking, occasionally making fists and blowing into them. Vapor blew out. Air was getting colder quickly.

A thousand seagulls blown in off the greenish-brown river stood huddled on the baseball field, away from the stretches of bare mud that were bearing muddy solace to a Puerto Rican schoolgirl running in circles wearing uniform Catholic School shoes she was determined not to care about. The gulls stood one-legged, with feathers puffed out in the stark green grass, round white balls with clicking yellow beaks and beaded eyes wary of a little checker-skirted girl running around and around and around in the mud, arms and backpack flying.

It felt like it was going to snow soon, the season's first, and hard. My breath was now making a cloud of vapor that trailed around and behind me. Looking through the band of soaked black tree trunks separating where I was from where the city was, I could see that the cars on FDR Drive had their lights on, windshield wipers swishing steadily. The sounds of the rushing vehicles and splashing tires came to me muffled. Be dark soon.

I decided to have one more thought before I let my mind puff out for the rest of the day. The thought came immediately. It came as more of a feeling, more of an impending — almost urgent — sense that (*you should do something*). I tried to focus, hold onto that thought, but I just couldn't. My eyes wanted to close. I couldn't think about anything.

When I got under the bridge I didn't stop like I usually did. Usually, directly beneath, it seemed that just being so close under this gargantuan structure might crush me, flatten all the thinking and head-hurting out of me. The roar, the clank of traffic and trains above me, the spanning steel beams… If it were night, or getting dark like this, I would be able to see window flashes of light from passing trains and giant white sparks jabbing down through the massive steel girders into the shadows.

You need to keep moving. So cold and wet. I knew if I stopped, I might not start moving again. A Russian freighter pushed upriver. Half a minute later, three expanding waves rolled into the seawall. Across the river in Brooklyn, big red neon letters on the side of a processing plant began to glow DOMINO SUGAR.

A tiny Chinese woman, lost inside a huge lavender parka with a white hood trimmed in fake fur, stood alone up against the railing and handlined for bluefish or the occasional striper, her tiny hands almost blue themselves.

Her face had a certain life-lived smugness, knowing that what she knew, the others didn't. On balmy days there were often ten or more — all men, all Rican — with full rigs and bells and fresh bait from the store on Delancey, men with Budweisers and packs of Newports, all *compas*. She here, today, alone…

A fit bluefish of nearly 20 pounds, hunk of rope through its flaring gills, hung gasping from the chain-link fence behind her.

"Boofish!" she said suddenly, darkly at me from beneath that hood to my unconscious stare as I passed. My boots did not splash in the puddles.

"When smell the melons, always you know, in time…" She shot a threatening look at a big bonus box turtle tied up inside a pink plastic grocery bag, its head sticking out and twisting around, not yet keen on soup. "Always you know," she said, turning back to the water, the monofilament coiled tightly — no kinks or snarls — and cutting into her blue hands. "You smell the melons, boofish running! Time for boofish!"

The rain crinkled off the struggling pink plastic bag. I hadn't stopped walking and her last words tried to catch up to my back, like something whispered from an alley.

As I got to the baseball field, the sky finally began to fall as snow. Thankfully, the little schoolgirl had gotten some sense and gone home to a warm apartment. May you always be safe, I thought. And have a really great life and future.

The first snowflakes fell like clumps of wet toilet paper. It felt like it wanted to snow so hard, maybe forever. The thousand seagulls huddled.

The wind changed, and for a second I thought I smelled something on it, something heavy, fruity, ripe, something almost like gone-over melons.

Then, just the smells again of the incoming ocean and river water, working freighters and tugs, and the usual, cooked-sugar smells of Brooklyn across the way.

I looked down at my feet. MUTATE AND SURVIVE read the spray paint on the tar path, glaring through the shallow puddle that stretched out along the pavement, absorbing the falling snow on contact.

I flicked on the light and happened to glance at the little metal sink that was tucked between the door and the kitchen bathtub. Tiny baby cockroaches were swarming all over the head of my toothbrush, sucking at its still wet bristles, even clinging to the handle, fighting each other to get them some of my mouth residue, their antennaes and legs twitching and scrambling for purchase.

"Ugh shit!" I said between my teeth, throwing my keys down on the floor and rushing for it, wanting to kick myself for not remembering to put it in the refrigerator. I pounded the toothbrush against the sink rim, turning the hot water on at the same time. The little cockroaches fell off in clumps and raced for their lives. I swiped them back down and down again, until the water got hot and steaming. It boiled them alive, and they collected in a dead, steaming mass at the bottom of the drain. I'd have to scoop the mass out. I swore to remember to buy Combat. It would be worth the six bucks.

As I wondered why the shower never got this hot, I heard a thunk of pipes in the wall, and then some tentative hissing. I turned around. The radiator was kicking on. The landlord was turning the heat on. Finally! It was so cold in here I could see my breath. Excited, thinking about a hot — well, warm — shower and stepping out of that into a warmed apartment, I grabbed the bar of soap and began lathering up my toothbrush, scrubbing it against my palm over and over again until sure I'd gotten all the cockroach spit off it.

The radiator thunked again and groaned loudly, then began hissing steadily. A thin spray of water vapor started shooting high up out of one of the pipes, clinging in beads to the green leaded-paint wall. That's what those brown stains were from. The water vapor gradually began to drip down the wall, a drop or two at a time. I looked at the dried lake-like ring with the white crusty edges in the bellied dip of the kitchen floor. That's what that was. I was going to have a lake in my kitchen.

I put my toothbrush away in the fridge, and went over and stood by the part of the radiator that wasn't spewing water vapor, holding my hands over the metal. I could feel a slim amount of heat. It would warm up more, I told myself. It has to. It just needs more time. And maybe the water vapor spray will lessen up once it gets kicking to full speed.

Pulling out my dollar-store broom and dustpan, I began sweeping the rough wooden floor. Old splinters from the sunken grayish-brown wood came out with each sweep. I avoided pushing any dust or splinters down the little hole in the floor in front of the refrigerator. You could see down into the empty apartment below.

After I dumped the dirt in the plastic grocery bag hanging from the doorknob, I checked the radiator again. Still no real heat. I wondered if Raul and Stein knew. I needed to tell at least Raul. But I hadn't yet paid this month's rent.

I've gotta make some money, I thought. I undressed, hung my wet clothes from the refrigerator handle, and climbed into the bathtub. I grabbed the hose and began squirting myself down.

Raul looked at the radiator and said he wouldn't be able to do anything about it, that he'd have to ask Stein to buy a new one. And that was not a good idea right now, since he'd already asked him to be patient with the rent. "Stein, he know how bad is the place," Raul said. "Long as you keep paying in, and make the effort. You don't get too far behind, you ok, you got me, papa? "

"Yeah," I said.

"Best thing to do, is wait it out. Spring is not that many months away. Next winter, you back on top; maybe Stein will do it for you. That my advice. You know, I work with him everyday. I know him. Anyway, the radiator, he been like that — no work too much — for a long time."

CHAPTER TEN

Luv Dancin'

The dance floor was set back in the dark, with no flashing lights or anything and I could just disappear into the blackness and dance, reduced to bone-vibrating rhythm beats and the anonymous crush of other dancing bodies. Lights from the front bar shafted through the moving silhouettes of people packed in around me. Buried in the crowd, I danced by myself in my own harder b-boy style until I worked up a sweat, making sure people knew by my body language that just because I could dance and liked to dance didn't mean I wasn't still a hard mug. The music, the thumping rhythms, the tribal beats were so powerful and intoxicating that more and more energy built up. I felt as if the DJ — hidden somewhere up there — knew he was capable of playing the crowd like we were helpless to it. Out of the speakers blasted powerful black women voices punctuated by beats and rippling musical scores, everything twisting together and separating and coming back together like pulsing strands of auditory DNA, sending tentacles into the crowd to overtake and command us. We were powerless to rhythm and glad about it.

Inside my own little world, I was still aware of the other young guys dancing all around me, close by, dark shapes of movement, some dancing with each other, some by themselves. I could smell their cologne and clean bodies, feel their body heat. I kept the bill of my ball cap down over my eyes. The dance floor was always packed; shoulders and backs in tightly stretched t-shirts brushing or lightly bumping into me. If somebody accidentally bumped into me too hard, he put his hand on my lower back or shoulder and, leaning into my ear, his neck, breath, scent close, said over the music, "Sorry, man." Sometimes I could see a flash of a smile, white teeth, in the dark, close up to the side of my face.

The Mars club in the old meatpacking district on the west side of town was the hottest thing; three floors, each with a different DJ, and packed with people, mostly young men, and some of their female friends. I stood on my platform on the second floor, hair slicked back, in a sheen of sweat like a second skin, naked except for a pair of shorts and my boots with the white socks poking up out over their tops.

A red light shined on me. The place was so packed I was trapped; even if I'd wanted to get down and take a break I wouldn't have been able to. I kept my sunglasses on. People came up and put dollar bills, or fives, in my waistband, but as soon as the bill was in there, I turned or backed up or leaned away, making their hands fall off me. They wanted to grab and feel; none of that shit was gon' happen, not with me. Maybe with some of the others — the three other dancers on my floor let people feel all over them for tips — but not me.

The house music —"Luv Dancin," "Work It To The Bone," "Pump Up The Volume," "You Used To Hold Me," and more — was so loud there was no use in anybody even trying to hold a conversation, and people just danced, or drank by the bar. The owner of the club came out of the stairwell and forced his way over to each dancer, saying something in each one's ear and handing him something or putting something in his mouth. He made his way over to me, said a few flirty-crap words and pushed an ecstasy pill into my mouth, while handing me two drink tickets. I used the tip of my tongue to push the pill between my teeth to keep it dry as possible. The owner went on his way, kissing people he knew on the cheek as they parted for him. He was the one who'd seen me dancing by myself at the club on St. Mark's Place, and pressed his business card into my hand. Soon I was working every Sunday night.

As soon as he left I bent down as if to tie my boot and took the pill from my mouth. I wrapped it in a piece of paper towel I'd hidden and stuck it in my boot where the leather upper met the tongue, so it wouldn't get wet from sweat. I made sure the boot was tied tight to hold it there. That pill meant an extra $25, sold to somebody.

As I stood up I noticed this tall guy with curly black hair and a silver hoop earring in each ear standing by one of the floor columns, staring at me. A girl was with him. He smiled. Having my glasses on, I acted like I hadn't seen him and kept dancing. This was just a job for me, three and a half hours a week. The only night the club was open was Sunday, and once I was up here on my platform, I usually stayed the entire shift. The money was sometimes all I could generate in a week. And after I collected my little $65 dollar pay, plus my tips, plus sold the little ecstasy pill, I went home, and buried myself in my foam mattress until utility bill collectors began calling in the morning, making threats into the answering machine, like "I know you're there" and "If you don't pay us now, you'll be in even more serious trouble later." The volume button was broken on my answering machine and stayed on the loudest setting.

After 5 a.m. Still dark. A Monday morning, after work, walking up 10th St. a few blocks in from the river. The gutted headless cow swung out on a hook from the back of the refrigerated truck, nearly hitting me as I passed between it and the sagging-roofed warehouse. I ducked out of the way and kept walking. A stocky man in a bloody white smock peered down at me from the truck bay, reaching a gloved hand for the large black and white unskinned carcass. The sidewalks and cobblestone streets of the meatpacking district had a fatty, congealed film on them, and the air smelled off, faintly like death and old coagulated body fluids. Some of the buildings were abandoned and cracked open. When you walked past, there was a gap in the air as if the dankness and must created a vacuum that wanted to suck at you, pull you in. Obscured in the shadows of corners or doorways, people sometimes stood, hissing between their teeth to get you to stop, maybe come over, maybe get into something or buy some drugs. Down by the river, and along West 14th Street would be all the drag queen hookers and the Wyoming truckers who'd just dropped off their haul and were looking to pay for some sex.

Another week passed, another night of work. Getting barely light outside, another gray, rainy late September dawn. I ducked into the timeless darkness of an after-hours club not too far from Mars. Sitting on a couch in a side room, just chilling, listening to the music, not wanting to move, I noticed the dude with the curly black hair and silver earrings come in. He came over and squeezed into the crowded couch opposite me, pulled out a cigarette.

He leaned forward, as if to catch my attention. "You look good up there."

"Where," I said.

"At the club. I've seen you dancing."

"Just a job. A little extra coin on the side."

"You trick?"

"Fuck you," I sneered. "Course not. What the fuck you ask me something like that. It's just a little extra money on the side. Dancing. That's it."

"Don't forget the ecstasy." He grinned.

Narrowing my eyes, I shook my head, not saying anything. I looked away.

"Hey, man, it's cool. Relax. I'm not stalking you." He tapped me on the knee, held out his hand to shake. "I'm Diego. I'm from Panama."

I sat there, being an asshole for no good reason. After a couple minutes, I decided to shake his hand. "Jihad."

"I know," he said. In the background, some R&B music was playing, New Edition or something. "The first time I saw you I noticed your eyes. I can't stop thinking about you."

I said nothing.

"Where do you live?"

I nodded my head east. "Over there."

He looked at me.

"Ok," I said. "Lower East Side. Why?"

"Because I might want to come stay with you sometime." He smiled. "That's all."

I noticed his lips were aiight. Full. Pretty nice looking. "I mind my own business," I said.

"Same here. You don't see me with a bunch of other people. I've only been with one other dude before."

"I ain't seen you before."

"Yeah," he said.

"I gotta go," I said, getting up.

I went to the back, behind some curtains, to use the bathroom. Coming out I decided to explore the dark rooms behind the empty stage. A plastic chair was back there on the empty floor. I sat down, putting my head in my hands, closing my eyes, listening to the background rhythm of music, tuning everything else out.

I felt heat on my face and backs of my hands and jolted up. The dude, Diego, was squatting down right in front of me, close.

I narrowed my eyebrows as if to say "What you want?" That close, we could see each other's face in the dark.

Putting one hand on my thigh, he leaned in and let his lips touch mine. I braced and almost pulled back; he pushed in. I gave in, and inside my head I heard myself saying 'oh nooo' as if falling down a tunnel where there was no return. For a whole life I'd told myself as long as I never kissed a guy, I wouldn't... couldn't be... that. He put his hand on the back of my neck; everything was warm. Unable to help myself, so unused to physical human contact, I arched into his hand, suddenly wanting more. He pushed further in. I gave up; my lips opened and soon our mouths were inside each other. His face, eyelashes, skin pressed into mine. He stood and sat down on me, straddling me. Full of each other's breathing and scent, we grinded. Jackets slipped off; hands went up inside each other's shirt, rubbing, roaming, arms circling around to hold tight, close, squeezing so hard everything else was pushed out. Never let go.

CHAPTER ELEVEN

Dead Man

Empty, I thought. I really feel nothing for him. Already. After only one week.

I looked down at his sleeping body half draped over mine, yellow skin against yellow skin. The contact felt good, but —

I just feel empty, I thought, my lip curling. I rolled my eyes up to glance at my West photo. My little car, now long gone, down there so tiny by the side of the deserted highway, dwarfed by the immensity of sagebrush flats and Western sky. My heart sank. The sunset bathing the open range in colored light, the silence, the air so clean and sharp and dry you could feel it energizing your lungs, the silence… It was so far away from me now. I had been alone out there, not a single other person for miles and miles. I could've stayed. Why didn't I just stop in the next town and stay?

I'm stuck, completely stuck.

The phone was thankfully silent. I wondered how long I had till the service would be shut off. I knew it was coming. What day was It? How much longer do I have before another rent is due, on top of all the back rent? Glancing up at the ceiling, I noticed the fly — the same fly?? — hanging upside down again on the peace sign mobile. He always chose the blue or yellow peace circle, never the red or green or purple ones. With him or her on it, the cardboard peace circle spun around slowly.

I looked again at the photo. I suddenly remembered that abandoned homestead in western Nebraska. How the early afternoon air had been a little cool, as if all the snow had just melted, the sky a fresh-washed blue, the sun strong and bright. The raw yellow-brown prairie grass had soaked up the sun. It had felt good to lie in it, as if there was warmth coming from the soil itself. I wondered what wild animals still lived in that secret place. There were so many secret places out in my West.

I just want to go. And never have to deal with any of this human shit ever again.

I pushed at Diego.

"Wake up. Come on, let's get up."

He murmured, his face flat on my stomach. He opened one eye and looked at me, smiled sleepily, then turned his face into my stomach, burying it there, still smiling. "I'm still sleepy," he said into my stomach. His voice vibrated in my belly and I could feel his jaw's stubble. I had to admit, the roughness felt a little good.

I pushed at his shoulder again. "Come on," I said, my voice a little softer this time. "Time to get up."

I stood up, knocking him off me, and pulled my drawers on, tossing him his.

I padded barefoot into the kitchen, careful not to slide my feet over the decayed wood so I wouldn't get any splinters.

After he left, I tied my boots on and went downstairs. The air was getting cold again, drier, that kind of air that rattles autumn leaves across the pavement. But there weren't any trees for blocks around here. Just litter for leaves. People were dressed in grays and blacks. Raul was coming down the block, and stopped me. I saw some homeboys up on the corner already wearing their goose down bubble parkas, hanging open because it wasn't that cold, but it shocked me. The year really was heading down to close now. It was something I always held off admitting for as long as I could. "J, you have anything? Stein is getting restless."

"I know, I know. I can have 50 dollars for you by tomorrow morning "

"50 pesos is gonna look like you can't do anything, like you are desperate," he said.

I looked past Raul's face to the gang of dudes up on the corner, their new white sneakers, their silver necklaces. I looked down at my ratty old boots.

"I know. I'm really trying. Maybe I can do 60."

He shook his head. "Stein, he will only hold on for so long. You have to come up with more. But OK, bring me the 60 dollars tomorrow morning, OK, before eight, before Stein get here. It's best he don't even see you."

We shook hands.

"Ok, I will. Thanks Raul. Good lookin' out."

I walked up the street, keeping my head down as I got to the corner and passed the group of guys my age with their fresh haircuts and new, clean clothes and silver jewelry. I stepped off the curb and crossed Houston, and walked up to A, then decided to shift course and head down to the East River. It was only around 5, and I didn't have to be at work till midnight. I would have to make some tips tonight because if I gave Raul sixty dollars, then I'd only have five left from my base pay. I walked east down 2nd street, crossing Avenues B and C, ignoring any glares or assumed glares, knowing I was being stupid to cross China Cat territory. Since I lived on Lucky 7, and was always out on the street, I was associated with Lucky 7, even though I had nothing to do with their H trade and didn't give a shit about any of them.

Later that night. The club again, down on the West Side Highway. Because it was so nondescript on the outside, you'd miss it any other night. Sundays, a big crowd formed beneath the old meat warehouse overhang.

The dance floor began to fill up with people. I knew I'd soon be standing above a sea of bodies crushing against each other. Already it was getting hot in here. Through my shades I checked out the other dancers. They were all built; they all worked out. I glanced down at my own body. Still skinny, I thought. Defined, but not built and buffed and bulked up, like the other guys.

Wearing white boxer briefs and a black g-string beneath that, I had snapped on an adjustable cock strap around the base of my nuts and dick to keep my shit in place. I'd learned that much from talking to the other dancers. I fixed my position on the platform so the red spotlight would accent my torso better, creating shadows and definition. Quick learner.

The other strippers were bristling with dollar bills sticking out of their underwear waistbands. But those guys let anybody come up and grab their shit, touch and feel all over them. I made tips, but not like they did.

The large room was now so full of people that the whole mass seemed to writhe and move and shake the floor as one to the pounding dance beat coming out of the DJ's studio.

I adjusted the dollar bills in my waistband, which were pushed over the sides to make more room. The hard crinkling paper was sticking me in the skin. A guy came up, holding out a dollar bill folded lengthwise between two fingers, and beckoned me closer. I gave him one step forward, but didn't bend down like the other dancers would. He reached into the waistband of my boxer briefs to slowly place the dollar bill. I tensed and made as if to pull back, to show him that was as far as he should go. With both hands he grabbed my ass and tried to pull me closer, as if hungry to rub his face in my crotch.

I flared and pulled back, then forced my anger down. I backed away, still in rhythm to the dance beats, and he reached out one hand trying to flutter his fingers beneath my balls. I turned around to face the other way, holding onto the black metal piping above my head. The red spotlight cooked my forearms. The light reminded me of a restaurant's heat lamp used to keep food orders warm. A voluptuous blonde girl in a black bustier, her hair pulled back into a tight ponytail, squeezed her way forward. She was one of the few females in the club and held out a five. Her name was Nova. I bent down and cupped my palm gently behind her neck, and she gave me a big hug around my sweaty back, letting her hands slippery-slide down to the top of my butt, and then stuck the five dollar bill into the back band of my drawers. I kissed her on her lips and she smiled white teeth bright against cherry lipstick. I stood up and grooved, back on autopilot, to the rhythms.

Need money, I thought. I closed my eyes behind my shades. Time to loosen up and get with the program if you gon make some money.

I spread my legs out a little. Kept my eyes closed behind the shades. Disconnected myself from my body. Soon hands began to tentatively flap up onto my body, and this time I let them. I grooved… All those hands reaching up, over my wet chest, stomach, ass, my crotch, up and down and around my legs… All those hands felt like a pack of feral dogs with no teeth pulling at me, mauling me. I again grabbed onto the black piping overhead, eyes still closed, and gyrated. And my drawers finally began filling up with the paper I needed. Make that money, boy.

My stomach began to hurt. Two and half more hours to go. With my fingertips I flicked off some of the sweat running down my side. Again felt those two little lumps. Behind my shades I opened my eyes.

I walked to the window to check the time on the big red digital clock in the apartment across the street. The oncoming sky was so overcast and dark. It seemed close to nighttime, but the clock said it wasn't even four in the afternoon yet.

I placed my hand on my side and felt for the lumps just below the skin. And on my stomach below my solar plexus, and on the side of my neck, just below my jaw. Weren't those lymph nodes? Hadn't I heard something about swollen lymph nodes being one of the main indicators of "The Bonus?" I felt jumpy. Like there was nowhere to go. I turned around in the apartment. Even though it was bare except for the foam mattress and one little table and the 70's yellow plastic chair I'd found on the street, the place seemed filthy, cramped, suffocating.

"Please God," I said softly, grinding my teeth and breaking a little sweat. "I was only unsafe the one time."

I felt my side again. What are you heading into?

I felt a hulking sense of danger all around me, as if it was everywhere, but I couldn't see it… It was just past the line of visibility in all the shadows that surrounded me.

I pushed all the thoughts out of me.

Diego was coming up the stairs. I had just tossed him the keys in a sock out through the front window. I opened the door to the hallway, wondering if Maria was peering out her door like she often did when somebody came up. Maria was our back hall neighbor, an old, thin Puerto Rican grandmother with missing teeth who often conscripted me to go down to Chinatown to get live chickens and carry them back in the cage for her. She loved to make fresh chicken. I never stepped foot into her apartment.

"Your phone is off," Diego said to me, panting, as he and his cigarette lungs reached the top of the steps and squeezed past Maria's obese, mostly naked, chain-smoking husband who stood in a cloud of cigarette smoke. *Abuelo's* grossly distended belly looked like some sickness, and his face sagged all around his bones. He was always out there, smoking over the railing, and I never saw him with a shirt or pants on, only boxers and flip-flops. His bloodshot eyes tried to read Diego's words. The old man didn't understand a word of English.

Diego handed me the balled up sock with my keys in it. "I tried to call you earlier. It says it's 'temporarily disconnected. No further information is available.'"

I went in and picked up the phone. No dial tone. I looked at him.

"Anyway," he said, and smiled. "Looks like my roommate's brother is coming back. She says I can stay till he gets here. But the good news is, I got us some weights, and I want to bring them over."

He lay down on the foam mattress, watching my face in the dim afternoon light. "Hey! That's good news! Aren't you gonna say something?"

I said, "Does that mean you're gonna have to move out?"

He sort of shook his head yes.

"Where you gon go?"

He leaned up on one arm, still watching me, and pointed at the floor.

I was quiet for a long time, standing by the window. The rust red bars of the fire escape latticed my view of the block and my city. The window was open. The late

October air felt good. We hadn't turned on any lights yet, and the approaching dusk began to fill the room. Diego and me and the chair became hazy shapes.

I went over and flopped down on the bed, rolling onto my back, folding my arms behind my head, keeping my boots off the mattress and sheets. He put his hand on my stomach, sliding it up beneath my comfortable, well-worn, black cotton t-shirt, and raised his eyebrows. "Well? What do you think?"

"It's cool," I said, exhaling, kicking off one boot and then the other. " I guess. But you know the situation. You'll have to help out."

"Hey," he said, pointing with his long finger. "I really like you. We can help each other out. We can make it. You're having trouble; I've got nowhere to go. It's just you and me now, anyway. Who else do you talk to? I hardly even see Jennifer anymore, and I'm supposed to be her roommate. And she and I have been best friends for years. I stay over here every night now anyway."

"You know," I said. "I don't really want to stay here. In New York." Or live with anybody, I thought.

"Well, we could go somewhere, once we get on our feet. I need a vacation, too."

"Ain't talking about no vacation," I said quietly. "Or going anywhere with anybody. I just need to go and be quiet. Alone."

His facial expression dropped. "Man, I'm starting to fall in love with you. We can make it together. You don't have to make it this hard. I know we haven't been able to find a job, either of us. But, we'll find a way," he said, zeroing his eyes in on me, "We'll find something."

"We could try to deal," I said.

"Yeah," he said. "But a steady supply, that's hard to find. And customers. Without getting caught."

"I know. The wholesale connection, that's the hard part. One we could trust. We don't got time."

Minutes passed, as we both thought about a lot of things.

"You ever been to Rounds?" I said suddenly, spitting the word out quickly. There. I'd said it. Just saying it made me feel sick.

He stared at me. I looked away.

"No," he said, strongly, shaking his head. I could immediately tell by the way he said it that the thought wasn't out of the blue for him. He'd been in the gay life since he was a teenager. "No, I haven't ever been up there. But I know people who have."

"It may come to that. I'm just joking, right now, cause I can't stand the thought of it. Selling yourself to all those disgusting old men. But it's up on 79th Street. East 79th."

"You've obviously been thinking about it," he said. "Just say, what if? What do you think it would do to us if we started going up there?"

I shrugged. My head was starting to hurt. Too much talking, too much thinking. I pushed all the worrying, all the ugly thoughts out of my head. A passout was coming on, and my eyelids fluttered, relishing the delicious onset of weightlessness, of going to the Other Side. I felt sexy and warm. I rubbed my arms.

"Don't make me say it again," he said, and his words filtered through the dusk that was enveloping us. "Man, I'm really starting to fall in love with you. It's like that Sinead O'Connor song, 'Nothing Compares 2 You.' Nothing compares to you," he said, lying on his back.

I rolled my eyes as I turned onto my side, facing him, and threw my arm around him. "I'ma take a nap," I mumbled, voice gurgling with sleep. "But we've gots to do something, bring in something soon. Otherwise, be homeless… for real." As I fell asleep I thought about the lake in the kitchen from the radiator. We'd named it Mira Flores, after a lake in Panama.

So this is it, I thought as we opened the black glass door to Rounds and stepped inside. I'm finally crossing the line. A dark vestibule gave way to a long, dimly lit, upscale looking bar with two open rooms in the back with tables and couches. The doorman was a brother, dressed in a suit and tie, sitting on a stool. He nodded to us. I immediately felt out of place. We were dressed in jeans and black boots, with white t-shirts and short baseball style jackets. We'd both wiped down our boots with a rag, and flattened out our clothes the best we could, and tried to steam them in the shower.

We were definitely underdressed, but I saw there were other young guys not dressed up. The older men, the ones I knew we would be trying to bait and hook, were mostly in suits or nice jackets and ties and expensive shoes, though some were dressed casually.

People looked at us as we walked down what felt like a gauntlet between the long wooden bar and the wall. People were lined up on either side. We went to the back, where a long brass rail separated the sitting room from the bar area. "Straight Up," by Paula Abdul, was coming out of the speakers, volume down low.

I stuck my hands in my pockets and moved closer to Diego, who was watching my face.

"So let's just act like we know what's up," I said. "Chill."

"I'm gonna get us something to drink," he said, and worked his way to the bar.

I moved back against the railing and casually scoped out the scene, checking out the other young guys and the older tricks. The old guys, white men in suits — even one in a tux, his bow tie loosened, partying loudly at the bar — bugged me out. I couldn't imagine touching any of them. A real bad mood came on. I doubled over to pretend to fix my pant leg over my boot and shook my face, trying to shake off the bad look I was sure was stuck on it. Looking like that, I'd knew I'd hook nothing, except maybe some S&M freak. People already thought I looked mean or mad all the time. Need to focus on the immediate goal: we desperately need cash.

I glanced at Diego, who'd ordered two glasses of ice water. What we could afford. I noticed the bartender giving attitude. Diego was smart enough to pull out a dollar tip.

A couple of the boys here were very young, and looked desperate and scared. I saw this one little boy probably only 17 being nearly smothered by this fat businessman who was pressing him against the wall, back by the jukebox. A flash of anger and disgust flared inside me. I wanted to —

Diego came and handed me my water. I drank half of it, pulling an ice cube into my mouth and crunching on it.

"Man, we're underdressed," I said under my breath.

"Maybe they'll be attracted to the street look," he laughed, raising his eyebrows. "But look, there are a couple other guys dressed like us. Look at him." He nodded at this guy who looked a couple years older than us, light-skinned black, wearing a t-shirt, baseball cap, jeans and hiking boots.

The guy was nice looking, muscular, tall. He didn't look desperate. I noticed something about the way he wore his clothes, or the way he stood, that said something different about him, but I couldn't put my finger on it. Cocky and self-assured, maybe. We were wearing jeans and t-shirts, but with us it looked like that was all we had.

As I drank the rest of my ice water I let my eyes scan the whole bar again, trying to make eye contact with some of the older men. Some returned the look, but then looked away. I passed over some of them and realized I was judging them by the way they were dressed, just as they were judging me. If something looked off, or somehow not quite put together right, it made me think they didn't have their money right, so I passed over them. I thought it was funny. I didn't know anything about fashion, but I could sense something.

"You guys should split up," said a nasally high-pitched, effeminate voice from behind. "They're thinking you two are a package. And trust me, they are afraid if they take you both together, you are going to beat them up and rob them."

Diego and I turned around to face this skinny white pasty drag queen in a dress, blonde wig, and pale red lipstick. "Hi, Diego," he — she — said.

Diego flushed, glared hard at her, and quickly glanced over at me. "Hi, Dierdre," he said. "What're you doing here?"

"I'm all dicked out," she said. "I had to take a break from the j-o-b. So I thought I might take the train up here and find you two." She turned to me, and smiled. "Hi, I'm Dierdre. You must be Jihad. Sorry she's being rude," she said, nodding at Diego. "Diego talks about you all the time."

('She?') "How you doing," I said. "I guess you all friends, huh? Diego never mentioned you."

"Dierdre, why are you here messing?" Diego said.

"Wait, don't worry about him," I told her. And I turned to D. "And since when you know all this gay lingo?" I looked back at her. "What you mean you're all 'dicked out'?" The thought of getting tainted like that worried me. The full scope of what was happening hit me. Once I crossed this line, selling sex for cash, I'd be polluted. I could forget about ever being worthy enough to meet somebody real, somebody on the outside, clean, masculine, who had his shit together, somebody who could match and challenge me, somebody I could really kick it with. I'd always be gutter after this.

If I'd always been dirty and second class to society, just imagine after I started doing this shit.

"Dierdre works down at Show World, down at Times Square. In the basement."

"She can speak for himself — herself. Whatever. So — You can make ends down there at Show World?"

"Only the girls do," she said. The real ones are on the top floors; we're in the basement. I stand inside a booth, with a glass wall with a hanging panel over it. The trick puts his money into a machine, the cover rises, and as long as he keeps putting money in the machine the cover stays up."

"And what do you do? Do you make all that money?"

"I stand there inside the box behind the glass wall in my fucking dress and pull out my dick and the trick pulls out his and jerks off while watching me play with my dick and rub myself while standing in my dress. I get $20 an hour. Show World makes two to three times that much off us, but it's steady work." She reached inside Diego's jacket, took out a cigarette and lit it, inhaling back, then blew out the smoke sideways through her lips, away from us.

"Oh," I said.

"I'm all dicked out because if I see one more fat, hairy pink belly and *quiveringly* ugly little dick — if I see any dick at all — I'm going to scream. I want some cake and ice cream is what I want. Butter Pecan. But I'll be better tomorrow. Gotta make those ducats, you know, honey?"

I didn't want to hear anymore. "I'm gonna go make some money," I muttered to Diego, nodding to the back room. "Don't leave without letting me know what you gon do."

I nodded to Dierdre, pulled my jacket collar up, and walked off.

"Just watch out for the Ice-Pick Man," she said. "Everybody who comes here knows about the Ice-Pick Man."

I stood around in the back with my hands in my pockets until, finally, I saw an opening. The suit on the back couch had begun to take notice of me, and through his wire rim glasses began to stare. I figured that was how they did it. Like shopping, they'd hold their gaze on the item they wanted. Then it was up to us to deliver. I went over and sat down next to him, trying not to cover up my nervousness with too cocky a step. To my absolute disgust he looked a lot like George Bush, complete with the same gold wire-rimmed glasses and hanging jowls.

He put his hand on my leg. "Are you cut or uncut, Emmanuel?"

"Cut," I said. "You get the whole ripe package."

"We have not discussed your price," said the suit, getting down to business.

"Just three hundred," I said, surprising myself. I'd noticed his expensive-looking suit and shoes, but didn't really know anything about all of that. I could just tell if something was worth a lot of money.

Up here at Rounds you could make up to $100 or $150. Or whatever you could get from them, really. I guessed that sometimes it was a lot less, judging from the barely-disguised desperation on so many young faces.

"That's fine," he said to my amazement, squeezing his hand on my leg.

"You're shaking," he said, expanding his power over me.

I swallowed and shook my head no. My stomach hurt.

In the cab, he asked me, "Do you like to do everything?"

I nodded, looking out the window. I kept trying to think of anything that would make me aroused, but I couldn't even seem to connect with that part of my body. I was going to be in trouble if I couldn't function.

The fucking Waldorf Astoria, I thought. Never in my life did it even occur to me that I might be stepping through these doors. Everything seemed made of gold. I kept my head lowered, staring at the floor. Thankfully it was late, not that many people in the lobby. Everybody must be staring at me.

Diego had already left with somebody. I wondered what he was doing right now. Fuck it, I don't care, I thought.

As instructed, I walked about 20 paces behind him, wondering if he was getting off on this, making a straight beeline for the elevators.

Upstairs inside the trick's room, like a robot I rubbed my hands over the trick's starched shirt chest, and pulled off his tie and shirt, trying not to breathe in. He smelled a little like lunchmeat.

He had long white hairs sticking sparsely out of his chest at all angles. He pawed at me.

I stopped. "Uh… I sort of need to be, umm, taken care of up front."

He cocked his head at me, then just like that got up and went into the closet and pulled out his wallet; handed me three benjamins. His hands were baggy and soft, pink, like they had definitely never held a shovel, the skin kind of see-though, accented by an expensive gold wedding band.

I took my time taking my shirt off, knowing that my swimmer's build would be enough to hold his attention for a few more minutes while I struggled again to find some feeling in my dick, at least get semi-hard. If I could do that, I could jerk off, and let that be the deal.

My stomach was killing me. It was hopeless.

He sat on the hotel bed, pulled off his pants, and motioned for me to pull my jeans off.

I turned off the light. *You got the money now. You should just bounce. You gotta get out of this situation.* I let him feel on me some more.

He pulled me downward, and rubbed his hands all over my dick and balls. I tensed, waiting for his reaction to the fact that my dick was soft. I had no intention of actually having sex with him anyway. I'd figured I'd just find a way to get the money, pacify him enough, and get out of there.

He turned on the light and propped himself up on a pillow.

"Here, just give me oral," he said, in a tone as if I was one of his employees.

You are one of his fucking employees, I told myself.

Why don't you just leave? Just run out. You scared? "If you got a condom," I said.

He put a hat on. I put my dry mouth on that dry, rubbery smelling latex, and let him watch my face go up and down on him for about five minutes.

"Yes, I like the way your nostrils are flaring. Nice lips, too," he said, staring at me. My nostrils were flaring because I was trying to hold my breath and not smell him, not because I was getting into it. My jaw felt like it was going to lock. I kept my eyes closed, thinking about the East River, the green water, the giant, roaring, clanking, light-shafting bridge overhead that I wished would crush me, thinking about anything, trying not to let the side of my face touch his water-balloon belly. When he put his hands on top of my head, I pulled back, glancing at the clock. The hour was almost up. Close enough, anyway.

"OK," I said, pulling my drawers and jeans on, and just tucking the laces of my boots into the rims. Pulling my t-shirt on and grabbing my windbreaker, I said, "Thanks."

"You did a good job," he said. The lamplight was shining off his very expensive gold wedding ring.

"Maybe I'll see you around," I said, pulling open the door.

As soon as the door closed, I ran down the hallway to the elevator. I jabbed the button. With a cocky bounce to my step, I flaunted all the way out the lobby of the Waldorf Astoria, thinking how easy that was, so glad, so so glad to have it behind me. This gonna be easy, I thought.

I got to a payphone and dialed Diego's pager. I punched in "42-30," which he knew meant 'meet me at 42nd Street and Lex in 30 minutes.'

I rode the train down, holding onto the swinging overhead handrails as the lumbering metal beast roared and screeched and shook from side to side in the tunnel, swaying me with it, flashing electric white sparks, fluorescent lights popping on and off. The subway car was deserted. An empty 40 rolled up and down the sticky, orange-tiled aisle, making that clunky beer bottle sound that I knew so well. I practically swung from the overhead bars. Three fat bills in my pocket.

CHAPTER TWELVE

Mira Flores

"Uh, I sort of need to… be taken care of first."

He stopped unbuttoning his pressed pin-striped dress shirt and looked at me for a second. He was a big guy, late 40s maybe, looked like he worked out, said he was here on business from Sacramento, wanted some trade. My wires were up with this one, but I had come to his house anyway. He had searched me before letting me in.

After the first trick, I'd gone a whole week before hooking another suit. This was turning out to be as hard as I'd originally thought. The Waldorf Astoria deal was a fluke, a stroke of luck. I hadn't made more than $150 on anybody since then, and it was usually $100 or less. These suits negotiated me downwards. Knew about their money, that's for sure.

I had to make something tonight. I literally didn't have enough for a token, and was planning on walking home if I didn't make anything. I thought of Diego, and hoped he was having better luck.

The trick laughed, and I knew right then that this shit was gonna go bad. "You're late on your rent, aren't you?" he asked.

I was over $1000 behind. I couldn't catch up, and lately had the feeling I was now past the point of no return.

He laughed again and continued taking off the rest of his clothes. He was tall, barrel bodied, and hairy. Probably weighed 60 pounds more than me. I could smell him from here. His dick was big and crooked, almost bent in half to the left. He stroked himself hard. This trick was going to be a problem.

"Because you're too good looking to be doing this. Do you think I'm a fool? You're not going to get paid until we finish. Take off your clothes."

We were in the living room of the extended-stay apartment. As I undressed, I scanned the place out of the corners of my eyes, checking out where the kitchen was, what objects might be nearby. My eyes caught sight of the wooden knife holder on the kitchen bar counter. All the slots were empty. Why?

I hadn't brought my own knife.

He rushed me, pushed me down onto the couch and fell on top of me, knocking my air out. He started biting and mauling me, and humping me. Like a trapped wrestler, I heaved him off with my left shoulder. He fell onto the floor. He got up and stood over me with his big pink dick pointed crooked at my head. Pre-cum was already coming out, and I realized it had slimed the inside back of my thigh. "I'm going to fuck you," he said. "And you're gonna like it."

I sat up on the slippery, dead-animal-smelling leather couch. It occurred to me that I was sitting naked and breaking a sweat on the ripped off skin of some animal's back. I imagined it twitching beneath me.

"I don't get fucked," I said. "And I don't suck, neither. For $100 you can get off, as long as it's safe. That's it."

He jumped on top me again; started humping away at me. "I make the rules here," he panted. He kneeled up and flipped me over face down onto my stomach, then again started humping and biting me. I let him, cause I could hear it was exciting him, and maybe it'd make him get his nut sooner. I needed to make that money. He tried to put his dick in my ass and I squeezed that door shut tight. He pounded away, but I kept him riding the crack of my ass, or between my legs, just below. He started moaning and then making these squeaking sounds like one of those dogs who'd had his bark surgically removed. My face and chest were mashed into the dead animal leather, getting pushed up and down with the force of his pounding, lubricated by my sweat. He finally got his nut, all over my back, and stood up to catch his breath. I could still feel his bite marks in my neck and back. I quickly got up, reaching for the towel that'd been on the table when I walked in. I wiped my back, and started to get dressed.

"Wait, we're not finished," he said. "I want to go again."

"Sorry. I gots to go. That was more than an hour. It's usually double if you run over."

He looked me right in the face. "No 'coins' unless we do it again."

What the fuck?! I hurriedly tried to assess the situation. But he pushed me down — and admittedly, feeling helpless, I let him. I had no choice; I needed the money. I was completely dominated. I let him go through the whole thing all over again; only this time it took even longer.

Finally finished, he wiped himself off then took the towel to the laundry room. I heard the washer dial clicking as it was rotated. Washer water started running.

Dressed, and by the door, I waited for my money.

He came back in the room and gave me a look like what the hell was I doing here. He picked up his pants, pulled out some folded 20s (but not from his wallet, which I'd noticed was not in either of his back pockets) and handed them to me. "Here," he said. "You need to leave now." He got dressed as I flipped through the money.

"This only $60 dollars."

"Man, I don't know what you're doing in my house. I tried to help you out, but if you don't leave right now, I'm gonna have to call the cops."

I felt like a flamethrower had been turned on inside of me, blasting from my chest up through my throat and into my head. "You owe me a hundred dollars!" I said, my voice so tight I could barely talk. My voice was shaking, and so were my hands.

He was dressed now, buttoning himself up. He walked to the phone. "Hey man, I tried to do a nice thing. Tried to help you out, but here you try to rob me? I gave you $60 because I feel sorry for homeless punks like you, but this is the thanks I get." He picked up the phone. "I'm going to have to call the police."

I whirled out of the apartment and slammed the door as loud as I could. I ran down the hallway and then down the stairs, unable to wait for the elevator.

Out on the winter street I pounded and punched the signs and mailboxes, newspaper bins, anything, as I passed, hurting my hands, bouncing off my inner walls, about to explode. I shook my head from side to side, half running, half walking, until I bottled it back up, once again, and shoved it back down inside me, once again. I slunk to the subway station, trying not to draw any more attention to myself. I'd spent my whole life trying to avoid 'men' like these, and now I purposely had to make myself sexually available to them. I was completely tainted, toxic now.

As soon as I found a secluded stairwell, I ducked down, unzipped, took from my jacket pocket the little 2 oz bottle of hydrogen peroxide I always carried these days, and splashed the fizzing liquid all over my dick and balls and up the crack of my ass and up my back.

Bursting into the smoky apartment, I threw the keys down in their usual spot on the rotting wooden floor and stormed into the front room where Diego was lying on the foam bed smoking. He jolted up onto his elbows.

"What the fuck you doing, smoking in here!" I smacked the cigarette out of his mouth. It went flying to the floor, shooting sparks. I stomped on it. I opened the windows and the cold air rushed in. "I told you, smoke outside. You and Maria husband, you can smoke together out there!"

He looked up at me, his dark eyes reflecting the hanging lightbulb from the kitchen. The radiator was spewing against the back wall. The trickles of water vapor were slowly running down, and Lake Mira Flores had overrun its usual banks in the sagging low point on the kitchen floor. Ice crusted around its edges.

"Well, did you make anything?" I roamed around the room, to the window, back and forth and around in a circle.

He got up and walked over to me in his drawers, and I thought he was beginning to look a little effeminate. "No, no luck tonight." He smiled sheepishly; tried to slip his arms around me. I pushed him off.

"I decided to just come home," he said. "I miss you. I just couldn't stand the thought of touching anybody but you tonight. Man — nothing compares to you. I just want to be with you."

I looked at him, trying to keep my face hard. "You know we bout to get our asses kicked out. Man, you need to hold your fuckin' weight. Speakin of weight, you need to start working out. We both do. You starting to look like a girl. Where's those weights you said you were gonna bring over?"

"They're still over at Jennifer's where her friend brought them. I'll go get them tomorrow. Hey. I'm sorry." He paused, standing there half-naked, looking awkward. "So. How'd you do?"

"I made a little. Under a hundred. That's it. But it was easy — I didn't have to do nuthin.' I didn't even have to let him touch me. I just took my clothes off and he just sat there on the couch and jerked off." I didn't look at him to see if he believed me.

I yanked open the refrigerator door, anticipating some organic carrots and tahini. There were only two carrots left. The little tub of tahini I'd bought at Prana up on 1st Ave was scraped nearly clean. The fridge was bare.

"Man, and you ate all my shit!" I slammed the door closed. I went into the front room to look across the street to see what time it was. The guy's clock said 2:13 a.m. "I'm gonna go get something at the Korean deli up on A. Some juice or something. Obviously you didn't bring anything back for the house; just ate up all my shit. I'll be back." My head burned. He didn't give a shit about his health. Why the fuck was he eating my food? He wasn't trying to be a vegetarian. Taking care of my own health was all I had left. Didn't need him and his dirty-ass fingers taking that from me.

Diego got back into bed. "You have marks on your neck," he said. I stormed out of the apartment.

I turned my head at an angle down to my right as I curled the dumbbell up in my right fist, relishing the pump in my biceps. I lowered my eyelids, concentrating on my body, how it was working, how lifting the weight made me 'swoll,' how it would make me strong. Shirt off, wearing only a baggy old pair of sweat pants, I stood in the front room, glad to be alone, going from one muscle group to the other, just like the book said. I'd been going to the Mid-Manhattan library occasionally, to escape into its hollow silence. From a book I had drawn diagrams of some exercises. Adding to my knowledge of vegetarianism, I was studying how the body worked, how it was put together.

I glanced up at the mirror on the wall, between the two windows. After a few weeks of working out my body was starting to show some changes, some real muscle appearing on my arms and chest. And I was getting stronger, able to lift more weight.

So glad to be alone. Outside, a few snowflakes fell from the gray afternoon sky. I switched to my left arm, pumping up, releasing more slowly on the return, exhaling with the exertion, like the book said. I kept up the intensity to break a light sweat because the temperature in the apartment probably never reached above 50, and often got cold enough to freeze Lake Mira Flores. I could hear the hissing radiator's jet of mist against the back wall. The steam caked the kitchen with clammy humidity but did nothing to warm the place up. The cheap electric stove couldn't help either, because coils don't heat the air like gas flames do, and the oven didn't work. I moved to the bench. The two plates, and a couple 25s and 10s, were all we had, along with an easy curl bar and two changeable dumbbell bars. I just did reps till I couldn't anymore. I stared at the ceiling, then at the peace mobile. Hadn't seen the fly around for awhile. Above the mirror I had tacked a big yellow poster of Malcolm X's silhouette that I had bought on the street for a couple dollars. It said:

> "I believe that there will ultimately be a clash between the oppressed and those that do the oppressing. I believe that there will be a clash between those who want freedom, justice and equality for everyone and those who want to continue the systems of exploitation, but I don't think it will be based upon the color of the skin."

I pushed out another set of 15 with real good form, breathing right, then carefully set the barbell back in its rack. I let my arms fall down past my sides, fingers brushing the floor. Didn't want to think about anything. Not how much a bind we were in, not how much an asshole I was being to Diego, even if he deserved it. *Nothing.* I just wanted to be a clean healthy body. No thinking.

And away from all this shit forever.

And never speak to anybody again.

Rounds again. Diego was standing over by the bar, a drink in his hand, laughing and joking with some trick in a monkeysuit tux. I stood about ten paces away. Suits passed me, or stood and hovered, glancing down at my boots at the same time I checked out their shoes. I thought it was funny how we all looked at each others' shoes. I didn't even know the first thing about dress shoes and name brands, but I could read a trick by his shoes and could tell whether they were well made or not. It was just something you pick up. And they were gauging me by my footwear too. At which point, it just became a question of whether each of us wanted to deal, or not.

I saw Diego getting the suit to buy another round of drinks. He was doing good tonight. The suit in front of me was giving signals, trying to find an opening with me. I ignored him. I needed Diego to get one more drink into his trick. Diego was acting real soft, on purpose, and for once I was glad he had been a part of gay life so long, unlike the first "just off the streets" image he had fronted to me.

Waiting for the suit to finish his drink, I walked to the back, slamming my shoulder into this fat businessman I had seen before, who was pressing up on this skinny little black Cuban boy who had a look in his eyes that his world was already over. He looked all of sixteen years old. "Oh, excuse me," I said to the fat trick. And looked him dead in the eye. "My fault," I said. I glanced at the little boy, giving him some back, some support, saying with my eyes what I couldn't say out loud about all these mutherfuckers without getting kicked out, and walked to the rear room. Rounds allowed all ages in here, from boys to men.

In the cab, Diego and I sat on either side of the drunk monkeysuit trick as we made it downtown. We stopped off on 10th between A & B to score some heroin with the trick's money. He'd asked us to buy him some blow because he "really wanted to party." Then we took him down to our place. They couldn't buy anything on the street without getting robbed, so they asked us to do it. We'd cut a little freeze into the H, but just enough to get them to continue inhaling through the little sliced straws. Heroin'll knock your ass out. After he became a drooling mess from all the "coke," plus the couple extra cocktails we served, we took his credit cards and most of his cash, dumped him in a cab, and sent him back uptown.

"The only thing you need to do is just watch out for the Ice-Pick Man," Damon said, in his cocky way. Damon was the nice looking, built, 6'2" black dude in tight t-shirt, ball cap, and sneaks that I'd seen the first time we'd come up here to Rounds. We'd run into each other several times after that, and started talking, when Diego wasn't around. But me and Damon were just cool. We weren't trying to holla at each other, we were trying to make some money. I liked to hang with him because he was intelligent and aware of world affairs. Even though we weren't in the same boat — he did this by choice, at least that's what he said — we were still co-workers. The thing that amazed me about Damon was that he didn't seem to care or be affected by anything, except for shit that was going on out in the world. Tricking didn't seem to bother him at all. Me, I felt my normal, tainted, wasted self. The only bright spots were when I was able to get over on a suit or even rob him.

In general, I felt like I had lost my chance in life to be young and sexual, to be clean, to experience the passion and caring of relationships that everybody else up in the outside world had. It had taken me so long to even own up to myself about my sexuality, and now I would never get the opportunity. I went right from craving to meet somebody who I could really vibe with, somebody to be really intimate with, to settling for Diego, who I realized did nothing for me, to becoming a prostitute, a hooker, a hustler, in a desperate grab for survival. I was tainted, polluted goods. As for Diego, my interest in him barely survived the initial pent-up sexual release. I acted like an asshole to him and couldn't stop myself. But we still had a few good moments occasionally, out of being forced to survive together, I guess.

Damon and I were riding downtown in a cab after work. His treat. He stayed on 5th Street, between A and B. We had both made bank quickly tonight, and gone back to Rounds. I didn't know where Diego was. Damon and I decided to bounce. As usual, he looked great. Real nice arms and chest, nice face, tight t-shirt.

"Why does everybody talk about the Ice-Pick Man?" I said. Whenever I ask about him, all people ever say is that he drives a blue van. And to watch out. Who the fuck is the Ice-Pick Man?"

"He drives a blue van," Damon said, looking straight ahead. "That's all any of us know."

I looked out the window, closing my eyes, letting the passing orange streetlights create side-flung hazy flares through my eyelids. Better than trying to imagine just who or what the Ice-Pick Man was or did.

"You know, man," I said, "I hate this shit. It's the worst possible thing to me. It's funny how when you're down deep in some shit, you not only can't see up on top, you can't see what it looks like from outside. You know what I mean? You can't see the whole picture when you in some shit. It's only now that I'm starting to see how low I fell. I mean, below rock bottom. I guess some big depression, and shit. I've been just trying to get through each hour of each day."

"Bruh, you can't let any of that shit affect you. Ain't nobody can do anything to me."

"You know, you seem like none of this bothers you. Me, in my past life, before this, when I finally began to accept myself, I wanted to meet somebody who I could kick it with for real. Shit. I was so craving for some real contact, some real sex, maybe even a relate. Maybe even a chance to fall in love, fo' real. But now, doing this, I feel like I lost everything. I fucking hate them. They stink. It's this huge weight on me. I feel polluted. I hate the suits. I let them pollute me, and I had no choice. They're really just the same people — things — that constantly harassed me and freaked me out when I was little. Now I have to go *to* them. Now I'm not worth shit to anybody up on the outside. In the normal world. If I ever make it back up there."

"Not me," Damon said. "I don't care. I'm all sexed out. It's just a job. Those old men, they just pay the bills. It's not sex. I'd rather eat than have sex."

"That exactly what I'm talking about."

"I fucked this dude tonight. Got $150 for that shit. What. What anybody really gon say?"

"You fuck? I wouldn't do that shit. Aw hell no. Couldn't do it. I can barely stand to touch them. And I gotta be absolutely safe. I ain't taking even a single chance. Hell no."

"Shit, you get used to it. And you can still be safe. You just slap two hats on."

"But..."

"Man, it's just a job that pays pretty good, better than most."

"*When* you hook something. It's not all that easy. Shit's pretty hard, in fact."

"Well, they know you ain't into it, and that you're only doing it for survival. It's all over your face. So you get the new ones, the occasional dabblers, the out-of-towners, and the freaks who don't care about getting the nut as much as taking the power from you. The regulars know I'll do it all, and I don't care, and that they're just getting semi-anonymous sex from some big, nice lookin' brother, so I make bank regularly. I have regulars, and I let some of them call me, too." He pointed to his pager clipped to the belt loop of his blue jeans. "I won't kiss them or nothing, but what the fuck about anything else?"

"Ugh," I said. I kept my voice low, aware that the cab driver was listening. "Tonight, I went with this dude who wasn't even old. He couldn't of been more than mid 30s or so. I kept wondering why this dude was here. I wondered if he had The Bonus. I think a lot of them that do have it, they come to the spot thinking that we're disposable, so they can come in, get their rocks off on us, and not feel guilty about it. He had no signs. Maybe he just wanted the thrill of buying somebody. I don't know. When we got to his place, I got him to give me the coronas first, like I usually am able to. But when we got naked, he suddenly grabbed me around the hips with both arms like he was wrestling me and lifted me up and started slobbering all over and eating my ass. That was the weirdest shit. I ain't never had nobody done that. I tried to keep my ass closed, but he kept spreading me."

Damon was grinning. "Men like to get that shit. It's good when you're with a lover. Of course you always take a shower first, but it's the best. It's a real private thing. But hell. Straight people fuck with the ass more than we do. They just don't admit it."

"I ain't goin' nowhere near nobody's ass. So, wait, you had a lover?"

"Five years, brother. Ain't doin' no more of that shit. I was ready to fuckin' marry that nigga."

"Marry?"

"Oh, I forgot. You're new. Lingo. Not marry like breeder straight people with the white picket fences and two and a half kids and all that shit; fuck that. You know, just in a real, on-the-low, down-to-ride, I got your back/you got mine kind of way… Anyway, what'd you do? With dude who was tossin' your salad?"

"It was just too weird for me, so I rolled him over, and humped on his back a little to force myself hard. I made him jerk himself off, too. His back was to me, so I acted like I couldn't take it much longer, and faked my nut, spitting in my hand and smearing it on him as if I was jerking my shit off."

"You're learning real good."

"Dawg, I just want to get out. I just want to go away. Go out West somewhere. I need to start my life over again."

"Where is the address?" the cab driver cut in, his voice sounding thick, as if he had a hard time swallowing. He'd been listening to every word we'd said. The meter said $8.50.

"It's in the middle of the block, on the left hand side," Damon said, not missing a beat. "Just drop me off, right there. Where that pole is. He's gonna continue." He turned to me. "Hey man, keep the faith. I'll see you around." He dapped me off. "I've also seen you down at the East River before, where I go running, but you didn't see me. I was already heading out of the park." He got out. Before he closed the door he handed me $15 to cover the cab.

"Thanks, man," I said. "But I see everybody before they see me. Trust."

"Be safe," we both said to each other at the same time.

A big draping snowstorm came, then partially melted, its remnants turning to gray sludge, then old, plowed, iced-over mounds. For Christmas, the guy across the street with the clock put white blinking lights around his fire escape. I could tell he was a homo. I realized I was getting gaydar.

Diego and I had gotten a full day's use out of that one trick's credit card. We got us some nice black Timberland boots that went just above the ankle that we could wear to work, as well as a pair of yellow buck work boots. Plus some sneakers, new jeans, and a little boombox radio. With work holding somewhat steady, we didn't get any further behind on the rent, and we were able to pay the $550 the next time it was due. We still owed $1200 on the back rent. But Raul was able to keep us cool with the landlord. We never saw Stein. I had privately given up on ever catching up in paying the rent, or even wanting to, and was now trying to save anything toward my big escape. The picture was on my wall, right above my bed.

Diego became smoking partners with Maria's husband. I had lost all feeling for Diego, though we still slept in the same bed. I couldn't stand the thought of *anybody* touching me. I didn't care who they were. I had also seen him using drugs, occasionally sniffing blow or making a coolie by putting it in his cigarette. I missed nothing, even though he and other people thought I did. He had started hanging out again with his old friends. I told him if he ever brought anything over to my crib, any drugs at all except X — unless we were gonna use them on a trick — I would cut his throat.

And sometimes we still had an OK time together, especially after we had scored another trick who wanted to party some blow and we switched that shit up with heroin and robbed him. Then we'd go out and celebrate, taking X, and I danced my ass off, while he drank (he couldn't or didn't dance). I'd have a single beer, a simple old cold Budweiser, and I was fine. I didn't even want to get drunk. And Madonna would sing her massive hit "Like a Prayer" — the gospel intensity of the Michael Connelly remix belting out of the giant wall speakers and strafing the building — and we were friends and lovers again.

In late December, coming in at 3:30 a.m., I flicked on the radio by the side of the bed. "U.S. troops have invaded the capital of Panama in an attempt to capture dictator General Manuel Noriega.... Heavy artillery fighting....

Wouldn't be surprised if Bush "accidentally" had him killed, I thought, especially since Bush has a lot to hide about certain *Contra* cocaine connections that supposedly didn't happen when he was vice prez....

Christmas passed. New Year's Eve came — the last day of 1989. The guy's Christmas lights across the street were still blinking. The air was cold and dry. Diego brought me the early edition of the *New York Times*. Its date stamp said *January 1, 1990.* I stared. It sounded so futuristic, and took a minute to wrap my mind around it. The 90's were here.

In February, the weather briefly warmed up. The fly (still the same one?! I still had no idea how long their life span was, though I'd meant to check in the library) appeared from his hiding place and hung upside down on the yellow peace circle again. Early afternoon; Diego had gone out. I lay on my back, feeling the hardened little lumps in my side, in my neck, in my stomach. I gauged the time by the light of the sky. I was just too tired to get up. I wanted to take a nap. I guessed I had a couple hours. I was supposed to meet a trick at his apartment at 5:30; it was only over in the West Village. Been without a phone now for a long time, it seemed. Probably would never have one again. I'm cool with that. The thought put a little smirk on my face. The silence, the removal from everybody up there in the world, above ground, out there... I would never have anything to do with them again, and I didn't care.

Needed to drop off, if only for ten minutes, go over to the Other Side. Pressing at the lumps, I gazed upside down into the pic of my long lost little car, out there by itself on the side of the road, way, way out West.

Mutherfucker's a goddamn walrus, I thought, gritting my teeth, heart beating from the adrenaline. I tentatively hit him in the face with the back of my hand, like somebody anxious to swim but needing to dip his toe in the water first, maybe a little scared to jump right in. My hands were shaking. Hated that shit. Why did they do that! I tried to will them to stop. Mutherfucker's a fat ugly human walrus faggot! I belted him again with the back of my hand. His face rubbered out to the side. The trick smiled, held up an index finger for me to pause, and quickly sniffed a hit of poppers.

I scrunched up my face, as if for a moment forgetting where I was. What was this about, I asked myself. I was in a trick's apartment. Why was I hitting him? The clock said 5:55. I liked it when all the numbers were equal. I felt sweat breaking out of my back and scalp. He had the heat on too high. I'd kept my jeans, t-shirt, and work boots on. The trick was naked. I wanted to hit him harder. Why was I holding back? *Scared you might totally let go? What's the matter, you afraid, boi!?"*

"Say, please!" I croaked.

"Please can I have some more, but can you make it harder?"

I compacted my fist but...

Damn! I felt like pouting. I couldn't get it right. This was too fucking weird. I was punking out. *What's the matter with you, bitch!*

Watching me, the trick spoke. "Umm... Hello-oh. Earth to Mr. Emmanuel. Can I have some more, please, and can you please make it harder? This isn't patty cakes, sir, we have a job to do. I do not like to be disappointed on my dates."

Harder? Harder?? My eyes flared, and behind them finally I saw the red I needed, craved.

I gave him a good blow, saw a nice red mark appear, but... but... SHIT! What was wrong with me? I couldn't totally let go.

The naked fucking walrus just kept asking for more, as if teasing me. I felt like I was being pulled over a cliff, and I couldn't help the fact that hitting him felt good, and I wanted more, but... *What the matter, dawg? 'Fraid you might kill him? Ain't that what you want?*

He smiled up at me from beneath his huge walrus mustache. One little hand still clutched the little bottle of poppers. He played with his dick with the other.

I stepped onto his chest with my hiking boots and balanced there. I put my boot on his face, pushing his face sideways into the floor. I stepped off, pulled back, and kicked him again. His body absorbed everything I gave it. He held up a little hand, waving his little stubby finger again, his little time-out flag. He unscrewed the poppers bottle, stuck it up into the big brown-gray mustache and took another big sniff.

"Please, sir, can I have some more?" he asked daintily.

Aaaauggh. I felt like I was falling down a tunnel. I punched him.

Still: "Please. More."

He sniffed some more poppers — but only after asking for permission politely, tiny erect dick quivering like some skinny pink rodent between his legs.

I wiped my face with the back of my arm. "Is that enough?" I asked. To my ears it sounded like I was screaming.

"Excuse me, Mr. Emmanuel? Sir, please will you speak louder?

Aaaaauugh. I put my hands over my face.

He pulled himself up and walked into the kitchen to get a drink of water. He offered me one.

I shook my head. "I gotta go. Can I get paid?"

"Oh, darling, of course not. Not yet. Come on. We're not finished. You must first come with me to the bedroom, where we must take a little post-connuptial nap.

Surely, you understand the after-embrace of romance." He limped his wrist and put the back of his hand to his forehead, as if it had a white lace glove on it. "Oh dear. I must lie down." He waddled into the bedroom, making a little flipping motion with his little walrus hand — his fucking flipper — for me to follow.

He made me take my shirt off. I lay on the bed with him, in my jeans and boots, staring at the ceiling, with the pummeled walrus snuggled up to me, clinging like a princess saved.

My rage began to build, having already been lit. I focused on its hot red waves. I tried to imagine the waves as cooled water, to force them down. I focused as hard on the cool water and waves, trying not to let anything else into my mind. But the rage wasn't only in my mind, it was all up and down inside my body, on fire, building. I tried harder to clear out everything from my mind, knowing if I let anything in I would want murder. Of who? This dude? *Or you, bitch?* I squeezed my eyes shut, scrunching my face till it hurt. I felt like I wanted to cry. And that was the oddest sensation. It scared me. I couldn't remember when…

The fat faggot fell asleep, his breath rasping in his chest. He started to snore loudly. I fantasized I'd done some damage. I smirked.

"What are you smiling about, darling?" the trick said, startling me. He had never fallen asleep at all. Had been faking it the whole time! "You can have the Benjamin — as you young thugs call it — in one more hour. But first, we must sleep some more. I'm the boss, let's not forget, shall we? Sir?"

"But, it's only supposed to be for an hour," I protested.

"Oh dear, we are simply exhausted. We must get our beauty rest," the trick said, and promptly started snoring, curling closer up into me, his mustache twitching at my armpit. And even though I had to stay there for way more than an hour, I still only got one Benj. He'd been the one in control the whole time.

Time passed. Signs of spring came. Cutting on the lights as I entered my dim apartment, I automatically checked for fat pigeons hiding and cucarachas scurrying. Sometimes pigeons flew in through the airshaft window, panicked and got themselves trapped. They'd startle the fuck out of me when I came in, jumping into the air and flapping around the kitchen like the end of the world, squirting shit and battering into the walls.

As for the little running-from-the-light cockroaches, the black plastic Combat traps had worked somewhat. But I knew the problem was inside the rotting walls of the building, and no matter how clean I kept my place, more would still come. Guaranteed.

Keepin' my body pretty clean, too, I thought.

But that still didn't stop problems from comin' at me. *Or from up inside you, huh?*

I hung the keys, went into the back and climbed into the closet, pulling the string to turn on the hanging light bulb. I put the toilet seat down, pulled down my pants, and sat on the hard plastic. As usual the damn seat tried to slip out from under me — it was only attached by one flimsy plastic hinge — but I held it in place with my ass.

I calmed myself down, took care of my business, cleaned up and flushed, standing so nothing splashed on me. The toilet was one of those geyser flushers. A lil' sleepy now, I sat back down. Didn't feel like moving. My back settled against the cold porcelain tank.

Somewhere, out through the open front room window, in the spring-warming up city, a car horn honked. Faint voices trailed up. The Kool Man Magic Man "Watch for our Children!" ice cream truck spread its tinkly music through the air. A few junkies were probably pacing.

My weight settled on the toilet seat. Minutes passed.

I slumped over, head falling onto my knees.

And I was driving. In the dark something shined off to the right.

I stopped the car and pulled over, turning the engine off. Silence flooded in. My eyes were weary and I had to strain to keep my vision clear.

I flicked the high beams on. Opening the car door, I fell out onto the dusty white road, lying there face down, fine dust collecting on my teeth. Something began to change inside my body, warming into me, tingling as I lay there. The more I breathed in the ground, the flatter I pressed myself, the better I felt. A thought came from somewhere: *You should remember this,*

I raised my head, thinking I'd (seen?) something. The high beams of my car cut twin tunnels of yellow-white glow into the moonless dark; further out, they merged into one and suddenly ended as if hitting a wall of night. It was so dark I couldn't tell what was on either side of the road, past the swath of headlights, past the rough green grasses ranging off the road shoulder.

Again, a flicker of something shining. Something yellow-green, dual, gliding low between the grasses, slinking in toward me. A pair of shining disembodied canine eyes loped into view and stopped, staring right at me.

I felt a sudden hooking inside my chest, as if pulling me outward *(come on!)* and I got to my feet. As I did, the black sky peeled back to reveal endless blue daylight, so clean I could see the curve of the atmosphere, and a great green plain stretching so far I could see the curve of the Earth. A slight wind picked up. Far off I thought I heard the tinny notes of a music box, playing over and over, getting farther and farther away, then disappearing.

I began to walk in the daylight, and I was getting smaller and smaller. The green grass was rough and luxuriant, soon up to my hips, swaying like water around me in the now steady wind. Birds and insects and small animals of all colors flushed at my feet, bolting only a few yards before stopping to watch me pass, eyes bright, noses twitching. Soon the grass got higher, and higher, until it was at my chest, and the sky began clouding up, condensing quickly into darker clouds.

I suddenly was not in the grass anymore but above it, in the air, buffeted by the increasing winds.

But when I looked down again, I still saw the black top of my head, just a child's head. I was still down there, walking further and further away. I could see as if from two pairs of eyes, simultaneously from up in the sky and down in the grass. The Sun suddenly lowered beneath the last overhang of rumbling clouds, flashing its blinding light across the entire land, a giant star.

I walked and it may have been miles. The grasses hushed and swayed all around, an ancient woman's robes, pulling, slapping at me. Thunder boomed over my head, enveloping me, filling my ears. Soon I could see nothing but grass and sky, the low, incredibly bright Sun inhaling me and everything else into it. The grasses gradually grew lower again till they only reached my knees, and the land became harder, rangier. Every part of my body felt loose and supported, muscles lubricated, organs clear, bloodstream and lungs calm and strong. Vital.

As the sky's light grew to a crisper, starker blue, the wind lulled for a moment. In bare patches there were rocks and scrubby bushes. Prickly palm-faced cactuses bloomed with bright yellow flowers and red fruits. A patch of snow appeared and melted before my eyes, a rattlesnake slid out of a hole and curled around a heat-swelling rock, flipping out a forked black tongue that quivered. Butterflies fluttered. Big sleek magpies dove black-white-and-green through the sky and snapped into the butterflies, eyes and strong black beaks gleaming. Freshly severed butterfly wings flipped over in the wind and floated to the ground like petals. The grasses changed from spring green to summer yellow. The Sun rose higher and hotter then lower again. But when I looked it was still straight out to the west, blinding bright and white.

Animals passed like shadows on either side, canines and felines with teeth and claws, hoofed woolly animals with massive black shoulders and curved ebony horns, or light, long-legged tawny antelope prancers. The wind picked up and the grasses rolled and quivered like a sea shaken out to the horizon. From above I checked below to see where my self had gone, and saw only a stick figure far off being swallowed in the open land and the great sinking Sun. Exhilarated by my speed in the high cold air, I raced to catch up; the land flew by below me. I bumped up into an air pocket and it flipped me over. Righting myself, I looked and looked but down below I was gone.

The music box sounds returned. The melody paused, then began playing over again. Dimly, I heard kids yelling and laughing, a metal gate being pulled down; farther off a warehouse alarm went off. Somewhere, somebody coughed. A car passed.

I lifted my head, opened my eyes. Out through the shotgun apartment, out through the front room windows I saw that it was still barely light outside, a washed-out yellow glow below a darkening sky above the tops of the buildings.

I climbed out onto the fire escape. Leaning on the rust-red railing, chin in my hands, I thought: Fuck humans. Fuck people, including myself.

I left the apartment, heading up and west across the city until I made it to the Hudson. Went out to the end of my favorite pier between Christopher and West 10th Street, climbing through the gaping hole in the sagging chain link fence like always.

I sat on the hanging concrete slab, the bottoms of my sneakers a foot above the Hudson River as it surged smoothly beneath me, its strength thrilling and unnerving me at the same time. The water was a flat green. I knew it was a deep river. I stretched the tip of my toe down and tapped the quickly moving water; a little eddy streamed around it.

I took my baseball cap off — the strong, late March wind might blow it into the water. The sky deepened to navy blue, with a yellow band of fading light over the Jersey horizon, marked by occasional planes and helicopters in the distance, city lights blinking, shadows of cliffs and buildings, and flapping seagulls. Spring grass had begun growing in the rotted wooden beams on the sides of the pier. Crushed cigarette butts hid in many of the splintered creases. A Circle Line boat was passing, playing loud, heavy metal music, the kind that sounds like one long continuous car accident.

I lay on my back and stared into the heavens, eking out the North Star overhead as it came out bright, and then, of course, looking west, over my West, where Venus glowed otherworldly above the band of yellow deepening to blue. I felt the curve of the Earth over that horizon, under that sky. I lowered my eyelids to slits, watching the last of the twilight sink into my West. Feeling my West, dreaming it, I thought *Nothing compares to you.*

CHAPTER THIRTEEN

Invasion

"One of the first symptoms an HIV-infected individual often notices is swollen lymph nodes, particularly in the neck and groin area. Other symptoms include night sweats, being tired all the time, stomach and mouth ulcers, muscle and joint aches...."

Huddled in the library, I pulled over the other book on the table. It said the same thing. You could carry the shit around with you and not know for years. But it was a death sentence regardless. Guaranteed. I thought about those hardened lumps I'd felt on my body.

I dug my elbows into the shiny dark wood and balled my fists into my temples, closing my eyes. What the hell is inside me? What had invaded me? Microscopic bugs oozing disease, filling me up, squirming around in there, feeding off me. Replacing everything that remained vital in my young body with filthy sickness. Had I been carrying this alien around with me all this time? Was I gonna get skinny with diarrhea, start developing lesions and open sores on my body? Was fuzzy mold gonna start growing on my tongue as I became a walking plague of infection?

The books said the virus could even fill up your brain and spinal cord tissue. I had been unsafe just that one time, so drunk, on 43rd Street between the parked cars. But that one time was all it took. I'd let that shit inside my body. What the fuck had I been thinking? *You weren't thinking; that's the problem.* Of course that dude had it; he was just out there, in the Deuce, not giving a shit. Older. Been around having unsafe sex for years, doing whatever the fuck, long before anybody knew about this disease. Fuck, you hadn't even heard about it.

I opened my eyes and looked out the window. The brightness made my pupils contract. Between the geometric shapes of the buildings, the sky was blue. People on the sidewalk were walking past, hurrying on with their lives. I suddenly remembered that time in Corpus Christi, after I'd let that dude pick me up on the docks, how the bright sky through the window had almost seemed to blue out my vision with refracted light. I remembered the dude squeezing my goddamn nipple and saying, right before I got up out of there: "If you take care of yourself, you could have a charmed life."

With my hands over my eyes, I stared through my fingers at the wedges of sky between the buildings. The sky is definitely a little duller here than out West, I thought. A *boricua* (Puerto Rican) couple walked past the row of windows, holding hands. He said something to her. She tilted her head back laughing, bright teeth glistening, her pretty black curls spilling around her shoulders. A fit black guy in a brand new white tank top and navy blue nylon athletic pants walked by in that sporty-thug kind of way, carrying a gym bag. His body was lean, cut, muscled. He took care of himself.

I heard whispering off to my right, sounding loud in the hollow library. Nobody else seemed to notice. I watched them through my fingers: couple leaning in close, their whispering lips by each other's ear, the sides of their cheeks touching. They were nodding, smiling big, eyes half closed.

I got smaller and smaller. The quiet, hollow library seemed to stretch away from me. I sat there, knowing secretly that the insides of my body squirmed with disease.

Diego was lying on the bed fully clothed when I walked in. I smelled fish cooking. There was a pot on the stove with a big chunk of fresh bakery bread by its side. He turned his bloodshot eyes up at me as I came into the front room.

Ignoring him, I peeled off my shirt and put on a white tank top. I plated the easy-curl bar with two dimes and a nickel on each side and began working out my arms, facing the windows and the cracked mirror on the wall, my back to him. My body began to warm up as the blood started flowing.

I felt Diego staring at me. I stared straight ahead, trying to concentrate on lifting some weights.

Finally, I turned around, bar pumped in mid-curl strain, and glared at him.

"I made you dinner," he said.

I glared harder as I noticed he was lying on my side of the bed, right under the photo of my West. I started to say something, but turned back around, finishing the set of curls. Remembering the pot on the stove waiting for me, I tried hard to soften, say something, but my pride wouldn't let me.

"Fine," he said, getting up. He stormed out the door, by habit swerving past Mira Flores like we both did, even though the lake was now a dried-up ring on the rotted kitchen floor. Raul had shut the building's heat off for the season. I was so glad winter was over.

After a few more sets of arms, I went running down by the East River. Coming back, I ran into Maria coming out of the building and she collared me to go help her fill her carrying cage with live chickens in Chinatown. Usually she wore a scarf over her head, but she must have been feeling the spring air. Her hair was pulled back in a steel gray ponytail. She asked me about my "cousin" Diego and said it just like that, too. She knew what time it was. We entered the squawking market and I changed the subject and asked her about her husband. "Fume mucho. He smoke too much," she said, frowning, nubbing her fingers up and down the rows of cages. Dirty, white-feathered chickens jerked their heads or bawked or sat bosomed against the fronts as customers crowded, pushing their feathered chests into the wire mesh. My stomach felt nauseous as I thought about them getting their necks wrung or heads cut off and blood pouring out. And the smell of their internal body cavities as they were opened and eviscerated. I knew what that smell was like, a clammy, dank, shit-and-death smell that didn't change until flesh started broiling, and then somehow it became just food.

The short Chinese guy reached in Maria's cage of choice and grabbed a chicken by her legs and yanked her out, holding her upside down for Maria to see. The chicken flapped her wings a couple times and hung there, lifting her head up so she could still think she was right side up in the world. Maria nodded and the Chinese dude stuffed the chicken into the carrying cage I was holding, and Maria picked out a second one.

Alone in the apartment, I contemplated the pot on the stove.

That was pretty nice of him, I conceded. I picked up the spoon, lifting the lid and leaning over to sniff. I was working at becoming strictly vegetarian, but every once in a while still ate a *caribe* fish dinner. Maria loved to cook for both of us, and she knew I wasn't gon touch her chicken or any other meat. She was a much better cook than Diego, but hey. I sniffed again at the pot of rich, thin tomatoey liquid with chunks of boiled yuca, fish, mussels in the shell, crushed cilantro and hot peppers. It smelled spicy and good, if slightly fishy.

I took a sip, anticipating the savory hot drip down my throat and into my stomach. It tasted a little different than usual fish soup, and not as good as it smelled, but I was hungry.

I tore off a chunk of bread, checking the stovetop for cockroaches. He shouldn't leave any food out. What was he thinking?

I dipped and ate into the soupy, spicy fish and soggy bread. I got used to the slightly odd flavor and went at it, hungry. I cracked open a mussel and sucked its flesh pod into my mouth, chewing its gritty texture into a paste and swallowing. It sort of grossed me out.

Definitely the Combat traps were working pretty good, I thought. I scanned the floor as I grabbed the pot and spoon and went into the front room to sit on the floor. I ate slowly, letting my mind drift.

Thirty minutes later I was about halfway through when my stomach began to bubble. What's that? I put the pot down, thinking I had been eating too fast. I put my hand on my stomach.

Bloating. I'm bloating. What's up? Suddenly I began belching disgusting sulfurous burps that rumbled up and out of my gut. My eyes began to water. I burped again. My stomach lurched and I knew. I raced to the back closet and kicked up the toilet seat in time to spew an ungodly mess into the water that splashed up onto my face. Another surge came. Gut cramping. Oh no.

The retching and burping continued, with cramping pain and more bloating, until little was produced. After a while, although my guts felt sore and unstable, I managed to stand and clean up my mess. Dude had fucking poisoned me.

In the front room picking up the pot like it was a bomb, I brought it back to the toilet and flushed down what was left, holding my breath for fear of even smelling it. Weakly, I opened the front windows then took a shower.

Diego didn't come home that night and I didn't expect him to. I threw up one more time in the middle of the night, but it was just eye-watering retching with some drool, stomach trying to shove and twist and squeeze itself clean.

I decided not to say anything. I could survive this. Next day, guts still cramping and sulfurous burps still firing up in periodic waves, I went to Integral Yoga Natural Foods on West 13th. After asking for advice, I bought some acidophilus caps and herbal teas. Thinking back to the clean spoon, clean plate, unbroken loaf of bread, I wondered how stupid could I have been not to notice he hadn't touched the soup. I would fast until I felt sure I could keep something down. I didn't care if I ever ate anything again, as long as this gas and bloating left me for good.

Diego came back the next day when I was out, I could tell by the change of clothes left on the bed, but was gone again by the time I got back. That night I still felt weak, but stable enough to go to work. Had to make some money. Got to Rounds early, by 9 or so. Lately, there'd been more young hustlers hanging outside the spot. They didn't go in. Some were from the piers. Some of them were on the pipe, and couldn't or wouldn't go in, knowing they were all raggedy. They thought they were scavenging leftovers leaving Rounds, but mostly they were the ones being scavenged by tricks who couldn't score in Rounds, or didn't want to pay Rounds prices. Boys out on the street almost never got more than $30. In Rounds, you never knew what you were getting into; but out on the street it was worse.

Entering the bar, I walked down the narrow, darkly lit hallway gauntlet and on into the main room. I nodded at the other young black and Rican hustlers who spoke. I thought it was sort of funny — I never used to even look at anybody. I thought it was weird how I sort of appreciated people recognizing me and wanting to say hi. I was a little "popular" for the first time in my life. I was now a regular.

That's sick, I thought to myself.

"Sup Emmanuel," Damon said, coming through the gauntlet and dapping my hand. "Man, I was all up on my couch and shit and just getting into Lao Tzu when the damn beeper went off." He flashed a roll of cash. "Buck fifty. One hour. Decided to come over here and see what's crackin,' since I'm already out and about."

A suit walked slowly past us, checking us out up and down, like he was in a supermarket. He looked at our shoes at the same moment Damon and I glanced down at his. We both had our sneaks on, so… It was up to the suit if he wanted to deal or not.

Diego passed by, and I just nodded, watching him watch my face. I acted like nothing was up.

Leaving Damon to deal with the suit, I went into the back lounge. I saw this tall, very nice-looking dude, copper-skinned, maybe a few years older, almost model-type, and wondered why somebody that on-point would be in here hustling. We began talking. He was an actor who'd come to Rounds to make some needed extra money. He'd done it a couple times before, had actually gone to Europe with one suit, but said he found himself disgusted with the whole scene. He only came here when he absolutely needed a little extra ends. As we talked — and we had both now shut out the whole hustling scene around us — I could see Diego turning purple across the room, standing against the wall, glaring.

I left with him, passing Diego who gaped at me. Alvan cabbed us up to his high-rise apartment building in the east 90s, a world away from Ludlow Street. He had a new-looking apartment with ebony statues and sharp silver and black metal decor. He ate crackers in bed, crumbs falling down the muscled gulley in the middle of his chest and abs. I passed out in his bed, my stomach shrunken and body exhausted, and we just slept together, no sex, just holding each other. It felt great to just be around somebody calm and quiet who I didn't have to brace myself against. The next morning he wanted to cook breakfast, but I told him I had to run. Stomach not ready for food yet, anyhow. He asked what I was doing later; I told him I'd call him, even though I knew I wouldn't. I was tainted, damaged goods, and certainly didn't belong in the company of someone that good looking, somebody who had his shit that together. I bounced, and just kicked it on the drizzly street all day, chillin' around the city.

I got home as it was getting dark. The bare lightbulb was on in the kitchen. Diego was in the front room working out, with his shirt off. The windows were still wide open from two days before, the air thick with humidity. As I walked in, I tensed up, but acted like everything was normal.

He continued pumping the dumbbells, looking straight ahead into the mirror at his body. I went toward the window. He threw the dumbbells down. I winced, worrying about the floor, and the noise. I hated attention drawn to us. He spun around. "You!" he screamed, and swung at me. I ducked, and tackled him. We fell to the floor, and he punched and tore at me. Diego was taller than me and I had to use my whole body on top of him, spreading my arms wide to yank in his flailing arms. I wrestled him to a squirming stop, sitting on top him, pinning his wrists against the floor up over his head. He strained his head from side to side and bucked. I bore down on him with all my weight. He got one arm loose and clocked me good on the side of the head. I grabbed his wrist and yanked it down under my right knee. I pulled back, cocking my punch, holding it with such strain I felt that if I slipped I'd smash his face into oblivion. My fingers began to shake.

"Go ahead!" he screamed. "Do it! Do it! Hit me! You don't care! Destroy my fucking face! I WISH YOU WOULD! KNOCK out my fucking teeth! DO IT! DO IT! I DON'T CARE! I WANT YOU TO!" He raised his head up toward me, his mouth falling open to give me his teeth. The cords and muscles in his neck bulged, straining at his skin; his face flared red. He started to cry, and slammed his head back onto the floor with a hard thud that had to hurt. He rolled his head from side to side as the tears came out loudly, shaking his whole body, vibrating into me.

The dirty yellow light from the kitchen shined on his wet face. Even though the windows were open, the air was dead still, the apartment stuffy and humid. Overheated with adrenaline and the strain, a drop of sweat rolled off my face onto his. I squeezed my eyes shut, trying to blink it all out.

I collapsed down onto him, breathing hard, letting go of everything, lying on him, my eyes dry as he cried and shook. We lay there like that for a few minutes. His crying slowly subsided, and we got quiet. Just the heaving of his overheated breaths up into my chest, and back down. Quieter and quieter.

He tensed and started bucking wildly again, knocking me partially off him. I flipped over onto the floor then jumped up, about to pounce on him, then stormed out the door, my shoe stepping in the middle of dry Mira Flores as I passed through the kitchen. I slammed the door behind me.

As I popped onto the stairway leading down, I noticed Maria's door was open. She was standing in her doorway, her mostly toothless face looking out at me, holding a bloody, half-plucked chicken by its wrung neck. Her fat old *merido* was standing behind her, naked as usual except for his boxers and plastic Delancey St. dollar-store flip flops; pot-bellied, purple-veined, bleary-eyed and probably itching for a cigarette.

I hopped down the flights of stairs three at a time and went out to my streets. I didn't go anywhere, except to both rivers, rubber-banding from one side of the city to the other.

"We need to take a break," I said, late the next afternoon. "Just need a week at least, to get my thoughts straight."

He seemed deflated, hardly said anything as he packed up his backpack. The situation was calm. He still was acting like nothing was up. He sure was a good actor.

I watched him go. He didn't look back. He walked up the street, thumbs hooked into the straps of his backpack that marked two black lines down the back of his white t-shirt. The top of his head moved up and down with the slight bounce in his walk. And I knew at that very moment the distance was widening, opening up, he was becoming a stranger again. He turned the corner around Katz's and was gone. Though I realized it was a passage, it was over with for real. I was glad.

My digestive system slowly came back, but I knew I had to be real careful with what I ate. I drank a lot of water, and ate soft things like mashed sweet potatoes with raw lime juice like Maria suggested.

On the weights, I worked out every part of my body, multiple times, until every muscle group was sore and doing that little twitch the books say you should work for. I kept going back at it, until well into the night. Then I showered, barely able to hold the hose up, then went out again into the streets. And realized that much of my depression had passed, replaced now by this sort of itchy desperation and restlessness. But it was still a cause to celebrate. Depression and desperation are two different dangers. At least I had a new sort of fury. There was some new strength here. Fire lit — even if it seemed to be propelling me into what was likely the brick wall at the end of my road. Cause I knew I still had *that* ...the Bonus... to contend with.

And the Shadow World again...

...music box sounds... Camptown Races melody, *doo-dah... doo-dah....* Diesel generator and small truck engine rumbling down below; a tinny ice-cream truck voice: *Hello? Hello?*

My eyes slowly opened as I came back into this world, taking in the Ludlow Street apartment. The peace mobile hung motionlessly, a fly hanging on it upside down. On the green peace circle this time. From the looks of the overcast sky outside, it looked like it was sometime in the evening. I wondered how long I'd been passed out. I'd come home around four or five. I could tell the ice cream truck was now parked right below our building, playing its musical rhymes.

I fully came to, realizing where I was, that I had left the Shadow World behind, I'd wasted this whole life; all the effort to survive was worthless. Just when it seemed I was getting stronger. God it's amazing, I thought, how you don't even know how low you've fallen when you're so far below rock bottom that it's all you know, and you can't see anything let alone the top rim or a way out.

Now, just when it seemed like I could get a grip on my shit, get a step up, it turns out I have AIDS.

I lay there, very still, my breath barely rising and falling. I looked over at my old Motobecane 10 speed bike in the corner that I'd bought for $30 when I took the bikemessengering job. It seemed like a long time since I'd ridden.

I glanced up at my West photo. I looked away. There would be no going out West any time soon. I needed to get my shit together here, first. I needed to get a job. But I would make it out there.

Keys rattled in the lock, the deadbolt tumbled open. Diego walked in. He'd only left a couple days ago, but it felt longer than that.

"Hi," he said, taking off his backpack and letting it drop to the floor. He kicked off his sneakers and lay down, propping up on one elbow the way he liked to do. "I couldn't stay away. I had the feeling you needed somebody. To talk to. I don't know. I just did."

"I'm cool…" I said.

We lay there in silence as dusk settled in. The ice cream truck left, and outside, on the street, in that Manhattan kind of way right at dusk, things seemed to get quieter, hushed for awhile, until night came on full. A slight breeze entered the open windows; the upside down fly spun slowly around on the mobile. I breathed out hard, staring at the fly and the ceiling, ready to talk now.

"You ever been… you know…."

"Hmm?" Diego said.

"*Tested.*" I whispered. There. I had said it. Out loud. "You know. For … that thing." It was so hard to even say, as if just bringing it into spoken language might let everybody know. Might even make the disease itself go full-blown, dripping sores and diarrhea and fungus and all that, at any time.

"Me and Jennifer went right before I met you. I get tested every six months. It's no big deal, except for the two week wait to get the results back."

I screwed my eyes over to look at him like he was some kind of alien with six heads. I couldn't believe how casual he was talking about it.

"Sometimes…," I said, "I worry." My head was squeezing so hard I thought my teeth might crack. "You know. That I might, you know, have it." Just then I realized he had no clue about all the extreme stress I'd been going through behind this.

"Man, you don't have it. You don't ever do nothing."

I bristled. "They say you could be walking around with it and not even know it. For years! Until signs…"

"No, I don't think you have it." He laid his head down and put his arm around me. "So I missed you. Even one day."

Flat on my back, I stared up at the ceiling, making sure nothing of my past anger toward him entered my mind. I had more immediate and important things to worry about. And I needed to keep this calm feeling going. The apartment was getting dark. After a while I said, "I think I'ma try again to get a job."

He'd fallen asleep. I lifted his arm off me. I mentally counted my money. There was $400 saved up. I'd kept the last hundred dollars Diego had given me for help with the rent payoff.

Staring at the fly spinning slowly upside down on the peace mobile, I mentally checked the month. April had turned into May. Time passing. Had to find a way out. I was going out West no matter what, though it might take me months, half a year, or more. That was the only thing I was doing now. Focusing on my departure. Stringing the landlord along, long enough to keep staying here. Trying to be as peaceful as possible. Working hard. And getting out of here. In the meantime, Diego would have to leave for good. It was over. I just needed to be alone. And to prepare for my departure. Out West. Where I would starve myself to death in the desert.

I opened my eyes, seeing that thought, that exhilarating image — like a clean black-and-white photo, liquid chrome — very clearly for the first time. At least I'll be pure. Purified. Whole and complete, for the first time in my life.

I saw myself sitting cross-legged in the desert, naked except for my drawers in the scrawny shadow of a scrawny desert bush. Everything was in sharp metallic shades of molten silver and black. My skin, my hair, my closed eyelids, the sky, the bright sand, the rocks near me, the bush behind me. I was so skinny you could see my bones. Obviously I had been there next to the bush for a while already. I got the feeling it was taking a long time for my spirit to pass. As I watched, I seemed to get skinnier and skinnier; I became a piece of gnarled, petrified ironwood with muscles corded and twisting around visible bones. I still didn't move. A couple more days and nights passed. Soon, I couldn't tell what was the wind and what was me.

Summer 1990 blew in bright and breezy, reminding me I was on a coastal Atlantic island surrounded by water. It was as if I had climbed out of a great illness, could stretch my arms and legs and breathe deeply, only to find another one looming.

The worst thing about my new job at the Paramount Hotel was the floor-to-ceiling mirrors opposite the elevators on each floor. As soon as the elevator doors opened, you saw yourself, highlighted in track lighting. There I was, sweating inside a black Armani jacket and white t-shirt, black slacks, fresh haircut and shave, shined shoes, and if I turned my head at all to the left the little AIDS knot-lump-thing in my neck beneath my jaw stood out in stark contrast. I became obsessed. I tried not to look, but each time the elevator doors opened, I found myself twisting my neck to see it, even as I hauled guests' bags to their trendy, tiny rooms.

Ian Schrager, some high-profile NYC entrepreneur who had owned and operated some of the famous downtown nightclubs, including the old Palladium, had turned an old Times Square single-room-occupancy hotel on 46th between Broadway and 8th Ave into a trendy new designer hotel. But the hotel didn't tell its customers about the size of the rooms. It was up to us bellboys to deal with the irate guests once they realized the hotel was all slick marketing and no substance. When we checked them into rooms so small there wasn't enough room for me and two guests to stand inside at the same time, they looked at me like I was crazy. They had to stand outside the door as I showed them how to work the lights and TV. Some left; some stayed and dealt with it. After all, the Paramount was supposed to be hip.

It had been hard getting a job, because I had no phone number, no work history, no personal or work references, not even a mailing address. There wasn't even a mailbox in my building's vestibule. But I'd taken a little of the money I'd saved, bought a discount button-down shirt and a pair of chinos and some black sneakers on 14th St., and made myself look as clean as I could. At the Paramount, I'd lucked out; they hired me at the cattle call. I'd learned how to tell in somebody's eyes without missing a beat when they found me attractive, and I knew how to keep an innocent face while discreetly using the situation to my advantage.

My shift was usually from 3 to 11 p.m. I took my lunch breaks up on the roof, or west down 46th a few blocks, where I sat on the stoop of some abandoned business called Dyke Lumber, which apparently was just somebody's unfortunate last name.

A black hooker often came and sat next to me, always wearing the same lime green shorts. She was short and thick, had lots of junk in her trunk, and was missing her front teeth. If she hadn't broke luck yet, she would try to turn me onto a blowjob, she'd even do it for five dollars, so she could at least get her "luck rolling for the day." I always had to say no.

I did my bellboy job well, caused no ripples, learned how to work the system, and when I felt a passout coming on, snuck into an unused room. We were always changing people into other rooms, so it was easy to keep a couple extra keys in our pockets during our shift.

I went up to Rounds a couple more times, and finally, never went back again. I put my foot down with Diego, and he moved out for good. It was over with, really, for good. There was no blowout, no nothing. He just nodded, packed up his things, I got his set of keys, and he left.

But I guess he thought about it afterwards, because he came back, and for about a week he caused a big scene on my block. He knew I hated attention drawn to me, and he used that. He was obviously high. He tried to throw bricks and bottles through my windows, but being that I was up on the third floor, he always missed. Glass bottles shattered against the old tenement bricks, and sprinkled back down on him. He yelled up that I had to meet him, had to talk to him. I finally agreed; we went up to the East Village and sat on some concrete steps, and he cried and blubbered, smoking cigarettes, his falling tears making the collar of his t-shirt wet. I tried to care. But I had no feeling left for him.

I began riding the old ten-speed bike again. And I was now working out regularly, or running down by the East River. I upped my miles. This way I'd be in good fitness when I went on my one-way trip out into the desert to starve myself to death.

On August 2, one week after U.S. Ambassador April Glaspie deliberately gave Iraq the go-ahead by telling Saddam Hussein the U.S. had no position on Arab-Arab conflicts, Iraq invaded Kuwait, which Hussein expected was Iraq's prize for fighting Iran. Newspaper headlines and the Bush Administration screamed about the invasion, conveniently ignoring facts behind it, and suddenly the country was on a massive, jittery build up to war. Saddam Hussein, the longtime friend and beneficiary of the U.S., was now foe and foil, and a president's perfect TV-op fight was picked, with oil spoils, war glory and massacred brown people the prize.

Jogging along the tar path in East River Park, seeking any breeze on this hot and sweltering afternoon, I ran into Damon. He always had this dog-like, stern look on his face. He peeled off his headphones and narrowed his eyebrows at me. His shirt was off; sweat glistened on the few curls of black hair between his pecs.

I took the shirt that hung from my waistband and wiped my face. The cloudless but slightly hazy sky added some blue accents to the gently heaving brown water. We said "what's up." He wondered where I'd been. I told him "around," that I'd just gotten a job at a hotel. Something flickered behind his eyes as I told him that. He was still doing Rounds. He was still the same Damon, so nonchalant. On the surface, anyway. That was the door I couldn't key open. I couldn't figure him out. Talk turned to the upcoming, we-knew-inevitable war.

We both stood there, looking at the moving river, trying to imagine the war, the hot urban sun beating down into our heads and bare shoulders. Broken glass glinted on the path.

"All that protective chemical gear they're gonna have to wear. In that heat." He said it almost like a gasp. "They're gonna get *sprayed*. And the Iraqi kids who live there, getting caught up in all that…"

"And the bombing," I said.

"It's gonna be hell…" he said, wiping his face.

"All around," I said.

He gritted his teeth. "I hate him. Bush. Got us into something that's not gonna end."

I nodded. We were silent, probably both hoping for any breeze to come off the river, fully taking in the impending war.

"Maybe I'll see you around," he said.

I nodded again, doubting it. And suddenly I knew I only had a few weeks left in New York. At last.

We dapped each other off and continued running, heading in opposite directions.

With arms folded behind my head, hot tarpaper baking into my back through my t-shirt, city blue sky all around, I lay on the roof and watched the world revolve.

My heartbeat tapped an even rhythm through my body, making a little jiggle in the frames of my sunglasses. I let my eyes follow jumbo jets that, to this world down here, were nothing but hot silver needles up there spinning wispy trails of puffy cotton-white pollution.

A heavy compressed bass beat began, loud, and the hard criminal raps of the Geto Boys filled the neighborhood. Eddie, top man of Lucky Seven, had turned his 4th floor stereo on, down the block, rattling the old buildings and priming the street for another block party.

I got to my feet, bits of tar gravel stuck to my shirt. I went downstairs.

The traditional block-long string of firecrackers was ignited, setting off tens of thousands of ricocheting explosions, a half dozen car alarms, volumes of smoke, fire, cheers, flying red shredded pieces of paper, more smoke, screams, and more smoke. One of the scaggy Allen St. whores from around the way straddled the line and gyrated wildly in front of the advancing explosions as if she was getting fucked by them. Her douche bottle was visible sticking out of her vinyl clasp purse.

Some of the kids on the corner opened the fire hydrant full blast. With a garbage can lid they redirected the spray at some disoriented tourists on the opposite corner, who had ventured over from Orchard Street, looking for Katz's deli.

"¡Mira the kids!" said two women in perfect Spanglish unison, two young grandmothers standing in a doorway, each with one hand holding a can of Budweiser with a paper napkin wrapped around it and the other hand resting on the aluminum handle of a stroller, gossiping, their hair lightened to coppery orange, the Rican version of blonde. A whole pig was roasting on a spit, and the smell of its burning flesh and sizzling, dripping fat turned my stomach.

The street soon filled with people and the smells of gunpowder, pork fat, baby diapers, warm spilled beer, smoke from blunts, and armpit sweat covered up with drugstore cologne and deodorant — Old Spice or Sure.

Eddie's black BMW was parked at the curb. A girl with huge gold doorknocker earrings snapped her chewing gum and bent over to comb her wet, freshly showered curls in the reflection of the tinted windows, knowing that she could still give cookies in those tight yellow shorts even though she was pregnant. The black spandex bathing suit she wore underneath held her belly like a soccer ball in a sling. She smiled at me. She was Eddie's girlfriend.

I thought about telling her and Eddie I was leaving, but turned and walked up toward Houston, threading my way through the crowd. The ice cream truck had pulled onto the block but because of the loud thumping rap nobody heard its grating generators and melancholic crankbox renditions of "Camptown Races" and tinny, sing-song voice "*Hello? ... Hello?*" played over and over on top of *doo-dah... doo-dah...* driving us crazy. Painted on its side panel was a smiling ice cream cone and THE VERY BEST! KOOLMAN-MAGIKMAN. WATCH FOR OUR CHILDREN.

At the corner sat the bony wheelchaired woman with the rangy afro-puff and no shoes who I'd seen so many times before. I knew she was dismayed by the street party's disruption of her routine, which included a much-needed daily $10 visit to Lucky

Seven. As she'd waited, hoping for things to clear out, her head had fallen to her chest, a long unlit Virginia Slims still clamped in her mouth. Her half-raised hand clutching the Bic lighter was faltering, dropping in notches to her lap like the arm of a reluctant wind-up toy. Once down, the hand let the lighter clatter to the sidewalk, and joined the other hand in finding the one place where the hands of all the discomfited and unconscious end up — the crotch — where warmth and a sense of protecting the security of oneself can be had at once.

Although anxious to get away from the crowds, I took an extra moment and walked over, bent down, and picked up her lighter. I looked at it; shrugged. I leaned down and lit her cigarette for her, then carefully placed the lighter between her lap-clasped hands. I gently shook her shoulder. Her head rolled upright for a minute, glazed eyes acknowledging me. The blue smoke curled around her face and sifted up into the angry mass of hair on her head, where it lingered, wafting. She tried to smile. I left before her head fell back down.

By September I'd bought an old silver Chevy Citation hatchback for $800 on Avenue D. I rented out my place, kept the money instead of paying Stein, packed up, stuck my 10 speed in the back of the hatch, and by midnight of September 9 was driving down the West Side Highway along the Hudson River, heading for the Holland Tunnel. There was no traffic. I pulled off on a side street and walked over. It was quiet. The highway and streets seemed deserted. I could hear the river gently slapping on the other side of the highway, against the concrete seawall. I leaned my back against a lightpole and gazed across the road at distant reflections of New Jersey moving in the dark water. Looking up West Side Highway, I watched the traffic lights changing one after the other like dominoes falling all the way uptown. The night was almost tropical. I could almost imagine palm trees lining this outer edge of Manhattan Island. Caught up in the moment, feeling well, with much unknown ahead, I peeled off my shirt; the breeze wrapped around me. The air cooled my skin and I thought: *This is where you are, right now.*

I looked up at the sky and saw a white and round haloed moon, then I saw a planet or star flung off to the side and beyond. It was then, for the first time, that I had the sense of depth in the universe. That I was here, the moon there, and the other planet or star farther out *there.* All these suspended bodies and bursts of light testifying to unimaginable lengths of time. And my flesh such a particle-blink in all of that.

"Is there a story to that?" I asked.

I looked down and saw myself as if from far off, this tiny figure leaning with his back against a light pole, bare chested, shirt in hand, orange streetlight enveloping him in a tight circle.

A PICKWAY FOODS 18-wheeler barreled by.

"Fucking faggot!!" the trucker yelled out his window, pitching a crumpled beer can out. It clattered to the pavement, rolling in the truck's backdraft.

The diesel wind danced in my hair.

Back in my car, before I entered the Holland Tunnel, leaving New York City, I saw graffiti that said:

FACE IT NY SUCKS AND
YOU STAY HERE CAUSE YOU ARE ADDICTED
AND THAT'S FUCKIN SICK
WAKE UP

And I was gone.

SECTION FOUR

"I was born on the prairie, where the wind blew free and there was nothing to break the light of the Sun… and where everything drew a free breath."

— Parra Wa-Samen (Ten Bears) of the Yamaparika Comanches,
   Treaty Speech of 1872

"It is the mind that makes the body."

— Sojourner Truth

"On a larger scale, the approaching dawn of a new millennium will inevitably create a sense of the beginning of a new age and the end of an old."

— Rupert Sheldrake,
   The Rebirth of Nature: The Greening of Science and God

CHAPTER FOURTEEN

Prairie Earth

In darkness, I leaned on the wire highway department fence behind the roadside rest area. Lights on two radio towers beyond a scraped-barren Pennsylvania hillside blinked on and off like a pole of lifeless red eyes. Behind me, a semi blared past, roaring, like the others before and after it, speeding boxes outlined in bright orange bulb lights. Were they part of the definition of America at night now?

Gazing blankly at the blinking red eyes on the radio towers, I felt the weariness of the land all around me. I didn't know what I was supposed to be seeing. Did this used to be forest? What was it like, when it was primeval? Everything seemed so used now. I turned back toward my car, my sneakers soaking in the damp night grass. I rubbed my finger over the lump under my jaw.

Driving hurriedly through the rest of the night, through Ohio and Indiana, "the Old Northwest." Not too road weary, mind drifting but alert enough to float down the dark highway. Ohio was a mute place for me. There were times early on when I hadn't spoken a word for weeks at a time. Driving through, I felt no connection at all to that time, or to that person who had been, had to have been, me at one time. The thought floated in and out of my mind like the others, dreamily, like the nighttime canopies of trees now overhead.

I imagined an unsettled hardwood forest jungle, the road a tiny narrow ribbon through woods leading west hundreds of miles until it hit open prairie country. I imagined silence. I tried to imagine this place before roads, before the noise of cars or any machines. Where in certain places one great forest stretched from the Atlantic to the Mississippi, the only openings before the Great River being the tallgrass prairie "barrens" of Ohio, Kentucky, and Illinois.

In daytime I'd realize I was passing through industrial cornfields, my imagined great forest actually a narrow line of accidental ditch trees. But for now…

The front seat of the Chevy Citation was all one vinyl bench across, and didn't recline. Why didn't I think about that before I spent $800 on this car? It was hard and uncomfortable. When I needed to pull over and rest I had to lay down sideways, with my legs folded and twisted into where the gas pedal and brake were, or, if putting my inner night watchman on high alert, taking a chance and leaving the door open so I could lie on my back across the seat, legs out, feet on the pavement. It felt good to stretch out my spine like that. But I had to sleep with my guard up just like sleeping on the subway or a park bench. Light sleep, hair-trigger rest, not real sleep. Watchman on.

In the afternoon, the car began sputtering and acting up. Leaving it at an auto repair shop in Hammond-Whiting, Indiana, an old industrial, sort of sooty smelling place, I rode my bike to the shore of Lake Michigan and swam in the sweet water, slipping off a wooden city dock.

Back in the auto shop waiting room, on the table was a *People* magazine cover article about a girl who had caught AIDS from just one incident of unprotected sex. In the photo she was staring at the camera, as if her soul had wanted to go somewhere else, but now hers was a life of 'no longer an option.' I had auto-shop waiting-room horror and tried not to think about it, but kept looking at her out of the corners of my eyes. I tried to focus on the immediate situation. Out another two hundred bucks for the repair. And now I had a little less than eight hundred dollars to my name. I was already existing on just alfalfa sprouts and sunflower seeds, not knowing what else I could eat that was vegetarian road food. *Money's not good. You will have to figure out something.*

In Humbird, Wisconsin, I sat in the grass by a lake. The afternoon was sunny, warm, a little breezy.

I told myself I wasn't going to think about the past couple years, especially the last year. You're just going to let it be. It was over with now. You just need to clear up your head. If any of it comes up, you're just going to breathe it back into the past again, like in meditation. I'd bought *Yoga Self Taught* at the Strand Bookstore on Broadway. I'd been studying it, realizing some of the positions were similar to ones my body'd been subconsciously pushing me to do anyway to relieve pain and pressure. The book just formalized it, gave me more options.

A farmer on a tractor with a load of hay passed a ways off. Did he notice me? I hunched and kept my head down. The little lake was barely rippling. I decided I wanted this whole trip to be like a conscious meditation, where I existed beneath the surface of anybody's attention, just a moving, unseen ball of nerve-centered feelings and senses.

Just going to *breathe* through the next six weeks or two months or however long you can stretch it out. Gonna spend most of the time outside, just let my blood, breath, thoughts flow through me on their own.

I already felt better, after only three days gone. Each morning, I found a hidden safe spot in some grassy area away from people and dogs, and did yoga, my shirt and shoes off, just wearing a pair of cut off gray cotton sweatpants, no drawers, following the pictures from my book. I'm a swami, I told myself, half serious, half delirious, not sure what a swami was. But I just listened to what felt right in my body.

The tractor guy was gone down the road, and it was just me and the lake. A Laurie Anderson song came into my head, *"Been getting lots of sun, and lots of rest...."*

I checked myself out. Darker, leaner, harder, since last winter.

I felt like I could have the capacity for extraordinary health. Just a few things (dark clouds) including a check-up and (*say it!*) blood test (so you know for sure). Just a few things, and some serious life alignments are all that stand in the way. Of course, it's obvious you can't live in NYC (especially the way you do) and still achieve this.

I drove a little more, getting restless in the afternoon sunlight. I stopped and unloaded my bike. Wisconsin is peaceful and calm, I thought.

Again I marveled at the freedom I felt in riding. It was the closest a man can come to flying with his own body. Occasionally a car passed me on the narrow, mostly deserted road, going fast. I kept my thin road bike tires on the white line, an eye out for rocks. There was no shoulder, just a three or four-inch drop off into gravel.

Sitting upright on the bike, freeing my hands, I peeled off my shirt and laced it into the loops of my knee-length baggy jean shorts. Getting back in forward position, I bore down harder on the pedals, picking up more speed.

Another vehicle was approaching from behind, and he was coming on fast. As I raced forward, I kept listening for his tires to let me know he'd be swinging out to give me more room. You can judge what a car is doing by listening to its tires on the pavement. Ears are a second pair of eyes. But he was coming straight on. I steadied my tires as far to the edge of the white line as I could. My stomach gripped against my spine, as if bracing for something it knew before I did. I held my course down to the last few seconds and inches of pavement.

This isn't happening, I thought. I felt air being pushed in front of him, like the air in front of a subway train as it barrels into the station. The hurtling pickup truck clipped my side, jutting me and the bike sideways. My front tire jammed into the soft gravel shoulder and I flipped head first over the handlebars, bringing the bike with me in a tangle of wheels, legs and arms slamming down hard, knocking the wind out of me. I skidded six or seven feet, gravel and cinders burrowing into my skin, before I reached the end of my little improvised runway and came to a stop. Straining my head up, I watched the pickup disappear down the road, the silhouette of a cowboy hat visible through the back window.

I worked to get air into my lungs, gasping, chest heaving. The shock shakes came on quickly, overtaking my body, jerking up through my legs and into my arms, making my limbs whap uncontrollably. I pulled my legs painfully out of the bike frame and wobbled to my feet. My right arm didn't feel right. There was a big gash torn out of the shoulder. Shreds of skin ringed the rip, which was just starting to fill with blood, which pooled out and began dribbling down my arm bright red, curling into the crease of my underarm and dripping hot onto my side. I tried repeatedly to stop my damn twitching arms and legs, but the shock shakes made me flap like a duck.

I focused on my bike. The front wheel was twisted. That was probably it for this bike. I bent down, and even before I moved my right arm it flared with pain. I hooked the bike frame with my left hand and pulled it up. My side was singed with itchy gravel burns. I barely noticed two cars blowing past me, their wind buffeting me, not even bothering to slow down. I stared at my blood with a detached horror, imagining it crawling with AIDS viruses.

Figuring I was about ten miles out, I next focused on the business of walking back. It wasn't anything I couldn't handle. The bent front wheel was going to be the main problem. The shakes were starting to smooth out a little, replaced by a big throbbing pain that rolled into my arm and upper right side and chest cavity. Clutching my hurt arm to my side, trying not to double over with each rolling wave of pain, I decided to cross the road, figuring walking would help spread it out. I could handle it.

A big old faded blue pickup came over the hill and pulled over. An old man in a bushy white beard and faded denim overalls got out and asked me if I needed to go to the hospital, told me to get into the back of the truck.

"I'm ok," I grumbled. "Just need to get back to my car."

"Is that your Chevy Citation up there?" he asked, nodding his head in the direction he came from.

I nodded, thinking that rural people note anything that's out of the ordinary in their regular routine.

"You rode a long way. Put your bike in the back. I'll take you there."

"Thanks," I said. I didn't like to take favors from anybody, but in this case I wasn't caring.

He got into the truck's big empty cab and waited for me to get into the back, watching me in his rearview mirror. My right arm was swelling, and the elbow seemed to be filling with blood (like a duck's neck after it was broken?). One-armed, I hefted the ten-speed into the truck's bed, then climbed in myself, still a little unsteady.

He drove me back, and the rushing air helped cool my roadburn and clot my bleeding. With my left hand's fingers and the rounded edge of my thumbnail, I began scraping out the bits of pebble and gravel in my skin. A lot of skin was peeled off my fingers and hands from landing like that, so it made it harder. But it was worse on my right. I wiped the blood on my shorts. In the back of the car I had a bottle of hydrogen peroxide and some aloe vera gel. Just need to get to a motel and shower, I thought. Clean my wounds. Just want to get some sleep. I needed to put my shirt on, but couldn't figure out how.

The old farmer dropped me off by my car, and I managed to get the bike into the hatchback. Finding the nearest town on the map, Chippewa Falls, I drove, working the automatic gearshift left-handed. There was a motel, one of those single-level, single-family-owned squat buildings. VACANCY glared in red neon over the office. Daylight was fading.

Covering myself with my t-shirt the best I could, I walked in, injured arm and shoulder hanging. Little bells on the aluminum screen door tinkled. It was a spacious office. Father and son — both Nordic blond and slim in an Upper Midwest kind of way — were in the back, standing behind a counter. The man stared at me, eyes widening, and his 9 or 10 year old son next to him had his mouth open, as if fascinated, as if saying "Cool!"

"Don't come any closer," the man said.

I stopped. "I just want to get a room," I croaked, clearing my throat. "One night, one person."

He reached for the telephone. His kid was smiling big.

"You need to check yourself into the hospital," the owner said. "I can't give you a room."

"I'm fine," I protested.

"I'm calling the police right now."

My eyes fixed on the beige telephone cord unwinding as it stretched to his ear.

I began backing up, cutting the dumb kid a look, whose face seemed to say "Awesome!"

Little aluminum bells above the screen door announced my exit as I hurried to my car, worrying about the cops coming after me, and them thinking who knows what, and doing who knows what to me.

Nobody was going to let me check into a motel. What was I going to do? Maybe my arm did need to be checked out. But I can't afford it, I thought. What if it's broken bad? Deal with it, muthafucka. Alright. Better drop some coins on this now, and not really regret it later. Just in case.

It was after 9 by the time I got to the hospital down in Eau Claire. I hate hospitals. Fluorescent-lit places of sickness filled with staff who keep you ill and feed you baloney, Jell-O and white bread. The parking lot was empty.

I brought in my bottles of aloe vera and hydrogen peroxide, thinking I could avoid their chemicals. A few women in blue scrubs were sitting around with some brown bags of McDonald's, reeking up the place. The front desk made me pay $300 cash before they would see me. The latex-gloved nurse who said "Come on" wouldn't use either of my two preparations and, rather unfriendly, hard-scrubbed my shoulder, arm, hands and side with this clear, brown liquid that was both cold and burning. She wrapped my arm and shoulder in a mummy-like bandage and gave me a sling. I thought she was being very rough, especially when she yanked my arm up to help me put my shirt on. She said it was likely my arm was just fractured. The cop in a khaki shirt was waiting for me outside, and I got nervous at the sight of him. I tried to act casual. I was already feeling like a wild animal out of place. He demanded my driver's license, ran my plates, asked me where I was going. He asked me repeatedly what had happened. I told him. He asked me again. I told him again, even gave him a description of the truck. "OK," he said, his shiny gold badge catching the parking lot lights. "I'm going to ask you one more time." I told him again. He told me I couldn't drive in my condition. But if I left Wisconsin tonight…

Miles later. Body aching and throbbing. Wouldn't let me sleep. I passed the night in the car at a roadside rest area, spasming, cramped in the front seat. I stared up through the windshield at the starry black sky, shivering, the car vibrating with the occasional passing of a semi.

By the next afternoon I was deep inside southern Minnesota, I followed a dirt road out through a tall green cornfield. Pulling under a cottonwood, I got out to walk, white dust getting on my legs, the last of the season's warm sunlight soaking into my skin. Long, shiny-green corn leaves flapped lazily in a breeze, and a duck rose out of a hidden pothole. I walked beneath the prairie blue sky, cradling my arm, bone-dead tired, drifting off, till something made me stop to listen. It was too silent. I realized I heard no insects. No grasshoppers, no crickets, nothing. The Minnesota prairie was false. There was no prairie, just a sea of false fertility, flapping long green leaves of monoculture cornfield pesticide deadness. Except for the potholes ringed by cattails, it was a dead, sprayed, silent plantation. So I got back in the car and moved on.

And then, on the eastern bluff above the Missouri River, I was finally on the edge of the American West, about to re-enter. The little flat-palmed prickly pear cactus sticking out of the dry, yellow-green grass stopped my footsteps. I was halfway across South Dakota, and I saw that the grass was rougher, rangier. Out of the grass spiked a couple yucca plants, their long narrow, serrated leaves leaving no doubt I was now entering into a different land. Even the dirt seemed drier, looser.

I'd been driving through mostly flat, mostly plowed country. But it was now shifting to rangeland, grassland. The light of the sky seemed very clear, and saturated with blue and yellow. I walked down a dirt path to the edge of the bluff. Below snaked the wide Missouri River, blue in reflected skylight. Across, on its western shore and beyond, the land appeared to stretch into an empty, rumpled grassland of breaks swooped in afternoon bluish shadows. A sign said BEWARE OF POISONOUS SNAKES. The other sign said Lewis and Clark had camped here, drying off in luxurious sunshine after days of rain-soaked traveling as they came from the east.

Had I sensed the land rising in elevation as I made my way west into South Dakota? I felt I couldn't be sure of anything; I hadn't been able to sleep. Nights were cold. My whole body ached. I'd drove, sat, walked a few steps, drove, sat, shivered like a zombie for a day and a half. At least keeps your mind off the fact you're dying of AIDS, I'd reminded myself, chattering and fighting recurring muscle spasms. I was very stiff, even though I tried to walk periodically to keep my blood moving. I was afraid to move my upper body. Everything hurt. Using my knife to start the rip, I had cut and torn off my dirty, bloodstained t-shirt, and replaced it with a red flannel button-down, which I was lucky enough to have. I kept it hanging open, half unbuttoned. It was too hard to button with one hand of peeled-raw, bruised and scabbing fingers. I kept my boots tied loose and slipped them on and off like that. In the evenings I put my jacket over my shoulders, without even trying to get my arms in. This and an old pair of jeans became my outfit. In eastern South Dakota, after seeing the cottonwood where the original 'Little House on the Prairie' had been built, I'd stopped for gas and a bottle of water in the cornbelt farming town of Mitchell. There was this "Corn Festival" going on, complete with a medieval, full-sized castle made out of dried ears of corn. Out of curiosity I'd decided to walk through the fair. My face had by then sprouted thick black stubble, which in addition to my off color, and the little silver hoop earrings caused people to stare. Everybody looked alike up here.

All the carnival rides, blinking lights, and pinging, screeching, popping, whirring noises, along with all the people screaming their heads off made me feel dizzy. I heard a disembodied voice calling off bingo numbers through a loudspeaker — from where I could not tell — N-31.... N-31.... B-10..... B-10... like some Muslim cleric hidden in a minaret calling his faithful to late afternoon prayer. I left and continued west, knowing that once I hit the Missouri River, I would be crossing the dividing line between east and west.

Now, standing on the Missouri River bluff in the exact spot where Lewis, Clark, their slave York, and the rest of them had camped long ago, I knew the West, my West — and its promise of silence (and what else?) — lay before me. Far out across the river, one single little cloud, a puff of white with an underbelly of blue-gray, floated over the western lands.

The weather shifted quickly. By the next afternoon, maybe 50 miles west of the Missouri River crossing, I stood in the roadside ditch bordering what was part of the Fort Pierre National Grassland, according to my map. The expansive sky was low and scudding with gray clouds over the ends of the Earth, dominating everything, especially me, the only human visible — a tiny two-legged standing upright, stiff and injured, arm in a sling, the winds pulling at his loose, half-open flannel shirt. The winds seemed to be from both the south and the north, battling each other, in the process of swinging from the south to the north, with me caught in between. All around, the land was treeless and rolling in grasshopper-green grass, with only a single dead tree visible in the distance.

This 'National Grassland' didn't look any different from the cow-burnt pastures I'd seen driving in. I stood there contemplating the barbed-wire fence before me, this three-strand barrier of hard-rusted bristling wires cinched between metal posts. It cut across the landscape, connected to others that crossed it, three strands or even five, others that crossed those, dividing and enclosing the entire Plains in square conquered sections. I now understood that this wide-open landscape — from here all the way down into Mexico, and back up into Canada — was strung up in bristling wires. This is the real American West, I thought.

With a lot of difficulty, I got down on my back and, holding my arm carefully on my belly, squirmed under the bottom strand of wires, nostrils flaring at the raw, earthy smells of dry soil and wild grass. Directly half way beneath, I paused and stared up at the wires splitting me, splitting the land, even seeming to split the sky.

Normally I might have rolled or scrambled under on my stomach, ducking my lower back to avoid getting gashed or snagged. I'd had lots of injuries in my life, but this one just seemed to make me a little stiffer than the others. I thought about the animals who must live out here. How are any animals, especially big ones like antelopes, supposed to get under without tearing terrible gashes in themselves?

As I got up, I noticed that this western grass did not completely cover the soil. The tops of the roots showed, their tentacles gripping down into the Earth. I started walking. There were small open stretches of dry dirt between bunches of grass, and understories of short curly grasses like yellow buffalo hair. I saw a lot of dried cow droppings around, velocity-flattened, crusted-over splatters, and much of the grass seemed punched down by hooves and pulled by bovine teeth.

A dead, barkless cottonwood tree, the one I'd seen earlier, stood in permanent half-lurch above a slough, and as I approached, two pintails and three mallard ducks jumped up, fighting the wind to gain altitude, and throttled away. A reddish-colored dead cow had moldered back into the white dirt, her skin like a hard blanket on the ground now, and slipping its hair. She had been dead long enough that even the maggots were gone. What was left was mostly stiff cardboard. I toed her with my boot. She skidded like a board.

I walked further out, the rough grasses switching at my pant legs. I thought maybe if I went further from the road, I would find a wilder area. But again, as in Nebraska, the land all around seemed sore, emptied.

I thought: Being out here makes me want to say it's beautiful, but that's not really the right word. Sometimes I feel like I could walk forever through the wind-blown grass of the prairie, but the bristling wires always shoot that impulse down. I always want more from a place like this. I'm always missing the full to-the-bone feeling I crave and need. And I know why. Something is missing — namely the whole thing. A vast, interwoven spiritual roaming ground. There are no buffalo, no free Indian people, no freedom, no mystical wilderness. Now it's just fences and cattle. Everywhere. I can't just get out and walk forever. It's so empty now, overgrazed and chained up, just dirt and patches of grass blowing, and big dried plops of cow shit. And these are the public lands that are supposed to be protected.

I plucked a stem of grass and put it in my teeth, chewing on it, trying to focus my thinking. I kept walking. A jackrabbit bounded out of a little recess up ahead, and I stared, watching him go, *feeling* his pumping bloodstream and big hind legs as he zigzagged, little puffs of white dust kicking up behind him. His ears looked like big wooden spoons turned outward, tough membranous ears covered in short silver-gray fur. Jackrabbits always look so much bigger in person, almost the size of a young antelope.

I walked under the low-sailing gray skies, letting the winds push me. A few songbirds blew across my path. I thought I might just… fall away. At some point, making it no more than half a mile further, I was down. On my back, in the raw, punched, grassy dirt, I stared up at the sky, stem of grass between my teeth. My hurt arm lay in its frozen crook position on top my belly. Some black clouds were undercutting the gray ones, as the winds continued to battle above me, and surely a big storm was about to happen. But it seemed too gentle, too quiet. Weren't Plains storms supposed to be giant, crashing, End-of-the-World deluges?

I drifted off, opening and closing my eyes. Soon I smelled ozone as the first few drops of rain fell, and I heard them plop into the white dust near my ears. A drop here, a drop there, on my face, on my bare chest through the opening in my shirt. I closed my eyes, ready for it all. Another drop plipped onto my eyelid, and it rolled down my face into my ear canal. Soon, I knew for sure, the giant skies would tear open, deluge me. Wind in my ears like an empty bottle. My stomach rose and fell with my breathing, pushing my slung arm up too. I waited, excited.

Time passed. Suddenly, like a giant vacuum, the winds stopped. I opened my eyes a slit, questioning. The sky had flattened out to a bare overcast gray. The drops no longer fell. Everything grew silent, even my breath, which was barely there now.

A rooted, spidery hand of warmth reached up into my back from the ground and seemed to pause there, grasping me, pressed by my weight into the grass and dirt. The warmth spread deeper up into me, moving around as if checking things out, then spilled into my right shoulder. I opened my eyes, listening intently. I could hear nothing. But I sensed this red-orange glow filling me up, loosening me up, tuning me, surging into the hurt areas, coming from the ground. After about ten minutes, afraid to move anything but my arms, I carefully lifted my right arm with my left, then found I could hold it up on its own. It was still hurting, but in a duller way. And I could move it.

I gingerly pulled off the sling, and for the first time extended my elbow, trying not to wince. I laid my bandaged arm down next to my side, and shifted over a little to my right, to allow my whole arm, elbow and shoulder full contact with the Earth. The warmth from the ground worked into my elbow, then down into my forearm, into my hand and fingertips. My body tingled. I lay there, arm and shoulder surging. I felt wet inside, maybe like a fresh melon. In another ten minutes, I again tried flexing my arm. I winced when my elbow dug into the dirt, but the arm worked. It still hurt and throbbed, but the pain didn't flare. It was still broken, still sore. But I knew I was on the other side of healing it now.

I sat up, breaking the seal with the ground, and looked around. I got to my feet, wondering how long I could carry the Earth's warmth inside me. I stuffed the sling into the waistband of my jeans, and found I could walk with my arm hanging regularly, if a little crooked. It took some getting used to. I kept trying to retract it to its injured, frozen position. It throbbed, but I was determined not to go back to the sling. The pain eventually came back bad enough, but I was able to get by with just holding it against my stomach.

Walking to the car, moving my fingers back and forth to work on them, I slid with little difficulty under the fence, them bristling, rusted wires reaching out to tear all flesh.

A gentle rain began to fall, and so did the temperature. Finding Interstate 90 again, the car and I pushed further west. The rain was nothing at all, just a steady sheeting down my windshield. South Dakota seemed to be saying there are few people in this world. I drove miles before another car passed, its headlights shining through the gray pre-dusk highway mist, a trail of tire-flicked spray in its wake.

The day ended in Kadoka, at the Leeward Motel, as I decided to treat myself to a room. The man who came out seemed surprised at my presence in his empty gravel parking lot. He let me have a room for $19. It was off-season, and South Dakota was empty. Shivering, I closed the room door behind me, thrilling at the prospect of a whole night indoors. I turned the heat on and pulled off all my clothes, letting them drop onto the old, stained, industrial carpet. I could see the vacuum cleaner tracks, and was suddenly sure that the maid had been the last person in here, and that had been at least a couple months ago. On second thought I picked up my clothes and put them over the back of the chair by the table.

I didn't want to turn the light on, yet. From behind the drapes, I peered out at the dripping sky losing its light. In a puddle in the gravel lot, reflections of the red neon arrow sign pointed at me, pricked by raindrops. There was absolute silence except for the occasional wet hiss of a passing car or pickup on the road out front.

I peeled off the wrappings and soiled bandages. My arm was still misshapen and swollen. It smelled like yeast. It needed to be cleaned. So did the rest of me. I went into the shower stall and turned the hot water on. Under the spraying water, eyes closed, I methodically washed my body down, hot, soapy, using my left hand.

Drying off, I made it to the foot of the bed. Pulled on a pair of drawers; began cleaning and dressing all my wounds (AIDS inside there?). My head began to droop. First a scrubbing with peroxide, letting the foaming soak in, burning and bubbling. After that subsided, I patted the wounds dry, then layered on a thick dressing of aloe vera, which always burns real, real bad in throbbing waves as it gets in, loosens things up, as it gets to work repairing.

I sat upright, in almost complete darkness now, listening to almost complete silence, no sound at all except the slight exhaling of the heater, and the barely audible pump of my heart. As I fell over, slipping down to the floor, I pulled the bedspread and covers with me and, with the aching and stiffness settling into a low hum, passed out.

Outside, the rain pattered on the motel roof and windows, and the sky went black. Much later, somewhere deep in the night, drunk with the first real sleep in more than a week, I made it back up onto the bed, and stayed there, in the Shadow World, where everything was permeating but effortless, nothing hurt, and there were no loud noises.

CHAPTER FIFTEEN

Sun Dogs

"Damn… They're Sun Dogs," I thought, looking out at the green plain of prairie dogs basking in the sun. The afternoon was filled with an almost painfully beautiful yellow and blue prairie light. And I saw that everything and everybody before me fit, was part of the next, everything connected.

A meadowlark warbled, a small flock of sleek, bubble-bodied mourning doves alighted in the dirt and bobbed their slender heads, a cottontail bunny hopped a few feet, accidentally startling a lizard who ran into cover, flushing a grasshopper that sailed away, stiff waxy wings buzzing and glinting back the sunlight. Prairie dogs grazed, groomed, sunbathed, played, and tumbled over each other. Spokes of narrow trails connected all the burrows. I caught sight of a little barrel-bodied owl with stark yellow round eyes peeking out of a burrow to the right. The burrowing owl bobbed up and down, and his movement seemed so odd I blinked. There were three other owls behind him, in separate burrows, each maybe eight inches tall full-grown. They weren't much bigger than robins, but their feathers were a rich, reddish-brown, barred strikingly across the chest with predator markings. I scanned the horizon. Red-winged blackbirds, flickers, nighthawks, little prickly pear cactuses, and large single-track lines leading into the center of the dog town. So much life here, even on this little piece of land. I guessed the large single tracks were buffalo trails coming up from the badlands behind me. I didn't see any buffalo.

Prairie dogs sound a lot like those little squeaky rubber toys. The closest prairie dog sat upright on his butt, back perfectly straight, short little black-tipped tail flattened out behind him. He was looking at me, his hands and long black fingernails hanging in loose poise in front of him. I could see the shine glistening in his alien-shaped black eyes and little black nose. Right then I knew I had to get close enough to all the Western animals to see the shine in their eyes. His sleek short tawny fur, golden tan with a white chest and belly, matched the colors of the dry Western landscape. His burrow was mounded up like a small volcano, with him perched on the rim. Some others started squeak-barking. One jumped up and squealed in a high-pitched voice: "Haii-yiiii" throwing her arms out and back, arching so far backwards I thought she might tumble over. But she was in perfect control of her body. Another, and another, and another prairie dog did the same thing, all jumped up and yipped, flinging their arms back.

The one closest to me shifted quickly to the side, facing west, staring hard now in the same direction the others were, flipping up his tail and twitching it excitedly. Before I turned to follow his gaze, see what they were all looking at, the entire prairie dog town erupted in a barking symphony. From the west, a golden eagle with a six-foot wingspan came flying in low over the town, no more than four feet off the ground. All the prairie dogs dove into their holes, then popped their heads out just enough to see, barking and squeaking. The eagle flapped his powerful wings once, then again, no effort at all, cruising over the town for a meal. It was obvious he was flying low to avoid high-definition detection against the blue sky, and hoping to snatch somebody by surprise just as he popped back up. The prairie dogs were not having it, and dove inside when he came near. The eagle passed in front of me, maybe 25 yards out, and even though they were underground I could still hear the prairie dogs raising Cain, their squeaking muffled by the topsoil. The eagle's legs were thick, corded with muscle, feet bright yellow, talons black and shiny. His great hooked beak was also partly yellow, and he had a luxurious golden sheen on his neck and along the edge of his powerful wings, offsetting the rich burnt sienna of his body feathers. The prairie dogs popped up again as he passed.

The grass inside the large oval of the prairie dog town was green, and shorter than the surrounding yellow brown late-September grass. I saw that the prairie dog town ended to the north, right where it met a line of barbed wire fencing.

A family gathered on a mound, standing like African meerkats, then suddenly tumbled into a ball, playfully tussling, rolling over and over. The half-grown ones ran around and around, tackling their brothers and sisters, tumbling, raising dust. Just as abruptly, they all bolted back up onto the mound, the mother grabbing the faces of her babies with her long, black, gentle hands and kissing them, her teeth clicking against theirs.

I was on the Sage Creek Rim Road in the North Unit of Badlands National Park. Behind me, off the rim, the land dropped down into badland breaks, gumbo mounds, white flats, and good grass. The sign said it was the only prairie wilderness left in the United States. I could see buffalo trails coming up to the rim. They liked to graze on the green grass of the prairie dog town. They could go as far as the fence. I looked around in the other directions and saw that I was in a large box. Unseen out there, on all sides where the park ended, were other fences. The sign said it was about 60,000 acres. Out of a couple hundred million acres of prairie, this was all that was left. And most of it was badlands.

I was thankful to be alone. One tourist couple had driven past on the dusty dirt road in a rental car, and kept going.

Again I thought about how quickly the weather changes out here. With the sky open, or closed with clouds, or the wind from the north or the south, the prairie is different each time. Right now, the sun was almost intoxicating in its late summer warmth and soft brilliance. Life was healthier out here. I changed my thoughts, not wanting to think about health.

Earlier this morning while walking down a dirt road I was startled out of my thoughts by a cloud's shadow coming at me, slipping over the low rolling prairie hills like a silent buffalo herd. One moving black mass racing up the dirt road till it enveloped me, swallowed me, then passed just as quickly. Yesterday's thick cloud layer was rapidly breaking up into puffy clouds that latched onto a wind and raced off. The chilly damp morning had begun drying out, warming up.

Walking west for about a mile along the Sage Creek Wilderness Area rim, scanning the open bowl of grassy badlands below me, I finally saw what I'd been looking for. That big black shape maybe a mile and a half out was no juniper tree. I checked my wrapped arm and re-secured the clasp in the ACE bandage. Though my arm had a dead weight ache inside it, I refused the sling. In Wall, at the "world famous drug store" tourist trap off I-90, I'd bought an ACE bandage. I'd really needed two, but my dollars were tight and getting tighter.

Dropping off the rim into this protected prairie space was like leaving the world behind, and going both back and forward in time. I kept subconsciously expecting to come onto some roads or power lines or barbed wire fences or something, but there was no hand of man anywhere on the landscape within. The weather and the wild animals were the dominant forces here. Buffalo trails, buffalo wallows, prairie dog towns, muddy white clay alkali creeks, rose bushes, sand plum thickets in the ravines, wind, erosion, heat, cold. All kinds of animal tracks everywhere. A young cottonwood tree had been felled by a beaver, still attached to the stump by a finger-thick strip of blond, unchewed core wood. The outer rim of the cut had been polished like stone by buffaloes rubbing and scratching their sides against it. Woolly wild hair with yellow brown curls hung in traces off the silvery bark edges.

I looked to where I had come down off the rim, coordinating my position with where I believed I needed to go to get to the big black buffalo. I made a wide half circle so I could approach downwind. The land was open, with only high gumbo mounds and some short breaks for cover. I walked fast, keeping my arm up against my belly for protection, wondering if I should have given in and worn the sling. Not able to see the buffalo at ground level, I kept to a half crouch. Periodically I checked my trajectory with my starting point on the rim. I knew buffalo were dangerous, and I didn't want to come up on him suddenly. But I had to see him up close. Had to. My legs switched through the grasses, my feet padded silently on the white dirt.

Getting down on my knees and one good arm, I began to crawl, holding the bad arm close to my chest. Crawling up a gumbo mound, I peeked over, scanning the country. The bull was nowhere to be seen. Looking to the top of the rim again, I guessed I was still in his vicinity and heading in the right direction. But he could be behind any one of these mounds. I zeroed my eyes on a mound about a quarter mile ahead, backed down, and on one arm began fast-crawling my way there. I hobbled like that until I got my rhythm, using my legs to help balance the uneven weight while crawling forward.

I had to rest periodically. The problem was that from ground level, I couldn't see the mound that I wanted, because others blocked it. Little stones dug into my knees, long grasses in the dips waved over my body as I passed through, but I hardly noticed them. I pushed forward through a low-lying thicket of wild roses, hurrying, oblivious to their thorns dragging at me, being as silent as I could. I realized if I took my white t-shirt off, my skin could blend into the grassland as good as any of the animals — the prairie dogs, the buffalo, the eagle, the owls, the coyotes, the prairie rattlesnakes.

I made it to the base of what I believed was my target mound and gingerly crawled up about 20 feet, peeking over. Nothing. I knew I was very close, because the land further to the east started to rise a little. Excited, I tried to guess which one he was behind. But shit, if I surprised him, he'd trample my broke-down ass in a second.

Again I thought of the AIDS inside my body, and my whole exhilaration slipped. *Fuck that. You're gonna go see him, and this gon be one of the best afternoons of your life so far. And yes, I said "so far."*

Something made me glance down at my legs, scratched and a little bloody.

Blood. Aaaarrgh.

I punched myself in the forehead with my good hand and flopped onto my back, digging my hand into my face, trying not to think about that blood. *Wipe it out your mind, muthafucka.* I lay in a narrow shadow cast by a mound I'd just passed, staring at the glowing blueness of the sky. The sky was a plain, a prairie itself.

I flipped back up and continued, keeping low to the ground.

I reached my mound, and began picking my way up over every little dried globule of gumbo, pushing my weight into the soft mass so I wouldn't dislodge a loud rivulet of dried mud balls. There was nothing to grab, so I had to use my weight to press in, hugging the mound close with two knees and one hand. The Sun was now low enough that a warm reddish cast was entering its yellow blast of light.

I peeked over the top and nearly fell backwards with surprise, sliding down a little, making way too much noise. He looked as big as a house. Almost, anyway. Broadside, right there, right here in front of me. Big black gigantic buffalo bull, dwarfing the little tree he was standing up against.

I clawed back up and just stared.

He was staring right back at me with his big black eye blazing, reflecting the red setting Sun behind me. His upward-sweeping Viking horns shined black like polished ebony, sharp points that could puncture anything. His eye was almost the size of a dinner plate. The giant woolly hulk of his head and chest, his sleek summer-shedded loins looking like a lion's, his ropy tail, were all motionless, seemingly rigid and relaxed at the same time. I looked into his eye again; hard to look away. I suddenly had the sense that he was burning up. Actually in flames, inside. That was red fire coming out of his eye. My head's elongated shadow reached almost to him.

That big eye was definitely looking right into mine. But how could he be? The Sun was right behind my head. I was just a stupid stick silhouette, an easily trampled one at that.

He saw you coming the whole way.

Dang, he been watching me this whole time.

He could kick your ass in a heartbeat if he wanted to.

I clung there motionless as minutes passed, the top of my head peeking over, soaking in his immense strength, his absolute perfection, his confidence, his indomitability.

I thought about all the fences. About this one last spot.

They've got you prisoner, I thought to him. Political prisoner in your own land.

The red Sun blazed out of his jet black eye, white pinpoint of light — of life — blazing back into mine. He twitched his tail suddenly, as if saying "*Well??*"

My stomach squirmed and I felt uncomfortable. My arm hurt. My head hurt. I might pass out. I had AIDS. What could I do?

Then you just another stupid stick-figure two-legged... Get the — He switched his tail again at me like a broom. His giant black nostrils flared.

Carefully, as best I could, I slid and slipped back down the mound, my chest pressed against loose balls of dried gumbo that rolled me down with a clatter. At the bottom I crawled backwards then just got to my feet and quickly headed back, opening space between me and him. I crossed alkali creeks, followed buffalo trails through wild rose and sand plum thickets and white mud flats, skirted mounds of Pleistocene gumbo and walked through good, yellow-green prairie grass that held large, flattened circles where buffalo-sized animals might have rolled and dozed. My face and arm and scratched legs were covered in white dust like a ghost.

Maybe 70 miles southwest as the crow flies, swallowed in pitch-black moon-lessness, I pulled off the dirt road. Hadn't seen house lights for a long time. Was somewhere way out on the western side of the Pine Ridge Indian Reservation. Just driving... till I could find a place to crawl into and sleep. But the night was completely dark. No moon, no lights. A wide open blackness.

I shut the car's engine off and the void rushed in; absolute silence. I started to crook my head out the open window to look at the stars when I found I couldn't move. I felt a jolt of fear. I couldn't move anything except my blinking eyelids.

Something like a flat hand pushed my head sideways down onto the windowsill, and I was stuck like that.

I rolled my eyes up to the gelatinous mass of single stars, planets, constellations, galaxies spanning the sky. The Milky Way hung beneath that like a cloud-slash of near stars. Maybe 20 miles away, a coyote screamed like a hot needle into the night. His howl set off another one near, who set off another farther, and for the next few hours coyotes for miles around pierced the darkness with their crying, sometimes so faint it seemed like a hallucination, other times so close it could have been just over the next rise. The howls and cries rose like heat into the black atmosphere.

I saw a shooting star and my eyes traced it through its downward arc. I could move my eyes and nothing else. I could only tell the passage of time by the slow rotation of the constellations. I could not sleep, though my head felt like it wanted to, stuck sideways like that in the open window of the car door.

But out of the corners of my eyes... straining to see but unable to turn my head... human forms thin and fluid and shrunken, streaming up out of the grass like fireflies, only to reach about waist high and hit something, be shoved back down again. By what I don't know. I only saw them — sensed them — rise and hit something invisible and impermeable. They were all around me. Trying to get up and out but unable. Unallowed.

Eventually I passed out. Maybe.

The morning sunlight struggled to take the chill out of the night; almost October. Frost soon. I opened my eyes and lifted my head, able to move now, bracing for a day of neck spasms. But as I got out of the car there was no crick in my neck at all.

I stumbled up a ridge and down into a ravine.

A sun-bleached buffalo skull lay in the gulley, upside down, washed out of the dirt, facing the rising morning Sun. He seemed to glow white.

He was left over from the old days, from the original herd, and I realized how rare it was to find something like this. A direct connection to when the world was a different place, wild, haunted, no cars — before any had even been invented! — no noise, vital with life in every corner and crevice. He was just lying there, probably covered and uncovered by rains and dust storms and melting snow mudslides over the years and decades. There were rings of blue lines in his molars, like tree rings. I kneeled down. Said something without saying it, asking permission. Upon feeling it was OK, I wiggled loose one of the blue-ringed molars and put it in my pocket. Then I turned him face up, so he didn't have to face the rising Sun upside down.

"The Wasicus basically killed us of everything," she said, eyeing me through her thick glasses as she buttoned her frayed jacket against the cold wind that had come on as suddenly as the low grey clouds. "This Wounded Knee grave site wasn't everything."

I looked at the long, rectangular mass grave at our feet, outlined in concrete, stretching all the way to the stone archway. Colored ribbon offerings tied to the chain link fence fluttered in the wind. On December 29, 1890, the U.S. Army had even used Hotchkiss cannons, which could fire two-pound explosive shells at a rate of fifty per minute. Shrapnel, unexploded shells, and rifle bullets ripped through the band of freezing people camped below under the truce flag. Children were called out from their dead mothers with a promise of safety then surrounded and slaughtered. Three hundred people were murdered. A blizzard came that afternoon, blanketing the area. On New Year's Day a big trench was hurriedly dug on the hill and local white settlers were paid $2 to dig out the frozen bodies, stack them in horse-drawn wagons like cordwood, and haul them up here and dump them.

"What do you mean?" I asked.

She pointed north to a little cluster of public tract housing. There was a small bunch of little beige or blue houses, many spray-painted with graffiti. Trash was everywhere; stray dogs roamed the unpaved streets. Down below across the road was a thatched shade on four poles, and an empty pullout for cars. Somebody sat in there, holding a few strings of beadwork, waiting for tourists that weren't coming. "That's the town of Wounded Knee. All the towns on the rez are like that."

I didn't say anything, my eyes following where her finger pointed.

"This whole rez is a POW camp. A concentration camp. You know, the 1868 Laramie Treaty still stands. That means all the land west of the Missouri in South and North Dakota including the Black Hills, a big part of eastern Montana and Wyoming, and a big chunk of the Nebraska panhandle is ours. We won that. It was ours to begin with, but we fought for it and won it in Red Cloud's War. We beat the U.S. Army.

Burned their forts, closed their roads. And they signed a treaty and guaranteed it. Got our country guaranteed back to us; that law's as legal today as any law on the books. And they still took it from us. We're still dying, but from diabetes and alcohol and heart disease and violence and you name it. Because we're so colonized." She pointed to other graves, more recent ones, on this hill outside of the mass gravesite. One of the headstones was for a woman named Ann T. Respects Nothing. The name struck me.

"Well anyway, down there is where the troops killed us all." She pointed to a wide circular depression in the land. "People once they got shot froze like wood. In all kind of weird positions right after they died. It was so cold, eeee, just dead they looked lying all over the ground. I could just imagine what that massacre looked like, all those dead bodies lying frozen."

Her long black hair was parted down the middle, with a few strands turned white. Her thick round glasses magnified her eyes. Her voice had that clipped, Western American Indian accent. "And you know we had a Wounded Knee in '73 too. Actually, it was a war, with tanks and tracer bullets and troops and FBIs. That's when they got Peltier. Right over here. Over there was where the holdout was. In a little white church."

I gazed in that direction. I held my jacket closed with my left hand, and huddled into my collar as the wind blew bits of dirt across the long grave and us. The right sleeve dangled loosely, my wrapped arm back in its sling. I wasn't punking out, I'd convinced myself. Just needed a rest.

"I saw some prairie dogs yesterday." It was all I could say. I wanted to tell her what else I'd seen since then.

"I'm surprised they didn't kill them too."

"What you mean?" I asked again, wanting to know exactly what she was saying.

"You know they came here in the 80's and poisoned off all our prairie dogs. I told you we're a concentration camp. We had lots of them. *Pispizah*. That's their name in Lakota. They were all one big town. I heard over a hundred thousand acres. Parks and Rec in Kyle was involved. Our tribal government's as corrupt as the U.S.'s."

"That's a lot of prairie dogs," I said, thinking about it. Quietly, I added: "I like prairie dogs."

Seeing that I was interested she said, "Supposedly it was the most that was left. Anywhere. All the way up the western side of the rez they used to be. My grandmother and her friends were sick about it. They said it was like the troops coming once again, and some whitewashed Indians joined in too, like always. The Indian cattlemen, they have all the power on the reservation. They all came in their pickup trucks and little four-wheelers and spread poison everywhere, geee. That's why there ain't even any more magpies. Everything died. They always wanted to make us cattle people, make it so we have no choice. Grandma said Pispizah was the only one who kept people alive during the Depression. Soup. A pot of water and a nice fat greasy prairie dog. That's all they had to eat. Prairie dogs don't hurt nobody. Grandma said her father told her we had to take care of Pispizah and everyone else, and Pispizah and all them would take care of us. It's them damn cattlemen."

"Sounds just like some of the Eskimos who want to help the oil companies drill the Arctic National Wildlife Refuge," I said, "when most of the Alaska Native people want it left alone and protected."

There was silence — except for the cold, moaning wind — as we processed our thoughts and began walking around the grave toward the stone archway. Down on the narrow little road, paved but unlined and dangerous, an occasional car passed, heading out to the next town of Porcupine about eight miles up. Some had turned their headlights on for the blustery cloudy day. Her little rez car was parked down behind mine. Hers had more mud on it. Out of the blue she'd just appeared, had come up here and started talking to me.

"What's your name?" I asked.

"I'm Beth." She held out her hand.

"Jihad." I shook her hand with my left.

"Like in Holy War?" she asked. I swore I saw her roll her eyes behind thick glasses.

"Like in War for what's Holy." I thought about it. "Maybe like in prairie dogs. What you told me makes me sick. I was in the Badlands yesterday up on the Sage Creek Rim and I saw how the buffalo need them, the prairie dogs, making all their trails up to the rim to graze there where it gets to be real prairie and not badlands. But aside from that last strip, they're all dead outside the fence. The best land's taken by the ranchers. Yet still, on this side, the prairie dogs...all this life... these birds I saw... everything."

She had her back to the wind and it was pushing her long hair around her head and into her face and flipping up the collar of her dark jean jacket.

"Actually," I said. "It's just a nickname I've had for years. I checked — its original definition is supposed to be about battling your private demons and becoming a better person."

"Nice to meet you," she said, pulling the hair away from her eyes so she could see. Her glasses almost made her look bug-eyed. "You know, I heard about these Eskimos who go out on their Skidoos hunting for seals. They take their snow machines way out onto the ice, and they're out there even when it's 40 below. I guess Indians and Eskimos don't get along too good. It's kinda like Minnesota and South Dakota I guess. We think Minnesotans are primps and they think South Dakotans are hicks. Well, this one young Eskimo guy who had this big Fu Manchu mustache was out hunting when he broke down; one of the rubber seals ruptured on his snow machine. He had his hood on and goggles on and his big skin coat and mukluk boots, and when he realized he couldn't fix it he began walking back. Everything in the world was all frozen and very cold, but up there, that's the way it is most of the year. He didn't wear his face mask or what you call it because he didn't think he needed it. He was a young Eskimo. But he had lost track of how far away he was from home. Well, it was a long time before he got back, and just before he got to his village he run into this old Indian guy who was out checking for tracks. The Eskimo's mouth and mustache was encased in ice.

"'Geeee, what happened to you?' asked the old Indian, staring at the Eskimo's frozen face.

"The Eskimo was tired from all that walking, and just stared back at the old Indian. 'I blew a seal, is what happened,' he said.

"'Geez,' the old Indian said and kept going, leaving the Eskimo standing there in his mukluks. 'Don't they have any girls in your village?'"

I looked at Beth. She punched me in the shoulder. "Laugh, man. It's Indian humor!"

I tried to crack a smile that probably looked half crazy, half wretched from lack of use. On our way down to our cars she said: "New York, huh?"

"Naaah. Actually Texas, if anything. That been my real home, if I have any. I really just live wherever I am. I been all around. That just says Nueva York 'cause I stayed there for a minute. And got stuck. But damn I'm glad to be out West again."

"I lived in San Francisco, for ten almost eleven years. We had every kind of people there is in the world. But I had to come back home. Out here you can see all the way to Nebraska," she said, jerking her head to the south like the state was just down the way. "Not that anybody'd want to see Nebraska, *eeeeee*. Hahahaha."

CHAPTER SIXTEEN

Dive By the Wreck

So in the back of my mind I knew I was slowly but surely dragging myself down to L.A. to get tested and meet my destiny, even if I couldn't say it to myself. Any time the thought came regarding the disease and me, I immediately shut it down, ran from it. But still, inwardly, I saw myself finally forcing the confirmation that I had The Bonus, and then just going back out into the desert to starve myself to death. All this drifting now was one foot-dragging play out of the last days.

I drove down through Thunder Basin in eastern Wyoming, then into Colorado, trying to take a short cut through the aspen and pine mountains (an odd, vertical world of cool black soil beneath a mulch of dead leaves and needles). My car struggled to make it up into the mountains, overheating repeatedly, slowly giving out, forcing me to wait by the side of the narrow winding road till it could go again. I pushed onward out of the mountains and down into the filmmaker's landscape of Utah desert sandstone.

I avoided people. My throat grew unused. I took walks at night off the side of the road. Little traffic. And I always saw people way before they saw me. As a vehicle approached I stepped back into the desert, not letting them know I was ever here. At one point a giddiness came over me, and just as a car or truck began to pass, I stepped into the calculated edge between their light beams and darkness, my open shirt and unraveling bandages flapping in the wind. A couple times I bared my teeth, fulfilled to see the jolt of heads behind glass windows turning in that instant as if thinking *What the hell was that?* or *Did I just see something?* I kept it up till I freaked my own self out and got back in the car and drove some more.

I got lost in the Nevada desert. On the map it was a dirt-road shortcut to Searchlight and the main paved highway, but on the ground it became little more than a scraped track that spurred off and petered out in all directions, all paths clearly unused for a long time. The heavily washboarded, unmarked tracks shook the car and me violently, making my arm hurt. The car engine light started blinking. I nearly got stuck in the sand a few times, but somehow gunned it out. I went up and over miserable hilly bumps jutting eight feet into the air that dropped my car down dangerously. I thudded through gulleys and washouts, bottoming out, and I knew the car was being damaged beyond its already faltering condition, but I was in too deep, there was nothing I could do but keep going forward hoping I'd find a way out. I went like this for a couple hours, fighting a low-level annoying panic, and I became aware that the adrenaline felt good, making me temporarily forget about AIDS. The car started overheating again as I came out onto a wider dirt track. I didn't dare stop now, fearing the next stop would be its last. The track began making a downward slope, then dead-ended in a dry wash. There before me opened up a narrow sea sparkling blue against the white of the cliffs and rocks and sand that buttressed the water on both sides. I realized it must be one of those big desert lake impoundments the government made during the Depression.

I shut the boiling engine off and complete silence rushed in, split only by the car's hissing and ticking. I opened the hood. I had two gallon jugs of water in the back but they were for drinking.

I opened the hatchback. The southern Nevada desert silence pulsed at me like heat waves off the white rocks. I walked real slow to the cove, not wanting to make a sound. I peeled off my clothes. I upended my body, split the blue lagoon as I dove headfirst in. And swam. My arm still hurt, but my mind was somewhere else. The day grew longer, and stretched the shadows of the rocks and thorny branches. I dried out on the rocks, then unrolled my blanket in the back of the car.

A night, a day, another night went by. I didn't eat. It was like I was in a partial passout that was ongoing. The lagoon was so blue, like a spring; hidden cool blue water. Old songs, songs I hadn't heard in a long time, began to surface as the clutter in my mind and memory began to unwind and cleanse itself in the silence.

I slept in the back of the car with the hatch open. I swam in the cool fresh water many times each day, and lay on the smooth October warm white rocks. Sometimes I swam at night.

I forgot to put my clothes back on. When it got too hot I crawled under a juniper and slept some more. I forgot about food, and just drank from my water jug. Once I saw a plane flying high overhead, my only reminder that civilization was still on.

Deep asleep late at night. Out cold in the back of the car, hatch open in the moonless night.

Somebody or something suddenly came up to me. I felt its presence, and heard it. I still had Watchman on, still slept on a hair-trigger. Always.

I slammed awake, but I couldn't move, couldn't sit up, body coursing with a strange fear that made my blood curdle. There was something very terrible, right near me. Had come right up to my feet. Stopped right there, hovering over me, looking down at me. But I couldn't move, couldn't see. The adrenaline froze in my veins. Is this what they mean by 'paralyzed with fear?' It's really real. I can't... fucking... move. What is here?..... What is it doing... just looking at me!?? Flat on my back I couldn't even move my eyes. I could only stare straight up through the top of the raised hatchback glass into the spackle of stars, trying to force my eyes to look down to see what was right there. I'd never been so filled with fright in my life; absolutely immobilized.

Though I don't know what happened in the time between, it became morning again, and I was fine. I didn't see any tracks at the base of my car. I have no idea what it was.

In a few hours jet skis and pleasure boats began whining and roaring up the blue sea, breaking the spell of my days here. I stared at them unbelievingly from my hidden cove, and realized my sparkling blue sea ringed in desert white cliffs was just Lake Mojave on the Colorado River, well below Hoover Dam, and that a weekend in early October had come.

I tested my arm. It still wouldn't straighten all the way out, and the elbow and wrist still hurt. And the whole upper arm was getting so skinny. Fuck. There was nothing I could do.

I put the LA Weekly on the bed, leaving it open. Even through the closed bathroom door I could hear the dripping of the faucet, which I had tried and tried to shut off. Years of slow-drip water had worn a black gouge into the porcelain sink. The sink was held up by its plumbing and a 2x2 piece of wood wedged beneath it and the floor, and though the sink's back was glued against the wall, I think it would have come down if somebody had knocked the board out from under it.

I got up off the single bed, which took up most of my room. It felt so good to sleep in a real bed. Outside the little barred window was a small courtyard about the size of three of my rooms, filled with all kinds of LA-style tropical plants, some potted, some in the ground, that nobody took care of anymore.

I picked up the newspaper again. An ad for the Women's Holistic Health Center in West Hollywood on Santa Monica offered testing, and it said you could get your results within 24 hours. It was the first time I'd heard of this medical advance. Like most people dreading AIDS testing, I knew once I took the plunge and got the blood drawn, that was it, I was on that one-way ride. And I just couldn't handle two weeks of that tortured waiting.

The fee was $45. Less, if you wanted to wait the normal two weeks. Grabbing some change, I used the payphone in the hall, down by the dirty kitchen. A woman answered. Her voice was calm and very soothing. I tried to keep my voice from betraying me. I hurriedly made my appointment for 3 p.m. Got directions. It wasn't too far.

There. It was done. Finally. I had set the ball rolling.

I began my fasting for real. Though I had eaten between the desert and L. A., I now would never need food again. My stomach was so acidic and unsettled I didn't think I could eat anyway.

All I needed for my plan was some water.

I went out into the lobby. Someone had written the rules of the place on the walls in black marker: "No Visitors, No drinking, No Drugs, No Drogas, NO Hanging OUT, No PROstitition, No Spicious Activity, Police will be Called, no Late payments, Payments Must Be Made Each 7 Day No Exeptions!"

Ibrahim, the hotel manager, heard me coming through the lobby and slid open his little wooden view door. I saw his pudgy, black-bearded face. He looked like the lord of a secret castle up here on Franklin, and he sat back there in his lair. I imagined he had a big easy chair, upholstered with dark green vinyl that had a permanent indentation from his weight, set up sideways back there, because his face was always sideways when he opened the little sliding view door. And he always looked out through the corners of his eyes. I could hear the sound of a tv. There was a little silver bell on the counter. There was a slot for people to put their rent in, which had to be money orders in an envelope. According to his fucked up calculations, the week was actually six days, so if you paid your weekly rental on Saturday, expecting 7 normal days, you had to pay on Friday of the next week, and then on Thursday of the following, and so on. No Exeptions!

The old transient hotel on Franklin had been my specific destination, affordable for the remaining time I would need, at most three weeks. Downtown Hollywood was as I remembered it, only two-dimensional for me now, because I was here for only one reason, and then I'd be gone. The side streets were still dusty and dirty, the little *tiendas* were still selling their dusty old products and bruised old fruit off mostly bare shelves. Hollywood and Sunset were still filled with the people wanting to be edgy and trendy, especially further west; few tourists ventured this far east. The alleys had piles of homeless who made occasional forays into the daylit streets but mostly waited for night. The homeless women pushed their shopping carts. Junkies and some peroxided, stringy looking hookers hung around the street corners trying to look purposeful. *Pelon* gangstas with shaved heads, baggy white jeans and short sleeve button-down plaid shirts drove by in their low, fast cars and, maybe rivaling, a black gang in tinted helmets on brightly-painted sport motorcycles roared up and down, until the police gang came and took over, temporarily squashing everybody back into whatever corner they came from. And at the 7-Eleven I used to go to, the same turbaned Sikh was still there behind the counter in his red uniform smock, a little older, but still selling the same 7-Eleven junk — Slurpees and Big Gulps, 75 cent hot dogs, candy, lottery tickets, and cans and 40s of Colt 45, the local favorite. I stared at the bottles of beer, wonderingly. But I only craved water.

After spending $145 for the motel, my money was now down to less than three hundred dollars. Still, I splurged on two 1.5 liters of Evian spring water. One for today, one for tomorrow after I went to the place on Santa Monica. The Sikh didn't recognize me; I didn't say anything. I had my sunglasses on. People only recognize me by my eyes, which I tried to keep hidden.

Soft melodic music, not muzak played in the background at the empty waiting room in the Women's Holistic Health Center. I sat on the black couch. There were plants, and lots of natural light from lots of windows. I kept my sunglasses and baseball cap on, and my head down. I handed my bogus-filled info sheet and the $45 cash to the gentle receptionist, who smiled in a doctor's office kind of way and said I was next, that there was just one other person ahead of me. That person was behind the closed door off to the right. Though the door, crafted and sanded out of light-colored wood, was probably designed to look soothing like the rest of the office, it terrified me, because I knew I would be sitting behind it very soon.

The door opened a crack, I heard some muffled talking, then a slightly overweight Mexican guy in a yellow t-shirt came out, his face stretched and shiny, his eyes wild-looking. I began shrinking inside. He'd drawn the bad card.

A quiet, middle-aged lesbian with a grey ponytail and a very clean face, no makeup, wearing a grey pantsuit over a light cotton turtleneck, came out. In the most soothing voice she said she'd be right with me, and went back into her room, closed the door.

I suddenly had the feeling that she had nothing to do in there at that moment other than take a deep breath and a few quiet seconds alone.

She came out, motioning me in.

She took my blood pressure. Putting a tray kit and some latex gloves on the stand next to me, she said I was her last patient for the day; this would only take a minute. I stared at the capped needle and the vial. My whole stupid life had come down to this one stupid little needle and glass vial. As she explained the procedure, and the counseling available, I listened half to her words and half to the hypnotic music. Flutes, with a sense of wind chimes, and distant drums lightly tapped, as if with fingertips.

She put the gloves on, scrubbed my arm with a cotton ball damp with alcohol, and prepared the needle. I had thought about this moment for so long, had imagined that I would look away, but I stared as it plunged into that bulging blue vein inside the crook of my elbow. Dark red blood — I imagined it so hot with viral loads that it would steam if exposed to the air — began filling up the shiny glass vial. I was officially past my point of no return. Just had to make it through 24 more hours. She tore off half a perforated piece of paper and handed it to me. It had a case number on it. She told me to bring it back tomorrow, when she would match it with my test results. She paper-clipped her half to my file.

I drove back and parked. I walked and walked north, carrying only the bottle of Evian water. The giant white letters of the Hollywood sign loomed up ahead, staked into the side of the hill. All around the sign was open chaparral hills and gulleys. I could make it up there; I just needed to get out of civilization. I pushed up through streets lined with houses, rising higher and higher in elevation. I kept thinking I would get to the end and get into Nature where I could begin the real vertical ascent, then another subdivision would appear. Finally I made it out onto unpaved ground, and I put my palms down into the sandy soil, thankful for its warmth, thankful for good, blessed dirt, then quickly climbed, trying to stay out of sight.

Later, I sat off to the side of the giant letters, watching the daylight slip from the sprawling metropolis below, as the straight-rowed city lights of the L.A. Basin came on, millions of them. I drank from my water bottle. A chill came into the air, but not too bad. I hugged my arms around myself. As night came on, I passed out, curling up in a ball on my side in the dirt and grasses. Hours later I came to, and sat upright again, watching the city.

A voice came into my head…

You fucked up big time. Just when you started to get your shit together, this happens.

I'm a pariah and a disease.

How do you know you didn't have this the whole time?

Born alone. Live life alone. Die alone.

I watched the lights of all the people down there. Cars visible by their headlights were still streaming up and down the streets of this gigantic city. Down there, nice looking people, fit people, healthy people, people with friends, with lovers, with families. People laughing, talking, hanging out, making love. People being normal, going to the gym or the beach, playing dice on the sidewalk or spades and dominoes down the block. People talking to each other on the damn phone, or shooting some fucking pool, or listening to good music together. People who had somebody, close and personal, keepin' each other warm and tight and not so alone at night.

Man, you coulda done some shit with your life. What a fucking waste.

I began to pray. I apologized for being so fucked up. And I made promises. Promises, that if my blood could somehow be negative, despite how impossible, if tomorrow I could just somehow grab one of the lucky numbers, I would make sure I never went backwards, would hold onto my path, would give my life to God, not to any rulebook kind of God but the God that is all around us in everything and beyond. Especially the Sun, the absolute physical manifestation and touch of God on Earth. And I would do so by being in the service of Mother Earth, who was His partner in Creation, who was hurting so badly, from the terrible things people had done to her.

Shivering, hugging my knees, probably more from being strung out with stress and lack of sleep than with the cold, I rocked back and forth. The temperature dropped as it does in the desert. Sometime before dawn, stiff with cold, with everything, I made my way down.

In my room... unable to sleep... listening to the stupid English house sparrows endlessly CHIRP outside in the tiny concrete courtyard overgrown with its untended plants. I watched the ceiling. Tried to think about who had painted it, and how long ago. They'd used a brush. Bad paint job. Swirls. Disease roared through my veins, as somewhere a few miles from here my squirming red blood was being pulled apart and peered at under a microscope or however they did it. Maybe they'd already done it. What time was it? Chirp. Chirp Chirp. Smoggy gray silence. Chirp Chirp. I got up and took a shower. I sat on the bed. It was still only 9 a.m. I lay on my back again. Chirp Chirp.

By noon, I was up and dressed in my nicest clothes — my newest white t-shirt and jeans. I put my sunglasses on and grabbed my ball cap with the curved bill I could hide under. I was ready.

There was a little church down on Santa Monica among the warehouses; I had seen it before, and it always had its doors open during the day, which I guessed might mean anybody could come in.

I parked down the street and walked up the block, acting like I was going someplace else, then veered and hopped up the steps. I passed through the open doors, keeping my head down and my hands close at my sides, wondering if somebody was going to tell me to leave.

The church was empty, except for two people standing near the back where I'd come in, a black dude probably in his late 30s, dressed in street clothes — Timbs, jeans and tight t-shirt — holding a baseball cap, and an overweight white man in a suit jacket, with a bald head and white beard. They were conversing quietly.

"May I come in?" I croaked.

"Sure, sure," the white man said jovially, keeping his voice hushed. He had round red cheeks. The black dude looked at me.

I nodded and walked up the aisle and slid into a pew.

I put down the kneeling bench, clumsily letting it bang, and it echoed loudly. I knelt, embarrassed, keeping my head down. I heard footsteps coming up the aisle; the brother came to me holding a tattered Bible. I looked up.

"Do you need to talk?" the street pastor asked, keeping his voice neutral, leaving it up to me.

I looked him in the eyes for a split second, then lowered my head, shaking my head no. "Thanks anyway," I thought I mumbled, but wasn't sure if any words came out.

Folding one balled fist inside the other, I pushed my forehead into my knuckles, bowing my head, closing my eyes. My mind opened up, and as I listened to my own breathing, all the thinking mercifully stopped, replaced with open white-lit space. My veins began to cool off. I became aware of the bench that my elbows were pressing into, and I began to sense it as a living, writhing tree, as it had once been, twisting upward in slow motion through life over the years, reaching for the Sun, squeezing its thick roots down into soil that got cooler and damper as it got deeper. I opened my eyes; they traced the life grain in the wood. I lifted my eyes to the front of the church, the altar, the statue of the bleeding, hanging man with his arms nailed and outstretched, and tried to focus there.

But something kept digging at me, distracting my attention. The front of the church was cold to look at. It was then that I noticed the church was filled with yellow sunlight streaming through the stained glass windows up to my right, and I turned my head. A Middle Eastern bearded man stood in the high middle window, in a strong stance, his head cocked slightly, surrounded by yellow stained glass, a gnarled olive tree behind him. His feet were planted firmly in the soil. His hands...

He had a plate-glass halo around his head. But his eyes. The sunlight was sparking directly through his eyes, in two piercing, slant-eyed shafts; they blazed hot yellow down into the church, right down into the pew I sat in, burning into me, burning into my eyes. I tried to look away, but couldn't. The eyes blazed, the Sun blazed through those eyes. And behind the Sun, so far out there in the sky, blazed God.

I prayed and prayed and prayed.

With my shades on, I sat again on the black couch in the empty waiting room, adrenaline ringing through my body, throat so tight I couldn't swallow. Tried to focus on the music, some kind of American Indian flute or pipes, but I was stone cold. The receptionist was gone. The Jodie Foster-looking woman who had taken my blood yesterday must have heard me come in. She took my piece of paper. She went into the records office, found a chart, then went into her room, saying she'd be right out. Closed that door.

I tried to get control of my breathing. Told myself to fucking relax. Accept your destiny, muthafucka. Think about the desert. The prairie beyond that. The wide open is sacred. Soon you will be out there, quiet, in peace. You can do this. Life is always a one-way street, bruh, just accept it and move on. If you think, I mean BELIEVE there was never any other reality than this, you will be ok with it. Promise. You gotta believe it. Just think bout you out in that desert plain, a hundred miles from the nearest person, and you can just go home. Think about it, man. Don't let any other thoughts come your way. No past. No present. Nothing but this, right here, right now. Never any other thing. Just this.

Behind closed eyes my color vision turned black-and-white again, back into the molten silver image I had during that passout on Ludlow Street, where I received the surety that I needed to culminate everything by starving myself to death. Once I got my diagnosis, I needed to purify everything out of me, the AIDS, the ugliness, the rage. Eyes closed, I again saw myself sitting cross-legged beneath the twisted little shrub in the desert, my body getting skinnier and skinnier, turning into ironwood, breath barely inside my chest, and finally, slowly, passing out and over into the old, original, real world. The Other Side, the Shadow World, once and for all. At last I relaxed, sitting in the waiting room.

Her door opened and my heart BANGED. I couldn't breathe. I broke into a sweat, scalp burning, on fire. She began walking toward me and she was twelve feet tall, holding tiny matching pieces of paper in each giant hand. I was trapped with the glass magazine table between us. In a second she was right there on the other side. I gaped in horror at her pant-suited knees. She came around. Her fingers released. The two pieces of paper flutter-fell in slow motion the last inch down onto the glass table.

"You're negative," she said.

My head slumped forward, the force of it so sudden it seemed I'd leapt out of my body and hit the wall. Peering down at the two pieces of matching paper, I fell back, the air gone out of me. I started to cry, and as soon as that shit opened up in me, boy I couldn't stop it and I bawled and bawled. I pawed at my face, trying to wipe it away, make it stop. I knocked my plastic sunglasses half off and quickly corrected them.

"Oh," she said. "You thought you had it."

She got up and left me there for a minute, then brought me a box of Kleenex. Told me to come into her office if I wanted to talk.

When I felt like my legs were stable enough, I got up and went in, sat on the couch, sinking back. I removed my sunglasses, looking at the floor, then forced myself to look directly at her. She didn't blink, looked me straight in the eye. The black blinds were closed behind her. I could see orange line-squints of late afternoon sun streaming through the edges and they kept distracting me. I asked her to open the blinds, feeling the need for contact with the Sun. She opened them for me, and it cast a glow around her head.

The gentle, serious woman with the cleanly pulled back hair said, "Why do you think you had it?"

"The swollen lymph nodes," I said, looking down, voice cracking a bit. "The hard ones."

"Swollen or hardened lymph nodes don't necessarily mean a health problem. Sometimes they just harden."

I couldn't say anything. Just tried to adjust my shoulders square.

She sat there calmly, her hands in her lap. The outside world was behind her, out on the streets, and I sensed that she had seen a great deal of it in here, and in her entire career, wherever else that may have been.

"Why else do you think you had it?"

I cleared my throat, and looked up at her. "I was… I just was unsafe. Just once. But I didn't know about this. You know. *It*. AIDS. And I was such a drunk. I had no control over myself. Everything was just too crazy in my face, and I couldn't handle anything or think about nothing."

"You can't blame yourself. A lot of people didn't know. It's not easy out there. What we have to do is try not to spend too much time blaming ourselves for past mistakes, even for all the times we were careless. *If* we can learn from them, from our past mistakes, we are bettering our lives. And often, a lot of people have an accumulation of many problems at once, and it overwhelms them. It builds up and, before they know it, they have fallen very low."

I nodded.

"People who come through these doors, I've seen the scars, the wounds that life has dealt them. My hope, whatever their experience in here, is that when they leave, they try to make the best personal decisions in the things they can control. We have so many things that we can't control in life, and yes, a lot of those things can be very bad, but we also have choices too."

I had the urge to slide off the couch and sit on the floor next to her legs. Lean up against her while she talked. I resisted it and stayed put, watching her, thinking about the streets out the window, watching the Sun sink behind her. Santa Monica Boulevard would be pretty busy with traffic right now. Its side streets would be mostly empty. But there would be people out there walking, or standing up against the wall, or ducking into a doorway or alley.

"What is it you want to do? You're clean, you're healthy, you're young, and you have your whole life ahead of you."

I cleared my throat. "I really don't know. I never even imagined I would live to 20. I still can't imagine making it to 30. I've just never been able to imagine the long-term future. I always assumed that if I didn't cancel me, something or somebody else would. I just automatically believed that any day, that would be it. That's why I've always just done things day to day, without any plans. But this year —" I shivered inside, realizing again that I really was negative. "This year I found out I really want to live. And I was afraid of dying. I wanted to look forward to something."

"Well," she said, pressing her hands a little tighter together, fingers out. "You're alive now."

Those words sunk in. The last of an involuntary shudder seemed to snap itself out of me, disappear out my shoulders and the back of my neck.

"And you likely will make it to 30, and even past that. If I were you, I'd consider myself blessed. I would use my life to great advantage, not let it pass me by."

I sat up on the couch.

"And I would try to enjoy life too. There is too much sorrow in this world. It prevents many people from ever living fully. Fear and worry too. If we can make the right personal decisions for ourselves, we can circumvent a lot of it." She paused, and again I sensed that the whole world behind her had entered her. I thought about tonight, about how many people out there will have sleepless nights. "Soon," she continued, "You and I will leave this building, and likely never see each other again. We'll both make more mistakes. But hopefully we'll avoid even more, because we looked out ahead."

This solemn, quiet woman and I talked for about another hour, and my sense of the falling late afternoon grew timeless. Though I'm sure she had plenty of things to do besides talking to me, she gave no sign of impatience. We had a long discussion. And she told me how she liked to go hiking up in Topanga and the other desert canyons north of town.

She talked to me like I was an adult, an equal, like I had intelligence and could follow a conversation and line of thought. It was the first time a person had ever talked to me like that.

SECTION FIVE

"Now picture a social struggle in which one side has a near monopoly on every resource, making victory for the underdog (us) seem a hopeless impossibility. Folk-song wisdom aside, mere truth and justice are not enough to carry a movement to victory. Evil routinely triumphs. Having a vastly superior strategy is our only hope of getting the upper hand in such an otherwise lopsided conflict."

— Mica Jacobin, *Earth First! Journal*

CHAPTER SEVENTEEN

Kingpin

I promise... promise....

My head rolled back against the seat. I could dimly hear the clatter of the train wheels below me as the Amtrak sped down the tracks, to take us eastward across the deserts and the plains and into the heavily populated half of the United States beyond, eventually dumping me back into New York City. I knew I was half dreaming, half awake, but... so tired. Kept snapping awake with drool in my slack mouth, then falling back, unable to keep my head up.

Behind closed eyes I prayed. Feel a little directionless right now. I was sure that at this point I would be immersed in preparing myself — getting up the nerve — for death. Shit, all those times you wanted to kill yourself when you was little, now you want to live, and you get this real second chance, for real you are lucky, and now you don't really know what to do.

I have so much to do. I have so much I *can* do. I have the rest of my entire life ahead of me. And when God decides to take me, I must, I will accept it as my simple fate.

I promise I'll be back out West as soon as possible. I'll be back in a few months, as soon as I can get on my feet. I promise I'll stick to the path. I know it's risky going back, I am worrying a little bit about it, but at this point, what choice or other chance do I got?

I promise.... I had promised I would keep myself clean, and hew to the spiritual path, never looking backward.

"¡Mira the lago!" yelled the lumpy woman to her kids across the aisle as she tried to stop them from bothering the man in front of them who was wearing a plastic shower cap over his Nu-Sheened jheri curls and eating smelly generic cheese crackers.

I pulled the hood of my sweatshirt up over my head and closed my eyes again, thinking about the last 10 days or so, trying to ignore my growling stomach. I had a pear and celery in a plastic bag stowed overhead. That food had to last me three days. It was probably good that it was all I had. Maybe clean out my liver or kidney or whatever that's back there. Right lower back had been bugging me. All that stress overload must've released a bunch of toxins, or something.

This train trip was going to take three whole days, with only 20 minutes in Albuquerque, 30 in KC, and four hours in Chicago. Eventually, after three whole days cooped up, it'd take me into Penn Fucking Station, New York Fucking City. Got 5 dollars left to my name.

I had replaced the valve cover gasket in San Diego, which stopped some of the leaking and, I thought, gave the car a little more life. Found somebody to do it for a hundred dollars. But what it needed was an engine seal, which meant they'd have to take the whole engine out, which meant basically I needed a new car.

In San Diego I'd slept on the beach rolled up in my blanket, or in my car. Either place, cops or dogs found me, pulled at me, kept me moving. In the car on a small cliff by the ocean, the cops found me and banged on my window with the butts of their flashlights, then shined the blinding lights right in my eyes. I was in such a deep sleep… so disoriented. Hadn't talked for a couple days. "Put some bass in your voice!" they yelled. They yanked me out of my car, asking me all kinds of questions, like what I had been arrested for, who else I knew in the area, if I spoke Arabic. They held me, searched the car, told me I stunk, which I probably did, after days without a shower. Then I remembered the trouble brewing in the Persian Gulf. They ran my plates and info, and finally let me go. As long as I left and made sure they never saw me again.

I drove down to just north of the border to wild, unsettled chaparral country. Pulled off the road into some bushes, spent the night raging at the cops, helpless anger, with a lot of it directed at myself because it seems I can never do anything during those situations. But I had to remember, like Lahumba said a long time ago when I was first in L.A., cops can and will do whatever they want to you. You just have to say Yes Sir to everything. And I know you are never to look them in the eye.

In this no-man's borderland, I soon found out that banditos and drug runners were all over the scrub hills. I could hear them running through the bushes, or driving along the roads with their lights off. Hoping to keep undetected, hoping nobody'd notice my little car hidden in here, I hunkered low, my wires on high alert, my six-inch Chinatown blade drawn. Not that it would have helped, as heavily armed as I'm sure they all were. Staying here was a very wrong move; I was lucky to escape detection and make it to dawn.

Drove down into Baja, Mexico. Left my car with this old grandma named Emma I met in very dusty Rosarito, 17 miles south of the border, who parked it in her dirt driveway. She kept calling me Muchacho. Rosarito was so scoured by dust storms that on very early mornings before people got up it looked like it had been abandoned for years.

Thinking about all this as I settled into my seat on the Amtrak, I visualized the ocean off Rosarito. I thought to myself: the ocean is a prairie. One evening, while walking along the Pacific surfline at twilight where the dark blue ocean broke onto the beach, I'd suddenly sensed something inconsistent with the rest of the water. In the next moment a wild dolphin exploded out of the waves real close and dove back in, followed by another. It startled me to unexpectedly see such large wild animals up close. Then, exhaling through their blowholes, and swirling their tails, they jolted back out to sea. The waves pushed and pulled, normal again. I had a sudden comprehension of the mystical ocean, but as a wild, almost survival-violent kind of place. The dolphins seemed like wolves.

I opened my eyes. Darkness outside. The train took a small curve. I glanced out the window. I could see the dim yellow cast of its big round headlight illuminating

the desert rocks in front of it, throwing back the shadow of the engine's blunt whale-like head.

This train ride back to NYC had become a sudden opportunity. I'd had no idea what to do next with my life now that I was going to live; I'd only planned on starving myself to death in the desert after getting tested positive for AIDS. Coming back into the States from Mexico, I'd woken up one morning in a dirty city park in downtown San Diego completely at a loss. I couldn't just drift forever.

Felt like I had been gone a long time; felt a little anxious about what might have happened since I'd left. And I was down to less than $20. On a whim I made a pay phone call to NYC, to the number I happened to have in my wallet, Dierdre — the drag queen friend of Diego's. $2.25 felt like gold coins leaving my hands. Dierdre gave me Diego's number. Turned out Diego wanted to get in touch with me and offer me a job. He had stumbled onto a big connect and was now dealing big time, wholesale. Had a pager, needed me to contact him. He sure had moved on up.

The pay phone took incoming calls. I paged him, and he called me back. Told me to come back to NYC. He said he'd explain more in person. Needed help with assembly, I'd make $1 per; it was real simple. He was doing quantity at wholesale and I'd make money. He had this worker, Camron, who was doing the retail, mostly in the clubs. He'd Western Union me money for a train ticket.

On the train. Five dollars left to my name. Opportunity land in my lap, and I don't even own a chair to sit on, hell yeah I'd better take it.

But what about your promises? Your vow to stick to the path?

You need to be in service. You made it out alive, and now you've gotta give back. You know somethin' ain't right with the world. Somethin's happening, comin' to a head. The next 20 — 30 years gon be the most crucial in human history.

Fuck, I can't pass up an opportunity like this. What else am I gon do, anyway? I'm not even supposed to be alive.

Exactly, muthafucka.

I went to the back, and stood in this narrow walkway by a big window, mindlessly staring at the dark desert rushing by.

"I'ma throw you off this train if you got a problem," the overweight train attendant said to my disgusted look as he tried to squeeze past me.

"I'm standing cause I can't stand to sit."

"If you get in anybody's way, I'ma throw you off, you hear me?" He looked like he had high blood pressure. He waddled into the next car.

I'ma cut that too-tight polyester suit off you when I cut you, I said silently. Then maybe you be able to breathe.

I looked back outside. We were somewhere in the middle of the Great Plains. Not a light in sight. It was a different world at night, a world of the imagination. We were supposed to hit KC by dawn.

If you get in, I thought to myself, you can't get in too deep. And no matter what, you ain't gettin involved in coke or crack, no matter what. If you stay on this side of that line, maybe you'll be ok. Just don't cross that line. Make a pact right here and now to never deal in coke or crack. Just make enough coins to get back out here to where you really belong. Your life in New York is over with. You got shit to do. You can only stay there a couple months, get some cash in your pocket. Then leave for good.

If the money is half as good as D says, you'll be set.

It's just that when I think back to everything that happened with him, I can't stand the thought of him. I'm trying to shake it out of my system.

But it sounds like he's changed. Somewhat.

He's still the same person.

Maybe we can exist — temporarily — as friends, co-workers.

Remember that he also poisoned you. And what about everything else? The fact that you and him are still alive — after everything — is stone cold testimony of the need to never forget the past. Otherwise, as the saying goes, you'll be condemned to repeat it.

I went to take a piss, and when I flushed the toilet, a hole opened up right onto the tracks. I couldn't believe it. 19 fucking 90 and raw sewage is being dumped right on the tracks, where it would run off into the watershed with each rain. For the rest of the trip, I stood between the cars where there was more room, looking out, because sitting drives me crazy. I couldn't stop noticing all the melting dingy white lumps of toilet paper out on the tracks.

GEORGE BUSH — *ASESINO!* GEORGE BUSH — MURDERER! GEORGE BUSH — *ASESINO!* GEORGE BUSH — MURDERER! Irresistibly drawn to NYC protests, I was hooked. The combined intensity of all these angry people pumping demands into the air, *protesting their government* and not getting shot fascinated and unnerved me with its boldness. The noise seemed deafening as people pounded garbage can lids and drums and shouted chants. We marched resolutely downtown. I stayed silent. When we passed between buildings, people ramped up the volume even more, and the steel and glass canyon reverberated and amplified the shouts of the crowd. The cops tried to keep us on the sidewalks but we kept spilling out onto the streets. NO BLOOD FOR OIL! NO WAR ON IRAQ! GEORGE HUSSEIN — SADDAM BUSH. The crowd continuously morphed. Passersby joined up for a few blocks; a few others heckled. A hideous giant-sized President Bush drooling oil from his lips and turkey wattles stalked through the middle of the crowd on stilts, bobbing his head and moving his hands in a maniacal grabbing motion. I pounded my fist in the air with each beat of the chant, swept up in the crowd. Although my throat wouldn't let me shout anything.

"You almost done, Jihad?" Camron asked from the other room, talking through the hanging sheet that Diego strung up across the doorway when we were in production. Camron wasn't allowed to see or know about this end of the business. "Come on man," he said. "I got customers waiting."

"Just finishing up your batch," I said through the curtain. "Give me a minute. Put on some music."

"One of my mix tapes?"

"I don't care."

I continued cutting the drugs as Diego had shown me with the razor blade, mixing and mixing till both piles of white powder from the two baggies were completely integrated. It was about a 3 to 1 ratio. I made sure there were no lumps and that everything was crushed to a uniform fineness. Using the torn off back flap of a matchbook, folded in half diagonally, I filled up and closed each 50 mg capsule, putting them in a new pile. House music filled the apartment with pulsing energy. After each 20 caps or so, I remixed the spillover powder back into the main batch, scraping the table clean with the blade of the razor.

Diego cuts this shit too much, I thought. I could make a better product.

Counting out 25 into a vitamin bottle, I got up and went into the other room.

Camron was sitting on the couch in shorts, a t-shirt, and unlaced high tops, nodding his head rhythmically with the music. He smiled broadly, coarse black mustache stretching across his face. "How bout that, Jihad? You like that? That is some good shit. I mixed that myself. When we make the real money, I'm gonna get those Technic turntables. Those are $300 bucks a pop, baby. I'll be spinning on three turntables at once."

"Here's your shit. Let me know how people like this."

Camron had somehow mistakenly gotten the impression that I was the top dawg in this business, the head honcho, that we only had this supply because I had brought it in from Mexico. And that Diego was my business partner, not the other way around.

"Great! That's great. Oooh," he said, looking at the brown glass vitamin bottle, pushing out his lips as he thought of something. He turned the music down a little. "I seen this fine looking Puerto Rican girl. Her name is Julie. You seen her Jihad? Oh my God. Damn." He cupped his hands under his chest. "She's real pretty. Short. Curly short black curls hanging off her head? Oh man I want some of that!"

"Naah. I ain't seen her. Only been here a week."

"But you been here before, right? Didn't you use to live up on Ludlow with D? That's what he said. Before you kicked him out. Hahahaha."

I didn't know how much Camron knew. "Man, I'm only here for business. I live out West. That's where my life is."

He sat back down on the couch. The underfed Rottweiller came up to him and panted, looking at him with sad eyes, then lay down. "Go on, dog," he said, petting him gently on back of his sleek black head. "Get out of here. I'm sorry Diego don't know how to take care of you." Camron and I had fed him two bowls of food.

I stood under the hanging light bulb in the 3rd floor apartment and glanced outside the window. Incoming traffic roared off the Williamsburg Bridge down onto Delancey. From the fire escape, you could almost take a flying leap and land on the bridge if you'd wanted to. At street level, if you walked straight out the front door and across the street, you'd walk right into the bridge's massive concrete base wall, which the law had a hard time keeping clear of graffiti. Diego rented this apartment. Camron had the one across the hall. Diego had turned into a fucking slob. I hated it here. He had bought a skinny Rott that he wouldn't take care of, and the dog had pissed and shit all over the back room where the mattress. And D just left the waste on the floor.

The apartment stunk. Before getting to work, I had put plastic grocery bags on my hands and tried to clean up everything, and open the windows to air the place out. Diego was a complete mess, he was using his product, smoking coolies as well as regular cigarettes, and drinking. His eyes were bloodshot. And he was trying to get back with me. I knew it was dangerous working with him. His m.o. was way too sloppy. I had $1000 cash now off this, and was starting to look for a place. A temporary place, cause I sure as hell wasn't staying in New York long term. Get me one of those single room occupancy hotels, Like Hotel Seventeen. Or one of them uptown. East or West Harlem. Don't care.

"You use you lose," I said.

"What you talking about," Camron said. "I know you can't deal and do at the same time. I might party a little every once in a while after work, but I'm not stupid. I'm about making some money!"

"I wasn't talking to you. Just thinking out loud." I went into the kitchen and got a glass of water from the jug.

"My sister lives in Denver. So what's the deal, anyway, with out West?" he asked. "I know it's nice and peaceful out there, and all that, and you seem like you want to be peaceful and left alone and all that. But it's boring to live! Here is where the money is. You just gotta keep me in product, man. I can move whatever you bring." He stiffened up his chest and stared me straight in the eye. "Diego's too inconsistent and fucked in the head."

I looked at him, checking out his nerve.

"Yeah, that's what I said. Face it, Jihad. Why don't you just kick D out? He's bad for the business, and bad for our safety. And I'll just work with you, and we can split the profits. You tell me what it costs per capsule at your wholesale price, we sell it for $25, and we split the diff. That way, you only split it two ways. Between you and me. And it's a lot safer."

I listened to the music, and narrowed my eyes. Fool Camron had pulled out some old high-pitched teenybopper Tiffany, mixed it with some jailbird Slick Rick, and added jazzy beats beneath and on top of that.

He grinned widely again. "Like that, huh?"

"What is it you want to do, man, anyway?" I motioned my head at his apartment. "I seen your artwork. Your paintings and your drawings. You got some real talent. I mean for real. You need to do something with that."

"Man, fuck that. I want to make some money. I'm talking about some real money. Only people who get theirs get ahead. That one pencil drawing I showed you? Took me over two weeks just to draw the grass. Yeah I know it's good. Better be. For two weeks all I did was draw goddamn grass. All them art classes didn't do nothing for me in Louisiana, and it don't do nothing for me here. New York is about making money. Other people say New York's just about fucking and killing, but I say it's about makin' some money!

"That's what I'm here for," I said. I didn't tell him that it was a one-shot deal. Once I made enough, I was gone, for good. West.

"Seriously. I know he's your boy and all, but I'm the man out in the public and you don't know how competitive it is out there."

"Ain't my boy," I said, dreading to have to go to sleep later in that disgusting bed surrounded by dog shit and piss.

"Security don't respect him, and I can hardly move anything cause I'm afraid I'ma get caught; meanwhile Miss Johnny gets the rule of all of Sound Factory. I know she's been around for years, but she probably makes three to four thousand dollars every Saturday night. Out of that, she probably has to pay security five or six hundred. The rest is take home. And she doesn't do wholesale herself."

"You don't know what she makes."

"I'm more than sure she gets hers very cheap. I know you could make a deal with Joel and J.T. We wouldn't even have to pay as much rent as Miss Johnny does, because we don't move as much. They'll know we are just building our client base. If they knew I was with you and not Diego, and we guaranteed them a decent rent each week, that's all I need you to do. Get things right with security, get me a constant supply of quality, and keep an eye out for my back. I'll do the rest."

"Just like that, huh?"

"Child, them white children are fiending for our shit. Especially all them Chelsea boys who come to the club, they come with a couple hundred dollars in their pockets. Even some of the uptown homeboys and the ones from Philly come wanting at least one, and nobody on the outside has even heard about X. The word ain't even got out on the outside and X is hot. On the inside, man, on the underground, X is the thing, boi! I'm tellin' ya! Everybody wants it. That's twenty-five bucks a pop. And if you want me to move blow or Special K or anything else, I can do that too."

My head was starting to hurt. "Naah, we don't have to do that," I said, remembering my pact not to cross the line. X was fine, weed too, but I had a feeling something bad would happen if I went too far, like with blow or whatever. I needed to be a moral drug dealer. "Look, I'm gonna get back to work, finish up. Thinking of getting a hotel room — one them weeklys. Need to get out of here."

"You can always crash in my apartment, too." He went to pop out his tape, then left it in. "I'm gonna go get dressed. But you can listen to this."

"Thanks, pa," I said as I went to the curtained-off room. "Whyn't you switch it to Hot 97 instead?"

He swatted his hand. "Pssht. Man, y'all don't respect *nuthin*!" and reluctantly flipped the stereo to tuner, where the night's guest dj on the ones and twos was scratching LL's "Mama Said Knock You Out!"

The club hit me like an exploding wall of bass beats. My mind was still out with the prairie dogs and the blue sky. I blinked my eyes, steeling my step, trying to put my thug back on as I walked into its giant interior. It was packed with thousands of bodies, and the tension of all that urban energy felt like a drug itself that could either get you very high, or make your head hurt.

In daylight, Sound Factory was an anonymous part of the warehouse district, but one night a week, Saturday, this spot on West 27th between 10th and 11th was *the* underground dance club in the world. House music had blazed into New York City from Chicago, got shaken up with new, 1990 street beats and high-energy tribal rhythms, and was at an all-time high. Nearly half the size of a city block, the club could hold over 3,000 people, all of whom paid the $20 cover just to get in. There was no guest list. Like a city below ground cast in dim blue light, it had its different 'blocks" and 'street corners,' even though it was one giant open room. Split into more or less regular hangout areas were the black and Latino homeboys from uptown, BK, Boogie Down and Queens, and Philly; then the voguing ball queens who competed in elaborate contests, usually pitting black or blatino gay gangs such as the reigning House of Xtravaganza against any other ball houses, then the hard-core music heads of all races, both straight and gay, who came just to hear Junior Vasquez, the High Priest of house music, spin (and get high with our product so they could feel the music to its ultimate); then the white muscle queens and Chelsea gym-bunny (or black snow bunny) boys in the far back corner area who took their shirts off and danced off their expensive drugs for the night and didn't want to go home. Interspersed among all these different gay groups were the fine straight women who loved them. Rounding this off were the straight, prison-hardened security guards who made sure that what went on in the club stayed in the club. Pity the person caught dealing who wasn't part of the program.

Many hoods would try to slip in unfamiliar workers to infiltrate, make some cash. The city's dealing world was a small place, an underground below the city's underground where the people who ran shit more or less knew each other, whether they liked each other or not, and knew where each's turf was. Those without turf who tried to break in, claim their own, ran the biggest risks. On this very limited but powerful level, word was out how lucrative the Factory was.

Because of all this, Joel, J.T., Anton, and Enrique had to run the tightest ship, and would almost always catch infiltrators. Plus, they each went home with hundreds of extra dollars in payoff rent from the sanctioned dealers. Dudes who got caught would get thrown out, their stash confiscated, and sometimes their mouths or noses would be dripping blood if they even tried to say or do anything.

Open only from Saturday night, actually early Sunday morning, from 2 a.m. to 10 a.m. or so, Sound Factory only sold juice and water. But people came to party. Everybody knew the success of the club meant access to something extra. The cops were paid off in a weekly 4:30 a.m. drop on 11th Ave. The deal? Cops stayed out of the club, and Joel, J.T., Enrique, and the rest would keep the peace inside.

I knew from the beginning that if I was going to get "in too deep", meaning when a person began his ascent into minor kingpin status, my shit would have to be so smooth on the 24/7 that I wouldn't raise a single ripple of suspicion anywhere, day or night, any time. Camron had a rep for being a loose cannon, but he was a good worker and people liked him. If I could just get him to shut his mouth at the right times. I had snapped to this real quick when I went to check into Hotel Seventeen and the front desk guy Billy smiled, told me he knew Camron, and asked if he could maybe get a few that night.

"What the fuck you tellin' people already bout me," I had confronted Camron.

"Man, sorry, man, but I had to let them know I wasn't with Diego anymore."

"We ain't even squashed that shit yet. And you need to keep my shit on the COMPLETELY DL. I decided yeah, I will supply you, but only if you keep my shit out of it. Only the inside-most peeps can know what the deal. So they know we're serious and not to be fucked with. And those who know will know cause I want them to know, not because you told them. You know my style. This ain't no party or game, Camron. It's a business, just a means to an end, and you fuck up, you fuck up everybody's shit. You wanna go upstate? I'm warning you: This the only way it gon work."

He looked at me straight in the face, unable to bear being berated. "Yeah, all right… aiightt! But what *you* gonna do about Diego? Diego is the main reason everything is fucked up. He's a mess. I need you to take care of that, and you're not doing *your* job, Jihad."

"I'ma take care of Diego. And when I need you, I'll let you know. I think I got it figured out. He's goin' on a little trip."

"Well, anyway, he don't know anything is up, yet, about you and me working together. He thinks you're still gone on your little trip to meet that girl in Montauk. I wish you'd hurry up, and I wish he'd stop coming over to my apartment. But you need to hurry up, because we're missing out on business." He lit a cigarette. As he blew out the smoke through his nose, he said, "Man, he's abusing that dog, too, and I don't have the time to take care of him. We're gonna have to find somebody to take him."

I took the N train and got off on Seventh Ave, just below Central Park. Walked up into the Park, crossing 5th Street, always glad to break through that boundary and get inside the Park's green embrace. I walked up and over the building-sized boulders among all the bare trees. The giant boulders had been stripped and scraped by glaciers about 11,000 years or so ago, and you could still see the marks. When I'd heard about that, I 'd gone to the library to read how it'd happened.

Once I crossed the 72nd Transverse, I discreetly let my eyes and ears scan the area for Alice. That was our name for the cops; they knew every other slang name for them but didn't have a clue about this one. Sometimes we'd spot a DT and just mention Alice, and everybody got real cool.

Pretty deserted today. And Alice was nowhere around, either uniformed or DTs. I made my way up along the east side of Sheep Meadow, between the chain-link fence and Dead Road, the short little bit of pavement that didn't go anywhere that skaters used for a hangout. My feet swished through the orange and brown leaves scattered on the still-green grass. Only one person was out on the big lawn, walking across. A few skaters bladed back and forth with their Walkmans on in the mild, early December weather. The burritos-and-beers woman was there, running her mouth in rapid-fire Spanglish to her *compa* sitting next to her on the bench. Not much business today, but she had her whole set-up out, her insulated compartments, her condiments, and her hand truck with its bungee cords. A couple of the regulars sat on the curb, drinking cans of beer. It was Friday afternoon. I kneeled down to tie my boot that didn't need tying. Out of its upper I pulled some folded hundreds and in a single motion pushed them up my jacket sleeve.

I spotted Anita from the Family up by the closed concession stand, her hands in her puffy jacket pockets, hanging back by the trees with a few friends. Two thug dudes stood next to her. She was a big woman, with round cheeks, who always wore a full-sized yellow or blue down parka that hung almost to her knees. The Family was a big extended clan who lived over in Hell's Kitchen in the Projects. They ran one of the biggest businesses in town, and only did wholesale.

Anita saw me and we met, back by the trees. "How you doin' today?" she said in a thick Nuyorican accent. "What you need today, papi?"

"Only two," I said. "I'll be over there, by the bench. Like usual." I nodded to the two dudes and walked away.

In a few minutes she came over and settled her heavy weight onto the bench. I moved my right thigh, revealing the folded bills I'd slipped under there. Her hand dropped two tightly wrapped, taped plastic rolls of powder on the bench and took the cash. "It's already mixed. We're gonna probably do it like this from now on. People been cutting the shit too much, and we don't like that shit. We try to trust people, but you can never trust everybody. Our reputation depends on quality and consistency. Just make sure you completely fill up each 50 milligram cap." She put her hands back in her pockets.

I slipped the product into mine. "Yeah."

"We thought about going to pills, the tabs, but they more expensive, and we the only ones with the capsules. And people like this shit. They like all our shit. We keep it like that."

Once I had shit on me, I got edgy inside, like I had to take a piss, and immediately needed to get moving. But I always remained calm, like I wasn't trying to hide anything. I hung for a minute. "Pretty soon I expect I'll be needing a lot more. You be able to handle it?"

"Yeah, sure. No problem. We got. We got. So whatever happened to your friend, what's his name, Diego? The one introduce me to you."

"He still around. I'm just gonna be handling things from now on over here. He's going to California. He says hi." I didn't know what the deal was between them. I also couldn't tell whether she believed me or not. Hers was a good, even great price, and I was really, really lucky to have this connection. I needed to keep it.

"Oh, that's good. Well, just lemme know, o.k. papi? It's best we always do it like this, know what I'm sayin'? If you need anything else, we gots that too."

I suddenly realized she was a lesbian.

"Guns, too, if you want. I don't know why I trust you, Devil Eyes. I usually don't trust, but I do, and I did, so we cool."

"Good," I said, getting up. I headed through the park to Central Park West, where I could catch the A train at 72nd. Always took a different route back from the one I came up. I rolled the tip of my tongue up over the gold tooth I'd bought down in Chinatown.

I sat in Diego's apartment, waiting for the phone to ring. The Rottweiller was lying on the floor, ears flopped down and long tail out. I remembered Diego saying he was going to get the tail clipped. I wasn't used to seeing Rotties all long tailed. But he looked all right. Just needed to be fed and exercised a lot more.

I looked out the window at the grey NYC sky, my stomach acidy. My stomach had never been the same since he poisoned me.

The big suspension cables of the bridge right outside the window made it look like I was looking out at the sky through big jail bars.

I wished the damn phone would ring. Paced up and down the old apartment, thinking. Thinking about everything that had happened since I'd lived on Ludlow.

Camron was in his apartment across the hall. I'd told him not to come over, that I was working. I planned to get this phone disconnected tomorrow.

The phone rang. I looked at it, placed my hand on it. Waited for it to ring a second time. I picked it up.

"Yeah."

"Guess where I'm at?" It was him. Right on time.

I tensed for the news. "You been gone a week. How is it? Where are you?"

"I'm in San Antonio! So far, it's been great."

"What? What happened to San Francisco?" I caught myself and quickly readjusted my voice. "Are you having the kind of time for yourself we talked about? You got people who care about you." Just like you cared about me when you poisoned me, I thought.

"Yes, I am. That's good to hear, and you were so right about getting out of the city for a while. Man, I just decided to go here first. What the hell. I got $4,000 on me. Plus I brought some product. It makes the bus ride a lot more fun. If they only knew, right? Hahaha. This ticket pass is good for anywhere for a whole month. I realize you were right. I needed to take some time for me."

"I'm just paying you back," I said. Damn straight I am. I dug up some sincerity, surprising myself at how hard it was, even though I'd planned what I was gonna say, to swallow my pride and lay out this shit like I meant it. "I just need you to be careful, man. If anybody smells that you got something on you, cash or whatever… you know what I'm sayin'? Be careful and not obvious. Just make it to L.A. safe and sound. Get you to the beach. Relax. You won't believe how much you did the right thing. I envy you. Life's for real better out there."

"Yeah. But you know, I still love you."

That's why you poisoned me. "Yeah, you too, papa. But hey, uhh, I got some news."

Drop in the line. In the silence I could hear the rumbling of the diesel bus engines behind him. Must be at the bus station. "I've been just hanging out," he said. "I went to Sea World yesterday. I'm going on the bus to L.A. tonight. Then up the coast. What news? It better not be bad news."

Man, what happened to you, I thought. "Man, cops busted up the shit. Everybody's scrambled. Anita, she ain't been seen nowhere around. The Family put a drop on everything. Sound Factory — there ain't allowed no going on at all anymore — the whole shit's canceled. We were all set to go for tonight, but it's done. Least for the foreseeable future."

"What?! What do you mean? I can't believe it. What happened? Oh man!"

"I told you. Somebody musta narc'd some shit. Or they had some DTs up in the shit, or what. But man, you lucked out. You're already out there. But thanks for the opportunity. I'm glad I paid you back the cash, so we even. Didn't make as much as I wanted, but I've got about a G. So I'm out. Haven't figured out what's next, but... It's cool." I paused.

"Wow..." he said. "What about Camron?"

"I don't know, really. I just gave him the news; told him I'm out too. He got real pissed and stormed off. You know how he does. He's your worker, not mine. All I can say is, just be glad you got out when you did. I heard a lot of heads got busted, locked up, peeps we didn't even know about deep in the scene. So I'ma just count my blessings and figure it out from here. I told you before I came back that I was through with New York for good, and it was just gonna be for a few months. So it's just a little sooner. Face it, New York sucks, anyway."

He thought about it. "How's Malachi?"

"Camron and I been takin' care of the dog." Feeding him some food, unlike your ass did. "We'll find a home for him, like we promised you before you left. Like we all agreed. Whether you stay out there or come back, it's for the best. He needs somebody who can take care of him."

"Well, I was gonna stay out here only for a month, but..." A grainy loudspeaker voice said something in the background, over the idling engines. "Hey, my bus has started boarding."

"You sure took the long route to San Fran. When you get to Cali, make sure you get to the beach."

"Shit, I'm trying to think. I don't know what I'm gonna do. Maybe I'll just let that apartment go. Oh, I don't know. Well, listen, I better go. I love you. How'm I gonna keep in touch with you?"

"I'll page you with my new number. Just remember my code: 05. I don't know where I'ma end up either, but I'll stay in touch when I get settled. You see a number with a 05 behind it, that's me. Aiight?"

"All right."

"Peace, then," I said. "Talk to you in a few months."

I hung up. My head was hurting. Pulled the phone cord out of the wall, and began packing up what little shit I needed.

"Come with me NOW!" yelled Enrique into my face, over the music, He grabbed my arm and shoved me, then tried to drag me.

I pulled off, my heart beating. "What! I can walk by my own self."

"Up here!" He pushed at me to climb the stairs. Sound Factory was one flight below the ground, with bleachers along one wall. Stairways ran up between them, to the fire escapes. Behind closed doors there were other rooms up there, off to the side.

Joel was inside. His ugly brute face wasn't playing. As soon as I walked in, Enrique slammed the door, and Joel swung at me. Instinctively I blocked him with an upward raising arm, but not before his knuckles clipped my cheekbone and slid into my eye, making me see stars. I stumbled backwards, knowing my eye was already swelling.

They pulled off my baseball cap, and emptied my pockets. Then pulled out about 50 pills I had left, and about four hundred in cash. Camron had just handed me some money. I had smuggled a pack of a hundred X in a tightly wrapped and rolled plastic bag taped up between my nuts and my rectum. Security searched and wanded everybody before they even let you pay your $20 to get in.

Joel screamed into my face. "Nobody sells in here! You're with Camron, aren't you?"

"Where'd you get this?" Enrique yelled. But it didn't come out as hard as he meant it. He was darker skinned Nuyorican black, the more muscular of the two; arms swoll in his tight desert tan t-shirt. His skin shined like burnt, polished brass and he wore a military beret. Joel — he just looked very hard core. Like he'd gut you for the fun of it.

I said nothing.

Joel was counting out the dollars. "We just got ourselves paid some more. Plus, what is this? 50 pills. Cool for us. What's that, fifty times twenty five dollars? $1250? Plus whatever JT pulls from Camron. Looks like we made some extra bank tonight. Your ass is banned from the club."

I sensed Enrique wasn't as hard as Joel, and I turned to him, going for reason. "All right, man. Yeah, I shoulda came to you guys first. Sorry bout that. This just a business for us. We're not meanin' to be steppin' on any tocs. And we ain't loud about our shit. And we got good product. I can pay your rent, if you let us work in here. More money for you." I glanced over at Joel. "Where is Camron?"

"J.T. has him. You both are banned from the club. And you best do some schooling on your boy, too. But don't let me catch neither of you up in here again. That shit on your eye ain't nothing." He tried to push me backwards with one hand. I stood hard and just looked at him.

He raised up his arms for a second, which lifted his shirt up just enough to show me he was packing a pistol in his waistband. "Oh, we got ourselves a hard one, don't we. Well this is my crib, and up in here, you're a pussy. A fucking pussy! You fuckin' hear me? Hear me??"

I gave a short, tight nod, resisting the urge to sneer or smirk at him. The wall was vibrating behind me with heavy bass beats. I thought of the dance floor filled to capacity and peaking with people and energy.

Joel's walkie-talkie crackled. I couldn't make it out. He said into the mic, "I'll be right there." He walked to the door, and made as if to jerk his elbow into my chest. I stepped back and he missed. He glared at me. I poker-faced back. He said, "Enrique, will you take care of this punk? And check with Miss Johnny. Ask *her* if she wants to share."

"Later, Enrique," I said, thug-nodding at him. I walked out on my own accord, collaring Camron with me on my way. I would handle this.

CHAPTER EIGHTEEN

On this Side

I sat in the middle of the low-elevation California desert, drawing my finger in the sand, alternately thinking too hard and letting my mind drift, seeking blankness. My overheating, engine-light-blinking car had warned me not to go any farther. So much for my return out West or driving into the plains. I had thought I could get to West Texas. Or at least eastern New Mexico.

You goin' back to NYC?, I asked myself straight up.

Yeah. Needed to take care of business.

There. It was official.

I'd be lucky to make it back to L.A. That's what I would need to do. Then fly back. I decided if I could just make it to L.A., I would abandon the car.

But I just could not think about that right now.

I'd walked maybe two miles out into the sands and greasewood that stretched across the wide desert plain. The quiet, and the warm balmy winds, were intoxicating. I saw only one jackrabbit, and two lizards. The woman at the little general store had said there wasn't much wildlife out here. People from the Chinese restaurants in L.A. had come out here a decade ago with guns and shot all the rabbits out and hauled them back to make moo shu pork.

Camron had been furious at me, because I'd "let" him get caught, meaning I hadn't paved the way in time for him to set up shop. Not a drag queen, Miss Johnny turned out to be a sweet, skinny Puerto Rican leprechaun in black tights, a colorful, shiny plastic windbreaker, and always some different kind of hat. She had said that all we had to have done was come up and ask her, instead of trying to go behind her back. She made mad for about ten minutes, then lightened up. She said there was enough to go around for everyone, holding her skinny wrist high and twirling it. Well, enough for two spots, anyway. Hers and ours. And no more. The other guy, the blond dude who came in sporadically, "He is out!" she said. There were complaints about his shit, anyway. And that was her final decision; she leaned forward to kiss me on the cheek, her beard's razor stubble dragging against my face. Business deal signed, sealed and delivered.

I tried to wrap my mind around the West, the outback out here. It's hard to believe this and New York are even in the same country.

I'd gradually seen that Sound Factory had become a home for all kinds of people who were in some way misfits in the normal world. Once you were searched and wanded for knives and/or guns, and walked down that long slope past the lounge area into the heart of that giant below-ground blue lit space floating in clouds from the hidden smoke machine overhead, you were in a different city all its own. Even the music — strictly tribal house — was different.

Out on the streets, hip hop's New Jack Swing was reaching its pinnacle, melodic and fresh, with Bell Biv Devoe, Guy, Wreckx-n-Effect, SWV, En Vogue, Tony! Toni! Tone! and others all characterizing the move from gritty, pavement-hardened late-80s into something sensual but still holding an edge, a sound that defined the early 90s. The new decade seemed to promise freshness, a new health just around the corner, something vital coming, as we felt we were in the last years of the sick, old, terrible millennium and on the home stretch toward something much better.

In Sound Factory, what struck me the most, at least in the homeboy crowd, was this hidden, underlying sense of sadness, loneliness, and longing. The hardest, thug-looking uptown dudes would come down, smelling great with CK One or Eternity, wearing fresh new white sneakers, new ball caps with the price tags still dangling, mustaches and goatees neatly trimmed. Maybe they'd let their jacket slip off one shoulder a little bit, showing a tank — wife-b or basketball jersey — and some skin, curvature of good muscles, strong shoulder and chest, crease at the armpit, swell of biceps. Or maybe they came in wearing a hooded sweatshirt with jeans or nylon sweat pants and rugged urban hiking boots, Timbs most of the time, left pant leg rolled almost up to the knee. Or overalls with only one suspender fastened, the other hanging, white-t or bare chest showing. And stand to the side, alone, or sometimes with a friend, nodding to the music, hoping to meet "that one," but knowing how slim the odds were. It was a life of just living through each day and week, working, slinging, whatever it took to stay alive, having to be straight day in and day out in a straight world that considered you disposable, knowing that most likely whatever was your life at this point was gonna stay your life, with few choices or chances out. The only thing that might bring some comfort, some excitement, something to look forward to, something more meaningful than all of the everydays, was the possibility of meeting somebody you could really relate to, call your own, fall asleep with, entangled in each other's warmth and strength through long, long nights.

Yet it was a catch-22 for masculine dudes because nobody ever was the first to speak, or it turned out that all somebody wanted was sex, or the ones you first thought were dl masc ended up being queens. Just queens in homeboy drag. Which left "real" dudes going back home alone, always alone, where night turned into harsh grimy daylight. And the hope of monogamous intimacy, being loved, hanging out on the low, just doing regular homeboy shit with another dude as hard and lived-life as yourself — finding comfort and refuge in one other human in this world — remained a yearning emptiness that nothing could quench or fill.

The Sun was warming things up. I got to my feet and headed further out into the desert. I loved the feel of this open country. The distant desert mountain ranges made me feel like I was on a different planet. The scrubby greasewood bushes were beginning to flower, tiny little yellow blooms appearing out of scraggly branches filled with stiff, turpentine smelling, waxy-green little leaves. Most of the bushes were about shoulder height. I saw a sidewinder rattlesnake's trail, how he had slithered just like his name.

Joel still made both Camron and me pay $20 to get in, even though we were paying $300 in rent every Saturday night, and as a start-up we hardly had even one-fourth the business of long-time Miss Johnny. That mutherfucker Joel sure didn't like my ass. I didn't like him either.

We had our own street corner inside, now. The idea was to carefully get the word out, and I would remain Camron's own personal security, keeping his back, occasionally checking in. I told Camron he still had to keep it cool, and not be obvious. There was always the possibility of some undercovers, even though all of us, the security posse, Miss Johnny's entourage, and myself, had pretty good copdar.

The main people who bought were the Chelsea gym bunnies and the music heads who came to hear Junior. Added in were some of the hardcore dancing/voguing ball queens, who danced wildly up and down the aisles, throwing high kicks and shit, just living for "the cutting up" and "the madness." The homeboy crowd rarely bought.

I wasn't immune to wearing a new baseball cap cocked or rollin' my pant leg up or letting my jacket slip off one shoulder, but, as somebody who read the newspaper fanatically now, I'd be standing in the club trying to focus on the moment and find myself unable to keep the real world thoughts from flooding in. I needed to be out West, away from everything. I knew nothing else mattered. I'd almost burst with anxiousness. All this club and music shit and finding somebody didn't mean anything.

I was afraid I'd begun to drive myself crazy over the war. As the countdown came closer to January 15th, I began to obsess. I found myself hating the president with an intensity that consumed me. He was like a rancher, only a rancher of the world. He was the "good ol' boy", grinning, always grinning, with death and destruction dripping out of his mouth like drool. And nobody could see. He wanted to drill, pollute, go to war for oil, kill innocent people, and he was always grinning, grinning like a monster with glasses whose face was falling off.

I drew my finger in the sand. I tried to put these thoughts out of my head. The anger was rising. Face it. There's nothing you can do. They're already over there, killing women and children who hardly even have shoes. Everybody in the U.S. is cheering. Remember that big fat redneck you saw wearing the t-shirt showing the silhouette of an Arab, any Arab, sitting on a camel, centered in crosshairs, and the words I'D FLY 10,000 MILES TO SMOKE A CAMEL written below? Fucking racist war. Racist America. Ignorant. Selfish…. Vicious.

I stopped myself again, looking up at the sky, *pulling* the Sun's heat and strength and clean vitality into my skin, organs, bones, soul. Mid-winter in the California desert, elevation key to everything, it was a little chilly.

I didn't feel completely right about this drug business. Not bad about it. But some nagging. It's a recreational thing for our clients. Most them make way more money than I do. I'm not pushing shit on anybody. It's not like I'm slinging crack or something. *As long as you don't cross* that *line.*

But aside from dealing, what are my options? There's a war going on against the Earth herself that's much bigger than the one in the Persian Gulf. And that's bad enough. I need to at least get on a playing field, even if it's never level. My head shuts down at least once every day. I have nothing to build on. This is my chance to make some money, get my feet under me enough to fight back.

I thought of Sound Factory again. New Year's was great. The dealers all sold out. Afterwards, everybody just hanging out, just chilling to the music. Had a good feeling to it. Around 5 or so, Junior suddenly hit the crowd with silence like a boom, as he shut down the output. Everybody stopped and looked up to the dj booth, to their High Priest, questioning.

And then, five hours into the year of 1991, fifteen days before we all knew the bombs would fall, loud and crystal clear through the speakers, Junior dropped some shit on us that nobody would've ever expected to hear in Sound Factory. People just stood and listened in amazement, because the moment was *on*, as if in that one moment all the world's angst and frustration and sorrow of centuries came out and boiled to a head. Eyes began tearing up as Bette Midler, Bette Fucking Midler, sang "From a Distance" out of the superspeakers of Sound Factory; her beautiful, aching voice rang through the cavernous club. And for those few minutes, people forgot about the party, forgot about their own personal shit, and inhabited Bette's imagined world.

I'd flown out of the city to California on January 31st, two weeks after the war began right on schedule. I'd set Camron up with enough product and personal trust to last him six weeks. "What was it about the West?" he'd asked me again. I tried to explain, about the buffaloes and the prairie dogs, and that they were having problems, and that the barbed wire represented the epitome of racist oppression and lies, but it didn't come out sounding like it made sense. Just in talking about it, I'd gotten all heated up. He'd responded by telling me he had seen on the news something about how they were going to let the buffalo roam free again, all up and down the middle part of the country, and people out in those "rectangular states" were all upset. I'd said, "Naah, that couldn't be. What about the Interstates? They must've been talking about some stupid Disney World idea for some theme park or something." He'd argued me that he really had seen it, that they were really talking about letting them roam free, but I didn't believe him.

Camron had a nice tv, and a big, black-vinyl reclining chair by the window by the mammoth bridge outside his apartment. In his chill time when he wasn't spinning new mixes on his two Technic turntables set up on the floor against the wall, he watched his favorite movie *Blade Runner* over and over, or cable news, and History Channel and PBS specials about historic catastrophic events like wars and natural and man-made disasters that had lots of grainy black and white footage in them. For a while there, he was focused on Pripyat, the radiation-bombed city nearest the Chernobyl nuclear reactor that exploded in 1986. 50,000 people had been evacuated, leaving an eerie ghost city of the apocalypse, and every once in a while he'd get quiet and say "PRIP-YAT! Now how about PRIP-YAT!" And one balmy day during that easy, warm winter, standing outside the apartment on Delancey in a t-shirt, he looked up at the sky above the bridge and shook his head, saying, "I like this global warming."

At that moment it'd occurred to me that global warming might become something real in our lives. Winters did seem to be getting milder in general.

Being back in New York, after all that getting tested and taking the train back and everything, I had felt uneasy. My promise to live a different life, in balance and *service,* kept nagging at me. I was supposed to live out West.

Now that I was back out here, in the desert, I told myself I would probably not be going back to the city again.

But of course I would. Had to now. Unfinished business. I didn't know exactly how shit was going to pan out, but I needed to do something. I had a sense that this was going to be my only opportunity to make ends.

I thought about all the stupid little flag pins everybody was wearing. Even the stewardesses, even the uniformed black woman who took my ticket before I boarded… Everybody was so war gung-ho. I'd gotten searched and checked twice, and I had to show ID. I sensed things were definitely going to change.

After the January 15th deadline passed, after a day filled with tension and waiting around the world, the bombs and shooting had begun. It had been deep night in Kuwait and Iraq, just past 6 p.m. in New York on the 16th. In nearly every deli, restaurant, bar and apartment, eyes were fixed on the CNN images of glowing green streaks of firepower searing across the screen, and the big flashes and big booms. On the tv it looked like a big sanitized video game. I didn't see no images of little boys and girls getting their eyes and guts blown out, which I'm sure was happening everywhere.

After deplaning in L.A., I'd gone to pick up my car at the motel in Rosarito, and Emma the owner had gotten me into a discussion about Bush and Hussein, how they'd used to be friends, and now they were fighting. She said that Saddam Hussein got his chemical weapons from Reagan and Bush and Rumsfeld. And that she wouldn't be surprised if all that oil spilling into the Persian Gulf was because of their own bombs, and they just blamed it on Saddam. She said if all the oil fields went up in flames the global climate itself would probably be altered, at least for a year, if not for a long time. She'd asked me if I believed in the Prophecies of Nostradamus. I'd told her I didn't know about those, but I really didn't think the world as we knew it would make it more than another 100 years or so.

After getting my car, I realized it truly was on its last legs, so I aborted my planned trip to the plains and stormed out into the California desert.

I took off my shirt, and it felt January good. Must be 75 out here. I tied my shirt around my head and kept walking, my boots and the lower parts of my legs getting covered in desert dust. I was way out in the middle of the Mojave Desert, south of old Route 66, at least 60 miles from any town big enough to have a motel. But there were some old railroad siding cottages here. Only about 20 people still lived in this little stop on the road. When I-40 had come through many miles to the north, the town had simply dried up.

Phyllis, the Mexican woman at the little store by the road, had told me I could stay in one of those cottages, and that was that. Just watch out for black widows and brown recluses, she'd said. We got lots of them!

I wasn't worried about spiders.

Miles out in the desert scrub, I pulled out my journal and began to write:

Many portents in our time. And I can see them speeding up. Too much ignorance, too many different wills, too many different, selfish interests. The world cannot sustain this. Chernobyl, Union Carbide, AIDS, Exxon Valdez, the Persian Gulf oil spill, overgrazing and barbed wire everywhere turning grasslands to sterile deserts, the destruction of the rainforests, the greenhouse effect, acid rain, factory farming, mega-agribusiness — the list is endless. And those are only the big news things. Every day more is lost forever. I forget the statistics on how many species go extinct EACH DAY! Already there is talk about how the weather is changing. Old grandma Emma had said, "I myself in my relatively young lifetime remember different weather."

I looked up at the sky.

It's almost like I feel paralyzed by the world situation, I continued, writing. *From top to bottom there are so many fucked-up things, so much that is so wrong... I'm becoming preoccupied, maybe obsessed....*

I made it to the bed of some railroad tracks. I turned around and looked to the little cluster of buildings out by the road where I'd parked at the end of my aborted trip. They were about five miles away. I sat down on the rail. Through the fabric of my jeans the iron was warm under my butt. I buried my head in my arms. Finally I began writing in my journal again.

All this... and more. And my feelings of impotence in the face of all this, feeling so ineffectual. I am really floundering. Feeling unable to do ANYTHING... Even severely getting down on myself knowing that if I feel so strongly about all these things I should be out there, doing SOMETHING, ANYTHING, if even on a small scale...

But the paralysis... what, fear of action? .... Why? Feelings that I can't possibly make a difference?

The part you have most difficulty admitting is the fact that you're lazy, that you don't want to carry your burden, your share, and that it's so much easier for you to just put it aside and go out to a club or something like everybody else. ... But deep down you know you are different... you are called to do something more.

Sooner or later you will have to act on these feelings... to grow up and shoulder your share. No more stagnation. Please!

I sat there till the Sun made it across the rest of the sky and dropped down behind the distant, jagged mountains. Venus first came out, so bright in the western sky not yet dark with twilight. A breeze picked up. A few native birds chirped in the tiniest of voices, as if in awe and appreciation of the sky, not wanting to break the mood. '*Help!*' I thought. I need a vision. Coyote. Jackal, you are brothers. Help. I need help right now. I need to feel the Spirit. Inside me.

I noticed a flash of movement, and it was gone. Out of the corners of my eyes, at the last second, I'd seen him. Rich, streaked, blond tawny fur. And eyes.... Yellow eyes. Coyote! Flashing into the bush. I shot my hand into the sky, almost in disbelief at the coincidence, savoring and thrilling to my first real, up-close sighting. I inhaled deeply, and actually caught the faintest whiff of his desert body scent. Etched it into my memory.

I replayed the image in my mind, realizing I was already familiar with Paco, my name for Coyote. I'd seen him many times in my passouts. But this time I'd seen him *on this side*. Not in the Shadow World.

As the blue deepened above, and the pale lemon yellow glow over the mountains sank till it was just an outline, more stars came out. And suddenly I saw a shooting star, not in my side vision, but directly head on, and I was able to watch the meteor flame through the atmosphere in a long arc for over a second, before it burned out.

Has to be a good sign. Has to be.

I heard a distant rumble. My hearing is very acute, and at first I thought it was a car. But there were no roads around here. Then I realized it was a train coming from miles away. I sat on the rail waiting for it. Soon I saw its massive headlight, and the rail began to vibrate against me. The train's headlight blazed at me in the night, coming on fast, light and noise obliterating everything. I knew I would jump off, but that oncoming obliteration thrilled me. 75 yards away and hurtling forward through the darkening desert, I'm sure its engineer was not even looking. Mos def the last thing he was expecting was to see some guy in a makeshift t-shirted *kufiya* over his head sitting on the rail looking up at him. The vibrations increased till they rattled the muscles in my body against their bones.

At the last minute I jumped off and stood there as the beast roared past me so loud and monstrous and fast. SANTA FE RAILROAD it said on its sides, clanking on the twin metal rails, blocking out sight and sound of everything else, each boxcar whooshing past, one after the other and another and another, cutting the dark blue sky into patches between each car, its wind flapping my clothes and pushing at me. I caught glimpses of train art, wildly looping graffiti, on the side of each car.

Disoriented in the mechanical overload, I dimly guessed the train was about a mile long. The caboose finally came up and rushed past and I felt pulled by its wake and stumbled after it, as if attached, then broke free as it rushed off into the almost dark night. The desert silence swirled back in and around, enveloping me and the night animals, left out here alone.

I looked down at the sand. In the last of the light, I knelt down and with my fingertip, drew a thin, sharp-pointed crescent moon and five-point star. It was my tag, my signature.

Lahumba opened the door to her Los Feliz apartment. Her eyes widened, and she rushed out. "Oh my God!" she said, giving me a big squishy hug. "Oh my God, Jihad! Where have you been!"

"Sup Lahumba," I said, trying to breathe and not to smile, as she squeezed my arms against my sides. I wiggled out and said, "Naah, it's like this" and wrapped my arms strongly around her. "Hey, you look real good."

"Look at you." She pulled back, checking me out. She rubbed her hand down my desert-darkened face, neck, arm, chest. "Nice brown skin." She was wearing some wide-legged white cotton pants and some kind of sheer white East Indian linen top with long sleeves. It made her dark skin glow, which had that L.A.-kind of clean-washed look to begin with. A black designer bra was underneath. Her long, straight, jet-black hair had grown to her shoulders. "Come on in. Come in. Sit down. Sit down. Can I get you something?"

I kicked off my dusty boots and tried to swipe off some of the dirt on my jeans. "I'm cool. A glass of water'd be alright. How you been doing?"

I sat down in her overstuffed love seat. She brought two glasses of water with two ice cubes in each and a lemon slice stuck onto the rim, handed me one, and sat on the couch on the other side of the glass table across from me. She was smiling, gazing at me, revealing perfectly whitened teeth. I sensed her perfume, strawberries, spices, incense. Her eyes were still those clear, warm black pools that, added to everything else, gave her a feel of an exotic, cultured but borderless woman of many far-flung parts of the world.

The ice water was great going down my throat.

"I'm so mad at you," she said. "I tried to get in touch with you, but that number was disconnected, and you never called me. It's been so long!"

I looked down momentarily. "I know. I just got caught up in some shit — some stuff. But everything's gonna be alright. What's going on?"

"Well, I'm doing a play over in Silver Lake. I'm the lead actress. I play this street person who became that way because she was wronged by her man, so she goes into prostitution so she can buy a big gun to take revenge. She wants a big expensive gun, because, you know, she doesn't want to just put a little hole in him. But her pimp is actually a very wealthy man, he only does this as a hobby, and soon she finds herself falling for him. She gets a taste of the high life, and soon finds herself faced with the dilemma: does she get the gun and stay true to herself, or move on and focus on her new man?" She hardened her eyes as if to show me the character.

"Do you still work at the call center?"

She sighed. "Yes. It helps out. I go a couple nights a week. But hopefully if I get these big commercials I'm up for, I'll be able to quit that. My manager is also booking me for some movie auditions, and there is this big play in Philadelphia, too. It would be for six months, that job. But get this! If I get that play, I think I will move to New York after!"

"Really."

"Yeah. We'll see. So do you want some lunch? I can make some scrambled tofu with black olives."

"Mmm, that sounds good. Food always taste better when a woman puts her foot in it. And you damn sure know how to put your foot in it. Haven't had one of your home-cooked meals in a long time."

She smiled, getting up and going into the kitchen. I followed her.

"I was wondering if you would take me to the airport later."

"What are you going to do with that car?"

"I have an 8:30 flight back to New York. I'm just gonna leave it on the street in Culver City. If you can, you could just follow me." I showed her my wire clippers, which I pulled out of my back pocket. "I already cut out the VIN number. Just need to take the plates off. Yup. Heading back to NYC. That car has bit the dust."

"Well, Brotherman, I might be joining you in New York," she said as she began cutting up onions and a ripe tomato, sniffling a little bit. She poured some oil in a big skillet, dumped the onions in; they sizzled. A cloud of steam rose into her face and she leaned back, eyes watering. The smells of fresh cooking filled the room.

"You know, Lahumba, my stomach been messed up. I get cramps, and it hurts, and sometimes, you know, I don't know, everything just feel so messed up, and I don't mean just my stomach. I mean everything. But my stomach, I don't know if it's stress, or I ate something, or both. I feel ok, right now, but I'm sure that will be temporary." There was no way I was going to tell her about Diego, or AIDS, or anything.

She looked up at me as she stirred in the crumbled tofu with the cutting knife. "You know, I found that if I squat down in the morning real low with my legs apart and breathe in and out, like in yoga, I can go to the bathroom real easy." She backed up and squatted down to show me, still holding the knife. She straightened her arms out between her legs, straightened her back, held her head up, and partially closed her eyes. "All you have to do is breathe deeply. Make sure you keep your feet flat, heels to the floor. And keep your knees in line with your toes. It opens you up!"

"Well, that wasn't exactly what I meant. I don't have that problem."

"No really, Jihad," she said, pointing at me with the knife as she got up. "You should try it."

I was silent as I watched her cook. She looked over at me, gave me one of her eyelash-fluttering scrutinizing looks. "What's really on your mind, Jihad? Why don't you tell me what really happened?"

For a moment... but then, "Naah, nothing, Lahumba. It's cool. I'm cool. But I am very glad to see you. You look so good. And that cooking smells soooo good."

"You really should let me read you your tarot cards." She stirred the skillet for a while, biting her lip. Sniffling, she looked up and pointed the knife straight at me again, dramatically. "Well you better not let anybody mess with you. That's all I'm saying. At my last call center job, oooh, I was so mad. I went in to pick up my paycheck, which I really needed, and they told me they didn't have the whole amount because they couldn't "verify my hours." And it turns out they did that to another woman, another black woman, too. Oh, I was so furious. But I had no proof. I went back in there, demanding my money. I leaned right in the manager's face, slapped my hand down on his desk, I really did, and I said, 'If I'm going to get fucked, I want to at least enjoy it.'"

Slightly feverish, I lay on my back on the old bed. Snow poured down the large, gray airshaft of the transient SRO hotel uptown on Central Park West between 106th and 107th. I felt on the verge of a passout, thinking so hard.

Over the past year you've become quite the scholar, I thought to myself. The information junkie. Read the New York Times every day. Scoured it for environmental news of the West. Got to know the writers and their styles, and the sense of their political views — whether they would slant things favorably or not, left or right — I trained myself to read between the lines. Looked forward to Tuesday's 'Science Times' section, which often had multiple stories on major environmental news globally, nationally and locally, as well as feature articles about everything from dung beetles (endangered) to black-footed ferrets (endangered, because they were dependent on prairie dogs and the plains-wide prairie dog complex had been shattered).

I often went down to the library, or the Strand or at Pageant Books and Prints on 9th. Upstairs at Pageant they had all kinds of old books for sale, tattered copies of paperbacks, musty old hardcovers, some that were first editions, all telling me in hundreds of thousands of words what the Anglo experience had been out West, from First Contact to Conquest and Settlement. I tried hard to find other voices about the West, American Indian, Spanish, Black, Chinese, Arab, whatever, but found next to nothing, even though all had played some part or other in the whole story. The descriptions of the unfenced, unbroken wild prairie, heaving with so much abundance and life, were heartbreaking. And the sheer numbers of animals and birds and all life simply too large to grasp. There were many books about Indians, but few by Indians themselves. Records of the Black experience out West were also limited. And that was mostly about the Buffalo Soldiers. What a great idea the Army had, I thought, disgusted. After the Civil War, suddenly finding itself with a bunch of black men with guns they didn't want around, they thought 'Hey, send them out West to kill Indians.' Pit the two most oppressed groups against each other, and solve a couple problems at once. With no jobs and little choice, the black men went. I was very curious whether there had been any moral qualms within the Buffalo Soldiers as they were put to work destroying other people of color, any sense of helpless anger in a fucked up world, any sense of disgust, empathy, solidarity, or refusal. In *Black Elk Speaks*, the Lakota Holy Man refers to "a black wasicu" that him and his boys had killed. *Wasicu* is the Lakota word for white man. But I knew the whole thing was much more complicated than that.

Anxious and restless, I returned to my daydreaming. My West… I projected myself out across the Hudson River over the curve of the East and the Midwest, returning back into those emptied lands. Yes, it was the land of sun, wind and grass. *Grass.* Blowing in the wind like the hair of a beautiful, fierce goddess…

She'd been critically wounded. But she was not dead yet. She was still wild, despite what people had done to her. Out there was the land of hail and blazing sun, torrential thunderstorms, searing heat and drought, boomeranging blizzards, wind and dust storms, great blue skies and towering white clouds …and the Earth-shaking rumble of hundreds of millions of ghost-hooves. What was it I'd experienced each time I was out there? What was the memory — of fertility, of prairie, of wild meadows and flowers and buzzing silence, discovery at each footstep? Where did it come from? The Plains — what did they have to do with me? What had been tapping at me every time I'd crossed them? Struggling, yearning. Like a wild vine trying to twist itself up into the sky, it — she—was trying to rise up. Fight the power. Shake it off.

I tried to remember what I'd known in Texas. The South Texas Plains, and remnant Coastal Prairie. Low yellow morning glories growing out of the dunes and sandy soil. Cactuses. Tall native grasses. Wire fences. Big cattle. The sunsets — those giant red sky-stretching sunsets — those were the biggest things I remembered.

I remembered the time I was heading back up to Corpus after that stupid little jail experience and stopped on the side of the road, my face yanked westward, transfixed by the sky. How I'd heard the coyote, and felt the pull of those lands westward, felt myself standing in a moment between the ocean at my back and the great open West in front of me.

The Earth Island Journal lay on the floor where it had landed, having slipped out of my hands as I'd begun to daydream, then passed out. Ran across it at Hudson News down on Broadway and 8th. Had an article on a new idea called "the Buffalo Commons." This must've been what Camron been talking about. The mag said some 149,000 square miles of western Great Plains counties had lost more than half their population in the last few decades, with the declines increasing. Many were now "frontier" counties again, with populations of six people or less per square mile. Some had less than 2 people per square mile, which was considered a population wilderness. The age-old cycles of violent weather extremes were reasserting themselves, making the old cow and plow economy unable to compete in the global economy. Two social scientists, Drs. Frank and Deborah Popper at Rutgers University, who had come up with this mapping, were calling for a Buffalo Commons. They suggested the prairies should never have been plowed and fenced, arguing that "settling the prairies . . . was the largest, longest-running agricultural and environmental mistake in United States history."

Those were strong words. The best answer was to put part of the Plains back to what it was meant to be: a wild, abundant sea of grass once again thundering with great herds of buffalo and all native prairie wildlife. The few towns that are still hanging on out there could work to create a sustainable, clean economy based on good jobs in restoration, eco-tourism, wind and solar power, and more.

As far as I knew, there was no wilderness out there, except for that one small Sage Creek area in South Dakota. And that was entirely circled by bristling wires.

The mag said the grasslands were slowly emerging, right under our noses, as "the nation's largest wilderness." Shit. It was probably a war zone.

My own spirit expanded like the horizon. A mirage of freedom lay out there, definitely. But there was something much more. What was I missing?

I thought again about the huge weather systems out there. I wanted to be held, tossed, shaken like that, by that power.

I thought I could hear the snow falling in the airshaft. My eyes fluttered. I felt drugged...

I began to see a land rolling off into yellow grass, but it kept momentarily shifting into rolling grassy sand dunes just a slightly darker, richer, redder color, then switching back again. I passed my hands over my eyes, clearing my vision in the hot sun. I realized I was naked except for a skin thong covering my genitals. The antelope didn't see me, my skin blended perfectly. I began running crouched, low and barefoot through the seared grass and sand, clutching my hand-forged spear. Suddenly I was on my hands and knees, but still maintaining my speed. Blue sky flew past my eyes and ears. My heart pumped what my body needed loud and smooth as my belly hugged the dirt, the rough grass barely rippling at my shoulders. A thin grip of sweat clamped around my temples in the dry, dust-hung air, drawing particles of dirt into my skin to make it look like I was banded, my hair somehow in a short tight afro. And before the antelope had seen me (*suddenly this close!*) I lunged the spear into his side right behind his taut shoulder — I could hear the puncture and see the ripple-pucker of stricken flesh, his bluish black tongue slapping out — and he died in a whirlwind of dust and rolled back eyes and kicking legs, tan-and-white flanks heaving.

Breathing hard, I walked up and looked at him lying dead and loose, the hot afternoon sun diving deep into the muscles of my back and shoulders. I felt consummation, penetration, perfection. At the same time a strong puncture of sadness opened up inside me and rattled me like wind-shook bamboo stalks. Both felt right.

Pulling out my knife to gut him, my eyes continued looking down at him, tracing over his sleek marked sides, down over where his taut belly creased into his thigh, providing a glimpse of his penis and testicles pushing out from between his collapsed legs. I suddenly blinked. For a second it was myself lying on the ground, my own belly waiting to be split by the knife, my own genitals about to get cut out. But no, it was just the antelope.

I looked around to straighten out my vision. But then I couldn't tell whether I was in the middle of the American West plains or the North African Sahara, both of which kept going from grass to dust under a high-in-the-sky burning ball of sun. I tried to shield my eyes to see better. And out of the corners of my eyes, the long-legged animal at my feet kept shape-shifting, and I got confused, couldn't tell if he was an American pronghorn or a North African gazelle. Or me. My head began squeezing, but it didn't hurt, it just—

My bare feet stumbled in the yellow grass or sandy dirt. A wind rose, swirling dust devils *and a woman's white flapping robes and veil* across the plain… I blacked out, floating effortlessly down but hitting the ground with a thud.

CHAPTER NINETEEN

Jihad

The shiny 7/8 crescent wrench had a nice heft in my hand. I holstered it into the back pocket of my jeans. I expected goons, rednecks, bat-wielding dudes from New Jersey, and worse, hundreds of thousands of them foaming at the mouth with racist war frenzy during their "Victory Celebration." The wrench was innocent enough (just going to help my girl work on her apartment, officer) and strong enough for some head-thudding protection if it came down to that. Better than my knife, which I was going to leave in the room. What was I gonna do, stab these rednecks as they came at me?

I pulled a Hanes tank on, tied my boots, folded the navy blue bandana into a square and stuck it all the way down into my left front pocket, and pulled the big floppy thug hat over my head. Picking up the white t-shirt that I'd painted front and back the night before, I carefully folded it lengthwise and slung it over my shoulder. Checking myself in the mirror, I agreed I looked dangerous enough, and got out of the little square box that was my room in Hotel Hell.

Noticing I'd picked up the New York 'hood rat's gait, the confident roll and drag that had become a regular part of my walk (how long had it been like that?) I made it over to Broadway and 103rd and the 1 train going down to the World Trade Center. It was such a nice sunny morning I decided to walk the extra blocks down to 96th and get the express. Still good for time. I'd change at 14th St. The big ugly celebrations for the war would just be starting, would last for hours.

On the train, I sat down and looked over the shirt in my hand. On the back, painted in black letters, it said:

Polarization?

Confrontation?

Damn Straight!

Compromise? (Hah!)

<u>Too</u> <u>Late</u>!

Time to REALIZE

the Real WAR

begins now…slowly,

surely, and BY ANY

MEANS NECESSARY

Five bloody bullet holes were added for effect.
And on the front it said.

WHAT GOES
AROUND COMES AROUND
Huh BUSH! ☺

With a little yellow smiley face next to that.

Inside, I was live with adrenaline and nervous energy.

Got off on Chambers and bounded up the steps. A wall of sound hit me, the sounds of tens of thousands of people gathering in the near distance, echoing and refracted by the tall buildings. I stalked the remaining blocks, jostled by increasing loads of people streaming everywhere, many in beachwear and carrying coolers(!). They still didn't know I was in their midst. The last step was to pull my t-shirt on. I scanned for friendly territory in faces, for any clues, clothing or signs, for other protesters drawn like moths into the flame. There would be some major protests down here, though dwarfed by the celebrators. I'd find them.

But I was unprepared for the sheer number of people massing at the lower end of Manhattan to celebrate. I stepped out of the streaming crowd by a bench, pulled on my battle shirt. Fixing the black floppy thug hat back down over my head, I turned my back to the crowd and tied the blue bandana around my face, leaving only a slit of my eyes showing. This is it, I said, and dove in, walking very quickly now, threading my way, knowing I had to find strength in numbers now, any safe place of others.

Immediately the attacks came. "Hey, what the fuck is this!" "Look at that!" "Hey asshole, go back where you came from!" I forced my cool. As long as nobody tried to put their hands on me. The immediate need was to find others.

Still, I wasn't anywhere near where the main celebrations were supposed to be, which I believed were by the river on the West Side Highway, but the streets were becoming too clogged. Somebody pushed me from behind, and I pulled out my wrench, clenching it in my fist without even turning around, keeping myself moving forward.

Getting up on my toes I noticed a disturbance ahead in the crowd, and I was suddenly reminded of the wild dolphins just off the beach creating a swirl in the heaving waters that evening in Mexico. It was a knot of protesters. They had been surrounded by swelling angry crowds and prevented from going any further. People shoved and jammed me as I squeezed my way through. I heard screams and yells and shouting. I pushed my way into the circle of protesters and as I broke through I felt a rush. So glad to be on a little island of friendly territory. Their faces looked strained. Folks were holding their ground here, abandoning any plans of trying to reach the much larger protests sure to be down further.

I nodded to others inside the group, and flashed my back to the angry crowd, letting them read my t-shirt, holding my bike-gloved fists up. Liquid excitement filled me. This was it. I was officially and *physically* on the opposing side. Hell yeah. I didn't have to sit silently by like some half-assed loser or take shit like a helpless victim or unwitting accomplice.

There were about twenty of us, only five who were guys including myself; the rest were women. It was a diverse little group of people. Some protesters held signs. A couple women wore Iraqi mourning veils, and held aloft empty baby strollers that had burn marks and 'blood spatter' on them.

Police shouldered their way in, erecting blue and white painted wooden horses in front of us that said POLICE LINE DO NOT CROSS. They shoved us back. "Just because we're doing our job doesn't mean we agree with you," said one very unsmiling way too-stereotypical bushy-mustached cop with mirror sunglasses. All but one cop left, and he went and stood by the building wall, his hands on his belt.

A few protesters gathered around me. "Thanks for coming," said one girl. She looked like a sweet little farm girl in her overalls. Her freckled, pale face was flushed. Heat from the sticky morning sun was magnified by the body heat of the crowds.

"Is this it? What happened?" I asked.

The Dominican guy with the anarchist circle-A tattoo on his coppery shoulder and a coarse black goatee said, "We had all found each other walking down, and we were trying to find where to go, and suddenly we got surrounded."

The rest gathered in like a huddle as the Indonesian-looking girl spoke up. "They're fucking rednecks. They're all drunk!" she said in a Long Island accent. "One of the women got spit on back there!"

"They're picking on the women because they ain't got no balls," I said. "Without their guns and machines, they're nothing. Where are the other protesters?"

"We heard there are a few other small groups like ours," said the tired-looking middle aged white man with a gray beard and flannel shirt, his voice sounding hoarse as he struggled to be heard over the noise. "And there's supposed to be one big protest, over by the river. But we're scattered; we're all surrounded."

"There's no way we gonna get any further," one of the black women said. "We gotta make our stand right here. And stick together, people!"

I nodded. I noticed a four-foot-long narrow box on the ground in the center, wrapped in a sheet or something. A few signs and some people's belongings were piled next to it.

A young, lanky black guy in a white t-shirt and new black jeans slipped under the barricade and joined us. People standing outside against the barricades screamed obscenities at him.

"Hey! Thanks for joining us!" said somebody. He smiled back an award-winning smile.

"We have to make sure the women stay protected." I said, especially to the guys. I realized nobody could see any of my face except for the slit of my eyes between the pulled-down floppy and the navy blue bandana pulled up over the bridge of my nose. "Dawg, we can handle it," the radical black woman said. "Fuck these people and their racist shit. What is this, a beach party?! Look at them! They're wearing pink and purple beach clothes! They're up in here in flip flops and coolers and beers!!"

"No, he just means there are more of you females than us," the Dominican guy said. "And with this crowd, we just gotta be careful. As men, we want to look out."

We decided that the three of us, the Dominican guy, myself, and the lanky black kid, who said he was 19, would take the front and spread ourselves out where most people were approaching. The three other guys would hold up the rear and the rear flank. Women would be in the middle and the sides.

Somebody smacked me in the head with a flagpole and I whipped around, the flapping cloth of Old Glory pulling back over my head. A band of about twenty New Jersey whiteboys with beer bellies, wearing — sure enough — flip flops, beach shorts and tank tops in those New Jersey bright artificial colors like purple and pink and orange, with those ugly iridescent beach sunglasses on their faces, had stopped to confront us. A Japanese film crew was right there, recording everything. There was no sign at all of any U.S. press. One of the Jersey dudes screamed at me, "Yeah I did it. What you gonna do about it!"

"Fucking murderer," I said.

"Take off your bandana! You're a fucking pussy! What are you afraid of, because you are bullshit, and you don't want anybody to see that YOU ARE BULLSHIT!" He jabbed at each word as it came out of his small mouth. "Get a life!" His friends shouldered in close to his side, ready. "Take off your mask!!"

He made as if to reach for it. The other two guys near me quickly closed in to my side. "He don't have to let you see shit, whiteboy!" the Dominican guy, whose name was Andrew, said.

"Let's see your face you fucking pussy!"

I ripped my bandana down and shoved my face right in his.

The New Jersey guy swung at Andrew, and I pulled Andrew back. Jersey tried to swing at me and I ducked as his friends pulled him back. I felt somebody pulling the wrench out of my pocket. It was Lantrell, the young lanky guy.

One of the other Jersey guys reached in and snatched Andrew's sign out of his hand, which said, NO BLOOD FOR OIL, STUPIDS! Andrew reached for it back, but was not quick enough. They ripped it into pieces. "Whatever," he said, raising his chin at them. I could see he was forcing himself to keep his hands down.

He came over, and tried to talk over the din. "Man, you don't have to do anything for them. Don't let them tempt you like that. That's what they're trying to do, get you to do something. Then they can brawl. And we're way outnumbered. We agreed beforehand; we gotta keep this non-violent."

"But man, we still gotta protect ourselves. And our women." I turned to Lantrell. "Why'd you take the wrench?"

"Because I knew you were about to use it," he said in the harmonica-raspy voice of a 19 year old going from the last vestiges of boy to man. "We ain't even about that, man. These fools, they're dead people. We don't even have to let them bring us down to their level. We just need to let 'em know we're here."

"They're end of the world people," I said. "Evolution took a wrong turn and hit a brick wall."

"And this splatter is what came out of that, and what we have-ta deal with," the farm girl chirped in.

In front of the barricade, a small, perky blonde woman appeared, maybe in her late 30s, wearing a business-smart thin white cotton sweater and turquoise skirt. She had a pleasant little Ms. Brady Bunch look on her face. In the same instant she ducked under the barricades and squeezed into our ranks. Our jaws dropped. She turned around to face the mob and suddenly shot them all the finger. She tilted her perky blow-dried head back at us and asked, "Can I have a sign?" flashing us a smile. Grins stretched broadly across our faces as one of the girls in the middle passed a sign up. Her name was Kelly and she stayed on the front lines with us. She said she had quietly followed the buildup and the war and the aftermath in the newspapers, the Highway of Death aerial massacre of surrendering, conscripted young men, many who didn't even have shoes, and all the rest of the story. Everybody in her office was all gung ho and she found herself gradually getting increasingly disturbed by the kind of talk she'd heard.

She'd come into her office this morning to catch up on some of her work rather than be with all her officemates who were celebrating, and had looked out and seen us down on the street. At that moment, she said, she'd felt something change inside her, and just calmly went out the door and down to the street to join us.

"Where'd you come from?" Lantrell rasped, cocking his head.

She pointed up at the World Trade Center. Heads tilting back, our eyes followed her finger all the way up the side of the silver sleek North Tower that seemed to reach not only to the sky, but through it. The high noon Sun was moving to the south behind it, sparking around its severe straight-line corner.

I pulled my bandana back up over my face.

Back behind me, I heard the women start chanting, facing off against the crowd coming at them on both sides. BOMB IGNORANCE, NOT BABIES! 1-2-3-4! WE DON'T WANT YOUR RACIST WAR! And POOR GEORGE — STUPID RACIST WAR WHORE! And always my favorite: GEORGE HUSSEIN — SADDAM BUSH! They had good rhythm.

Attackers darted in and tried to punch us, or snatch our signs and then run back. They particularly targeted the women. When the women turned their backs they'd come in and smack them on their heads or their faces. We tried to form a circle around them, but the women wouldn't have it. Beer bottles, ice, drinks and drink cups, spit, all kinds of shit was thrown at us. The cop looked the other way. But some people in our group made a stink about how the cop seemed just to be protecting and listening to the goons, and went up to tell him about it. Two other cops arrived to give the cop backup. We were the problem, not the attackers. Hours wore on. For some reason, my presence seemed to especially drive people crazy. Some incoming partiers had to be literally held back by friends grabbing each arm. I wondered if it was the little yellow smiley face I had painted at the bottom of the front of my t-shirt, beneath

WHAT GOES AROUND COMES AROUND. They would lock eyes with mine, and suddenly they'd go berserk.

At one point some of the women had gotten too close to the barricade's edges and goons had attacked them with fury, hitting them, spitting on them, and yanking their hair. The three of us guys from the front fought our way between them and, besides separating them, had to resist contact with anybody of the mob — which immediately would have spilled into all-out violence. One woman had a bloody lip from where a half-full can of beer had hit her. How I wanted to swing. Only the knowledge that violence would ensue, and that we'd be the ones injured and facing certain jail time, kept us in pure resolute defensive mode.

But still! It was amazing to see how fiercely angry and strong and together the women were. They were mad as hell, and determined not to flinch, and seeing them like that made me stronger, filled me with pride.

Another partier got close to me, got in my face.

I said to him, "Why don't you go home and jerk off to one of your child molester videos. Partying about this killing, about your big machine power over others, it's the same thing."

He came for me. The constant strain of the day had worn in on me and I grabbed for my crescent wrench ready for real this time to crack a skull. I only put my hand on it, but that threw him into a frenzy. The cops couldn't hear him; they were listlessly holding back another part of the crowd. At this point I didn't care, I wanted to bust loose, but Andrew and Lantrell rushed in and blockaded, pushing him back. The barricade almost collapsed, then held. The cameras whirred. Some of the attacker's friends pulled him back. "But he's got a wrench!" he yelled, hoping the cops heard him. "He's got a wrench!" he yelled. It came out like a whine. His shouts were drowned out by the din of the crowd.

The standoff went on for hours. Not one of us broke ranks, or wanted to, even if somehow he or she could have made it out safely. I wondered how the others were holding up under the strain. I felt fine. We were all filthy and sticky from all the shit that'd been thrown on us. Jet bombers buzzed overhead for the war display celebration. The world was defined by the cumulative drunk aggression of hundreds of thousands of people. Finally, as the afternoon wore on, we knew we had to make a break for it.

After a quick huddle, a few of us engaged the main harassers at the front. Other protesters bunched up behind, getting ready. Suddenly, there was a loud *whoosh*, causing even those of us who knew what was coming to jolt around.

Courtesy of one of the mourning ladies, the white sheet over the narrow box — and now the box itself — were roaring in flames. The box was a little coffin, a child's coffin, painted black. As the sheet quickly burned away it revealed a very realistic child's skeleton inside. The flames took over rapidly. Through the heat waves the child's grin-grimacing skull seemed to be shaking in a final fit or paroxysm. For a moment, the crowd went silent, creating a sudden loud vacuum. We were momentarily as transfixed as the crowd, then snapped out of it. We shoved one of the barricades over, using the long board to push back the attackers, who were still thrown off by the sight of the little coffin and child writhing in flames. The wooden horse came apart; the boards clattered to the pavement.

Bolting forward in a tight knot, we pushed and broke into a brief open space then ran for a less-peopled side street. A few of the goons gave chase, but gave up in the crush of partiers as we broke up and scattered as planned. I rounded the corner and glanced back. Cops with fire extinguishers had moved in on the coffin; the flames were extinguished in one big *hisss*, tendrils of gray smoke curling skyward. The momentarily silenced crowd erupted into cheers, yelling God Bless America! The last I saw of our group was the WTC woman; sweat-streaked, dirty and sticky she gave me a thumbs up as she ran, but she wasn't smiling.

I quickly peeled off my sticky t-shirt and bandana, ducked into the crowd, and headed uptown. I knew then, truly, like Malcolm X had said, like on the poster hung on my wall back on Ludlow Street, that all causes were connected. And there really is "only one fight, that of the oppressed against those who do the oppressing."

Early spring 1992. Night-driving thoughts on the road to Odessa, Texas. Behind me now, New Mexico and another enraging, distant encounter with a war-booming, coyote-killing helicopter. After a couple months in the Western outback, getting adjusted to the car — a van this time — again was a thing I needed to work on.

Where the hell are you?

Followed by: *And how the fuck did you get here?*

Couldn't talk. Throat not working. It was like that for me in the backcountry West, least in the outback. Soon as I got out here, I'd begin to grow mute. Within a week, literally lose my voice, unable to speak. Needed to readjust now.

I thought back to the little New Mexico town I'd mistakenly tried to hide out in, approximately 40 miles north of the border. Very remote. Except for one couple of Mexican descent, the people in that town were ghostly pale with thin dry skin that showed networks of blue veins underneath. I was the only one under 30, under 40 even. Most of the locals were two or three times my age, except for the sheriff's deputies, who didn't live there anyway. I kept to myself.

Coyotes, hawks, lions, rattlesnakes and more were shot on sight and left to rot. Many of the locals were direct descendants of Confederate families who had left the South after defeat, but brought their plantation ways and race and class assumptions with them. They only spoke to each other when it was necessary. The old dragonlady who ran the tiny one-room Post Office had this way of smiling that let me know clearly there was no smile in any of that. Once I caught her opening and reading my outgoing mail. She sat all day on a stool behind the counter, listening to the shortwave radio or crooking her neck out over spread-open copy of the Albuquerque Journal. One day when I walked in, without lifting her head, she hissed, "I *hate* environmentalists. They've gone too far!"

Had I raised suspicions?

After arriving in that town and shutting the ignition off, I hadn't driven the vehicle once. As the days passed in silence, I became sensitive to all stimuli, every sense exaggerated, every nerve-ending super-heightened.

I didn't need the van. I had my feet and my new, red, Specialized mountain bike. The van had become this metal Industrial Thing sitting out front in the overgrown grass and dead weeds, at any possible moment a loud belching alien monster that would disrupt and break every natural rhythm I had achieved. It gathered dust beneath the dry heat lightning as the early spring sun warmed the afternoons in this part of the country.

Even though I was running out of food and the nearest grocery store was only 50 miles north, I resisted driving. I began eating plantain weeds I found growing green by an old inactive windmill, great big bunches of the palm-faced plants that cooked down like spinach. They were good raw, too. Though I considered myself a vegetarian, I killed and ate a rattlesnake. I needed to eat something, and I ended up eating somebody. I asked him for permission, not that he was really going to say "Yeah, o.k.," but at least it was a way of being respectful. Wincing, I hit him with a stick, breaking his neck. But rattlesnakes don't like to die, and though I hit him again in a few other places on his body, only those parts died. I tucked him through a belt loop in my jeans, and he squeeze-circled his muscled lower body around my thigh like a living rope marked with diamonds as I cycled back. I simmered his clean, pike-like flesh with jalapenos and little doughballs of blue corn meal. I stayed strict veg after that.

Black-haired, skin yellow in the winter, near black in the summer, I turned a different shade darker every day. I was the only human outside. I spent my days out in the grassy desert-like terrain, blending into the landscape, learning, seeking answers, trying to get a handle on my anger, sensing the ghosts of native animals and native people no longer there, wanting war, reacting, recoiling, roiling, not sure what I could do.

Something was happening to me. All my senses were pinging out in different directions, as if my inside self was unformed, like putty, being pulled outward through my skin.

One twilight, after a long day hike up the flats toward the Animas Mountains, I was walking back along the deserted tar road that came north from the border, my mind alive with the ghosts of Apache people and jaguars, all gone from the landscape now. The long day was in my skin and soul, and I felt good, that rare, good, healthy feeling. My night vision easily read the gathering dusk and thrilled at the bright stars appearing in the sky. I heard the car coming from behind, and steeled myself. It roared up and passed.

I kicked myself for being sloppy and walking back along the road, instead of off a way in the bush.

The unmarked car sped past me, but I *felt* the release of the gas pedal, and I knew. The car braked maybe 50 yards ahead, red taillights flaring, and spun around. Blinding me with his high beams, he floored it straight at me, cutting diagonally across the median line; I was the coyote in the headlights. Before I could even get out of the way he was upon me, burning rubber to a stop a few feet from my knees.

He jumped out. I still did not know who this was; I just expected another redneck. I grabbed for my knife, quickly getting into defensive stance. He yanked out his gun and yelled, "PUT IT DOWN! PUT IT DOWN! HANDS UP!"

I slowly put my hands up. "What… the fuck!" I croaked. Nothing audible came out.

"Sheriff's deputy! Drop the gun!" He saw it was a knife. "Knife! Drop it right now or I'll shoot. Speak English!? SPEAK ENGLISH!"

I dropped it to the pavement and backed away a few steps. Strained to get out the words. "Just… out… Just… taking… a (muthafucking) … HIKE!" I pushed out the last word. It sounded like I was shouting. My blood was roiling.

"What?" he said. "Speak up! Hike? Way out here?"

He walked over, still pointing his gun at me, asking me questions. I found my voice, and growled out whatever sounded good, not breaking my stance. He suddenly looked unsure, glanced at his watch, and got in his car. Sticking his head out the window as he turned around he said, "Thought you were a wetback. You better be careful. Better watch where you walk next time," and peeled off, speeding north up the narrow two-lane blacktop, his twin red taillights piercing through the distance and winking out after four or five miles.

As I drove toward Texas, I got angrier and angrier again, thinking about it, dwelling on shit like this, like I do. People tend to call my mixed ass any Third World or race slur they first think of. And they blame me for it. I didn't know who the fuck he was. Unmarked car attacking me. Fucking plainclothes in an unmarked car. "Better watch where I walk next time??" Like I had no right to be out there walking along that state road which bisected more than half a million public Bureau of Land Management — I mean "rancher-owned" (in their mind) acres? They think they own everything, especially that which is not theirs. It's very clear who the cops protect.

Whatever little "higher road" thoughts I had left vaporized. All's fair in hate and war, I thought to myself, liking the sound of that.

After that incident, I became the insurgent, sneaking out of the settlement, returning overland, always hidden, and got my first exhilarating taste of cutting fences.

The area was a mix of High Plains and Chihuahuan Desert. There were cattle or signs of their destructive passing everywhere on this fragile arid land. I had even begun to hate the stupid bovines — admittedly misplaced aggression — because they represented the "bloated ranchers" and their absolute reign. In an area so devoid of human population, signs of the Conqueror like a cancer everywhere, even twenty miles out from the nearest paved road. Rampaged landscapes, denuded stream banks, destroyed soils, shit everywhere, like an ungodly plague of hoofed locusts.

I tried to release myself from this pressure by striving to stay as far removed from the ranchers' and cops' control, their world, as possible. When I would re-enter my little house under the cover of darkness, sometimes it would take me hours to turn on a light. So in tune was I with every natural rhythm, even the lights began to seem… disruptive. For light, I burned those tall voodoo-Catholic candles you get in city bodegas and Mexican tiendas. I'd brought some with me. One time in my house, flashlights from outside suddenly flared through the windows into my face, making me jump. The deputies demanded I come outside, searched the car, but couldn't find anything.

You're really pushing your luck here, I told myself. The night breezes blew the ancient chintz curtains like a transparent old hand waving fingers over the sink.

At last, crossing back into Texas. "Nothing between us and Canada but barbed wire" is a favorite West Texas High Plains saying. With the winds regularly swinging from north to south, cold to warm, and back, ruled by winds we are, the weather can change at any moment. Except for the hot south wind summers, for most of the year it can be cold and hot in the same day, and back again, with winds from Canada and Mexico battling it out in a constant tug of war. Add in the moist air pushing inland off the wild untamed Gulf of Mexico, which explodes into the dry Canada and Mexico winds fighting it out on their own front, well, that's why they call this part of the country Tornado Alley.

I'd bought the pale yellow van for a thousand dollars from this Chinese guy out in Queens. Paid a guy a hundred dollars to install metal bars across the back windows and put those impenetrable cast-steel puck locks on the doors. I got the van instead of a car because I could sleep in the back, as well as secure my bike.

It'd taken me all the way to January to get out of NYC. Hotel Hell was barely livable, the bathrooms — one to each side of the floor — were so filthy I had to climb flights to find a usable one, but at $450 a month it allowed me a NYC-affordable place of anonymity, privacy, and month-to-month arrangements so I could leave whenever I wanted. Business had been OK, though Camron was constantly on my ass about me not committing more. He felt we should really go for it; he was always complaining that I seemed "distracted."

I'd bought me a high-end red Specialized Rockhopper Comp mountain bike for $900, and it was great to ride again. The bike greatly increased my business mobility.

Camron and I pushed on. We became good work friends with Miss Johnny; she even bought wholesale from me a couple times. Joel still acted like he was the toughest thing even though we all found out his very real-looking girlfriend was a drag queen with some serious work done. Then in the summer our supply line went dead, the Family wasn't doing anything. They told me to just be patient. I scrambled, looking for product, forgetting that desperate people make mistakes. I finally found somebody who said yeah, he could get me a little. It'll least be something, I'd thought, stupid to not pay attention to how quickly he'd said yes. Taping the two thousand dollars in an envelope to my lower back beneath my shirt, I bicycled down to our arranged meeting place in Hell's Kitchen. I went around the corner with him to do the deal, three others jumped out of a car and they all jumped me. One landed a good punch, closing my eye, but like a wild animal I managed to hold them off until I could get on my bike. One snagged his hand inside the little black bike bag I had around my waist and yanked hard at the same moment I dug hard into the pedals, and the canvas belt parted at the stitching. I took off, expecting a bullet; they took off for their car, expecting they had a lot more than just a beeper and $19. It all went down in a couple of minutes. Hah. For days I enjoyed the thought of them opening up the bike bag, seeing nothing in it. On thinking about it, they probably thought that *I* had come down to rob *them*.

By the time I left NYC, I had maybe five thousand dollars of accumulated profit, which was way more money than I'd ever had. Camron was upset about me leaving, and I made no commitments about my plans, but again I gave him trust and product enough to take care of things for a while. Told him he should've saved some of his money instead of buying all that expensive new spinning equipment and partying so much. He'd spent a couple thousand on his new sound system. Me, once I got into the devastated outback, I started getting mad at Al Gore for deciding not to run for president, handwrote him a letter asking him to please reconsider, and drove to a town that had a post office so I could Express Mail it. The postage was just drug money, which never seemed like real money anyway. Shit, with all that time on your hands, sometimes the outback will make you think too much and your brain overheat.

Daylight, south of Odessa. Much of Texas, the drier parts, always has this under-lying African feel to it. In its own scraggly rough way, it has a certain wild post-apoc-alyptic attraction, my no-man's land. One of my no-man's lands.

Winds strong, plastic trash from the oil fields snagged up in the roadside barbed wires, thorny mesquite everywhere, ravaged, scorched Earth, hard soil, grass strug-gling, desperate for rain and relief from cattle, still too early in the season for rain.... oil jacks nodding their heads up and down in the distance like gone-loco metal horses...not a person in sight... the roads empty for miles...

I pedaled, so glad for my mountain bike.

Riding is great, I thought. Shit, when my bike is taking me on more than just a ride, that's even better. Hah mutherfuckers.

Used to be all grass. Buffalo eat grass, not bushes, not mesquite, not seeds. Cattle, while not as bad as sheep and goats, eat everything, and they evolved in wet Eurasian climates, so their hooves and milling compact and ruin arid lands in an unnatural way. When the cattle came through, they consumed everything, and shit out the seeds, including the sparse mesquite. Woody brush grows well in disturbed, damaged soils. In parts of Texas mesquite has spread everywhere, rampaging over the grasslands in the cattle's wake.

Outside Odessa, I noticed a remnant prairie dog town, just a couple acres in size. It was an oval oasis, completely free of shrubs and woody invaders. I stopped at the side of the road, straddling the red bike. I could tell by the presence of grass both in and outside the oval, along with the absence of cow droppings that for some reason this little pasture had been free of cattle for quite a while. The grass on the prairie dog town was clipped and short, but greening, thick and healthy, not bare dirt like it would be if cattle had been here. And the site was crammed with wild grassland birds. Even this little prairie dog town held so much life, I thought. And it was only maybe two acres. At the turn of the century just one of Texas' prairie dog towns stretched 25,000 square *miles*! Thinking… if there is 640 acres to every square mile….

In some years more than 125,000 men had worked to poison as many as 20 million acres of prairie dogs. I heard it takes three days for a poisoned prairie dog to die, orifices boiling out in burning drool, and they are wracked with so much pain their normally loud outspoken selves sound like mourning doves, cooing and moaning with pain. If even on these couple acres there was so much health and abundance, I could just imagine all the other life that had thrived on that massive prairie dog town, an unimaginable explosion of life in size and number.

I smiled as I watched some prairie dogs act all kind of crazy, running, squeaking, rolling, tumbling, sitting up on their hind legs and yelling, or stretching out in the warming graces of the Sun to bathe.

"What's up Little Fatsos!" I said. "Don't let nobody mess with you or try to tell you who you are. You just keep bein' you. We need your little fat selves for the future!" I continued riding for miles, grabbing my turnoff onto a deserted road. The land in general was still very dry; it was the middle of March and not much was greening up yet. As I rode my bike down the back road under a faintly blue, cloudless sky, I finally found what I'd been looking for. *You're really stupid, being out here in broad daylight,* I told myself.

Ain't nobody here. I'm just some dude on a bike. They got a bike shop in town.
Man, you get caught… Why can't you wait till after dark?
Want to be long gone after dark.

Sure that there was nobody around, I hurriedly lifted my bike over the fence, then hopped over at the strong point next to the post, making sure I only stepped on grass or stones where I wouldn't leave footprints. I knew my tracks could be traced, if they found any and it came to that, but that would mean they would have to have suspicion, widespread investigation, evidence, me, and my vehicle. Not likely. And besides, I had taped the bottoms of my shoes with duct tape. Hah.

Grabbing my bike and ducking my head and shoulders down, I rushed away from the road about 50 yards before I laid the bike down and slid it on its side under a mesquite bush.

There is hardly anybody else out in this part of the country, anyway, I thought. Even on the paved roads I could ride for ten or more minutes without seeing another vehicle. The great thing about ranchers is that they almost never go anywhere on foot, they use their big shiny new pickup trucks to go everywhere. A careful *guerilla* who is mostly on foot can easily escape notice.

As far as I was concerned, I was the invisible man, my body molded with the land. If I wanted, I could slip in anywhere, private property or public, and nobody would notice. They were too busy stuffing their faces with Cheetos and burgers and bloody steaks and donuts.

I headed south onto the plain, winds slowly shifting from the south to the west. I didn't bother bringing water because I didn't plan on being long. I scanned the horizon 360 degrees. The thorny mesquites were at most about shoulder height; they offered extra cover. I suddenly had a thought, and placed my hand over the Bic lighter in my pants pocket. I should just set this whole thing on fire. It's dry enough. Fire cleanses and heals the prairie. That would clear out a lot of this mesquite, recycle the nutrients back into the soil and the grass. Fire was a prairie animal, too. I thought of this 19th century painting I had seen on the cover of a book by Peter Matthiessen called *History of Wildlife in America.* "Herd of Buffalo Fleeing from a Prairie Fire," by Meyer Straus, showed a great herd of buffalo thundering across a dry tawny sage-green plain, their tails held high, racing with some antelope and black wolves away from a giant prairie fire blazing orange-yellow-red that lit up the sky behind them like a flaring sunset. Dust was flying, breath was steaming out of the bulls' nostrils, the wolves' tongues were hanging out and red, the sky above was roiling in black smoke like an approaching thunderstorm with only a thin line of blue sky visible at the opposite horizon. It was a thunderous, extremely powerful image, one taken from real life in the not too distant past, from an area just like where I now stood.

I decided to stick to my original mission. About a mile out, I began cutting on the fence, keeping low, working on every few sections, cutting between posts. Since I had a lot I wanted to accomplish today, I didn't peel each section back, just some of them. This rancher had five strands of fencing, all the way down to six inches off the ground, so it took me longer. There were once at least 40 million antelope out here, "prairie ghosts" as they used to be called, along with 65 million buffalo and 5 billion prairie dogs. A couple of books had theorized why the antelope had hardly rebounded, once the wholesale killing had stopped. It was the fences. Antelope were strict open country animals and when an object came in their way, they simply walked around it. They didn't evolve in woods or brush, like deer, and never learned to jump over things. When faced with the new barbed wire fencing, they tried to crawl under. Many got snagged, the others simply were put to so much stress trying to survive in the overgrazed and fenced new world. Without places to live and spread out, they never were able to rebuild. With the fence wires strung so close to the ground, life became very difficult. I cut faster, new energy fueling my determination. *You really should be doing this at night,* said a voice inside my head.

At one point I stood up onto a bottom second strand, holding onto the weathered wooden post, scanning for any signs of my enemy. Sometimes you could come up on a house hidden in a ravine or behind a little roll in the land, even this far out.

I have to remember to be careful, that they are the lords of this land now, I thought, grimacing. They waged a war against the Indians and the animals for it; they'll use whatever means they need to keep it. All's fair in hate and war.

The cutters bit in, fought the tension. Bite, pierce, pop. In the distance, pump jacks nodded up and down, pulling oil — the Serpent World, according to Northern Plains Blackfoot legend, and not to be touched for fear of setting off great harm — out of the ground.

Bite, tension, pierce, pop. Pull the wire strand back. Spreading liberation a few feet at a time, I made my way down the fence line, glad for the little black cotton gloves I'd bought at a truck stop for $1.19.

Again: Wonder if I should just burn this whole thing down.

I felt for my lighter in my pocket. It was there. Never went without it, because you never know when you might get caught out. Least you can always make a fire.

Would those oil jacks explode?

You don't really want to do that… Might set off huge black clouds of burning smoke and flame like those fires the war set off in Kuwait?

Naaah…..

I exhaled. Stupid, brushy, ravaged, scraggly, flat country. I can hardly even tell what you used to look like, I thought.

Used to be straight-up grassland. Now you have to go all the way up to the panhandle to get away from the mesquite takeover. It's so bad that you get excited when you actually see grass left in areas. That grass can still grow.

Desertification is happening, at least this far west and south. Acknowledge that. It's spreading.

There's no goddamn Buffalo Commons. It's all in ruins. None of those people out there in the mainstream world or in the media have seen or even acknowledged what's really been done to the West. The land is dying. Not dying. Being *killed*.

Does that mean it's hopeless?

The wires pressing into my soles shifted and I swayed on the fence. I rebalanced. A little higher and I bet I could see a hundred miles. In a way it's still beautiful. With a little effort I can still imagine what the Earth used to look like. Maybe how it could be again with some work. I wish a big storm would come, with lightning strikes and everything.

I continued to cut, but of course the fenceline got longer and longer, the land got bigger, and I got smaller and smaller. Near evening, I finally gave up for the day and sat with my back against a fence post, absently pushing into the wood, enjoying its loose hold in the soil. I watched a big flying saucer of a storm cloud slide in, leaving only a rim of sky low at the horizon visible for 360 degrees all around like the edge of a big bowl, exposing a band of blue to the east, blue and yellow to the north and south, and blazing red orange like a prairie fire to the west. The underside of the cloud was contracting like a speeded up movie, as if wanting to start something. After all, it was late March in Texas.

I suddenly noticed an arrowhead, a tiny bird point lying in the dirt a few feet away. I reached for it and turned it over in my hands. Little more than the size of a penny, its blades sharp and paper-thin to perfection, it had been hand-carved out of flint by a master with stone-tool skills I could hardly imagine. I was honored and awed to touch something like that, in my own hands, that had been held and worked by rough hands hundreds if not thousands of years ago, right here on this plain.

The same winds that blew on my face had blown on that carver's. And on all the wild animals'. These same winds had blown into the hearts and faces of an alternate universe, when everything had been sacred, connected, primeval, haunted with life, eyes shining, and people and animals spoke with each other without having to speak.

The great orange ball of the Sun dropped below the storm cloud spaceship's western rim, sending a blare of orange and red light rippling across its roiling underbelly and liquefying my Odessa plain with clear light. The Sun's round bottom began to drop below the Earth's horizon. A streak of silent lightning flashed in the black cloud above, thrilling me.

I hid the bird point in the soil for another thousand years.

I began heading back, seething and toxic with anger.

I remembered reading how some of the settlers and rangers/militias were freaked out by the big sky and open prairies. Made them feel small, I guess. Such timid men, I sneered. To me the big open sky was like a wind-cloak around my shoulders, and I felt more comforted out in immensity than anywhere. Especially with the Sun blazing into me.

My mood changed, as I thought about the darkness of the night coming. Nights were hardest to deal with, but that wasn't because I was afraid. Hell, I've inhabited the dark my whole life.

Admit it. You're alone. And night reminds you of that. And maybe you don't want to be alone as much as you think you need or want to be. I conjured up another night sleeping in the back of the van, far from here. All alone as usual. Another night like a chasm to cross.

Fuck that. You're not alone, I told myself. What about the animals out here? You got it easy compared to them. Man up and quit your whining. All the surviving animals out here never get a break. They live under constant threat of persecution and danger their entire lives.

It's like a racial thing for the ranchers, I decided.

At least the coyotes and some of the antelopes are still here to carry the torch, although they have to live under extreme fire, especially coyotes. The buffalo survivors are imprisoned; they're America's longest held political prisoner. The wolves of the prairie and the grizzly bears (originally Plains animals), are all completely gone. Killed, not gone. They're killed. Dead. Not a single one left on the entire prairie from Mexico to Canada.

Nothing like militant thoughts to focus you on what's really important, I smirked to myself. I kept walking, the legs of my jeans scraping against thorny branches of mesquite. My taped hiking boots stepped carefully on grasses and stones, avoiding where possible the dry red dirt.

Not alone... All you need is God and Earth.

I am in Your service, I mouthed, voiceless, heart beating stronger than ever. I moved faster.

I looked down at my dusty jeans, boots. The animals are your brothers and sisters, wherever you go.

We're in this together now, you and them, feel me?

Further south, two days later, I stopped the car and got out. A female mule deer was hanging dead from the bristling wire fence off the side of the road. As I investigated, I saw that she had tried to jump over and gotten her left leg caught and twisted up in the top strand. It was snapped at the shin and hanging loosely, her black hoof pointing skyward. It must have been a horrible death, of shock, dehydration and struggle. Who knew how long it had taken for her to die? She was rigor-mortified cardboard now. Insects had gradually eaten out her asshole, then hollowed her guts out. From the signs of animal tracks in the dirt a few feral dogs and coyotes had nibbled on her, pulling out some of her guts, but I found it strange that they had left the most of her untouched.

I retreated further south, to the desert canyon lands of Black Gap east of Big Bend. I only meant to stay for a couple days, but again the quiet… The sense of being so hidden, so far away. The days and nights came and went. Not a single plane flew overhead for weeks. I couldn't leave. I climbed. I walked. I swam in the Rio Grande. Time stopped. Soon I couldn't tell whether it was Wednesday or Sunday, soon gave up trying. Weeks went by. I scrimped on food. A hundred miles of wild desert Mexico lay only a swim across the river. Huge four-foot-long catfish swirled in the muddy water. I felt exhilarated, and every time I thought about the outside world, and the rancher-politician-polluter hell, I quickly changed the subject. When I had a good mood swing, sensing opportunity and enthusiasm as wide as the sky stretching from here to that distant butte on the horizon so far away, I thought of the possibilities. When we rebuild the Earth's great wildernesses, there can even be room for wild aboriginal man again. When that happens, at that moment, I will disappear into the bush without once looking back. I'll forget the English language. I'll create my own. No wait, I won't even need to think in words anymore, but in sinuous emotion and feeling like the animals do. My hands and feet will know every rock and plant, every spring and streambank, every animal's way of being, every mile upon mile I walk through the grasslands and deserts. I will become the future-primitive, with every sense, every nerve, every molecule of my being and soul so precisely tuned it will be complete and effortless immersion into the primeval ancient wild, like — (*like what, like in your passouts? Then that means you'll finally be dead. Passed into the Shadow World once and for all, muthafucka.*)

Sweet acacia trees along the green banks of the wild Rio Grande buzzed with super-fragrant yellow puffball flowers and bees nearly shouting spring's firm arrival. Along each side of the river, long bands of fifteen-foot high river cane like giant grasses undulated, danced in unison with the winds blowing down from between the flat-topped buttes. I didn't know if the cane was native or not — I had the feeling it was probably a harmful invader — but it offered a jungle. The days soon grew hot. I became Jungle Boy in the canebrakes, and Desert Plainsman out in the open country, swimming, climbing, trekking, learning, thinking, thinking, thinking. At night I could hear the river water moving, when the wind temporarily stopped making the hollow cane stalks knock and flap their long green leaves. Each night I heard the javelinas, small barrel-bodied native black pigs with sharp tusks, running past me like little buffaloes, their hooves thudding the earth, and jumping into the river, squealing and splashing. I knew from reading that the Jumano people used to live here and would head north onto the plains to hunt buffalo. I found some of their *metates*, corn grinding holes, carved into riverside rockbeds. One night, when the wind stopped, I thought I heard singing or crying beneath the slow rapids. A woman's singing or crying. It's said the Jumanos were driven to extinction; the last that was heard of them was in the mid-1700s, though supposedly a few mixed-blood descendants were thought to still be living in the area around Ojinaga.

I kept glancing north. I knew the Southern Plains began about a hundred miles north of here. *Are you shirking your duty? You going crazy?* Everytime I closed my eyes I saw buffalo running into bristling wire fences, determined to tear them down, faces streaming red with blood, eyes blazing with anger.

But here there are no people. I can disappear. Live perfectly in balance with God and Earth. I can revert, *right now*, disappear for good, never speak again, become aboriginal. I know the plants to eat and wear. This desert is a garden. I can make shoes out of lechugilla fibers. There's a hundred miles of wild Mexico right across the river, just right over there. And nobody would ever know. And that would be that.

With a sharp stone I cut a willow sapling that was about half the thickness of my wrist. I sat and scraped the bark off, and shaved it down, then began working on a spear point, using my knife where needed, trying to push the images of the fence-tearing buffaloes out of my eyes.

Buffalo. America's longest held political prisoner, I thought. I scraped methodically at my emerging spear.

Nothing can live for long, perpetuate and thrive, under the bootheel of The Rancher.

I'm glad for this now, because I am *ready*. Come for me, I thought to my enemies. I'm ready. I've always been asked, 'What are you doing here!'

My mind began to overheat, as I thought to myself: I've never even seen a rancher walk more than ten feet. Outside of his monster new pickup truck, he is a fat, soft-bellied, belted and buckled, sunglassed, eyes-darting, constipated little man, I thought. But surrounded by his machine of steel, with all his guns and traps and poisons and wires and weapons of mass destruction, he is a Big Man, with the cops on his side. He is a man with KILL A QUEER FOR CHRIST bumperstickers. Inside his truck he is the Big Man with the ten-gallon hat who runs the bicyclist off the road or slows down and glares at the young man, demanding *"What are you doing here!"* He is the man who is threatened by somebody walking. Walking is subversive. You are not where you should be: in a car where you can be kept an eye on. He cannot and will not understand a language that includes integrating with the land/animals/ plants/ dirt/wind and all that is wild. He can't understand the importance of hearing a beetle scratching across the dirt 15 feet away. He is the Big Man who can sit back in his truck on a five-foot long tube of backed up shit and smile with that rotting beef jerky grin of his, look out over 100,000 acres of public land and gloat, "I own all that." Never mind that saying one can own *any* land is like saying one owns that cloud, or the sky, or a part of that star up there. Once his cattle spread out over the land, chew all the forage to the ground, starve the wildlife, trample everything, shitting everywhere; once his government agents in planes, helicopters, trucks, and on foot shoot, poison and trap the remaining wildlife, the Man feels himself spread out over the entire land. There is not one creek, stream, pond, river or lake in the West where a thirsty, exhausted person can drop to the ground and drink straight from it without getting giardia or some other disease.

I put the tip of the whittled spear in the fire, hardening it, then brought it back, working on the shaft and the tip more, scraping, honing.

The Grassland Earth is like this beautiful brown-skinned mother with long yellow grass hair who's been knocked down, beaten, strung up with bristling wires, raped....

But at some point her strength will re-emerge. She will rip those wires off; her natural cycles will return. Her spirit will come into people, propelled by the strong pumping adrenaline of her heart. Because the so-called "men" who shoved her down and drove their rusted stakes through her failed to reach her heart. As deep and painful as it was for her, they completely failed to understand that the Life Force was within, stronger and with more clean, fierce power than anybody could imagine, even herself!

I scraped and scraped furiously, hunched over the spear in my lap.

As she finally struggles to her feet, she'll clench in her fists those bloody coils of barbed wire she has ripped from her shredded womb. And she will stand there and look down at herself, at her body, and tears will begin to flow, so clear, so blue those tears from a deep spring; tears of relief and more than 500 years of sorrow will wash down her, run in rivulets first to those places most hurt, in need of cleansing, healing. She will stand there, drying in the Morning Sun, and she will know and accept that there will be scars. But dew sparkles, and like the new shoots of wild grass scattered after a thunderstorm and LEFT ALONE, hope and wellness will thrive over the scars. Like a native wild rose bush blooming over a barren dirt burial mound, her womb will bring forth new fresh Seed.

I put down the spear. I felt my lips curling. My teeth... they're—
I am in Your service.

A couple days later the river near me was assaulted by a group of slob fishermen, who drove in on big monster trucks. They tore up the delicate water hole that so many animals had depended on, threw beer cans and trash everywhere, and took shits everywhere, leaving their shit and toilet paper lying there.

I picked up a beer can I found by the torn up waterhole and walked silently up on one of the fisherman. His head seemed to wobble as I startled him. I thrust the crumpled can at him.

"You dropped something," I croaked, using my voice for the first time in weeks. My fingers were not shaking.

His cheeks puffed out and his face seemed to turn purple-red. He looked like he was thinking about a gun he had in his truck.

"This place is sacred," I grunted.

He looked at me like I was utterly crazy. My eyes glazed over his distended belly pushing at his shirt. He definitely had guns in his truck. I thought of the two knives

I had on me, my street knife in my pocket, and my buck knife attached by the sheath to my belt loop. I breathed hard.

I dumped the trash at his feet and walked away, unsure of myself in the company of people. These so-called humans.

I packed up and drove a mile or so back on the 26-mile long dirt road that would take me to the even-longer paved road that went a hundred miles further before civilization. The thought: *How pathetic is this? Even if you blew their truck up, you'd still be doing nothing.*

SECTION SIX

"It's really a wonder that I haven't dropped all my ideals, because they seem so absurd and impossible to carry out. Yet I keep them because in spite of everything I still believe that people are really good at heart. I simply can't build up my hopes on a foundation consisting of confusion, misery and death. ... I can feel the suffering of millions and yet if I look up into the heavens, I think that it will all come right, that, that this cruelty too will end, and that peace and tranquility will return again."

— Anne Frank, age 14

"There was no hope on Earth, and God seemed to have forgotten us."

— Mahpiua Luta (Red Cloud) of the Oglala Sioux

CHAPTER TWENTY

Crack Between Both Worlds

TROOPS ENTER RAVAGED LA said the Albuquerque Journal headline, dimly lit by the single fluorescent tube inside the tiny New Mexico town's closed gas station. It was getting dark. I'd made it back across the state border, back into New Mexico once again.

Earthquake? Out in the Big Bend/Black Gap backcountry, I'd been in a news blackout for weeks. I peered closer. Pictures of the City of Angels in flames. Rioting. Looting. No earthquake. The cops who'd been caught on videotape beating the crap out of Rodney King had been found "not guilty."

So that's why when I'd tried to call Lahumba from the payphone the recording kept saying, "All circuits are busy now. Please try your call again later,"

I went back to the glass pane phone booth. It stood by itself in the middle of nowhere at the side of the deserted road. A couple of its panes had long ago been busted out by the wind. It's folding door still closed, but why would anybody need to close it? For privacy? The next nearest store was 50 miles away.

Oh, I thought. The wind.

I called the operator and asked, "Do you know if this payphone takes incoming calls?"

Having done this — the discreet drug dealer payphone check — many times before, I mouthed her exact words in tandem with her as she replied, "No I do not, sir. But if you hang up, I can call you back. If it doesn't ring, then you know it doesn't." In some ways, things were easier in the early 90's for drug dealers. This would never happen now.

With the phone good, I called to the other coast, paging Camron, using my calling card, and put in my code O5 after the number. I settled down to wait, watching the occasional car pass on the secondary highway, knowing it would take Camron a while to call back long-distance.

Finally, he called. Everything had gotten all fucked up. He'd gotten people mad at him — something about him insisting he should've been let in free at one of the other clubs. And something with some other dealer's girlfriend. Also Joel and JT needed to meet with us. I shook my head. I knew it. I just knew he was gonna fuck shit up again.

Camron started getting loud at me on the phone. Why did I leave him hanging, he should take all the money but he didn't, he needed me to come back ASAP and mop up some things, because that was my job. He was the front man, I was "the one who is supposed to guide and handle and manage the business behind the scenes, and above all, you hear me, provide some back. Without *back*, Jihad, I'm just a single person small-timer out here against everybody else who's got crews. You need to come and handle your business, Jihad! I've been sitting around here, with nothing, waiting for you while you're out I don't know where doing what the fuck what! So you're gonna have to face it: I had to use some of this money to survive while I waited for you. You left me hanging."

I was starting to grit my teeth. Man, I hated all this. Leash around my neck. I had way more important things to be concentrating on.

"Alright, Camron," I said, "I heard you. Calm the fuck down."

"What's the fuck wrong with your voice, anyway. And you don't need to tell me to calm the fuck down."

"Nothing. I just had a little hoarseness. Guess from talking too much."

For some reason that seemed to quiet him down. "Yeah, I know you got it rough too, handling things on your side for the business, dealing with all them big-time folks out there in Cali and Mexico. They probably are real high-maintenance, I'm more than sure too. I just need you to come back so we can make some MONEY!"

"Well," I said, resisting inside. "I'll be back in a few days."

"Good. It's about time. You know how long you been gone? Almost half a year!"

"Naaah, it ain't been that long. Can't be."

"Yeah, man, for real. The whole world is changing, and it's gonna pass you by, too. You need to catch up, boy! Oh, by the way, I've got some bad news."

"I hate bad news. What."

"Miss Johnny died." He paused. "You know she had The Bonus, don't you? Well, yeah, she passed. We had a little thing at the club for her memory."

"Oh," I said, marking this point in time that the first person I knew had died from the disease. A gusting wind pushed into the phone booth, swirling grit, wobbling the remaining panes.

"Anyways, Joel and JT say we're top dogs now. So hurry back, all right?"

"Like I said, I'll be back in a few days."

"Now that's what I want to hear. Hit me up as soon as you get in. Travel safe. I'm out."

I concentrated my attention on the nearly subliminal, steady humming of the jet airliner as it flew east across America through the night sky. Every once in awhile, down on the ground below or far off, I saw a little cluster of pink-orange lights. As we flew out over the Plains, the clusters below mostly vanished into sprawling darkness.

I knew all below me was emptiness. I felt a thick longing to be out there, down there in the darkness, out between the far-flung clusters of lights, unseen. I felt like I was looking at the country from a satellite. So much had happened down there, and tonight, all was silent, dozing. I believed we were passing over the Texas Panhandle now. I was sure that was Amarillo down there.

In the book *Adobe Walls Wars: The Fascinating Yet True Story of the Last Indian War in Texas*, by Amarillo newsman and historian Bob Izzard, buffalo hunter/Indian fighter/Army Scout Billy Dixon says: "I heard a familiar sound. It rolled down into our ravine from the flat land of the plains. I had heard it often. It was deep, moving and not unlike the rumbling of a distant train passing over a bridge. This was what I had waited for. I had strained my ears for weeks and now it had come. I rushed to the top of the ravine and ran out where I could see across the flat prairie. There wasn't anything to see. I knew that, too. But the sound was enough. The buffalo were coming."

It wasn't until mid-morning that Dixon had seen the first few arriving bulls. He rode past eight miles of buffalo that only constituted the front of the herd. "You never forget seeing a herd of buffalo," he said. "I rode into the mass until, as far as the eye could reach, south, east and west of me there was a solid mass of buffalo. There were thousands upon thousands of them" all slowly moving north.

It was 1874 and the numbers were thinning rapidly now. In the Southern Plains alone five million had been killed between 1872 and 1873 when the price was 50 cents a hide. Over in Fort Worth, auction sales in 1873 and 1874 were off the chart; at one point over 200,000 hides were sold in two days. During the hot season, buffalo hunters would line the Canadian River that cut across the Texas Panhandle, and as the buffalo would come in to drink, shooters would blast into them. Buffalo can go two or three days without water, and can travel vast distances, but they still need to be within a couple days' walk of live water. The survivors would run off, only to be forced back by thirst to try to drink again, and get shot at again, and in this form of torture, with survivors eventually driven mad by thirst and the smell of water within reach but unattainable, they would all be killed.

By 1874 the price was two dollars and fifty cents a hide. Kansas hunters had come down to join the slaughter, thinking all 'their' buffalo had gone to Texas (but what had really happened was those buffalo up there had mostly been shot out already). Dodge City, the nearest white settlement on the Southern Plains, was 150 miles north of Adobe Walls. The only roads were wagon trails and Indian horse and foot paths. Dixon shot enough buffalo to keep the skinners "busy for several days." Skinners made fortunes — at twenty-five cents a hide. Marianne Goodnight, wife of rancher Charles Goodnight, who "owned" the 3 million acre XIT ranch, was being driven crazy by the constant rifle shots of the sharpshooters killing buffalo day in and day out across the High Plains prairie. She pleaded for her husband to save some buffalo, and that's how a few animals of the Southern Herd were saved.

"Face it," Dixon had said to Bat Masterson. "There is no sentiment in this business. It's dollars against tenderheartedness and dollars won."

In Lubbock, TX there is a historical marker sign in Yellowhouse Canyon:

1877 Migration of Wolves

From 1877 until 1880, large packs of wolves were seen in the Yellowhouse Canyon vicinity. Traveling northwest at a rapid pace, they were presumed to be leaving the area in front of encroaching human settlements. Don Biggers, an early booster of Lubbock, described the scene: "It was of course impossible to ascertain the number with any degree of accuracy. But there must have been several thousand of them. They were probably twenty abreast, and the pack must have been two or three miles in length." W.S. Glenn, an early buffalo hunter, recalled seeing the wolves at another place, still traveling rapidly toward the northwest.

No such thing had ever been witnessed before, or since. The buffalo wolves, known for their superior size, superior intelligence and otherworldly perceptions, knew their End Days were at hand. Desperate for food, poisoned, burned, dragged, pulled apart alive, and shot on sight, the remaining wolf nation struck out on their exodus in front of the horsemen of the Apocalypse. As they reached into New Mexico and Colorado area, they were dispersed and hunted to extinction.

Eventually we passed over Oklahoma City or Wichita, and the light clusters began to increase, then expanded rapidly eastward from there. Then, Kansas City loomed, and we were completely out of the West. The lights were back on.

You can usually tell a crackhead by his face. Not always, but usually. The face is shiny or waxy, looks stretched, Often there are a couple dark red almost purple spots that look like pimples but stubbornly stay around, the skin being the barometer of the body's internal health. But mostly it's the eyes.

A crackhead regularly shifts back and forth between three phases. When the person is straight, when they're not actually on the pipe, unless the person has become physically emaciated by long use you wouldn't notice a thing. The second stage is when their mind has suddenly shifted to thinking about getting high again. That's when the danger begins because it's seamless and can catch you off guard. There's a dark hungry desperation inside that thinks (but doesn't reveal) "I would easily kill you for three dollars, actually I would love to do it just to do it if I didn't have at least some self-control." The third stage is the demon itself, the high, the Pipe, the crazed zombie takeover of the individual, the teeth-gritting, eyes-popping, sweating, slicing, slashing return of the living dead.

One night I was crossing 10th Avenue and this overheated crackhead came zigzagging at me wildly in the middle of the street with his knife, just zeroing in on my abs for no reason: It was like he just had to cut out my abs, just slice them wide open, and that steaming pile of agony would be the most satisfying thing. The traffic lights changed and cars honked as they raced down around us and I danced out of his way, leaving him to stumble blindly to the other side, his skin shining darkly in the headlights.

As I went to press the button to be let into Hotel Hell up on CPW, the hazy midsummer NYC sun burning into my neck, I noticed Cindi standing inside the glass doors, waiting for somebody. She pushed the door open and smiled "Hi Cutie" in her grainy, part-time crackhead voice.

"Thanks," I said as I passed, looking at her out of the corners of my eyes.

The front desk shifts were fitting for Hotel Hell, that is, they had to be hell. 6 a.m. to 6 p.m., and 6 p.m. to 6 a.m. Only Bangladeshis applied for the job. Amjad, the young guy who was constantly super-horny and drooling over every fat sweaty white female —"Oh I must get some!" "So much to love! Oh fuck I cannot believe it" — did the long graveyard 6 at night to 6 in the mo'ning. Two other guys worked part-time and between them split the open shifts. Susan the British bitch manager only came in during the day, and that was to count and pinch every penny and yell.

A gaudy, oversized, hanging glass chandelier, some mirrors on the wall, the elevator, and the stairwell going up to the left of the elevator shaft made up the small lobby. Two payphones (which took incoming calls) were stuck to the wall by the basement stairs.

Heading up to my room, I hopped up the stairs two by two, on each landing passing an overflowing garbage can, eyes wary for tossed-in-the-trash glue-trapped mice with their quivering eyes bulging out, till I reached the sixth floor. This plainsman didn't need no machine to carry him up stairs. I went down the dark blue carpeted hall, took a right and went to my room. It had a sink, a bed, a little round table with a chair, and a chest of drawers. It was just a small, stanky square box, but it was private. It didn't occur to me that I could've gotten something nicer like an apartment share. Sometimes, buried assumptions of inferiority built in long ago permeate your day-today without you even knowing it. Maybe unconsciously it's all I thought my "dirty, less-than" self deserved. Plus, the anonymity, privacy, and freedom to come and go at a moment's notice without having to mess with anything official or aboveground was my main priority. My real home was out West anyway.

I locked the door, let the drape loose over the window, and went to lift out the half-full plastic grocery bag from the little trash can. Reaching down to take out the rubber-banded stacks of money I'd hidden beneath the bag, I got down on my knees on the floor. They were in thousand dollar stacks. Two piles were in hundreds, eight others in twenties. One was the miscellaneous pile, unfinished, with 5s, and 10s. I lined them up, and pulled open my backpack. Sticky, hot and humid in here. Couldn't turn on the fan yet because it'd blow the loose bills around. Sweat trickled down the middle of my back, making my t-shirt stick to my skin. Pulling a wad out that was folded in half, I quickly went through the new stash and aligned the bills all right side up, then began thumb-flipping the 20s, 10s, 5s into piles on the floor, counting them out like a banker pro. After adding in the new $1200, I separated out the grands I needed, then put everything back in the bottom of the trashcan beneath the plastic bag. I packed up my backpack, and set it on the bed.

I peeled off my shirt and went to clean up in the little sink. As I splashed water on my face, I wondered what else was going on in this old hotel, all these little rooms stacked on top of each other, separated by walls so old that you could sometimes hear rats tumbling down between.

Least in Hotel Hell, nobody asked about nothing. That privacy made it all worth it.

I went out into the hall to go down to the bathroom, glad I didn't have to take a shit. It was a struggle to find a clean seat in this hotel. My floor's bathroom usually had a problem and I had to climb flights to find a usable one, my bottles of hydrogen peroxide and rubbing alcohol in hand. Most of the time, the bathrooms had backed up toilets, shit floods, razors, blood, needles, urine smeared everywhere. Maintenance would eventually clean it, only for it to return like that sooner or later. Shortly after I'd returned to the city, I had gotten knocked out of commission for nearly two weeks from touching my right eye after touching the faucet. Fifteen minutes later my eye was infected, running and bloody; it felt like glass was under my eyelid. It spread from one side to the next, and back. Each blink was painful; I could hardly see. Finally it went away.

I peered around the open door into the prison-white bathroom with the cabinet door that wouldn't close. It was clean, except for one puddle of urine in the corner between the toilet and the shower.

I took my piss, by habit still conscious of where I stepped, then went back and grabbed my gear and bike. Susan said I should be thankful for 6th floor inside, which I got because I was now considered a regular. Others got the lower ones, and faced outside directly onto the noisy street. Hotel Hell's top floor was the cleanest, mostly old bag-n-cat ladies who'd lived there year-round for a long time. The rest of the hotel was occupied by mental outpatients, crackheads, hustlers, prostitutes, political refugees from Iraq, Pakistan, Bangladesh, and Afghanistan, and a group of tall black drag queen hookers who clacked their tongues at me and who fought amongst themselves over everything. The girls would share cab rides down to far West 14th Street, where they worked nights soliciting truckers with license plates from places like Wyoming, bitching all the way.

Throwing my bike over my shoulder, I hauled my ass down the stairs, again two at a time. Stairs were nothing compared to the terrain of plains, deserts, and canyons.

I went out into the Saturday afternoon, the thick, steaming air enveloping me. The Sun was a ball of burning haze through the smog. The northernmost end of Central Park was directly in front of me; forty-foot-high rock formations, scraped down by the glaciers thousands of years ago, had raggly trees growing out of their tops and formed a makeshift wall to the 105th, 106th, and 107th blocks of Central Park West. I fixed my bike glasses on, looked down CPW at the city, and gritted my face. Standing up on the bike I slipped one foot then the other into the traps, bore down on the pedals, and shot off the wide concrete step, landing on the sidewalk, then hopped again off the curb, the fork RockShox cushioning the contact as I hit the street. Speeding downtown, dodging traffic and pedestrians, snippets of conversations whipped into my eardrums telling me the news and mood of the city's day. As I got down into the wealthier part in the 80s and 70s, my bike velocity began setting off the first warning clicks of parked car alarms as I sheered past. Click-click, click-click, click-click like dominoes. In no time, I was in the 50s, and cut over to Hell's Kitchen.

"Normally, we don't have people come up to the house," said Pops, the white-haired, white-mustachioed *don* of the Family. "But it's ok. It's why I ask you to come. Take a seat." I leaned my red mountain bike up against the wall by the door and sat down on the edge of a lounge chair. He pulled over a chair from the dining table.

The public housing apartment was spacious, though cluttered in that Puerto Rican extended-family way. A young girl, nearly swallowed in an overstuffed green chair, cradled her baby. Small fans whirred from bookshelves and tabletops with lacy coverings over them, creating an artificial but comforting sense of coolness and fresh air inside this space sixteen stories up. His wife sat on the couch, staring at the tv, the top a garden of family photographs framed in gold, some planted a long time ago.

The grandma brought me a plate of yellow rice and peas with moduros — ripe, black, fried platanos — wedged onto the side.

"Thank you," I said, peeling off my bike gloves. Behind closed doors was great — if you had sufficient trust that you wouldn't get caught in a trap. I had gotten used to doing my acquisition business outside, often in the Park, acting like I was fixing my bike, in the anonymous ebb and flow of people.

"You know and we know that you are doing a good job, you keep your hands clean, and you do not get yourself involved in all the mess. This is why we invite you up here. You are a good client who handles his business," Pops said.

Eating, I nodded.

"But you know, people are starting to know about you."

"What do you mean?"

"Is no problem right now, it is going to happen. Pero we just want you to stay at your level of exposure and no more. You understand, right? No mas."

"Don't worry. I just ride my bike. I'm just a bike athlete, just the dude who rides and keeps to his self."

"It's good. We just need you to remain the anonymous, you know what I'm saying?"

"All good. You know I keep a close eye, without looking like I'm keepin' a close eye. I ain't like any of the others. I don't care about any of that flashy shit." And I thought: Nobody notices anything, but I notice everything, and slip through everything. I appear only when I need to, to make sure shit stay straight. Where I need to put a back on some things. That's it.

"We have many business operations, Jihad." He pronounced it Yihad. "I'm sure Anita tell you this. We don't like attention."

I heard the grandma washing dishes. The tv and the fans seemed to blend into a background of low humming noise. The young girl rocked her baby, her bent-down clean face a moon with slicked, pulled-back Latina hair, hovering over a smaller moon. Outside it was getting dark. "I'm cool," I said. I put the empty plate down on the coffee table and the grandma instantly came to take it, aware of everything going on in the apartment but acting like she was in her own world.

"That was very good," I said to her. "Gracia."

She nodded and smiled.

"OK. We don't have to say more. I know you sell to a lot of those gay people, and some can get loud. Miss Johnny, we knew her, but never sell to her. And she don't buy from us. The problem — too many people know — knew — what she do."

Yeah, but sometimes I sold your stuff to her, I thought. "She had her own connect," I said. "So, the reason you bringing this up — there been some problems?"

He glanced out the window, and I had the sense that he was seeing his whole extended *familia*. I knew they'd been up in this apartment and in this biz a long time.

"Everything is fine," he said, as if deciding right then to change the subject. "You have to come to Puerto Rico some time. Come visit."

I nodded, knowing that both of us knew that would never take place. We weren't tight like that.

"So what you need today?"

"A thou."

"That's good." He pulled over a black bag. "You should not carry these with you, when you go downtown to meet Martin."

"Pops, I almost never have anything on me. I keep product on me the shortest amount of time. Like I said, I'm just 'the bike guy'." I nodded confidently at him. I knew everything was chancing shit, that no matter what, it was all a big risk, but each time, I calculated that risk and made my next move and decision from there.

We exchanged money for goods. My dealings with any of the Family were the only transactions where neither party counted the money or the product as it passed hands. That did say something about the trust — though I always checked afterwards, and I'm sure they did too.

"You remember Martin. Meet Martin at his house, then you can go from there. You pick up your client, and then go to Steve, on Bleecker Street. Steve is the white guy who has the pills, the tabs. Martin he know where the address is."

"I know it'd be easier if the customer'd take the caps," I said. "But he only wants the tabs. Too afraid of people cutting."

"Like I said, is OK. You just have your client leave the money with Steve, OK?"

"There he is," I told Martin, finally seeing the new client in the last of the daylight. "Wait here." I crossed West Broadway, just south of Houston. Ralph, this white dude from Philly, was in the payphone, the phone to his ear. Something about him looked different. He looked disheveled. He was wearing a blue flannel shirt and some old jeans. I moved in on him.

"Sup," I said sternly, as he saw me and hung up the phone. Something about him… "You got everything? The money?"

"Hey how's it going," he said. "Yeah." Was that perspiration on his forehead?

I put it out of my head. I needed this money. Big wholesale deal. The thing about deals was to just get through the pressure of the actual transaction as soon as possible, which only took a couple minutes most. The buildup stress to those few moments was what often fucked shit up.

"Come on. That's my partner Martin." We began walking. I prepared him. "Everything's gonna be straight up. We go over to Bleecker, meet the connect, everybody lay their shit out on the table like grown folk, we each count, and we go. 1 —2 — 3, just like that."

A car passed in front as we crossed. I automatically held my breath past its backdraft to avoid inhaling its fumes, and for a moment thought of how I'd become so ingrained to the street that I'd stitched myself into its rhythms. Half of me was the wild outback man who hated the whole 'humandustrial' world and did everything to keep separate from it; the other half was so attuned to every big and minor aspect of urban life it was natural and second-nature. Only when I went against my own intuition did I fuck up. Nothing could touch me otherwise. At least on the street. What mattered, and was still unresolved, was my West.

"Martin, this is Ralph, from Philly."

Martin cut his eyes at me. "What's up," he said to Ralph, almost sneering. "How'd you get here?"

Ralph said, " I took the train. But hey, I don't know about having two people. You guys could jump me."

"Look, you want this?" said Martin. " We don't have to do this. It can be some other time. Hey Jihad, this is your client. Where'd you meet him?"

"All right everybody. Relax," I said. I turned to Ralph. "We do this the way we need to do this — straight and out in the open. Calm, cool, and collected."

To Martin I said: "He came to us through a contact of another client.

"Well. I don't know," Ralph said. "I came all this way."

"What are you acting so nervous for?" Martin said to him.

"I'm not nervous, I just — "

"What?" I said to everybody. I wanted the money. "I said, relax."

This needed to smooth out. My wires were starting to go up. I ignored it. This was a pretty big deal and I could net 4 Gs profit. "Come on," I said. "It's just a few blocks up, let's get this over with." I just wanted to get to the other side of the deal.

"We can do this some other time," Martin said. "It ain't no thing."

"Come on," I said again, putting the shoulder strap of my simple duffel bag diagonally across my chest.

Martin and I walked forward, with Ralph following in the rear. Martin was a no-bullshit, dark-skinned dude, with low cut hair, rarely wore a cap. He was engaged to a very pretty Dominicana named Rafaela.

At the building we took the elevator up in silence. Ralph smelled like lunchmeat.

Steve opened the door as we knocked.

"Hey Steve," I said. "How's it goin'?" Martin just nodded to him.

He looked out at us. "What's up, guys. Come on in." There was another guy in the apartment, standing behind him. You could tell that Steve was gay. They both were.

Ralph crowded in behind me and Martin. "I don't feel comfortable going in," he said. "We need to do this right here."

"Look," I said. "Like I said. We go in. We sit down at the table, each count out our shit, steady and calm, like professionals. Then we leave."

"Are you in a hurry?" Steve asked Ralph.

"Well, sort of." He seemed to be getting redder in the face.

"Man, come on!" Martin said. "We don't do this in the hall like this."

"I'm not coming in," Ralph said.

I gritted my teeth and turned to Ralph. "Look. You got the money?"

Ralph nodded.

Martin looked at Steve, then at me. We were all sweating in the hot hallway now.

"Lemme see it," I said. "Rodger, you got the product?"

Steve's friend held up a brown paper shopping bag with corded handles on it.

"I think we need to say we tried, and just call it a day," Steve said.

Ralph pulled out a folded-over large white envelope from inside his shirt. "The money's in here." He held it back, close to his body.

"All right," Steve said, half-turning to take the brown bag from his friend. "This is not how we do business. We'll count it right here."

Ralph lunged and snatched the bag, tossing the white envelope at him. I whipped around at the motion. He bolted down the hallway, opened the EXIT door, and disappeared down the stairwell.

"It's just cut out pieces of paper!" Steve said, ripping open the envelope.

"Hell no," I said, racing after Philly dude.

As I hurtled down the stairwell two, three, four steps at a time, I heard the door above swing open and Martin follow. "I bet he's heading downtown," I yelled back, catching a glimpse of a blue flannel shirt out the door. "I'm on him!"

"Right behind you," Martin yelled.

I tore out onto the street and ran. Fuck. Fuck! No fucking way! Ten thousand dollars wholesale worth of shit in there. I turned the corner on West Broadway. Man I fucked up. I saw a glimpse of him rounding another corner. I geared up my pace, knowing I was in better shape.

He turned on Spring Street. Behind him by about thirty seconds I followed, gearing in harder, running down through the warehouses in SoHo, the sticky night air streaming around me like a molten fitted mold. He had a good headstart but I was slowly gaining. He was running for his fucking life. Hah. I glanced behind me and saw Martin following, far back. The streets were largely empty, a few cars, people, nobody paying any attention.

I bolted across Broadway; saw dude turn right on Lafayette. He ran diagonally across the street. He was in reach now. I bore in some more, pounding down the sprint. He pulled out a knife and held it up as he fled, shiny blade glinting back the streetlights, his arm swinging by his side, the other clutching the bag like a football.

I caught up to within ten paces of him and he shot his eyes back, looking crazy at me, his eyes wide. He ran harder, brandishing the knife.

"Throw the shit down!" I yelled between breaths at his back. Without losing pace, I reached into my bag and pulled out my big stainless steel, black-handled buck knife as he swiveled his eyes back again at me like a hunted cow. His head jerked with the realization that I also had a blade. I ran even harder, still ten full strides behind him. I held that distance and pace momentarily, giving him the option of throwing the shit down.

"Man, talk about a fuckin' punk!" I yelled to his back, gulping down air. "You a fucking pussy. You gon'… get yours… and so… your friends. You don't cross me … over anything, let alone… some fucking services. Just throw the shit down!"

He jumped into Canal Street between two cabs speeding west. I shot right through behind him. He ran across the eastbound lanes, then back west across Lafayette to the corner. He suddenly slowed and I nearly ran right up on him just as he threw the bag down and swung fast around at me, slashing the blade. I braked as hard as I could at the same time tried to throw myself into reverse and jerk backward. I fell off the curb, tripping, my back hitting the oily pavement with a thud, my knife flying out of my hand. He jabbed his knife down toward my stomach and I knew this was it, I saw the blade coming, it was going right into my abdominals. I scrambled to push back and gain some distance but knew it was gonna be too late.

A wire mesh trashcan appeared out of nowhere and slammed into his torso. Martin had suddenly appeared.

Dude fell backward, dropping the knife. The half-full trashcan rattled to the sidewalk, spewing litter and gnawed chicken bones. Martin overshot and nearly fell over both him and the trashcan, but caught himself. Philly dude jumped up looking like worn-out wild-eyed hell, grabbed his knife and ran down the subway stairs.

We ran for the paper bag, snatched it and ran into the street. A yellow cab was coming, its 'available' roof light on. We tried to flag it down, it slowed, then saw us close up and sped off. We ran across Canal, and as we got in the shadows of the buildings slowed momentarily to stuff the baggied drugs into my bag then jammed the paper bag into a trashcan. We ran as fast we could up the cobbled middle of Wooster Street, then jumped onto the sidewalk, heading back toward Bleecker, not knowing if the Philly dude had others waiting for him, might be coming back, or what. I realized I'd left my knife where I'd fallen.

Running full speed, Martin said, barely audible under his breath, "Man... we lucky."

Out of the wall of an abandoned building right into our paths stepped two heavyset cops strapped to the nines in guns, clubs, badges and everything a cop could ever want or need.

Their eyes jumped in surprise and they grabbed for their guns as we literally slammed to a halt less than two feet from hitting them.

"Drop everything! Hands on your heads! Right now! Against the wall!"

The words sounded like the whole world was a cavern, not just this deserted old street, not just the hollow hard pounding sweating thudding of my racing heart, but the whole world. A cavern, and I was now... slammed to a halt. Arrested. Blown out.

I collapsed face first into the wall, lacing my fingers behind my head, spreading my legs, gulping air, streaming sweat, trying to catch my breath.

Martin was doing the same thing.

I heard only bits of what the cops were saying... only dimly felt the one on me, his hands molding over every part of my body... "This guy's heart is beating so hard I can feel it through his back..." Questions... Unable to answer... From what I could tell, Martin neither. They moved him paces down from me.

I could hear them unzipping my bag, dumping everything out. A notepad. A bunch of baggied drugs. What else did I have in there? Shiny-shoed feet crushing and grinding open a couple of the bags. Asking each other, "Can coke be made into pills?" Calling on the radio for help. Radio crackling about a called-in report of somebody being chased by two suspects with knives. Squad car was going down to Canal area to check things out. Asking Martin questions.

Suddenly I heard Martin telling the cops that it was us who had been chased by the guy; it was the guy who had the knife; the dude had pulled out the knife on *us*.

(Which was true.) That's why we had been running. Dimly I thought Martin's voice sounded different. He was acting odd.

Cop cars rushed in, filling the street, though we didn't dare turn our heads. Sirens died down; cop car lights flashed white red blue strobes, making my shadow against the brick wall seem to shake and dance.

What the hell are you doing here! You're supposed to be out West. You really fucked up this time.

Cops talking some more. I could hear them poking, peering at the smashed drugs and my belongings. Again, more talk, wondering if coke could be made into pill form. I closed my eyes, willing my heart rate down.

I saw my little bed inside my little room in Hotel Hell, a paradise of sanctuary all my own, where I could close a door behind me, be all alone. I saw myself on my expensive red mountain bike, the nicest thing I'd ever owned, and the freedom it gave me. I saw my upcoming prison cell, it was too late now, no toilet seat, everything stunk, everything bare metal, my cell mate taking a shit right next to my trying-to-sleep head, cigarette smoke, filthy white bread food, cramped for, what, five years? Seven years? Not a minute of privacy or sunlight, for years now. My head wouldn't be able to make it. You just gon have to make it. You fucked up. Man you fucked up. I thought of the sunlight out West… the sunshine…

Again, dimly I heard Martin, and this time realized he was talking to me, but loud enough for the cops to hear. And he was talking in a sporty, caring, boyish voice, when Martin was basically a stone-cold thug. "You o.k., baby?" he said in a nice, loud-enough voice. "Don't worry. We made it. The officers will figure everything out. We're just lucky neither of us got stabbed or even killed. Boy I can't wait till we get home. You gon' take a shower with me, huh boy? Don't worry. Everythin' gon be alright."

My heart rate dived lower and lower. I kept my eyes closed, trying to think. My head was a little tight, but I could hold on. No passout coming right now… Thinking hard, that's all. A voice, insistent: "*You have to THINK!*" Mentally I pictured the act of my eyes closing, and that helped, that opened something. My West… Shower… Shower? *Martin's actin' gay!* Cops talking… all up in your bag, in your business….The West. Being healthy. My West. Sun. The sunlight. Sun-*shine*…

"They're ZINC," I blurted with calm exasperation, loud enough for everybody to hear, my eyes closed, forehead pressed against the bricks, hands loosely clasped behind my head. "I got them at Whole Foods. Right up on Prince Street. The large economy bottle — $19.99. TwinLab brand. 50 milligrams. For my friend *Sunshine*. It's just zinc. We're supposed to go out to Queens tomorrow to see her. I just packed them like that because they're easier to carry. Sunshine and her moms haven't been feeling well, and Whole Foods has the best deal. So I got them a supply. You're supposed to take two a day… with meals, because if you take zinc on an empty stomach it might make you nauseous."

"And we were just coming from dinner in Chinatown," Martin chimed in, "when this crazed white guy with a knife jumped us like he was on crack or something, and he almost stabbed J here when he fell. We barely escaped! That's why we were running so fast. We'd just gotten away, but weren't sure. You got the wrong people. You're letting the real perpetrator get away!"

I thought I began to notice a confusion rolling through the pile of cops behind us. I heard another cop car pull in to the already jammed block. A woman lieutenant walked up, talking to the officers, handing them something. A knife had been found down on Canal.

"What's this knife, then?" one of them asked me, coming up to my side.

Eyes still closed, I said, "I work out West part time. It's just a fishing knife. I just got back not so long ago. I missed my boy, here. It's just been in my bag since then and it fell out when I fell. Dude almost killed me. If Martin hadn't been there I'd be dead right now."

I imagined the cops looking at each other as to what to do. They conversed. Minutes passed. A car door opened and closed.

"There's a law against knives in the city," the officer said. I felt something passing in the air. I would not allow myself to hope. He seemed uncertain about fishing knives, even though it was an all-purpose buck knife. I heard cop cars leaving, pulling out!

Finally, one of them said, "Ok you both can put your hands down. Pick up all your stuff and go home. We don't want to see you out here this late at night. You," he said to me, "I'm gonna have to confiscate your fishing knife, and write you a ticket, but you can just pay the fine, I think it's like $50. You guys need to be careful out here."

"Yes sir," we both said. "Thank you."

"Sorry about the mix-up," Martin said.

As I cleaned up all my belongings and stuffed them into the bag, the remaining cops left. I was too stunned to think or say anything.

"Here, give me a bag of those," Martin said. "Steve need to be glad he gettin' any of his shit back. This is our pay. You need to take one too." He glanced at the smashed white powder on the sidewalk. "The cops wrecked two bags, but this is still everybody's lucky day. Except for that Philly dude. We need some info, and we ain't finished with him."

"Man, I first thought somethin' was wrong with you," I said. "When you started talkin' like that."

"Shit. Back when Koch was here, and way before him, the cops acted however they wanted for years and years. But when David Dinkins came in as mayor, he made the cops take training about them gay people. Those were specific orders." He smiled, a big, silver-capped smile. "But still, you best go home and say a prayer of thanks. I will too. Zinc?! Where the fuck you come up with that! Shit."

"Not to mention me tripping over that curb and almost gettin' my guts cut out. Thanks, man. Why people always trying to cut my stomach, anyway?"

Man, if this ain't a warning sign, I don't know what is. What the fuck you doing? You supposed to be out West, in the outback, fighting that battle, and looking for what you supposed to be looking for.

Sand Creek Still

A bike really is more than a bike, for real. It's freedom and spirit.

After 2 a.m., at the lower end of Manhattan. Soon I'd be gone again out of New York. That thought lifted me like the whitecaps off the waves in New York Harbor. Need to get to the heart of the West. Need to have it permeate me to the deepest level of my flesh and blood and soul. Need to become it, through sacrifice and supplication, whatever it took. Maybe then I would finally find that one last sacred, safe place that I knew in my passouts.

It was the only thing that mattered.

I rode around and around in circles and figure-eights on the great empty plaza at the base of the World Trade Center, dimly illuminated in the lower yellow lighting, bike tires silent on the smooth slate. The mid-Atlantic night was warm for November. I looked up at the Towers. So high I couldn't see their tops from down here.

Riding a bike is like conscious meditation. It not only takes the edge off aggression, but it helps you think.

It was November 1992. Least Bush is over with, I thought with relief as I left the Towers.

Thanksgiving was coming up…

Fuck people and their Thanksgiving. I knew the real story now. This year, 1992, made it 500 years of genocide. Last month all that big celebration of Columbus Day. 500 fucking years. Back before being wrecked, this land, this whole continent, something about it was so sacred, so silent, no noise, no machines, everything intact, so much going on here. Before everything was shattered, I bet something really was going on here. So much life, so much intricacy, every square foot, every living being connected in holiness, a spirit of something so powerful… the world had been a jungle and a plain of open and evolving secrets, one wrapped and inserted into another and another, everything connected, silent, glowing with secret life, sacred. You could even drink straight from every lake, creek, river or stream, kneel right down, put your face right in and drink. Now disease from just a drop. Everything violated.

I wondered what happened in that exact moment in time upon contact with Columbus' ships. When the first animal and Indian eyes looked out to sea and saw those ships approaching, did a ripple of dread reverberate backward across the heaving continent? Did the heads of every passenger pigeon, Carolina parakeet, salamander, luna moth, buffalo, prairie dog, wolf, wapiti, panther and pickerel suddenly turn inexplicably to the east, sensing something with a great, horrible foreboding, and shudder?

I thought about Columbus, and then the Spaniards, and then the Pilgrims, all armed with greed, hate and quivering fear. Puritans called it "the waste and howling wilderness." New people then spread across the land in an orgy of killing like they were possessed by demons. How could they have hated something so beautiful and indescribably holy? It was like they were rabid, foaming at the mouth, to destroy everything. Why? Why?? Barry Lopez wrote in last month's New York Times, on the 500th anniversary of Columbus' arrival, about the difference between imposing and proposing. Nobody had seemed to think anything was wrong with this killing and killing and killing. Things could have been different. People could have acted differently, set examples, shown true leadership, people from all races could have shared ideas equally, and the world could have evolved into the modern era without the race wars, the horrors, the killings, the wanton slaughters and massacres and destruction, defiling and violating everything.

Instead we have de-evolution.

But wait, hasn't that been total human history from the get-go?

Well, I thought, gearing down on my pedals, if they want war, they got war.

I rode and revved myself up over all the world's problems until I got completely exhausted. My mood dropped abruptly. Just want to find one place, hide, disappear, be quiet forever, disappear into my West where in places you can almost touch how it once was. And leave everything and everybody behind, once and for all, forever. Put an impermeable wall between me and them.

On the road again. Can't stay in the city. Had a little '82 Toyota Corolla now; bought it in Vegas. Cold, crackly-dry, windswept Colorado plains… It was the 128th anniversary of the Sand Creek Massacre on Colorado's southeastern plains. On November 29th, 1864, something very bad happened at Sand Creek, in the middle of designated Cheyenne and Arapaho buffalo hunting grounds that were supposed to be permanent between the Arkansas and Smoky Hill rivers.

Out of a blur of gore two images stick:

A little Indian girl, maybe 5 or 6 years old, runs for her life up the dry creek bed. Her sleep-tangled long black hair flaps behind her. She had no time to put on her moccasins. But she doesn't feel the sharp stalks, burrs, and rough brush that scrape her legs and soles of her feet as she flees for her young life. She only hears the screams and wails of relatives and repeated rifle blasts advancing rapidly behind. Horrible other sounds — familiar voices of sisters, mothers, aunts, playfriends — pleading, the sounds of bodies being split open. The continuous boom of guns. And the eye-rolling terror of *these* sounds these footsteps right behind her, the pursuing footsteps of big grown men running after her, coming to hurt her, attack her, they won't leave her alone they just won't (oh please please no please leave me ALONE!) leave her alone. Catching up to her.

The little girl throws herself face down into the creek bed. Like a bottomfish she squirms back and forth into the sand, digging frantically deeper, trying to bury herself, hoping, praying, *praying* they don't see, didn't see her duck out of sight in the sparse cover of grass.

The creek sand is cold and wet. Down as far as she can go. She snaps the trembling out of her body, staying motionless as possible. Sand in her mouth and nostrils, full of terror she can barely breathe. She hears the footsteps of a soldier close, running. She can feel the light thudding through the ground. Now the footsteps stop right by her head. Her entire being freezes in that back-crawling, eye-scalded Moment — split second — as she hears through the sand the muffled sound of him barking at her in a language she doesn't understand.

The soldier cocks the rifle, excitement flushed high in his curly-brown bearded pink cheeks. He blasts his rifle pointblank into the mound of sand shaped like a face-down arms-clapped-to-her-sides little girl. A thick geyser of sand and spine and organs erupts.

The soldier reaches down through the sandy dirt, grabs a thin wrist, and hoists the little girl up like a dripping trophy pelt. The yellow pale winter Sun is just clearing the morning horizon.

"Nits make lice!" Colonel John M. Chivington, who led the militia attack, had retorted, when asked about the propriety of killing children.

The other Sand Creek image in my mind: After a successful day's massacre, the soldiers reveling. They had mutilated most of the bodies, and cut out vaginas and breasts and decorated their hatbands and saddle horns. Progressing on to Denver, the company partied, parading their trophies on a vaudeville stage. Prior to the attack, the able-bodied Indian warrior men had been told by the officials at Fort Lyons that they should go out hunting for buffalo, so only women, children, and elderly were left in the camp. Easy pickings.

As I drove eastward in the pre-dawn darkness out toward the site, in my mind's eye I kept seeing the photo of the "Fighting Parson," as Chivington was called. He was a Methodist preacher. Well-liked, they said.

I tried not to stare at his face in the darkness, centered between the car's head-lights. Ugly, purple-black flames of racial hatred kept rising in me like puke in my gullet as I stared into his face. In his face I recognized the look, the same look I'd seen on the faces of ranchers and cops out West. A look of hate. It seems to actually take over a person's whole appearance. The skin becomes pallid and puffed, with bad color blotches. The eyes stare straight forward, beaded, slipping in and out of focus. The tiny lips clenched inward, disappearing entirely into the beard.

Looking into this face, I wanted to hurt him. Unleash something onto him.

I hate this feeling, I thought. It's an infection. It's what they are all about. They pass it on. Hate is the only thing they know and can relate to. I can't be infected by it. I need to remove myself from all this pollution. I remembered reading about an old Tohono O'odham grandmother's saying, from one of the Arizona/Mexico border tribes: "Keep your hair out of your eyes and don't be like the enemy."

I rolled the window down part way. Only in the ever-changing weather of the Great Plains can the temperature suddenly start rising in the middle of the night, in what's supposed to be the coldest hour. Everything depends on which way the wind is blowing. The night was dry and clear, moonless; I could smell the dry rough grass; a clean, prairie Western smell like slightly damp straw. Moisture from recently melted snow.

Darkness and space loomed over the entire universe. There were very few lights for great stretches of the road. I felt like I was heading out into the bush. I passed through a few dessicated, boarded up, barely surviving towns. The moon rose late. The headlights flared occasionally in the chocolate-drop eyes of zigzagging jackrabbits. Twice I got out to do a short sprint and inhale the air. I lied down on my back in the middle of the old road and crossed my ankles.

Around 5:30 a.m., I found what I was looking for. I pulled off to the side. The car's headlights illuminated the large, timber brown, wooden-plank sign. Painted across the top board was a scrim of snow-capped mountain peaks with a sky-blue background.

SAND CREEK MASSACRE

November 29, 1864 was an unforgettable day for the Cheyennes and Arapahos, on the banks of Sand Creek, 8 miles north and 1 mile east of here, stood a camp of about 100 Cheyenne and some 10 Arapaho lodges established by what may have been taken as orders of the U.S. Army Commander at nearby Ft. Lyon. (sic) According to Indian tradition, early that morning Cheyenne hunters reported that soldiers were coming. Black Kettee (sic) a leader and spokesman for the camp, hoisted an American flag to convey that the camp was peaceful. Ignoring the signal, volunteer militia, led by Colonel John M. Chivington, attacked, killing all in their path. With many of the men away, organized resistance was impossible. When the tragic day was over, more than 137 Indian people, mostly women and children, lay dead, their bodies mutilated. The brutal attack was denounced in congressional hearings. But none of the participants was punished.

Erected by the Colorado Historical Society, the Colorado Native American Heritage Council, and the Colorado Dept. of Highways through the endowment of Mrs. J.N. Hall Endowment. 1986

A dirt road led in from there. I drove down the rough-graded track, my car and teeth shaking from the washboarded surface. About seven miles in, a big red stop sign demanded that I STOP, that I was entering private property and that I must pay $2.00. "Collection fee charged for non-payment."

I looked around. There was not a person or building in sight.

Dutifully, I got out and folded my two crisp dollar bills into the slot in the metal box.

A mile or so further, and up a slight winding rise, and then I was there, in the dark on the bluff overlooking the famous horseshoe bend of Sand Creek. I knew the place so well from descriptions, drawings, and photographs in library books. Down there in that bend was where the encampment had been. The shadows of large bare cottonwoods traced the course of the creek in the pre-dawn. There hadn't been trees along the creek banks in 1864. Big, regular prairie fires had still roamed the living plain, fire being an essential prairie animal like the buffalo.

I blew out my breath. It was still cold. Right where I stood, from the southwest had come the troops. It's said that a woman early-riser first heard the sound of hooves approaching and thought that some buffalo were coming into camp.

I shivered a little in the cold, and also from the jaw-taut wiredness that sets in after a long night of driving and no sleep. Fasting, I hadn't eaten in 36 hours, just so I could be more *connected* when I got here.

The stately ranch house sat squarely on the land down to the east. No lights were on inside. I could just barely make out the gleam of its glass windows, palled in drapes. The front yard was dimly lit by a tall, flickering fluorescent lightpole casting an ineffectual pool of greenish-white light.

Up on the bluff I felt exposed. What was I going to do here, anyway? It was the anniversary of the Massacre. I'd only come to pay my respects. I was surprised that no one else was here.

I dropped down off the bluff, my eyes peeling over the familiar horseshoe bend, the expanse of shin high grasses I knew would be color-blended in tans, yellows and browns. Dawn was coming. Hurry, sunup, I thought, shivering. It was good to be moving my body, getting the blood up. I again had that feeling I always got when out West, of stepping into black-and-white history suddenly turned to full 3-D color.

I made it down into the dry creek bed. Everything was the same. I lingered, quietly absorbing, until the Sun came up, bringing little degrees of warmth. One hundred and twenty eight years ago, at this very moment, unspeakable things were happening right here, all around me. Strangely though, the feeling was calm. I picked up my pace, wanting to get my blood up, my legs brushing silently through the grass.

My wires were up. I was in a big bowl. Up on the rim, from where the soldiers had come, anybody could look down. Even though I was dressed to blend, I needed to put some distance, make myself smaller. I had an underlying sense of hostility emanating from that rim's direction, and the ranch house. I was vulnerable. Needed to get distance, and then to a low spot.

I walked due north. Noticing a small herd of cattle grazing to the east, I was glad to see that the land wasn't too overgrazed, at least what I'd seen so far. Grazing cattle here under any circumstances must take some nerve. The alien beef, tools of the conqueror, is fed by these remaining native grasses, which in turn are fed by the blood of slaughtered babies, mothers, grandmas and grandpas. Have you had your break today, America?

I came onto a dilapidated barbed wire fence. It was old and sagging with half its spindly wooden posts leaning and dried out. In a low spot I jumped it. It was so decrepit that I could've quickly destroyed a mile or more of it. Just pull or push against it and many of the posts would come down. Wouldn't even need to cut it in most places. Not like some of those public land barbed wire fences where you have to break out of Alcatraz just to cross, let alone take it down.

Walking outside on the prairie is a guaranteed antidote for depression, I thought. If we let her, Earth will take care of folk. Even if she'll throw a tempest fit like a tornado every now and then, she'll still for the most part take care of folk if folk take care of her.

Africa. Again I was having that African feeling. The yellow tawny sweep of rough-stalked grassland, the sandy soil, the bluff to the south, the savanna of big gnarled cottonwoods along the length of the creek that you can see through to open unplowed grassland again. I realized I was thinking Africa. I was walking in a great ancient plain, like Africa, that kept hinting at a sere bush wildness. Only without all the animals. The place was almost entirely empty. I noticed some tiny mouse footprints in the sandy path I was following.

A string of small teardrop pools lay in the otherwise dry creek bed. As I approached, a hawk lifted out of one of the giant trees. I was glad to see her.

As I got down into the actual creek bed I saw that the pools were heavily trampled and torn up by cattle. I stopped, thinking hard, thinking of the ranch house, something burning again in my chest. I tried to put it out. I walked faster. Each pool of ice-crusted water reflected the morning blue sky, making a nice contrast with the tawny yellow land.

I hit a sandy patch grown up in little bluestem. I stopped.

I closed my eyes and stood still. I breathed full and slowly.

Suddenly I fell to my knees. Then face first down into the ground.

Working from side to side I began to wedge my way into the sand. A few inches down it became cold and wet. I didn't go deep enough to cover myself. I just lay there, eyes closed, face flat in it, breathing all the smells of hundreds of years of damp Earth, right in my face, watching with my ears.

Say she had somehow continued to live. Maybe right here. An old, old woman now. Raven hair gone to white. Eyes clear like the ice reflecting sky. Skin like the sand plums in winter. Ancient smile wrinkles at each corner of her mouth.

I turned my head out of the wet sand and glanced back.

The rancher's pickup truck was on the rim, bright, new, shiny, metallic.

Violated.

He'd either already seen me, or would as soon as I stepped out of the riparian cottonwood savanna.

Keeping low, I rolled up to my feet and stepped out on the other side, but kept close to a trunk. Checked the rim again.

The truck backed up and drove out. It reappeared down the hill. It occurred to me he might have done something to my car. I decided I'd better head back.

The rancher's truck climbed down off the bluff and reached the dirt road at the bottom.

To my surprise the rancher drove right past and headed east. About a half-mile further, he pulled over and stopped, truck nose facing north. He still hadn't seen me.

I kept low. I was almost to the dirt two-track when he saw me. He backed up fast, raising dust, and sped toward me. He'd been looking for me.

Since my time was up for now, and something ugly was surely coming my way, I quickly tried to digest the overall sense I got from Sand Creek.

Not anger or terror emanating from the sandy soil like I had expected. From the grass and sagebrush holding my feet I felt a faded exhaustion, maybe tanned over by something more earnest, like a strong desire for healthy physical growth and life. This part of the Earth had an exhaustion and desire, dealing in things like patience and time, in that this was once a great inland sea, and things die, new things are born in their place, and others reborn into theirs. The vicious cattle culture was thankfully dying after 150 years. Buffalo had been alive, I thought to myself, through one long connected chain of being, for millions of years. And though almost driven to extinction, the buffalo has far more people praying for him every day, many times a day, than has the bloody-handed cowboy.

These affirmative things, healthy and Powerful things, adamantly rejecting the negative, are what came to me out of the deep roots of Sand Creek as a new morning met the Plains sky. Maybe it was because most of the couple hundred people slaughtered were women and children that this affirming *female* energy of the place came on so strong. Women forgive, women tolerate, women take pains to take care. At least more do so than men, anyway.

The rancher skidded to a dust-blowing stop a few yards from me, truck idling. He had his foot on the brake; I could see the brake lights. He rolled down his window. I stopped and turned around, not wanting my back exposed. I took off my baseball cap. I decided to try to be friendly.

"Hello," I croaked, my jaw locked up in the cold, plus from fasting, plus not having said a word in a few days.

"I've about had enough with you!" he screamed, slamming the gearshift into park.

I noticed I couldn't see his lips, smothered in the thick gray beard.

"If you don't leave right now, you and I are gonna go at it!!" His small eyes darted around the truck, looking for something.

(Say what??) I took a few steps back, at the same time marveling how quick he'd gone over. Or maybe, he'd already been there. My mind hit the street, sizing him up while at the same time blinking at how loco this was.

Maybe early 50s, heavier, and taller. I was undoubtedly quicker and more agile, and most likely stronger, although insane hatred can fuel insane bursts of physical strength.

A couple scenarios flashed through my mind. If he had a gun, all bets were off. It would be split second as you go. *That's what he's looking for, stupid.*

I looked into his face.

Something very bad was happening there.

I took two steps further back. I switched my cap to my left hand. The only thing I could think of was start over, try again.

Like somebody who done lost his mind, I stuck out my hand. "Hi," I said idiotically. "I'm — "

"GIT OUTTA HERE!!" he screamed, shooting his left arm out the window at me and pointing.

By instinct I ducked the swing, even though I knew I was just out of his reach anyway. On the rebound I found myself staring with something like amazement, being this close to something like him. The mortal enemy. His eyes were seething with real, live, in-my-face hatred. The whites of his eyes were grayish and dull, with little spokes of red. There was something really fouled up in there.

I began edging away, morbidly fascinated, not wanting to turn my back.

He dove forward, groping for something under the seat.

I backed up quickly, and the last I saw before I turned around was him still groping, and I suddenly had the image of his hand flapping around down there like it was disembodied.

I hurried toward a footpath going straight up the bluff. My back crawled and squirmed, waiting for the first pucker as the bullet pierced, then the punch as it threw me forward and exploded out my throat or chest, followed by the echoing boom. Dirt crumbled beneath my feet as I made it up to the top.

I heard him yell loudly: "If you turn around, or say one word…." He left the rest to my imagination.

I resisted the death wish temptation to look. It's funny how the senses get tempted to do something your mind knows they absolutely should not do.

As I got onto the level area, I could hear the truck rumbling up the hill, coming for me again. Striding quickly, I let my ears gauge the shortening distance. I rushed for the car, unlocked the door, got in, started up. Raising dust, I spun down the dirt drive to the washboarded and tooth-rattling graded road and turned right. Nine miles to the paved highway.

A few miles down, bumping along, dirt and sand scissoring up off the tires into the fenders, I realized what it was about him that had snagged in my mind.

That rancher looks like Chivington. Living back there all alone, lording over the site of the Sand Creek Massacre, he carries on the good will of the Fighting Parson. He has, in proxy, become him, both in looks and temperament. It's all there, the size, the hairline, the messed hair, the beard, the missing lips, the puffy, blotched face, and especially those small, darting, on-the-verge eyes.

CHAPTER TWENTY-TWO

On the Other Side

"Jihad, I'm worried about Cam. Whenever you are gone, he seems to get himself into trouble. I love him — as friends, we're just friends but — I worry about him. He exasperates me. I just have to say this quickly while he goes to the bathroom."

The back of my head was starting to squeeze a little. Sitting in the dark Lexington Avenue bar, I looked at Julie as she told me this. Her full lips were almost plum purple against her light olive skin and black hair in shoulder length curls. Never any makeup. Cute and pretty as hell. She had a voluptuous body, and in the winter always wore luscious, form-fitting sweaters.

"Things cool now?"

"The problem is he gets himself into trouble without even being aware of it."

"What you mean?"

"Well, he opens his mouth, or does something without thinking. And it turns people off. When you're gone, or not around, he starts acting like he's this big time dealer, he wastes all kinds of money trying to impress people, that he's top dawg of the whole game. I just want you to talk to him if you can. He's going to get himself hurt. Not to mention your business. You know how small New York is. We have our own little world beneath everything. Outside the club world, people on Delancey, or uptown, or wherever don't even know about what's going on, they've never even heard of E, or anything, and they think *they* are the underground. I think Anton was gonna throw him out a couple weeks ago."

"Like what specifically?"

She took a sip from her Rolling Rock. "Well, the big thing — most recently. He decided to take it upon himself and go up to the Bronx, start getting his own supply."

"What?"

"Yeah. You need to know this. He wanted to start selling coke, too, and I know you said you're not going to do that. Well he got his ass caught in a stairwell with a gun in his face, they robbed him of all the money he took, and he had to run for his life. He didn't tell you that."

My head was squeezing. I glanced to the back of the deserted bar, where the bathrooms were. Camron had come out and was leaning over the jukebox, one arm up on the big glass globe, the little revolving purple and white disc light inside spinning off his cheeks. He pulled out a wrinkled dollar bill and straightened it out, back and forth, over the edge of the top of the machine.

She followed my gaze, then placed her hand on my knee. "Also, stupid things. Like messing with Jose and Luis Xtravaganza. Why is Camron even messing with those bitches? When Madonna tapped them for "Vogue" to be her dancers, and her movie, you know how big their heads got. Who cares!"

Camron came up, grinning beneath his baseball cap, as a Kate Bush song — "Babooshka" — came on.

"How you like that?" he said. "Thought I was gonna play Donna Summer, didn't you."

I put my hand over my face.

"Well, don't worry, Donna's next."

Julie got off her barstool and gave Camron a big hug, standing up on her toes. He put his arms around her nicely sweatered waist as she kissed him on his cheek, and for a moment he swooned at the contact, eyes fluttering, the only heaven he needed. She glanced at me over his shoulder. "You know, Camron," she said, pulling back and lightly hitting him with the ball of her fist on his t-shirted chest. "Sometimes, when you are talking, I don't know if you are totally insane, or a total fucking genius. Either way, nobody can understand you."

She gave me a hug, her beautiful natural breasts pushing up against me, and kissed me on the cheek also. I could smell her perfume — warm roses and clean skin — and it gave me a little bit of the shivers. "Get some rest, J. You look tired, ok?" As she went out the door, pulling her down parka on, she turned around and waved to both of us. "Bye, boys." She smiled, her full lips pulling back from bright teeth.

"So how the fuck did you end up in Montana?" Camron said, jovial for some reason today. "And you left your car there? That was stupid."

"You don't even know what you talking about. I was in Colorado, and then went up to pay my respects to the buffalo at the National Bison Range in the Flathead Valley. But it was just a little theme park shit; then my car broke down so I came back while it's getting fixed."

He over-dramatically shook his head from side to side at his beer, snorting. "I can just picture you. Here you are, this big time drug dealer, and you're driving and riding your bike and hiking all over the West doing or looking for I don't know what." He looked at me. "You know, and I been meaning to tell you this: Have you ever considered that you've become too specialized, like some of those animals that are dying off on the Discovery Channel because they can no longer adapt to the world around them? I could live on the ground floor facing 42nd Street, with all the traffic roaring by day and night, but you couldn't. Have you ever considered that maybe the world has just passed you by, and the shit we're in is the shit we're with? Like in *Blade Runner*?"

I sneered at him. "Don't worry about me. We need to talk about business."

"What about business? Oh now you want to talk about business. I've been waiting for months and years for you to talk about business seriously."

"Don't press, Camron, I'm not the one. Look, New York is very small, everybody know each other. Every player respects the other's territory. That's how we all got this shit carved out with no heat from the outside. Nobody in my hood has even heard of

E. But they will, and people everywhere will, soon enough. X gon be the big thing. But for now, we get things straight because we been on the dl, and Camron, you gotta, I'm telling you, not asking you, you have to keep it that way."

"Oh, Julie was talking your ear off?"

"Don't mind what Julie and I were talking about. She's going for her Master's degree in Art History. I can just tell about you. When I come back, things always seem worse from when I left. The people I get to supply you while I'm gone are concerned, also the security guards — even your outside clients."

"Well, if you wouldn't leave your business behind every time." He jabbed his finger at me and I parried it away, irritated. "Let me tell you something, Jihad. You got responsibilities that you don't live up to. You're a big time NYC drug dealer. You got responsibilities. People depend on us being steady and regular. That's why I went up to the Bronx. I decided to take shit into my own hands. Make some real money. Cause you're never around! I bet it was Orion who told you. Fuck him."

"Man, you've got this idea we this and we that. This ain't about being big time or whatever. That's all bullshit. It's just a job. All that shit, about who's big, all that's in the movies. I ain't goin' upstate on a 15-to-20 bid behind some stupid shit. I told you, I don't live here and never will. I live out West. I just work here and commute. It's just a job."

"You don't treat it like it's even that. It's like you don't even care. At all."

"I make my money like this so I can make my own war; aiight? There. How the fuck you like that? That's all that matter to me. I'm funding my own shit to strike back at the rapists and the destroyers. I make my own rules. The only rules I gotta follow is by God and Earth. And I'm sure I fuck up even there sometimes."

"I'm more than sure you do." He peeled at the beer bottle's label. "You take shit way too seriously, anyway."

"I don't need you to tell me what the fuck. I'm eventually moving out West once and for all and never coming back. But I'll make sure we both taken care of in the meantime, if you just act right and handle *your* side of the biz. And no, it wasn't Orion. Orion is always gonna be cool. He will tell me what's up if he has to, but it wasn't him; it's me telling you that you need to just worry about keeping things cool on your end."

"Bartender," he said, shaking his head at me and raising his hand. The fat guy in the flannel shirt looked up from his conversation with the two ladies smoking cigarettes at the other end of the bar and came over. "Two more." He turned to me. "Maybe you should drink more. Maybe you'd fuckin' relax more. And handle your business better."

The bartender clanked two icy beer bottles down on the dark, scratched wood surface, and lifted a ten out of the scatter of bills between me and Camron. I twisted my lip. "You don't need to tell me about drink. I drank enough for all of us. I'd tell you about it but I don't remember."

He tapped me on the arm with the back of his hand. I looked up, and he nodded his head out the window. I looked across Lexington Avenue. A white New Jersey-looking hooker with long stringy bleached hair, wearing a short skirt, stockings, and long white boots was ducking down into the stairwell as she reached into her clasp purse. She squatted down, faced toward the building, just her head visible, nervously checking for people coming on either side, and hurriedly douched herself.

"Why'd you move up here?" I asked him.

"I like this little area. It's so boring nobody thinks of anything. But still close enough to everything. I'm a different kind of incognegro. I got a little hotel room two blocks up, at 31st and Lex. For some reason, though, all the Jersey hookers come to this area. Just like how all the drag queen hookers got the West 14th St. area and the meatpacking district on lock. Funny, huh? Funny, right? " He tapped my arm again as he said it, sharing what he thought was one of his inside jokes.

I rubbed my face.

"You know," he said, swallowing beer. " The cops got me the other day. Have you noticed? Giuliani isn't even inaugurated yet, but there's a new heat out here. Something tells me some shit's gonna change."

"Cops always been a problem. But New York cops are Nice People compared to cops other places. Here, they mostly just focused on the big shit, and only occasion-ally blast one of us for no reason. Try L.A."

"Yeah, so far. I think we've been lucky. But the other day I was walking up Clinton Street; I'd gone back to check for a piece of paper with some numbers on it. And these two cops pulled up and put me in the back seat and took me to the precinct. They said they were looking for this Dominican guy who was wanted for robbery. I don't even look anything like Dominican!"

"You didn't have nothing on you, I take it."

"Nope." He scratched at his temple with the perfectly cut nail of his fourth finger. "I was pissed off! But I didn't show it. After they questioned me, I made them take me in their big shiny police car to where I was going."

"Man…" I said, shaking my head. "I can't even talk to a cop. They make me feel like I'm starting to choke."

"That's because they got you so dominated. I'm more than sure you don't even look them in the eye."

"You're not supposed to. That is the law."

"Man, fuck that! Fuck them! It's their job "to protect and serve.""

"Protect and serve themselves," I said. "Just themselves. Don't be stupid. They can and will do to you whatever they want to. Whenever."

The rack of Kate finished and Donna Summer (She works hard for the money!) was coming on.

"Jihad, I know you care all about the animals and environment and shit. I know you're a fucking vegetarian, and I'm more than sure you can't sleep at night sometimes thinking about all that goes bad in the world. By the way, I saw on Connie Chung about your Buffalo Commons again. You know what, Jihad? For real. I really would like to see that happen out there, those buffalo come back. Even if I don't go see it myself. But what can you do? I know about the West; from when I went to visit my sister in Denver. I watch the History Channel and PBS all the time. I know all about Union Carbide and Exxon Valdez and PCBs in the Hudson and Tuskegee, Alabama and My L'ai and PRIP-YAT and what the fuck. I know all them companies and the government are polluting and raping the Earth and killing people like there's no tomorrow. But Jihad, they're always gonna get over. That's the way it is."

He swigged from his beer and thunked it down on the bar. "So we need to just focus on getting ours."

The wire springs in the Hotel Hell mattress creaked as I slightly adjusted my position, flat on my back, staring into the 7-day white wax candle. The flame in the tall glass tube burned straight up to a fine point, refracting through the glass rim. Lahumba had said white was for Spirit, and yellow for Manifestation. (Green was for money, but I didn't think it was right to burn a candle for money.) I didn't blink, and the flame grew a soft halo, larger and larger. Somewhere inside my eyes, not too far below the surface, I sensed water. But the surfaces of my eyeballs were as scratchy dry as the Sahara Desert. I clutched my pillow to my chest and stared.

Again, I thought about the wild animals, back when the continent was primeval. What had it been like for them? It's a wonder anything — any*body*, animals are not things — survived the onslaught and conquest at all. What was it like for them? How had it been? When, from the Atlantic to the Pacific, there was not a single engine or mechanical roar... and hundreds of thousands upon hundreds of thousands of generations passed through life and death within the prairies, forests, lakes, streams and skies... At moments I can still feel — almost get a sense of it. What? What was it? Maybe God was here. Right on the ground. In the grass.

Back before all the noise, the Earth was haunted. That's what I think. But haunted with life. And it was somehow all the way up into the Universe. Something was going on down here. I think everybody saw in the "dark." Spoke through their blazing eyes and strong chests. Everything was alive in some way, had their own living spirit, even rocks, trees, water, and dirt. And spirits walked everywhere, unashamed; everything quietly hummed with open secrets reaching up through the ages like ancient twisting roots through good dirt. Things that would be considered supernatural were normal. Natural. Part of everyday life, day and night.

What was it like, as the realization of the terror to come shuddered westward, gripping the land like a plague of unspeakable proportions? The crash of ancient trees being cut down, the millions and millions of gunshots, the ripping up of the virgin prairie, the crushing of the babies' nests... the onslaught... the endless murder of native people... the gluttony ... some unspeakable indescribable insatiable monster chomping and destroying everybody and everything in its path. The horror, the fear and knowledge that the world was actually ending. Animals and people, the Earth herself, actually experiencing the Apocalypse. For some, the Apocalypse had already come. The changes, when they came, happened so fast, that the world some were born into was utterly and completely destroyed within a span of years. People and animals had been shot on sight. Everything defiled and violated. Survivors stressed, harassed, scrambling to adjust to the war zone...

My chest began heaving as I comprehended it. A choking gurgle came out of my throat. I gripped the pillow fiercely to me. Why did it have to happen?

The animals surviving today struggle tooth and nail just to make it through. They do not choose to live like this; in the confined spaces, ravaged fragments, noise and desperation that people have left them; they do so because they have no choice.

I tried to let my mind go blank, but was helpless. The photos, stories and descriptions kept flooding in. A black-and-white image of some shawled and starving Blackfeet kneeling outside a one-room slaughterhouse, hands upraised and begging before the slats in the outer wall. Streaks of blood dripping down the sides of the building from those slats. And hardly even getting that. Reduced to begging for ladles of blood from the new cattle rancher kings, anything to eat, to stop from starving.

Another image — of one of the remaining herds of pronghorn antelope — in the Red Rim country of Wyoming fleeing a winter storm in the 1980s, trying to make it to their winter range, as they had for millennia but getting snagged in a rancher's 28-mile fence. Thousands of pronghorn got stuck and died. The looks on their rigor-mortified faces as they softened and rotted when spring came. So many pronghorn died huddled along the Red Rim fence they never were unable to get a full count.

The buffalo killers… Back in the early 1870s people shooting so many buffaloes their rifle barrels would start to melt. Just shooting them, one after the other after the other. The prairie dog poisoners. They'd gone mad. The monster had arrived, and was in full gear, consuming everything…

I rolled onto my side, rocking, trying to shake something out of me, burning my eyes into the solid white flame of the candle. *Please help, Dear God. Please. There's nowhere for me to go. I can't take this. Anything I do, anywhere I go, everything and everywhere, I can't shake this. Please. Please let there be some hope. Dear God. Mother Earth. Thank you for my life, my health, and my wholeness. I am sorry for all the evil I have committed and participated in. Please give the wild animals the strength they need, and the homes they need. Let something happen. They've never done anything to anybody. Please let them have some place of peace, of cleanliness, where they can be vital and LEFT ALONE… Maybe our society can fix things. But if not — however. Do whatever. Crash everything if you have to. Please. Take me first. Thank you. I am in your service.*

I lay there on my side on the uncomfortable mattress, breathing hard, listening to the muffled sounds of the hotel. Somebody pouring something liquid out the window, hitting and splashing on the mess of junk below. Distant voices on some TV program. Tumble of something soft and not so small inside the wall, nails scratching, scrambling.

My eyes traced the ceiling's square edge around the room. I prayed for a passout. I let my breathing and heart rate drop very low. Had gotten very good at that. Still… nothing. Earlier, in the bar, I could have. If I could've just found a quiet place.

I leaned off the edge of the bed to reach the tape player. With the rough pad of my index finger I pushed in the black PLAY button.

Stared at the flame. Firelight. Fire. Sun. God.

The room gradually filled with sounds of "Storm on a Wilderness Lake." The night animals, birds, and insects made their normal voices as they went about their business. I heard a warble. A grunt. The steady up-and-low scissoring rhythm of crickets and all kinds of wild insects mesmerized by the night, multiple tandem layers of sounds. A wind began to pick up; storm coming. I heard it through the grasses and the trees. It blew and blew, getting stronger. The animals' voices changed. Thunder rumbled in the distance, then suddenly lightning crashed overhead. Drops of rain began to fall, hitting the surface of the lake, plopping onto wild green leaves and wild green grass. The sky opened up, and it rained hard. Thunder again, shaking the world, vibrating in every cell like water quenching the thirst of a desert man. The storm gradually passed, then silence again. Dripping… Everybody momentarily silent in the wake of the storm, except for an occasional waterlogged gurgle or throat-piped note. Wind… falling off to a breeze as the storm began to move out, pulling in a vacuum of dripping stillness behind it. A few crickets squeaked. A loon cried out something holy and piercing across the lake. Frogs and toads peeped. And then, howling into the night sky, a wolf. He moaned, head thrown back, he moaned as if unable to control his voice, he cried, then howled all the despair and hurt and sadness and loneliness that had come onto this land, that had ever existed in this world.

Need to make a sacrifice… was the thought that came into my head as the cassette tape of wilderness sounds finished. *Need to give something of my physical self back to the Earth. Need to give.* An image of me cutting off my finger, and burying it way out on the prairie, flowed soothingly through my mind. *Need to give.*

I'm going to cut off my little finger, and bury it in the Earth. That's what I'm going to do.

And at last, I passed out.

I opened my eyes a slit, cautiously turning my head into the red Sun. My head fell back, but still I stared. I'm floating, I thought. *Am I finally dead?* The Sun was blazing red, so clean and sharp, hanging directly in front of me in a sky so severely blue, blending to darker blue, everything in hyper detail, an open-ended universe of rich deep blues stretching into the universe above forever. And beneath the Sun and myself a soft, pillowed white plain stretching out to eternity. Groggily, I stared, my eyes transfixed by the severe high-altitude clarity… I'm finally….dead… floating across a pure plain of… clouds? Warmth of the red setting sun on my cheek through the window, parallel out there. The crescent moon with Venus to its upper right starkly bright in the blue up there, pointing…

Windows?

My forehead was stuck to the window.

I sat up out of my slump, shaking my head clear, as I noticed I was now descending through clouds. I looked down at myself, then to my right… People sitting across the aisle.

Oh. I slumped back. I'm in an airplane.

Closing my eyes again, I rubbed my little finger, encircling its base with my thumb and forefinger. Right where I would sever it.

SECTION SEVEN

"One wonders... who, indeed, were the savages."

— William McPherson, *The Washington Post*

"Dearly beloved, avenge not yourselves, but rather give place unto wrath: for it is written, 'Vengeance is mine; I will repay,' saith the Lord."

— *Romans 12:19*

CHAPTER TWENTY-THREE

Red Mist

Browning, Montana. Center of the Blackfoot Indian Reservation. Just south of the Canadian border, east of Glacier National Park and the Rocky Mountain Front. Drunks stumbling around, frozen plastic bags and other trash stuck to the hard mud ruts of the dirt streets. Stray dogs with sharp yellow teeth and mangy hair scavenging… Clusters of public tract housing, blowing trash, graffiti… Frozen barrenness.

I dug into my books. Again I looked at the turn-of-the-century black-and-white photo in the book I'd bought at Strand. It crystallized the whole West for me. It made me sick. Stark, overgrazed High Plains surrounding a makeshift slaughterhouse, no bigger than a barn. Slats in the walls, black streams of blood dripping down. Starving, shawled Blackfeet Indians kneeling on the hard ground up against that wall, begging for offal, ladles of blood, anything at all to eat. The ranchers inside patronizing them with an occasional splatter of blood tossed out.

Further east, the Little Rockies rise suddenly out of the High Plains on Fort Belknap Indian Reservation. George Bird Grinnell, who was supposed to be a friend of the Assiniboine and Gros Ventre who live there, swindled them out of the lower southeast corner of their reservation, cutting out the little mountain range, which happened to contain gold dust. Pegasus Mining has chopped off the top of the mountain, and soaked tons of crushed rock with cyanide to remove the gold dust, poisoning the streams. "The deer have yellow, distorted livers," Mike Fox, director of the Tribe's Fish and Game Department, told me as we sat in his living room in the tiny village of Hays at the base of the mountain. I had gone to the Tribal office and asked if I could talk to somebody about buffalo and prairie dogs, and I got referred to Mike. I was here at last, in what I thought was the remotest section of the Great Plains. Certainly it was said to have some of the worst weather in the country.

"Our people are afraid to eat deer anymore, one of our traditional foods." We were surrounded by plastic gallon jugs of water on the floor, his little son playing on the carpet. People were obviously afraid to drink the water, too. Mike was a young guy, probably not that much older than me, with buzz cut hair. I noticed a couple rap CDs in the corner by the stereo.

Walkie talkie blares. Poachers have been spotted shooting at antelope and golden eagles in the northern end of the reservation. He is heavily armed. Asks if I want to come. We jump into his truck. Binoculars sit on the seat between us.

Driving fast up the main rez road under low cloudy skies, I see the Bear's Paw mountains to the west, where Chief Joseph had come through, had made his last stand and almost escaped into Canada before he and his band were hunted down and captured. Where he'd said his immortal words, "Hear me, my chiefs. My heart is sick and sad. From where the Sun now stands, I will fight no more forever." Earlier, Mike had shown me a 10,000 year buffalo petroglyph, partially covered by a thin crust of snow, overlooking the valley.

"I need to see the buffalo get their freedom back," I said.

"Well, you know the buffalo is just singled out because he looks a little different. Like any other race."

"Like a political prisoner," I said, nodding. "He's big and black and refuses to submit. The ranchers and politicians are afraid of what might happen if he got his freedom back. The public might get inspired, might actually find out what's really happening on their public lands, and challenge the ranchers' control and killing of the American West. The buffalo is America's longest held political prisoner."

"You're a True Believer, huh," he said, cracking a smile over the steering wheel.

We rolled up over some low hills, where the former prairie in the central part of the reservation was striped in big yellow bands of harvested dryland wheat, alternating with equal-sized swaths of black frozen plowed ground.

"If it warms up a little, it might snow. We got some of the worst weather in the country," he said, grinning. "No place like north-central Montana."

We didn't find the poachers. I was considering the offer to join the poacher patrol on a regular volunteer basis. "We've got 5,000 acres for buffalo now, and hope to be able to expand, if we can get the fencing," he said. "I'd like to get some of them endangered black-footed ferrets too, for our prairie dog town, but I don't know if the Indian ranchers will like that. They hate the prairie dogs just like any rancher."

"They poison them?"

"No, not right now. Least not that I know of. But they let white guys from Texas and California come up here to spend big money to shoot them."

"What do you mean, shoot them? For what? To eat?"

"No, they never even go out to touch them. They just set up their shooting tables. Some of them got these big expensive guns, costing up to $10,000, they got ear guards, elbow pads, and all that. They shoot them for sport."

I was staring at him as he talked. "You mean, on top of the poisoning, they — "

"Oh man, it's a whole big sport. They do it everywhere. Colorado, Kansas, the Dakotas, Wyoming, your Texas, too. I'm surprised you didn't know. Our tribal government makes money off selling permits to shoot. The shooters even have their own little groups; I think they call themselves the Red Mist Society or Varmint Militia or something. The — "

"Wait, what??"

"Yeah, the Red Mist Society. It's a whole sport. They have different names for the types of kill, but basically the prairie dogs get blown up by the high-powered rifles. They use deer and elk rifles, or even bigger bore. That's why they call it Red Mist. It's for IVG — 'instant visual gratification.'" He gave a laugh, shaking his head like he wasn't really laughing.

I tried to clear my constricting throat. "They do this on sacred Indian ground, and Indian people let them?" I could hardly talk.

"Man, nothing's sacred. Not when you're tryin' to run a cow-and-calf operation."

Later, I found out that the tribal government not only sponsored aerial gunning of coyotes, foxes, and badgers, but also marketed itself as a destination for rednecks to come and blow up prairie dogs. And that these Red Mist militia groups really did have different names for the types of impact the bullet has when it hits a dog in all these different ways. There is the 'Hoover,' which sucks the dog out of his hole if he's been peeking out of it at the same time the bullet blasts off his head. They have the 'Chamois' where for some reason the bullet knocks him right out of his skin, and the 'Spaghetti' that basically splatters open the belly and all the noodle-like guts come flying out. They have contests. They even sell a video, *Exploding Dogs*.

I bolted out of there.

Further out into eastern Montana, I walked into worse. The frozen prairie dog town was silent. Rigor-mortified exploded bodies — dismembered fur and gore cardboard caricatures of prairie dogs — were on nearly every mound, or thrown back a few feet. In some cases I could see where the bullet had gone right through the body; the prairie dog must have been standing on the rim of his burrow. There was a hole bored into the packed clay dirt of the opposite burrow wall with a blood stain dripping down, dried in time like Indian paint. Many songbirds had also been shot, just for the hell of it, and lay there as mangled clumps of feathers, next to the belly-gore blasted, twisted, barely recognizable shapes of prairie dogs. Strange thing; not a single shot body was touched by a scavenging predator. They wouldn't touch them, as if recognizing something bad had happened here. All the bodies and pieces of bodies lay, flattened, dried, frozen in blasted, twisted death, to gradually abrade away with the seasons.

Didn't see any live prairie dogs. If there were any left, they were probably too stricken to come out anymore, unable to understand how or why merely stepping out into the glorious air now caused them to explode. These Sun Dogs had had their God taken away from them, and now cowered in darkness, their immune systems and life vitality withering.

The Big Open, they called it. Big Sky Country.

Fingertips numb, dangerously close to frostbite, my face wrapped in a black rag, I crawled over the hard-frozen buffalo grass, before dark, up onto the small hill. Ancient tipi rings, smooth stones placed in a circle by aboriginal human hands, likely women, when the Earth was an entirely different planet. When it had been time to pack up and move, the tipi flaps were just pulled out from under the rocks, leaving a series of rings as silent testimony. One stone ring was much larger than the others. They looked like stone crop circles, mythic, mysterious, powerful, of another lifetime and another Earth. But suddenly none of that specialness seemed to matter. Though there was no human habitation for miles, cows had trampled all over, shitting over everything. The native grass was grazed bare. Their shit was frozen in big splatters even inside the sacred tipi rings, and the sign of their presence on the grassland was not just like a swarm of hoofed locusts, but a disease.

You spend most of your time trying not to go crazy, I thought to myself.

I couldn't find any leghold traps in the Charles M. Russell National Wildlife Refuge, along the Missouri River Breaks, though I searched and searched. I cut as many wires as I could. On the rises, where the trees were, snow was deep. I stayed in a motel up along the Hi-Line, the northernmost railroad route in the U.S. With the cloud cover gone, the temperature plummeted to 40 degrees below zero, the wind chill 20 or so below that. The air itself seemed to freeze in bluish-green vapor clouds. I discovered pockets of moisture on my body I did not know I had. Tiny crystals froze in any pore even briefly exposed; my eyebrows, eyelashes, mustache and goatee froze like black iron. Snow so dry it blew like sand, and drifted into dunes, creating mesmerizing shadows and ripples. Sun so bright I almost got snow-blind. I wrapped up like the abominable snowman on my High Plains that became Jupiter for me, the low, short daylight of the Northern Winter clouded in frozen blue and green vapor, an odd pale white-yellow sun hazing through as it made its way down to sunset by 3:30 in the afternoon. At the convenience store in Malta, where I took a motel room, I bought a gallon jug of water from the refrigerated cooler, and noticed its 45 degrees was so warm in comparison to the outside temperature that I slipped it inside my parka to add warmth.

Wyoming: Trying to make my way southward. Trying not to go crazy with anger and hopelessness as I passed an elk, a deer, and two snow-white jackrabbits stuck dead in the endless bristling wires. Passed a pickup truck with men in the back driving along a dirt road, dumping poison-laced sheep carcasses along the side.

I fled to the desert. *You've lost your courage.* Just need to go to ground, hide out, disappear.

I holed up in a tiny one-room shack with a wood stove that had a tin smoke duct sticking out through the roof. Nipton, California, population maybe 50 people. Seventy miles as the raven flies south of Las Vegas, in the California Desert, right next to the Mojave National Preserve.

Open desert grasslands at 5,000 feet... cattle and barbed wire... no escape, not even here.

I huddled around my fire, the late winter nights freezing at that elevation, unable to eat, stomach sick, fasting... veins cold from lack of food...

Winter rains alternating with chilly sunshine... walking out into the desert, warm daylight bright sunshine, miles ...still tormented by images of bristling wire fences. I imagined buffalo running into them.

Shutting the visions out. Just walking. Came up over a rocky pass and below, a wide valley stretched out for maybe twenty miles. I noticed a raven; no, he was a crow, flying over me. He circled. His shadow cut across the desert like a scimitar. I scanned the basin, eyes catching and focusing on these thick-looking sticks in the ground down there standing straight up, higher by half a foot than anything else. I gazed for a minute, realizing there were hundreds if not thousands of them. I sat down, trying to think. How? Way out here? Desert wilderness. What are they?

I unsteadily stood up. Noticed the crow was still with me. Black feathered oil and sharp black beak in blue sky. "Still with me, Crow?" I croaked. "Stay wit me, papa. Stay with me. I am in your service. All of you." Made my way down through jagged rocks, greasewood bushes, gravel sandy washes to the first stick. It wasn't a stick but a plastic pipe stuck into the ground, some kind of marker. Open mouth 4-inch diameter pipe. I remembered hearing something: big gold mine planned… cyanide heap leach mining, dig up the whole desert… many tons must be crushed and soaked with cyanide to produce one single ounce. Like in the Little Rockies by Fort Belknap Reservation in Montana.

I spun around and hit the pipe with a rear thrust kick, sending it flying out of its hole, the soil loosened by recent, fading moisture. Kneeling down, I peered into the pipe's bottom end. It was blocked. I saw feathers. I wedged a stick in there and pulled the mass out. Three dead birds were matted together in varying stages of decay. Their stricken wide-open eyes, sunken and shriveled, relayed to me in frozen time what had happened.

The bright, sunlit blue sky seemed to wash out my eyes. Crow shot across my vision.

I came in for a landing on the tallest perch around. Expecting a solid grasp for my feet the breath gets knocked out of me as I fall down a shiny dark tunnel, jamming and breaking a wing. I flutter wildly. I hit bottom onto something soft and stinking. Body numb from the sudden shock I do more damage to myself as I try to flap my already broken wing, but there's not enough room. I flap and squirm and try to jump, eyes bulging, overheating with panic until I collapse, hot little heart beating wildly in my feathered chest. I can see the bright blue sky way up there through the end of the plastic pipe, my home free out there, but stuck down here, unable to do anything. I realize I am lying on top of other birds, dead birds, who had fallen in like I did. New panic surges up through me, as I beat and struggle and kick, trying to get up and out, at least get up on my feet. Finally, exhausted, my overheated body pounding with exhaustion and shock, I lay on my side on top of the dead, rotting birds and squirming maggots which are already trying to crawl onto and bite into me. My broken wing is wedged painfully out of joint, breath and super-fast beating heart failing, staring at the hole up there into my bright blue sky home out there, so far away, a circle of blue brightness that washes out all else. Then, something moves beneath me, and I realize one of the other birds I'm lying on top of is still alive, just barely alive.

I grabbed a foot-long rock and leapt onto the plastic pipe, feeling like I was flying I was so lightheaded from fasting, and slammed the rock down onto it, splintering it. I fell backwards from the force of my thrust. I leapt again, landing on top of it with both my feet and jumped on it until it smashed into plastic splinters. I buried the birds in a sandy grave and placed grass stalks in a cross over them.

I went to the next. Kicked it down. Pulled out a snarled bunch of dead birds. Went to another one. From pipe to pipe I found cactus wrens, different kinds of finches, flycatchers, even a yellow-billed cuckoo. Destroyed the pipe. Prepared a burial. Moved on to the next. And the next. The hidden monstrous corporation in all its evil began to grow bigger and bigger over me. The winter-changing-to-spring Sun moved in a big arc across the southern end of the sky. A singular cotton cloud passed in slow time. I counted an average of three dead birds tangled at the bottom of each pipe, with a lot of pipes having as many as six or seven bodies. Death was here, and an even bigger death was coming.

As I broke and crushed each pipe and moved on, still more appeared. I tried to shut out the knowledge that there were at least a couple thousand pipes like these stuck out here by a multinational corporation announcing its coming benevolence. I jumped, broke, crushed, and moved onto the next, jumped, broke, crushed, getting weaker and weaker, but obsessed and desperate to still find one bird, even one, who had just recently fallen in, was still alive, who I could rescue, provide escape and release from the horrors of man. I got smaller and smaller, the pipes got bigger and bigger, and doubled and tripled in number, and harder to break. The Mojave Desert plain sprawled out before me, behind me, all around, ringed by mountains that certainly didn't guarantee an end to the pipes.

The mining corporation would likely chew up the mountains too, like they did the Little Rockies in Montana. There was no end. The birds and I were a dust speck, and they were going to boil that dust speck. Boil that dust speck! I suddenly looked up for Crow, having forgotten about him. My heart sank. Even he was gone.

Months passing in the California desert… full spring now, things heating up quickly. Evening sun cast a halo behind the head of Teresa, the Apache woman with the Russian military rifle who was hunting some old gray-bearded white man who she said had tried to molest her 8 year-old daughter, April. She said, "I've traveled all over. People all over the world know what is wrong, what they're doing to the Earth. Everybody knows the bills are coming due, even if they tell you they don't. Some don't care, but most people just don't know what the hell they can do, so they shut it out and go shopping."

April, who liked to climb on my shack's roof, hung upside down over the door frame, wearing fake glasses and tapped a ruler like a schoolteacher: "Get to work, young man. Get to work!"

"Get your skinny little Indian ass down off the roof, before I whup it," Teresa said as she shouldered the Mosin, and aimed at the tin wash bucket filled with sand that was out behind her trailer 100 feet away. She blasted another perfect hole through it and it sprayed sand out the other side like spit.

At night, Las Vegas, 70 miles away on the horizon, was a half-bubble of artificial light, pushed down by the pitch-black desert sky pricked with stars and constellations and the Milky Way.

A desert windstorm picked up, came on fast, the strongest one I'd ever felt, taking over the night. It rattled and shook my cabin. I was sure the winds would collapse the whole thing in on me, and it excited me. It was the middle of the night, late, late night. Who else was awake? Could anybody sleep? The winds pushed and howled, and I began to sense a rhythm and beat to it. Beat in my veins. Pulsed in my body. Wind blew, howled. I opened the door; it flung out of my hands and slammed into the wall, the sharp sound muffled, snatched away by the straining wind. I jumped out into the windstorm, helpless to it now. It pushed at me hard. I began to dance, in tune with its beat, trying to stay upright. I danced harder, spinning, hitting each beat, raising my heart rate, breaking a sand-gritted night sweat, the little glow of Las Vegas washing across the corners of my eyes as I turned this way and that. I shut it out, sand stinging my eyes. I bobbed my head, dipped my shoulders, first the right, then the left, I jumped and stomped, danced harder, whirling, staying in rhythm, pounding it out on the desert floor and in the wind, leaping higher and higher, till I could for sure fly away.

The wind stopped and I fell hard to the ground sprawling face down, heart beating so loudly in my head and in the sudden silence I could hear nothing else.

The settling dry air immediately began wicking the sweat off my body through my cotton clothes. I dug my fingertips and face into the dirt, scrunching up my face, praying, praying as hard as I could, putting my whole being into it. *Please Please Please...* Gasped for air, mouth and nose inhaling sand, until it was draining in a scratchy slide down my throat. *Please God, let it be so. Let it all be over with. Let us ....* *be back in Time Primeval... Let it be so. Let Earth... back wild again. Everything shut off. Please. Let us be passed through... back or forward... into a real Time....again... Please.*

Clenching my eyes shut and afraid to look, I fought to lift my head, wanting to stay face down here forever where it was dark, where the lights were off, but knowing I had to see, to be sure. *Please.* I raised my head an inch, breath bellying into the ground, body a taut vibrating wire as I braced myself for the truth.

I dropped my head back down onto the sand. The world's lights were still on. Las Vegas was still there, its giant half-bubble glow still lit up on the horizon — still there like always.

I heard a noise, and lifted my head up off the ground to look behind. A woman a few cabins down had opened her door, sensing something out there in the night, or just checking to see the desert storm had passed. She shook her head, I'm sure swearing at me in some Spanish curse, and pulled back inside closing the door.

The next afternoon, a few miles out, tired of cutting fences, and worrying that it was time to move on, I dropped to the ground for my coyote scramble beneath more barbed wires. Good contact with the ground prompted me to flop over onto my back, rest there for a moment, soaking in the contact. Looking up, I noticed I was exactly halfway under; the bristling wires split me vertically in half, from head to toe. My right side was north; my left side was south. My head hurt. Narrowing my eyes, I stared hard at the wires splitting my choices. Left — disappear once and for all down into Mexico; right — go back up into the Plains to face my call and never look back.

"Bleh," I groaned, tongue falling out of my mouth.

The stupid wires.

You've been thinking too hard. You can't get those buffaloes out of your mind, desperate for their freedom, running into these damn stupid barbed wires everywhere like a perpetual crucifixion.

Where the hell are you? And how the fuck you get here?

Why can't I just go to a club or the beach and hang out like other young people do? Am I crazy?

So what is it, muthafucka. Left or right.

I thought of my escapist desires to disappear south into Mexico. Maybe I can still find one perfect place. Disappear forever.

I thought about the remaining buffalo that lived behind the fences in the north country. And were completely shot out of the Southern Plains except for one tiny herd. I thought about the reservation tribes equally imprisoned up there.

You know what the problems are; many people do. But nobody's taking the first step to actually do something on the ground. Just think what it could mean. Everybody's waiting for somebody else to do it.

The Buffalo Commons. It's just an idea. People talked about it, but that's all. There's no Buffalo Commons. Nobody is paying any attention to what is really going on out here. The Commons means reclaiming huge, abandoned areas of the Great Plains back to their natural condition; in other words restoring the living ecosystem enough to allow the return of wild, free-roaming buffalo to the West, and getting people to evolve enough in their souls to live healthily alongside that. As part of that.

Well, that ain't nowhere in reality.

The Buffalo Commons reminds people that history is not just something in a book, but continually evolving right now. Big changes, getting well again, are still a possibility.

Man, just think… What if we could heal the Earth and, right in the most devastated outback, let that be a whole new model for civilization? If we could do that, we could heal ourselves, heal our communities, heal the very way we relate to each other and the Earth herself.

I think the Buffalo Commons idea means we can do better. As a civilization.

But how?

I closed my eyes. My gut wrenched again as I saw those big black buffaloes in my mind, ramming into the fences, trying to get out, trying to catch somebody's attention. Behind them I could see great open horizons of green grass, silent, emptied, killed of life. I saw prairie dog killing contests.

I opened my eyes and as I stared up at my split sky I saw Texas turned thorny and overgrazed. I saw machine-gunned coyotes, bristling wires choking an entire Western landscape, poisoned prairie dog towns, countless carcasses of birds and animals deliberately strung up or caught in the wires. I saw beaten overgrazed land for hundreds of miles, swastika tattoos on cowboy wrists in Nebraska gas stations—

I lay there on my back, beneath the wires and blue sky. I stared up at the braided metal strands of bristling wires that split me in half. Suddenly, I felt strong and clear. I held onto it. *If nobody else is going to lead, then that means — guess who.*

What the fuck. Leave me the fuck alone.

You have to do it.

I momentarily sensed great capability. I saw myself inspiring and exciting people of all cultures together into a great new movement for change. Me? The image quickly faded as I sensed how overwhelming the problems were, not least my own self-doubt that I could interact with people on a regular basis, eye to eye. How me? How the fuck me?

Yeah, that's right. *You hate everybody, including yourself. Remember? Don't forget that. Everybody can die, for all the fuck you care, including you. Don't forget that. Just die.*

I felt so overwhelmed I wanted to crawl somewhere hidden and go to sleep for twenty years.

But I rolled over to the north.

I need to make a real sacrifice. Bodily sacrifice. Then maybe…

I need to cut my finger off. Then maybe….

I began my public writing career, unhinged, and not so public, with an anonymous piece in the Earth First! Journal, the radical rag of the direct action movement. Handwritten on a couple sheets of paper and mailed to the Journal without talking to anyone there, it felt odd connecting with others about something that had been so private. And when it got published, it was unnerving and exhilarating to know that my voice, my militant radical voice, was now broadcast out into the world.

Earth First! Journal   Eostar (March-April) 1993

The Great American (Festive) Cowboy
By Yellow Grass Dog

George Wuerthner says, "Ranchers are not evil people."

Dave Foreman says, "My heroes used to be cowboys."

The New Mexico snarling bag of bones postal lady/ranchwife says, "Environmentalists make me angry. They've gone too far!"

The Kansas rancher who shot the black boy in the back of the head claimed self-defense, he said he thought the black boy — this "negro" — was "wearing his baseball cap backwards and coming to attack" him. The local Kansas jury — made up of mostly ranchers themselves — of course agreed with the defendant; the rancher/murderer was acquitted.

Against efforts to protect and maybe even heal a shred of Kansas prairie, another rancher wailed. "We are today's Indians!" (This one really made me quiver.)

Rancher/former Montana state senator Pete Story, after a Yellowstone wolf reintroduction hearing, screeched, "Those of us (ranchers) who are affected, we feel like the Jews would, listening to an affable Nazi talk about Auschwitz."

Earlier this century, after the few remaining Indians who had somehow survived the slaughter and starvation campaigns were safely locked up on "reservations," the ranchers then looked around, their eyes widening, and squealed "WOLF!" In Montana alone, in less than 20 years, over 100,000 wolves were poisoned, trapped, shot, and burned alive with flamethrowers during the government's systematic campaign of extermination. *Canis lupus nubilus*, the Buffalo Wolf of the Great Plains, biggest wolf on Earth, became extinct. Another Heaven and another Earth must pass before her own throat may again keen the Stories across the Grassland. Did somebody say *Auschwitz?*

General Philip Sheridan, that Great American Hero, said "Buffalo hunters have done in the past two years and will do more in the next year to settle the vexed Indian question than the entire regular army has done in the past 30 years. They are destroying the Indian's commissary, and it is a well-known fact that an army losing its base of supplies is placed at a great disadvantage. Send them powder and lead if you will; for the sake of a lasting peace let them kill, skin and sell until the buffaloes are exterminated. Then your prairies can be covered with speckled cattle and the festive cowboy, who follows the hunter as a second forerunner of an advanced civilization."

And so:

Starving Blackfeet beg for entrails, guts and blood through the slats of a "speckled cattle" slaughterhouse. Overweight ranchers demand more; the Dawes Allotment Act is passed. Indian people lose more than half of what little land they have left.

The great Yellow Bear, *Ursus Horribilis,* originally a Plains animal, knows the sun-drenched grasses no more; at the sight of the cowboy hat she has shrunk in uncontemplating horror, run wild-eyed for the hills.

Today, the prairie dog remnant-towns of Buffalo Gap National Grassland, just outside South Dakota's Badlands National Park, like all the others, are laced with rodenticides and barbed wire. The BLM (Bureau of Livestock and Mining I mean "Land Management") office in Wall declares emphatically, *"These lands are multiple use! The prairie dogs pose a threat to the ranchers!"*

Black-footed Ferret, just the faintest breath of a whisper now, just barely... (*still here*) twitches through the long-winding burrows and tunnels, hunting, comes across the still-warm (but candy inside) body — easy food in the moonless night.

In January 1993, so late in the Millennium, and yet, still, *still...* South Dakota ranchers demand a $20 bounty be placed on each dead (sacred brother to me) coyote's scalp, to be added to all the millions of public dollars already laid at Rancher's feet. The measure is narrowly defeated in the state legislature. Which only means Rancher won't be paid this extra money; the coyotes will still die.

On the sparsest, most fragile deserts, the cattle graze.

On the wildlife refuges, the cattle graze.

On the National Forests and National Grasslands, the cattle graze.

In many National Parks, the cattle graze.

Has anybody ever seen a wild valley?

Can anyone even imagine a Great Plains Wilderness?

Everywhere, everywhere, mile upon mile upon mile of the Bristling Wires, the once virgin prairie stabbed through and ripped open and strung up. Freedom is a bloody, strangled piece of agonized and torn flesh.

The land is sore, nubbed raw, trampled, pockmarked with shit and clouds of flies.

Every creek, stream, river, pothole, pond, lake is shrunken and infected with disease. Boil or beware.

The ancient, unrenewable aquifer drops. And drops. Drought returns.

Surrounded by grassland and winter forage, the great black Buffalo Bull, breath billowing in the cold air, snorts and shakes his massive woolly head. His herd is close behind. An age-old instinct wells up inside, throbs like drumbeats in his soul. It says, "*Move. Fan out. Shake the ground. Roam...*"

Just recently, the great Bull, followed by his herd, steps across the imaginary Yellowstone National Park line onto other public land. He has left the political square in which he must remain. The Festive Cowboy throws his pink-swollen hands up into the air and SHRIEKS! Government, rancher, and private bullets burn through living flesh. "Like shooting parked cars," they would say later. Hundreds of massive, snorting hulks crumple to the ground; life leaks out into the snow.

Wolf is again sneaking across the imaginary line that lies to the north that is Canada. Rancher hefts up his gut over his belt buckle and snivels to the good old boys, "Shoot, shovel and shut up!"

Across the entire West, spring-loaded cyanide guns sprout like flowers.

Carcasses are laced with black-market strychnine, cyanide, thallium sulfate and compound 1080.

Steel-jawed traps are set.

The good old boys grab automatic rifles and unplugged shotguns, go out for a helicopter joyride.

Newborn, nursing coyote and wolf pups are fish-hooked or dug out of the mother's den; fresh soft skulls are smashed with a shovel or the heel of a cowboy boot. The mother is shot.

Eagles, hawks, vultures, ravens, crows, magpies drop from the sky, poisoned or spattered with lead shot.

And standing dead-center in the killing fields of America, Rancher slowly turns around, tips his 10-gallon hat, and smiles.

And Happy America settles back into big, soft, easy chairs, pushes the button that reclines the chair back. Eyes are closed, feelings are warm inside, dreams are sighed... ("My heroes used to be cowboys"...) The Great American (festive) Cowboy.

Late at night, pushed and cornered and stressed and harassed, and alone too, survivor-coyote crawls exhausted to the hilltop. There seems no hope, or end in sight. With a sudden burst of the last of his energy, fueled by a life's — and half a millennium's — worth of Rage and Anger and bottomless Sorrow, he throws his head back; he cries and cries and cries. His voice spills up out of him. It rings off the hills.

Earth First!ers shuffle their sneakers in the dirt, hands in pockets.

Who is it that's got blood on their hands?

And "Animal Damage Control" gets another year's budget of $30 million.

CHAPTER TWENTY-FOUR

Political Prisoner

I spiraled back onto the Plains…

No hope… everything… every part of this planet has been attacked, impacted, hammered in some way, and people are celebrating it….

In the Oklahoma panhandle town of Boise City, the cattle hauler semis were all lined up and rumbling at the diesel side of the truck stop's filling station, their tall cab exhaust pipes spewing bluish fumes in the searing summer heat.

Inside the metal slats, I could see the wide eyes of sweaty, foamy cattle peering out, their face fur wet with sweat and feces and vomit. Some seemed unsteady on their feet. The stench was acrid. Cattle smell stronger and worse than any animal, and when crammed together, it quickly becomes overpowering. The sides of the cattle haulers were streaked with splashes of liquid shit and vomit that had flung up, out and back, even reaching the tops of the slatted hauler.

I heard yelling. I walked out past the pumps to get a look around the other side. A truck driver was jamming a stick into the trailer, yelling at an about-to-pass-out cow to stay up on her feet. I could hardly see, but I guessed that once she went down, she'd stay down, and probably others would follow, and die like that, leaking vomit and shit and urine in one big pile on top of each other, expiring in the filth, stench and heat.

"Why you hitting him? Her," I said.

He glared at me. "How would you like my job?" he said, wiping at his grizzled, dripping face with his arm. "I don't get paid for dead cows."

"The question is, how would you like their job?" I said. He was black, too, a black trucker in overalls. I wanted him to see that he could look at this differently from the rest.

He sneered and jabbed with the prod again, screaming, "Get up I said get up!"

I backed away. There was nothing I could do. Again.

Some parts of the plains reek for 30 miles or more from giant sprawling cattle feedlots, especially from Garden City to Scott City to Dodge City, Kansas. Hundreds of acres of cattle crammed together at each confined feeding operation, standing and eating in their own waste, casting a sickening plume of waste into the air and water-sheds, polluting everything for miles around. Yet I saw people, blond TV family-looking people going about their daily business as if they couldn't notice. The smells where rendering plants were added were indescribable. Burning blood, offal, shit and death. They even have a regular Burning Blood Day.

I thought: How can people sit down to dinner, work in their yard, send their children out to the playground, make love and sleep amongst this filth? Are they completely dead people? Do they hate the Plains so much, and hate anything of any value in life? I mean, they will actually choose this over any sustainable and healthy economy, because this way at least they don't have to share?

Days, weeks, months passed. Rabid now in my quest to find one undamaged spot, I lost all connection to civilization and drifted hopelessly, pushing on without any plan or reason. I was still coherent enough to know that I was dangerously close to insanity, but I was too caught up in this whirlwind to get out.

Outback dirt roads. Signs of coyotes, their scat stained the bright red of cactus pears. I passed many ghost towns, weathered dwellings and one-room stores now barely recognizable in some nailed-together order of a town once imagined. Houses and shops of grayed wood holding up roofs no longer there, walls pulled apart and shrunken, wind and weeds rustling through. Abandoned two-story schoolhouses of yellow prairie limestone, caved in by the weather like a bomb had dropped, a wall or two standing, rubble scattered in the surrounding jumbles of weeds, rusty nails, boards, coils of wire, grass and snakes. Days burned well over a hundred degrees. Nights dropped to less than half that. Drought persisted. Swarms of locusts rattled through the dry stalks of grass. Cows died right where they stood, belching up their tongues as they fell, or getting stuck in the mud of drying creeks and deciding to die right there before they even keeled over, faces jammed into unnatural positions. On the bloated, stinking bodies, the buzz of thousands of metal blue-green flies, and squirming masses of white maggots.

In southwest Kansas, I found adobe-mortared remnants of Black Freedmen settlements. Some of these had only part of a single building left. Their location perplexed me. Even today, these places are hard to get to. I couldn't imagine black folk coming this far out, on a level plain with no towns or settlements for miles and miles around, enduring frigid winds in winter and broiling heat in the summer, the nearest flowing water a couple miles away. They came with only horses and carts, and their own feet, for transportation. How did they come to think that this was The Place to build a new life? The South had to have been *that* bad. Little did they know that the West as well would grow in white supremacy, hate and intolerance.

All around these silent, abandoned places, in the exhausted soil wild sunflowers grew and stretched their round yellow heads to the sky. It's eerie how they keep their faces turned into the Sun as it passes across the sky. And in the middle of the night, hours before first light, sunflowers switch back around to the east, unable to control their excitement and anticipation, waiting for the Sun to return.

Something about being in the western High Plains for weeks unending, with no shelter, no trees, just a constant wrath of burning plains sun, hot wind, hot dry grass, hot dry dirt, sears into your soul. It gets into the back of your eyes, as if you have just stepped in from the bright into a dark place and you're not sure what you're seeing, yet you're out in the open in broad daylight. No shade… skin turned black like charcoal-fired wood.

But still, the outback High Plains, something softer than the desert… a softer prairie blue light in that unforgiving cloudless sky. Dust storms whip up, created by

Adrián 2006

clueless farmers plowing fields in the middle of a drought-stricken afternoon with the winds blowing 25 mph, ancient soil disappearing in the ceaseless wind. Hell, I thought, these big dryland farmers know they can at least farm the government if nothing else, taxpayer subsidy checks guaranteed.

So much of the land is overgrazed, unable to grow back from lack of rest. Starving wild animals try to get to the strip of grass on the road side of the fence, get hit by cars, or snagged in the wires.

Me... staying far away from people... not knowing or caring whether I was trespassing or not. Where other people would be overcome by the lack of shade and open horizon on the High Plains (and I'd read of many settler people who had gone crazy out here), I felt like the Sun and sky were a protective hand around me, even as it broiled into my bones. My skin was meant for it.

I remained hidden. My senses were so attuned I always saw and heard people before they saw me, so nobody caught me. On autopilot now, knowing I was nearing the end of something, I still searched and searched for life, the life I had visited in my passouts. My stomach hurt so much of the time that I often couldn't eat, or would purposely fast. I grew as lean as possible. Most of the time, I was light-headed. I knew now that if I could just find the center of even one area that was pure and pristine, and not snarled up in the bristling wires, I could sacrifice myself. At the least I could cut my finger off, give myself fully to Grass Earth and God. I was hardly aware of any other motivation. I just propelled myself to keep moving, sometimes holing up for a few weeks, then moving on. Pretty soon, I ceased to smell like sweat; my skin took on a dry earthiness of grass and dirt. I was once again just another animal out on the land, trying to survive, hidden, seeing and gone before being seen.

A mother badger popped out of her burrow, and the way she charged me like a flat bristling little bear I could tell she had much love for her babies, and that she had never met a two-legged before. I met all kinds of rare birds. Lark buntings, long-billed curlews, a sandhill crane. I could smell a coyote den before I saw it; from ten feet away I could smell whether a prairie dog burrow was still alive and active or not. I found ancient arrowpoints, big fluted ones and tiny fragile bird points. I marveled at the artistry and hand dexterity that had created them, thrilled hold in my own hands a direct connection to the primeval world. I found a stone ax head north of Middle Springs on the Cimarron/Santa Fe Trail. Mostly, I left them where they lay.

In flat parts of western Kansas, huge swaths plowed, and harvested early, the cut fields of winter wheat a moonscape of lifelessness. Not even sounds of crickets in the evening by the roadside; the ground must have been soaked with poisons.

Nearly every place on the Plains that is flat is plowed; it's the rolling, or broken or bluff country that's still unscalped grassland and used for cattle-overgrazing.

Occasionally I came across a microclimate, a large oval that had gotten some rain, and it was weird the way you could step from one world into another, from dry, crackly yellowed grass, to green growth, even some flowers, then out of it again. In a microclimate in eastern Colorado lying flat on my stomach I watched amazing life at the green roots: ants, aphids, caterpillars, tiny bugs I didn't know, a miniature grass forest twelve to fifteen inches tall so complex, so beautiful, holding the soil; in cut banks I could see their finger-like roots reaching deep into the ground, holding everything together. *Imagine what it was like back when the world was wild.* Multiply this diversity a thousand times.

How could it be that nobody saw the value in grassland? Everywhere you walked, looked, there had been life. How could they have broken such a valuable thing? It was a homeland and nursery and promise for millions of years and billions of lives.

But wait.

Life was still here. The animals are still here. *Some* of them. They're still here, carrying on their cultures as best they can, even though their lives are filled with constant danger and a never-ending tooth-and-nail struggle to survive. Have they gotten used to this? It's all they know. This is the modern-day Great Plains.

Prairie light at any time of year is unmatched by any light on Earth, but especially in September. September gave way to fall, and fall to a half-frigid, half-warm winter, depending on what the winds were doing. Sometimes, at least in the north, it was 40 below zero; sometimes it was 60 above.

I fasted constantly. I went to South Dakota, into Montana, back down to Nebraska and Colorado and Kansas and Oklahoma and Texas and back up to South Dakota again. I stayed on Pine Ridge Indian Reservation in South Dakota for a while, where I made friends who showed me the buffalo herd they have in a canyon pasture. One of them, who worked at the Tribal Parks Department, told me how she kept hearing this loud knock at night — "You know how a cop knocks?" — but there was never any one there. Things like that happen regularly on the rez. The supernatural is just part of the natural. Some of it's bad and threatening, some of it's good and nurturing. On the outback plains the Indian reservations became for me the only safe place of human inhabitation. People offered rides, invited me over for supper, smiled, laughed, joked. I saw that those smiles weren't just a tough-yourself-up way to handle life in the midst of grinding poverty, rampant drug and alcohol use, and domestic and gang violence that mirrored the worst in America's deepest inner cities, but a radical refusal to live beaten, even inside what people commonly refer to as a POW or concentration camp. Many people don't have running water, the outhouses use trash paper and phone books for toilet paper, public tract housing is ripe with black mold because the BIA sited them carelessly. If a car doesn't have a windshield but runs, and it's 40 below zero, hey, wrap in blankets, strap on the goggles and go. At least it's a working car.

But I couldn't stay put. I kept moving. I had to keep looking for that last wild place. Somewhere in the outback wasn't damaged, there had to be one piece of pure prairie where I could sacrifice myself.

I went in circles and half circles and devised routes. In Wall, SD, I bought the book *Where the Buffalo Roam,* by Anne Matthews, which was nominated for a Pulitzer Prize. It detailed the trips that Frank and Deborah Popper, the professors who came up with the Buffalo Commons idea, took through the Plains when they first were advancing the thesis.

I thought the book would provide some clues for me, but everywhere I went my experience was the same or worse. No Buffalo Commons. Nowhere. Everything imprisoned. Sometimes in winter the land was so damaged I couldn't tell whether it was plowed or just overgrazed.

And I began to question myself. Out here I had fallen so far from the human race, except for my few Indian friends, that I just couldn't see any future. I was at a standstill, a complete loss as to what to do. I had planned on my eventual and final escape. It was the only ticket I'd bought. And I had reached a dead end. The city was a distant haze. Had I once been a homeboy with a gold tooth?

I thought about all the people out there, on the coasts, in the cities, doing their daily lives. They had no idea what it was like out here. Everything was A-OK-all-right in the world. They were worried about what they were going to wear to dinner, if that new red dress would show the booty just right so Terrell would finally make his move, whether they were going to be able to go buy those new shoes in SoHo in time, or dudes buying sneakers and Tommy Hilfiger and fresh colognes, ready to roll with their boyz, wondering what new pussy they were gonna be able to get tonight at the Tunnel, or who saw who where. Etfuckingcetera.

But out here it was a war zone, fucking Afghanistan, right in the middle of their own goddamn country, and nobody knew, and nobody gave a shit. That whole world out there seemed so far away from me I might as well be on another planet. I doubted I would be able to even fake fitting in on the peripheries of that world, even in its underground like before.

I was a wild animal in the West. Worrying about my brothers and sisters the prairie dogs and buffaloes and coyotes, trying to find a place to... *to what? Eat a fucking elk and live off the land, aboriginally? You're a fucking vegetarian, first of all, and second of all you're about to turn to dust, because you can't get anything done out here. Because in one way or another it has been turned into a wasteland. And so have you.*

Well, if I make a sacrifice, maybe there will be—

The last of another winter moved into a warm early spring, which arrived in five minutes. I drifted southward again, heading for my Texas. In western Oklahoma, near the overgrazed and oil-drilled Black Kettle National Grassland, I stopped at the Black Kettle Museum in Cheyenne. A mountain lion — a large tom — was stuffed in a bad snarl pose inside a glass box. He'd been the first mountain — I mean prairie — lion who'd made it back onto the Oklahoma prairies in decades. It occurred to me that most of the animals I'd seen in my life were dead — shot, mangled in some way, laying beside the road, strung up in fences, poisoned.

A rancher in a navy blue button-down shirt stretching over his protruding belly walked in. I lowered my head, holding my breath. Suddenly trapped in this small room in close proximity with The Enemy. So close. Out through the window I could see his giant shiny new pickup truck. I tried to edge back toward the wall as he went into the other room. I turned around holding my breath as he passed, not wanting to even breathe in any of his exhalation.

Just as I prepared to bolt for the door he stopped and turned around, came up to me. I cringed. He pointed his short swollen fingers at the big cat in glass. "That's a mountain lion," he said, the fleshy drooping folds along his jaw wiggling as he nodded knowingly. "Not much good for anything."

He lifted his head to peer at me beneath the 10-gallon cowboy hat rim. "What're you looking for? Work?"

Still unable to turn my head to look at him directly, I just shook my head, willing him to move away from me.

"Black Kettle," I said.

"What? I didn't hear you."

"Heard me," I grunted.

"Oh I see, you're one of *them*." He nodded his head. He walked out the door.

The curator came up to me, motioned at the lion. "Likely he came up from the canyons in Texas following a river, maybe even the Canadian in New Mexico across Texas and into here. But the local ranchers around here say the government is coming in black helicopters at night and dropping them on us. That it's a ploy to get the Endangered Species Act enforced on them and take away their land and grazing rights on the national grassland."

"Black Kettle survived the massacre at Sand Creek," I said. "Only to be slaughtered four years later by Custer out here by the Washita. What do you think? You're the curator. You're supposed to at least be objective."

He eyed me straight. "I think this lion got pushed out of old territory as a young male by other lions, came scouting for new lands, and with our decrease in human population and the comeback of some really fat deer, got away with it here for years till he got caught." He stared at the glassed big tom. "Local people are just nervous. They feel like they can't make anything work. Unfortunately, some people will shoot anything they feel doesn't belong here. The old culture is dying hard, and people are scared. But they're mostly good people."

"But who was here first?" I protested. "Why can't there be some effort to at least allow some room? I mean, why do they have to have the entire thing, the entire thing, every last bit of it?"

"I have to get back to work," he said, grimacing. "But please make sure you sign the guest book before you leave." He turned his back and walked away, shoulders a little slumped.

I sputtered down into Texas, out into the Panhandle. The Llano Estacado is flat as a table. It was a million year old grassland until being plowed. Abandoned farmsteads in slow, decades-long collapse.

On the Rita Blanca National Grassland I found nine dead aerial-gunned coyotes dumped in a pile, big ragged holes blasted out of their necks or backs or ribs. All their mouths had fallen open, frozen in a jagged white-toothed gasp or grin of death, black lips pulled back.

Squatting by the nearest one, I examined his face and body. His slanted yellow eyes were sinking and clouding over. A fly buzzed into his mouth, crawling jerkily on six graphite-like legs over his tongue. The hole in his neck had soaked a ring of blood into the still-winter thick, yellow silver and tawny fur. The electric-blue peaceful fly flew up out of his mouth in a winding circle as if drawing the path of a vine up into the sky, then buzzed in a straight line down onto the blind eye of the next corpse.

I palmed the pads of the coyote's paws. Rough and cleanly lined, like my own hands. Fleshy, padded, black, cold. I wet the pad of my thumb with the tip of my tongue and polished his short dog-like fingernails, getting the dust out and the shine back in. The black nails shone against the yellow-blond fur of his dead, once-strong legs.

Sound travels far in the dry country, I thought to myself as I heard the very faint buzzing of a plane that nagged at an otherwise perfect silence. Then the concussive bangs of high-powered rifles firing. And again.

What would you do if one of those flew over you?

If I was armed, and we were very far out, I'd probably try to shoot his ass out of the sky, I thought to myself. And they'd fire at me and — well — whoever hit who first wins, I guess. I shrugged.

What'd really be best is if I could get one of those "really big guns," like they called them and kept out of sight up in Indian Country. Surface-to-air shoulder-fired missile launchers. I knew that a few Indian people had them, just in case. I mean, they'd been attacked before. Hell....

Still in the Texas Panhandle a week or so later, increasingly weak, unable to eat, I staggered into an abandoned farmhouse, knowing I'd reached the end. I surveyed the roof. Pretty good roof. On the rafters were built-up cones of bird guano, from birds roosting in the exact same spot. All the inside walls were knocked down or fallen in, so there was only one open area. A stained mattress lay on rusted coil springs in one "room". A porcelain doll's face, grimy and smudged, stared at me. I turned it away so her eyes looked into the baseboard. The slight wind whistled through the cracks and holes in the outer walls. On the outside, the people had plastered mud adobe-style into the cracks around the wood boards, but most of that had fallen out. The boards were still in pretty good shape. I guessed the house had probably been abandoned in the late 30s. There was a pile of newspapers, the most recent from the 70s. The Shah of Iran stared up at me from one of the brittle newspapers. I wasn't the first squatter in this old abandoned place.

My stomach hurt so much I was afraid to ever eat again. I pulled out my knife and a yellow candle. I placed the candle in an area shielded from wind drafts, and lit it. I would stay with it till it burned down. Lahumba had said yellow was for manifestation. I collapsed onto the stained, nasty mattress on the loose springs, but it sagged and was so lumpy I felt like I was laying on a couple dead bodies. I found a wood shelf that may have been a built-in table nook or something, and flattened out on my back. I watched the sky through the cracks, and listened to the winds whistle in, stop, blow harder, fall silent, go soft, then hum; the house creaked and groaned.

A couple days and nights passed. Occasionally I stumbled outside to piss. World grew hazy. I was becoming bones. Even the drool coming out of my open, half-dead mouth dried up. Pretty soon I got confused whether it was night or day, because I saw spots, and sometimes I thought the light coming in through the cracks was spots. Or the other way around. I think.

Sleeping. The candle was almost burned down in its glass tube. It had been friend and God, fire equaling energy equaling light equals God… Sleeping… I knew it was night. Too dark in here.

I jolted awake as somebody thumped me in the chest, then again pushed his hands down into my chest, knocking the air out of me. And thumped me a third time. I felt my skin and hair bristle as I looked around wide-eyed. Nobody in the room. Only candle light. There was no wind or sound of wind. Absolute stillness. And again somebody slammed down on me. I gulped and almost swallowed my tongue. I clamped down on it with my teeth. Ice and fear surged in my veins. Completely vulnerable. Completely weak. Drained of all strength. Whoever you are, you got me, you got me now, for good this time. I could do nothing. Unable to move, my eyes darted around, out the slats, up and down the room, stared up at the dark guano-piled rafters, the vaulted roof. All the shadows…

I lay there frozen with fear. Completely vulnerable, bracing for the next attack. *I … can't … see … you! Who the fuck… Are… where…*

The candle flame flickered. *But there's no wind.* Bright point yellow fire light. Flickering now. Clean. The center of the room. Center of the Universe. Fire. Light. Sun. God.

I began to pray; pray so hard. I noticed my veins warming up; able to move my fingers now. I prayed. Or vowed. Or swore. Didn't know the difference. Silently, but loud, inside my soul and chest — *I reject all that is hateful, ugly, and life-destructive in the Universe… I reject all that is hateful, ugly and life-destructive in the Universe… I reject all that is hateful, ugly and life-destructive in the Universe…*

As I repeated it over and over silently, swelling it out of my sunken chest, pushing outward, I felt something big and dark, monstrous, hovering right over me. Suddenly it budged. It scared me. I couldn't see it, but I could. Like a mass of black right there. I got defiant. *I reject all that is ugly, hateful and life-destructive in the Universe.* It budged backwards another inch. I couldn't see it, but I could see through it to the yellow flickering candle flame, and that flame seemed to flicker more and more excitedly. And I thought my eyes were watering, because there seemed to be a glowing halo around the flame… softest glow. *I reject all that is hateful, ugly and life-destructive in the Universe!… I reject all that is ugly, hateful and life-destructive in the Universe!!…* Over and over I swore it without mouthing a word, and whoever it was that had attacked me kept getting pushed further and further back, towards that flame. I pushed with all my soul, my chest, everything inside me, repeating it over and over again, all night long, for hours, and the dark cloud-like monster moved backwards inch by inch. And then, right when I thought it must be near or over the flame, suddenly — I knew it was gone. I was alone. Except for the flickering flame. The flame settled out, grew still, pointed straight up to the ceiling in a perfect motionless spire.

Jaw aching, shivering from cold and exertion, I got up, a walking skeleton. Peered outside the slats, still a little careful about exposing my back. Still a few hours before dawn. I went back and lay down. A gentle wind seeped in through the cracks, silently. I felt it on my eyeballs and lashes. The candle flame flickered.

During the day, I tried to poke around outside, but was just too weak. There was nobody around for miles. Outside I found a shotgun-blasted hawk that had dried to a hard-feathered mass, and I brought him in with me. For days longer I lay inside on the wood shelf with the hawk, wrapped in a blanket, cold and hot, shut off in complete darkness, except for the slats that whistled when the wind blew and sent in sideways bullets of light when the sun shined. I grew too weak to move. My head swam in blue and green spots behind my eyes. I passed in and out of consciousness. I could barely take sips from the bottle of water at my side. It was my last gallon jug. I wondered if my car outside had been reclaimed by wild grasses and flowers. The thought made me smile. Paint me a beautiful painting, before you go. At night I thought I heard the patter of paws or swoosh of a low body outside in the grass and weeds.

This time my passouts were almost blank, filled with nothing but air and the blue and green spots, like bubbles. Usually I went on vivid trips, but here I was floating in empty clear space. Just me and those hard little blue and green bubbles. I was bubbly. The thought made me laugh.

I thought of nothing. Except sometimes the bubbles. My breaths slowly gasped down to what might flutter, at most, a flower's petal. The candle burned down and went out with a hiss.

A couple more days of blankness passed. On the sixth or seventh day, I became conscious of an image floating behind the blue and green bubbles. It had probably been there for a while.

The image made me giddy. It looked like a little hard worm, maybe a quarter-inch long, dun colored, just floating by itself in the background. *People eat worms, you know. Good protein. Hahahah.*

What? Shut the fuck up.

If I looked at it for too long it started to steam. I began thinking about a handful of those little hard worms clumped together in a small steaming bowl.

I focused on the bowl. I looked from the bowl to the blue and green bubbles and back to the bowl again. Behind that, flickering in and out of view I thought I saw a man who looked like he had supple flesh on his bones; he looked strong. Eyes and teeth bright. But he was see-through, and as quick as I saw him, he vanished.

I pulled my arms over my face and pressed hard, trying to block out everything. I was too weak to turn over. The images kept coming. The stupid dude, and the hard little steaming worms.

And finally, a few hours later I decided that I had a small plastic bag of brown rice in my car. The rice kernels looked like little hard worms. And a blue cooking pot. I could almost smell the aroma of cooking rice. I was hungry!

For the rest of the early afternoon, I planned my trip to the car. Before evening I had dragged my body off the bed, made it outside. My stiff, air-filled movements seemed awkward and in slow motion, but got easier with each step. I saw the afternoon sun not filmy but unfiltered and bright. A yellow butterfly fluttered past. The car was not part of a beautiful painting, tangled up in vines and flowers. It was just my damn Toyota sitting there.

I made a fire. Modern technology. The lighter in my bag. So not all modern things are bad, huh? Made a fire right inside an old tin washtub, out of the wind, using a pile of sticks from a wood rat's old nest.

In another hour, the grain was boiling; its steamy, nutty aromatherapy filled the cabin. I opened the creaking door to add the evening sunlight in.

Soon, I sat in the doorway in the red setting sun, a skeleton without a grin but a hungry belly. Yucca stalks and grasses spiked long sharp silhouettes in front of me. I poured some blackstrap molasses — iron and phosphorous-rich — over my steaming bowl of rice, and held the warm bowl close to the center of my belly. Two, three, four grains on my fork at a time, I ate the entire bowl, my strength returning like a small fire building inside.

I felt different. Cleaned out. I had passed some point, and also passed something out of myself. *So you've decided to live?*

I thought of my body. I was still a young man. Something (what… human need?) stirred inside me. Let it go. It was too early to think about rejoining society just yet.

I thought of my Plains, and as I did so I realized it was with acceptance. The past was over with. I let it go.

But that didn't mean history was over. It was late spring 1994. Nelson Mandela had just become the first democratically elected President of South Africa. Night began to fall, bowl of darkening blue lowering overhead.

The wind stopped. I wrapped myself in the blanket like a mummy and sat in the doorway. A few crickets picked up, holding onto the remaining warmth of the spring day, perched on the soil between the roots of the grasses. I listened to them sawing their waxy wings, ticking and clicking and rasping, picking up a rhythm, getting faster, then buzzing down to silence, only to start again. As they did so, new crickets joined them, a discordant band of insects playing parts of their own bodies, jamming at the grass roots, sending a message up into the deepening sky.

The land all around was feral, ragged, tangled, plowed at one time but long fallow and grown in weeds, recovering native grasses, flowers and vines: a grassland post-apocalyptic version of that Henri Rousseau painting "The Dream." Last year's matted dead growth was being replaced by new spring green grass. Soon, the sky would have more stars than blank spaces. I thought about each of those stars. How many of them might be suns like ours, all part of the Great Sun? How many worlds, how many souls out there?

A shooting star pierced the distant sky... not a real star. Meteor burning as it dove into our atmosphere.

I suddenly thought about a woman's white robes and veil blowing in the wind — blue-black skin and eyes shining. Now it seemed as if those robes, that head wrap, that hand could sweep across the entire night sky in a flash.

We have no evidence of any other place like Earth, I thought. Not a single other place.

The number of crickets increased, from hundreds to thousands, then into the tens of thousands, then even more. Their voices were rising, their scratchy wing and leg music as precise as warm needles stitching together a great quilt of living sound. New crickets joining into the jam raced to catch up with the ones already singing. As the plain filled to the horizon with insect meaning, I at last heard them all as one, veins and shiny black bellies full of green plant life, hundreds of thousands, millions of them, chanting in unison from one horizon to the other, somehow exactly in tune with each other, their voices rising and falling. Rising and falling... Chanting, chanting, chanting, working themselves harder and harder into it, sending their message?... story?... up through the grasses of this million year old plain, up into the night sky, up into the atmosphere, up *through* and beyond the atmosphere into the black Universe filled with galaxies of stars. They were telling a story, letting somebody know. Who? Old friends and relations? What did they know, right now, right here, as millions of their lidless black eyes gleamed up between the shoots of grass, into the twilight, antennas perked?

As I made it back north up through the Texas Panhandle and crossed the Canadian River, I knew that the Sun wasn't up in the sky, like people thought. It was straight out parallel to here, a massive, boiling ball of white-yellow fire blasting unimaginable heat at our little planet and beyond.

I was a microscopic plainsman in that blast. So powerful, this Sun that we are ruled by, blasting 93 *million* miles away, and so perfectly calibrated is Earth that less than a half mile change in elevation makes all the difference in the weather.

One thing I knew: As long as I had Sun and Earth, I was not alone.

Morton County, Kansas. Southwesternmost county in the state. Outside the little town library I sat down on the curb and thought about what I'd just read in the glossy picture book *Kansas People*. Head bent into the book, staring at the quote, I didn't know what to make of it. The sharp black letters on the shiny white paper seemed to move on their own. My mind drifted. I forced myself again to focus. The quote said:

"I guess if you've never seen or experienced open land such as we have here, it would be difficult to accept. It's just peaceful. Gets you away from the strains of life. You have to adjust to the quietness out here. And, really, loneliness and isolation at times. If you learn to live with yourself, you're going to be all right."

— Elizabeth Rogler, Chase County rancher

But she's a rancher. How could she have *any* feelings?

How could a person from a ranching family be expressing such heartfelt familiar feelings? Here — right from The Enemy — words of wisdom, and feelings you've had yourself?

I remembered a paragraph in the book *View from Officers' Row*, a book that tries to gauge the perceptions of the military officers mounting the Western slaughter campaigns against Indian people. There was one account of a group of officers that'd been traveling with an Indian scout, and the Indian man was remembering something painful and started to cry. The officers had been amazed. They had no idea that Indians were capable of exhibiting emotions.

I again remembered a saying. Had I heard it? Read it? Some Indian grandmother's saying... from a border desert tribe, the Tohono O'odhams, or Papagos, as they used to be known: "Keep your hair out of your eyes and don't be like the enemy!"

Against the concrete pavement I rubbed the soles of my sneakers back and forth, getting antsy. *Maybe Kansas is here to teach you about your own self. You automatically run from or shut off somebody if they exhibit any of a long line of red-flag indicator traits. Maybe the whole world is fucked up and never was perfect, just like you. Gotta get through the bad to get to the good. Doesn't mean you have to compromise. But instead of running, maybe you should work toward finding some common ground. Meaning you have to get past and over your own prejudices.*

I will never compromise my beliefs!

You don't have to.

I refuse to accept that history is over with!

Who said you have to?

I refuse to accept any so-called limits on what is or isn't possible, what can or cannot be done.

Huh, I thought. Maybe it will be in this manner that we will — or won't — as a species make it to the Future.

I looked out, down the street, past the edge of town, to where the land opened up again into its big bowl of universe, sky, grass, emptiness. My Great Plains. Dry, dusty, worn, tired... You damned old field. You're going to be my garden.

I scuffled my feet some more. I got up, started to walk back to my car, then whirled around and sat back down on the curb, furrowing my brow, needing to think more about this, oblivious to the mostly empty street. I paged mindlessly through the book. *Watch me make it grow.* Watch me make the prairie bloom again. I'm going to bring the buffalo back, and he will for the first time in a hundred years be truly a Buffalo, meaning not a ward of man, but a wild Buffalo free to roam wherever he chooses. We're going to have a true Buffalo Commons where people and wildlife live alongside each other in health and balance. A World Heritage Site. A place big enough to hold its secrets intact. A shining example not only to the nation but the entire world. Remember the bumper sticker you saw in Albuquerque: IF THE PEOPLE WILL LEAD THE LEADERS WILL FOLLOW.

The thought finally formed out of all the subconscious naggings of the past year and floated to the surface: I'm going to start my own organization.

My manic enthusiasm dropped as suddenly as it'd risen.

In the morning, I'd gone into the local Cimarron National Grassland headquarters to protest.

"This is cattle country!" she had said.

"Wrong," I'd said. "It's buffalo country."

We have no leaders, I thought, snapping the book closed in my lap. I felt crazy with frustration. They just don't understand. How can I explain that the land needs to rest, that it is hurting and sore, that it is so tired, just wants to be left alone, that constantly putting all those cattle out there is like putting acid on a wound?

A woman was walking in my direction down the sidewalk, a red-haired redneck female in a sleeves-rolled-up white t-shirt with her hair cut tomboy short. She was holding a cigarette and waving it at the air. She came right up to my feet, which stopped in mid-antsy scuffle. I gave her a look that said either she or I must be crazy.

She waved the cigarette at me impatiently, then jutted it into the corner of her mouth and said in a heavy drawl laced with alcohol and a lifetime of smokes. "Hon, can you get me a light? I'm already late." Her wrinkly arm skin was as reddened as her neck and face and messy hair, only disgustingly see-through, almost blue, and I could see her veins.

"Ain't smokin'. Don't got a light," I said, looking back down at my feet, then remembered I did; it was in my pocket next to my knife. "Uh, yeah, wait. Think I do."

"Oooh, good," she said through cigarette-pursed lips. "If I don't get my smoke my finger'll start itchin'. I can feel it already startin'!"

I looked up at her as I dug for the lighter in my jeans. She was holding up her right hand, specifically where her pinky would be. It was gone. Just a stump. She only had three fingers and her thumb. I couldn't help focusing on her missing finger.

"Hon, what you starin' at? I told you this shit's about to start itchin' agin, so can you hurry it up?"

Shaking my head, trying to figure out what to say, I started to stand up and flick it for her but she snatched it out of my hand and lit the cig herself.

Puffing the flame into her Merit, she tossed the lighter back at me. Smoke streamed up into her face, making her blink. "Thanks. That damn fuckin' peckerwood of a boyfriend bit it off. Then he called the cops when I tried to shoot him. And the cops arrested me when they came, accusing *me* of making "terroristic threats" against *them*! And the damn thing still acts like it's still there. It drives me crazy day and night!" She turned around and walked off like a man, in her tight faded jeans, rubbing her hand, trying to scratch a finger that wasn't there anymore.

CHAPTER TWENTY-FIVE

Everything Will Now Come Your Way

New York City seemed so long ago. I shook my head, trying to remember how long I'd been gone. Almost a year? More than a year? My thoughts got distracted by the big city; still so familiar, but different. Me too, I knew, as I drove in, approaching the island skyscape looming with glass and steel like spines on a dinosaur's back. I contemplated its honking, gridlocked traffic, screeching subway trains, and river-in-motion throngs of humans striding uptown, downtown, crosstown; chrome and metal sparking eye-painful angles in hazy hot sunlight. Hidden in its humid bowels seethed the city's crumbling tenements, and drug lords on sidestreets off Brooklyn, Uptown, and the Lower East Side. Hidden in its covert corners of warehouses, parks, and beneath bridges, pretzels of hard black feces anguished out of homeless human bowels, formed hard and black from scraps of processed food and refuse, scavenged to make a belly full.

People said NYC was the "Island at the Center of the World."

But I knew its name was originally "Mannahatta," "the island of many hills," named by the Lenape Indians, and that Midtown used to be a wild thicket of berries, flowers, vines, deer, and wolves.

Whenever I'd previously commuted back to NYC, I'd dropped right in, hit the street running. But this time....

Central Park... green lungs sucking me into its soft, damp breath and pulsing tissue, catching me up like a bug in a Venus fly trap.

I kept to the shadows, edging into the Park from 72nd St. after coming down Central Park West from 106th and Hotel Hell.

Dead Road in the middle of the park was live with people glad for a car-free space. Young people of all different ethnicities skating, attractive and vibrant, agile on their Rollerblades or quads, dancing to high-energy tribal house beats I could hear dimly from this side of Sheep Meadow. I could see some bike riders hanging out, straddling fresh new mountain bikes. Black and Rican, some had heavy-duty blue-and-white BMX-style gloves, those doing the hardcore riding up and down the two-story glacier-stripped boulders further up. I could see the burrito woman with her hand-truck and ice chests — what was her name? My mind drifted.

I leaned on the chain-link fence, watching the scene from about a hundred yards away. It was Sunday in Central Park. The Capoeira dancers were sweating out the day's practice of the slave-invented Brasilian martial art. By the benches, the Haitian drummers worked the tightly packed crowd to a frenzy as weed smoke wafted into the air. The dancing and drumming got more and more furious. I looked at all the people hanging out in Sheep Meadow, or walking through the park. The city rose behind them, around them. I glanced into the western sky, in my mind's eye following the curve of the Earth westward. I doubted that a single person here was thinking about buffaloes or prairie dogs or aerial gunning, let alone the presence of the ancient island right beneath their feet.

Maybe they have their own issues, maybe they aren't oblivious to the world's problems, but they know how to balance their lives. They take time to hang out, have fun. Together with their friends. With other people. Maybe they balance their shit.

Halfway around the world, the Rwandan genocide was occurring. With machetes. Nobody was doing anything about it, least of all the superpower U.S., and our damn military could stop the whole thing with .22's if they wanted to. I couldn't seem to get my mind around what was happening over there. *You short-circuiting?* The world was an endless war zone. I realized a new layer of numbness was forming.

I noticed a white oak tree behind the dancing skaters. I wondered how old it was — maybe 70 to 100 years? I could see the tops of its roots and I knew they reached deep into the ground. My eyes followed the trunk stretching up into the sky and the limbs reaching out as if swaying sinuously in very slow motion. The oak was dancing like the skaters, only each little move took months.

I felt exposed leaning on the fence, and pulled back. Seeking shadows, I ran right into Martin, who was walking down the path toward the concession stand and Dead Road.

"Oh snap! Look who is! Man, J., where you been?"

I grunted. Then realized how that sounded, and tried again. "West." I looked him straight in the eyes, beneath the bill of his NY Yankees baseball cap. He cocked his head at me. "Aiight. Well, I don't know, but you get what you need out there? This time?"

I dapped his hand and headed off, not saying anything.

"Hey J-Man," he said to my back. "Pops been askin' bout you. When you comin' back to work?"

My mind didn't feel like it was really working right. Having trouble staying focused. City, everything, still a little overwhelming. I shook my head and kept walking. Suddenly it seemed like people were crawling all over the park, bumping into me, heading into me, crossing right in front of my path. I tried to get out of all of it. Get out of their way.

At night, on my bike and back in the park, only further uptown in the North Meadow, I coasted on the path. This big open field just south of Harlem's North Woods always reminded me of out West because of its open space and one prairie-like knoll that rises to the north; from here I could see all the way down to the lower tip of Manhattan and the World Trade Center. Just off the 103rd Street entrance, past the Loch and the cattail-lined lake, this field usually held few people, and was empty at night. I rolled up to my secret black walnut tree, the only one I knew here, near the mud-and-cinder horse trail, and crashed out next to it in the grass, touching its rough familiar bark with my fingertips. The black walnut tree embodied the Midwestern prairie/forest edge, as well as being a direct cousin to the Texas native pecan. One of my secret sharers. Sometimes, on foot, streaming down from Harlem and out of the North

Woods and into this open space, I felt like Hiawatha stepping from his primeval forest onto the prairies. Black walnut trees are to me a part of a group of plants and animals including the sunflower, luna moth, buffalo, prairie dog, passenger pigeon and northern pike who embody the original garden fertility of the North American heartland.

Drinking up the cushioned silence, letting the hum of the city stay out there beyond the lung tissue walls of the park, I could see one star in the sky, and one planet that I thought was Jupiter. The rest of the night sky was washed out from the great upward heaving of city light.

I flopped over onto my back in the grass. Everything was ok, or at least better, when there was physical contact with the Earth. Nobody could see me here; still I kept my senses alert. I wanted nobody to come and violate this momentary claim of private sharing. But I knew my senses were so automatic now in being able to see or hear people before they did me, I was covered.

After lying there for about 20 minutes, I again thought about all those people this afternoon, all those people being active, looking good, feeling good, hanging out, maybe meeting new lovers or old friends. And how the chain link fence had bit into my forearms, digging into my skin, but I didn't move until I needed to slip back into more cover.

Why couldn't you gone and joined them? Or just talked to somebody. Just see somebody you think might be cool, just make a new friend?

Oh well. Maybe we just gotta accept certain things. People have certain lots in life.

Well what are you even back here for?

Finding myself alive and ok in Texas, I'd suddenly taken a look at myself, and thought, "what am I doing?" I'd grown restless and tempted. Needed a break. Felt my oats. Maybe I wanted to be around people, just be young and urban for a moment, clean myself up, put a temporary separation between me and the ugliness, sorrow, and crushing weight of the American West. Just a breather. *Maybe meet somebody? What about that side of you?*

So, on the spur of the moment, I'd decided to drive back to NYC just for the summer. Maybe I could deserve a summer's respite? Having passed something out of me, I was sticking to my new thinking about trying to find balance. For the first time I devised a plan. I knew I definitely needed to spend the rest of my life out West, but I didn't know where. I decided I would move to a small city in the fall, and see if I could blend my urban and outback natures. I thought of Texas, but something compelled me for now further west. I decided that after my little break I'd move out to Pueblo, Colorado. It seemed reasonable and nothing I should feel guilty about, like I was abandoning the battle or losing my militancy or going soft or some shit. Maybe living in the West didn't have to mean total abandonment of the human race and civilization. I realized this was a huge evolution in my thinking.

Though I'd never been there, Pueblo seemed like a good compromise, a small diverse city of about 100,000 people on the western edge of the Southern Plains. Not too far from the five state area of Colorado, New Mexico, Texas, Oklahoma, and

Kansas that had some national grasslands and good potential for restoration. Maybe I could set up there. I knew I needed to get settled.

I was going to start an organization. That was my answer to the impasse I'd come to in the West. There was no safe place, so it was up to me to create one. And I needed to find a base to do it. My hell and self-torture in the outback were over. I would chill the summer, just see what's up, go with the flow, then in September move back out for good, get a house, and slowly begin starting my new organization and new life. I was really going to do this. Though I really didn't know the hell how.

I flipped over onto my stomach, face down in the dirt. Lay there, breathing, like a child on a mother's belly, breathing in and out.

I got up on my knees, looked up at the star most visible, pressed my forehead into the ground, and prayed, palms flat against the Earth, still breathing full. In… and out.

I shaved my head. Kept my room in Hotel Hell clean and organized as possible. I bought a gym membership down at the 24 hour club "Johnny Lats" on 17th St. I began working out five times a week. And riding my brand new Specialized Rockhopper Comp FS-1 mountain bike 200 miles a week, nearly 30 miles a day. Built my body; toned that shit up. Learned more about natural supplements, and began taking spirulina, a super-blue-green algae rich in beta carotene, iron, vitamin B-12 and GLA that for centuries nourished people in Africa and North America, but only recently had been marketed as "the world's healthiest superfood." If I was really gon be the new soldier I began sensing I could be, I couldn't just eat healthy and work out; I needed to build and renew my body on the inside too.

I still had some cash money left, more than 20Gs left from the business. I'd be cool. I had a plan. And once I got out to Pueblo, my expenses would be almost nothing.

Just a little longer, I thought to myself, before I move back out West, once and for all.

You think there's something left for you here, in New York, don't you? What you missing?

Her dark eyes shimmered like Egyptian stillwater pools in moonlight. She knew their spell. She pursed her lips into a Janet Jackson-like smile.

"Yes I did, Jihad! I drove across all by myself, in my baggy sweats and baseball cap," Lahumba said in answer to my question. "I looked like a trucker!" She said it proudly. We sat side by side on the edge of her bed, which was ringed in lit candles. Her windows were open; the curtains moved gently. I could smell incense and essential oils. A cab honked outside. Her hands were placed on top of her rounded thighs, her fingernails painted clear shellac. She was wearing a white linen blouse and pants, and the herb-oiled black essence of her skin smoked through.

"I don't think you looked like a trucker," I said, nodding at her figure.

She took a confident deep breath, exhaled dramatically and smiled like a movie star. "Now you listen, Brotherman. When I was driving over one of those states with mountains, I think Colorado, I was coming down this really steep hill, and suddenly

I looked out and my U-Haul was starting to catch up to me alongside me, out my window! I was so scared I almost screamed! I had to drive out into the right lane and then back to the left and swerving all over, and cars and truckers were getting mad at me, and I felt it was whipping me back and forth, but I finally straightened it out!"

I had my face buried in my hand, shaking my head. "Why didn't you take a more southern route to avoid the mountains? Like I-40."

"Oh I just did what the Triple A people said. I don't know."

I rolled my eyes.

"Oh, and by the way, Mister Brotherman. I *could* play a homeless or street person in a film. A true actress can get down and dirty as much as she can play the Queen of England. In fact, my manager just called with an audition for a play where this woman ends up being a streetwalker after her husband leaves her, and then she takes over the block and street corner. It's like a reverse rise to fame, only through her downfall. I think that's what they said. Only thing is, it's down in Philly. Maybe I mentioned it to you?"

Trying not to roll my eyes I said, "You gon take it?"

"Mmmm. I don't know sweetie. I just met Sterling, and things seem to be going good. I have to audition for it first."

"You like living in the theater district?" I asked, remembering all the hookers and Times Square stuff. But the place was changing, at least during the day. And most of the old businesses on 42nd Street between 7th and 8th were being shut down and boarded up one by one. Supposedly Disney or something was going to take it over; word was a whole reconstruct was about to happen. But a lot of the streets above and below were still like they used to be. That little hole in the wall TRIX was still here. I'd gone in, out of curiosity. It was still as empty and desperate as ever, one of the lowest class hustle joints, hardly a step above the piers. Most who tricked here also tricked the streets. Skinny little black and boricua hustlers swarmed around the lone fat white man in a business suit, while a skinny doped-out "dancer" stripped on the bar naked except for his little tighty-whities. Place was nothing but a seedy, deserted, narrow slot in the wall that served beer in cans, with a jukebox that only had a couple scratchy songs each from Paula Abdul or Jody Watley.

The whole thing seemed insane to me. I could hardly believe I had been an insider in that world. But in a way, in a weird, solidarity kind of way, stepping momentarily into that very hidden bar, so removed from daily American life, had felt comfortable.

Lahumba was talking. "...but Sterling doesn't know. But Oh My God, Jihad. When he went down on me, or should I say came up on me, from the bottoms of my legs up, right up between my legs.... And then right as he, um, got there, he stopped, and rose up to my face and teased me by kissing me on the lips. I can always tell if there's potential by the first kiss. You can tell everything that's important about a man by the way he kisses."

She had her head turned towards me, seemingly flushed by what she was describing.

"So that's my story. I'm back in New York. Sterling is helping me out with this apartment. But I met somebody else!"

"I don't know what to tell you," I said. "I'm not the expert. My name is Single and Celibate. I'm still tryin' to get the image of you fish-tailing down the Colorado mountains out my head."

She rubbed her hand over my freshly-bristled head and instinctively I turned my face into it before I stopped myself, the sudden human physical contact sending shock waves through my body. "The only reason you're single and celibate is because you're afraid of getting close to people, Brother Man. You are so closed off, you push people away. You're unapproachable. I see how people look at you, and they would like to get to know you, but they look and hit a brick wall. My friend said her brother said you walk down the street with a look that says "Fight me."

"People always think that shit. I'm sick of it. That's just the way my face is. I'm just a serious person. They thinking I'm ready to thug on somebody when really I'm thinking about saving the bunnies. My mind is a million miles away."

She laughed and clapped her hands together. "Oh, come on, let me read your tarot cards!"

"You always want to read the damn tarot cards," I said, twisting my lips into a dumb smile. "Naah, I can't. I gotta go. I just came by to say hi. And that I'm glad you made it here safely. It's a big move for you."

She got up and slinked into the kitchen. A slight breeze blew her curtain, tugging at the folds in her linen pants. She really was so beautiful.

I heard another cab drive by down on the street. I smirked to myself that I still had it: the ability to tell the difference between cabs and regular cars a lot of the time just by the sounds they made. She opened the fridge and came out with two fortune cookies, handed me one.

"Well, open it. I had some amazing Chinese food today, sesame tofu and broccoli, with brown rice! It was just amazing!"

"Almost as good as your L.A., huh?"

"Oh, and I had a glass of white wine, too. Shaaa-blee. It was perfect."

She cracked open her brittle fortune cookie, a few crumbs falling onto her lap. "It says: 'You will have pleasant surprise in your search for the pot of gold!'" She smiled. With her fingertips she picked out the crumbs from her lap and placed them in her mouth, eyeing me expectantly.

She popped a piece of the shiny-glazed hollow cookie inside her mouth and reached over and grabbed for mine. "Here, let me, if you won't," she said in between crunchy bites.

I pulled back. "Ok, ok." I cracked it open, and unfolded the stiff little piece of pink paper. "It says: 'Everything will now come your way.'"

"Everything will now come your way," I thought with a luxuriant swoon, sitting in the twilight on the curb in front of my house on the Lower East Side of Pueblo, Colorado. I had made it out of New York for good. Summer'd passed, I'd rode my bike every day, grew restless and anxious for battle which, as always, helped shunt off any deeper personal yearnings, and boom. Popped out of the city on a moment's notice in mid-September. And here I was at last, with everything behind me, and ready to dig in and start building up an organization. I'd been thinking about this for a long time, and really felt I could now do it. It would be called Great Plains Restoration Council. There was nothing else to do on the Great Plains but restoration. Everything was shattered. And it needed to be a cultural movement, not a biology project, involving black, Indian, white, Hispanic, everybody. It needed a mission to rebuild health in the widest definition of the word, with practical specifics and applications. There was work to do.

My house was at the end of a dead-end street; a railroad ran right in front. Long September-yellow grass grew along the embankment; a meadowlark sang, everything was bathed in glorious red sunset light draining the dry blue sky. The High Plains air was balmy, still, warm, perfect. I had made it home at last. I could now settle down out West with my own place. Ready to build a base.

My rent is $250 a month. I have twenty thousand dollars left.

My stomach and veins surged with warmth and excitement. You've made it. You've really finally made it. You are home.

I gazed at my little house. I looked at my white sneakers on the clean, dry, but slightly dusty concrete. You've got enough cash to figure things out. Plus take some time to chill. Build your organization up. Learn. Figure out exactly what it is you need to do. And most of all, you can just chill in peace and quiet, out here on the Southern Plains. It's not Texas, but even wilder. This will work.

I looked up at the western sky over the mountains, where the big Sun was lowering. "It's like a painting," I murmured. "A painting by God… so beautiful."

I decided to go for a bike ride. There were 20 miles of bike path along the Arkansas River. A half moon was coming out.

I rode through the long twilight heading west up along the river, inhaling the distinctive dry-sweet smell of riverside cottonwoods and coyote willows. The southern winds blew. I was a healthy man ready to start his next new life on the western edge of the Plains, the winds filling me with vitality and promise. I achieved an endorphin high that was barely containable, everything in my body working perfectly in sync with the mountain bike and the Southern Plains winds rustling the deep green, heart-shaped leaves of the cottonwoods. As I flew back into town a couple hours later, an unseen mountain lion screamed from under an outcropping up the bluff to my right, thrilling me with wild chills, capping a perfect night beyond anything anybody could ask for. Earlier today, east of the mesa, I had seen five antelope out there in the dry grass plains. Practically in my front yard. I had a perfect base.

Everything will now come your way.

Jack, the old landlord with the white gold-miner beard, knocked on my door the next morning. The city had rejected his repairs to the furnace, and he would have to replace it. I had to move out immediately, because he could get a major fine. It would only be temporary, until he could get the replacement.

I checked into the Kozy Motel, south of downtown. My neighbor was a big man, living off a car accident settlement; he looked like he was from India, but said he was from Greece. The owner of the motel was Vietnamese, had lived all over the country, buying and selling motels, though he was only a few years older than me. He made side money by renting soft-core porn videos out to his customers. I helped him when he needed to work on his car, though there wasn't much he needed help with.

I waited. And waited. I grew restless. I hung out. Bored. I read USA Today, sitting in back alley curbs with my bike in the mostly empty downtown. I went to the public library, which was very impressive for this small Southern Plains city. They even had subscriptions to newspapers from all around the world, and the librarians seemed fiercely knowledgeable and independent. Good for lil' old Pueblo, Colorado, I thought.

As I paged through the Des Moines and London papers, I began thinking that what I wanted to do with this new organization, Great Plains Restoration Council, was a very big undertaking, and I needed to make sure I was as solidly anchored and prepared as possible. My stomach tightened. It was a huge challenge.

A thought came to me. I remembered what another wholesaler had said to me, a long time ago, when I asked him what he did with all his money. He'd bought himself a few things, like a shiny SUV, and his girlfriend a nice sportscar, but he said mostly he kept reinvesting in the business, always having his money making more money. Course last I'd heard he'd gotten locked up.

Dangerous thoughts began building up on my uncertainties. Should I go take the money I have, and try to double it? Triple it? Am I just wasting time here, sitting around, waiting? After all, it's a finite amount that I got left. It's not going to go that far.

But it's still enough to get you started on what you really need to do in life. And you're already here. You're set if you chill.

But what if I run out before I even have the chance to build the organization up?

Twenty thousand is still a lot of money. Still a lot of money.

Wonder what's goin' on back in NYC… Wonder what Camron is doing. Wish my house here would just be ready so…

Should I go back?

I checked myself, scared by how anxious and restless that thought had come on. I concentrated intently on myself, how I was feeling.

I decided I'd call Camron later. Just to check in. Nothing more.

It suddenly seemed like I could become trapped in that little house. Even bored out of my mind. Here I was, in the middle of a strange town, with half the population so conservative and out of touch they couldn't even say the name of their own town right; they pronounced it "Pee-eblo." Even though half the town is Hispanic, and all of southern Colorado used to be part of Mexico, the Anglos here are so incapable of noticing anybody else's culture or viewpoint they never even took the time to learn how to say the name of their own city.

Are you being too hateful?

No, fuck that. Why should I cater to somebody's self-assumed superiority?

I shut my eyes, trying to think. I tried to latch onto something, anything that would bring clear thoughts back. It was all jumbled. All I knew was I couldn't wait. And I was suddenly worried I wasn't prepared enough to really jumpstart this group, in case I found myself stuck in an unexpected trap. What did I know anyway? Maybe I should go back to NYC and try to double my money, just to be sure?

You might fuck up —

Fuck that. I'm climbing the walls here, waiting and waiting. I'm wasting time. I don't know when the house will be ready. I can go back to New York for a little bit, and just pay the rent here for a few months. $250 ain't nothing. Make a lot mo' money, anyhow. And maybe by then old Jack the landlord will've gotten his shit together. On *my* house. Which should've been right and ready in the first goddamn place before he ever thought to rent it.

I walked, taking a long roundabout trek to nowhere, thinking, weighing my decision. On the way back to the motel I boldly took a short cut through enemy territory — the officers' parking lot of the Pueblo Police Department — and regretted I did. Four bumperstickers on the largest, brand-new-shiniest pickup truck said: "Insured by Colt," "North American Hunting Club," "I Brake for Animals, I Eat Them and Wear Their Skins," and " A Cat Almost Always Blinks When Hit in the Head with a Ball-Peen Hammer."

"Jihad," Camron said. "The city is different now. Especially the club scene. You don't know cause you're not on the front lines. We have to add Special K and blow to our product line. We have to! I can't get people to come buy if they can do their one-stop shopping over at Kirk's and the two little goons he's got selling for him.

"And everybody is on the lookout. Since Giuliani came in, man, there has been so much heat that everybody is actin' all jumpy."

"I don't like to hear that," I said. "People fuck up. And they fuck up others, when they jumpy. You need to stay out of it, far away from that jumpy and anybody who is acting like that."

"Well, if you're not gonna get me the bumps and the coke, I'm gonna have to go get it myself. And you will just lose out. I'm sorry, but that is what I'ma have to do."

We got to the apartment where we were making a special delivery. Camron pressed the buzzer.

"I told you I didn't want to get involved in any of that. We stay with what we got, then—"

He swung around to face me. "You're not listening to me! I said, we need it to keep this business going! You want me to come up with this money, but if you don't come up with the product that people are buying now, then I'm — " The door buzzed and I yanked it open. We headed up the stairwell.

"They're still buying E. They always will."

"But not without K, and coke. They want the combination. And some just want to do K."

We walked into the drag queen's pink, very dimly lit boudoir apartment. She had a couple homeboy thugs hanging in the back shadows, like they thought they were bodyguards or some shit. I gave them a sneer and sat down on the couch. Camron shifted into his happy, friendly, club-kid mode, a front-line business professional, kiss on the cheek — *mwah* — so funny to see from a straight boy. The drag queen and him got down to their business. I gradually tuned them out, thinking about nothing, just listening to the trance house music coming softly out of the speakers.

As I did so I realized there was a zebra skin rug, cut out in a circle, right in front of my feet. I blinked my eyes, and stared. Had it just twitched? I suddenly had the sense of the zebra's back muscles shaking off a fly or some dust, while he stamped his hoofs and bent down his head again to graze. I wrenched my eyes away, tried to pay attention to the transaction now in progress. The drag queen was not made up, and with her hair pulled back at the hairline with some kind of band or tape, and her over-sized black-market silicone lips, she looked like a cross between a dude and a female. The coffee and dining room tables were glass, lined in black steel, the walls were pink; the big round boudoir mirror was spanned in front by a counter with dozens of beauty products set on it like chess pieces. Camron and the drag queen were talking at full speed. One of the thugs shifted on his feet back there. I discreetly shook my head, trying to clear my focus. I was in a New York City high-rise apartment. There wasn't a green, living or natural thing in sight. Except for… *this animal, right here sprawled at your feet.* I resisted until, out of the corners of my eyes, again I thought I saw movement. A back shoulder twitch? Sides breathing? I slammed my eyes back down to the zebra, to see, to check, trying to hide my staring by cupping my hand over my brow.

I didn't feel good about the eight-ball of blow I had in my bike saddlebag as I rode back down Upper Broadway from Washington Heights. I'd sworn long ago that I would not cross that line. But Phil, the owner of Sound Factory, had opened up a new club called Sound Factory Bar on 21st between 5th and 6th, and it was fresh, clean and packed. It had the same quality of music, only it was open for regular club hours, and it served alcohol. And the crowd, especially the Friday night crowd, needed their "services." Thursdays were Puerto Rican/Dominicano night "Factoria Venta y Uno," Friday was White night, which was jammed and now the biggest dealing night in the city, and Saturday was Black night. The Friday night job was our main gig now; with all the Chelsea boys and the Fire Island crowd swarming the place, we could make good money. But our rent to the bouncers was steep — $400 a week, due every Friday whether we worked or not. And product was scarce. Giuliani's cops were really cracking down.

Commotion up ahead. Flashing lights of police cars. I rode into the traffic jam, trying to thread my way through. Not a rubbernecker, I had to get off and walk the bike through the crowd. I glanced across the median to the uptown side of Broadway. A large, overweight woman with iron-gray curls was flat on her back in the street, lying in a pool of blood and clear body liquid. Big flat strips of yellow fat hung out of her body, still attached, reminding me of chicken fat. It seemed like she had been split at the seams by the impact of the car that hit her. Gloved paramedics were trying to keep her together in order to get her on a stretcher. They began trying to slip her into some kind of plastic wrap. Her head was jutted backwards into the pavement in a spreading circle of blood.

In the lobby of Hotel Hell, I checked my voice mail on the payphone. Martin had called, saying to page him. It was important. I didn't like the sound of his voice.

I did so, and waited by the phone in the narrow walkway under the fluorescent tube, watching people come in and out of the glass doors of the hotel, shaking off or bracing for the cold January rain. It was after 11 at night. I bet not a single person in this hotel has a regular, 9-5 kind of job, I thought to myself.

My stomach was acidy. The tone in Martin's voice was eating at me. Something was up. I knew it would take him time to get to a secure payphone to call me back.

The phone finally rang. Waiting till the second ring, I picked it up.

"Sup."

"Can you talk right now?" His voice was low and agitated.

I felt pretty secure about these phones. I knew which ones were hot and which were cool up here between 106th to 110th, and on Manhattan Ave., and throughout Crack Valley. But that didn't mean I didn't need to be careful. "Yeah. What's up? Talk cool. And it's cool."

"Can't. Look. The Family got raided. I don't know the whole detail, but some people broke in, with fucking AK's and shit. I'm not joking. Shot them up, robbed them. Took everything. Personally, I think Alice was involved, maybe set up or payback. It was a big thing. I don't know the whole detail. People are dead, others locked up. The killers didn't get everything. I hear there was still product, weapons, and loot that was hidden. I can't find out anything more cause Alice is all over the neighborhood, investigating. I know some of my shit — something of mine — was left up there. But people got shot up, man. It's over."

My throat constricted, scalp hot. I caught my breath. "Alright. What you gon' do?"

"Gone, dawg. Leavin' the city. You should too."

I exhaled. "Where you headed? When?"

"Hey man, peace. I gots to go." He hung up, and the dial tone buzzed high and loud into my ear canal.

I heard a female scream from the first floor hallway. I hung up the phone. Amjad came out of the office in time to meet this tattooed white guy — shirtless, jeans unbuttoned as if just pulled on, boots untied — running into the hotel lobby. He looked like that dude Axl Rose from Guns-N-Roses.

"Fucking rats!" he said to Amjad. "Ugh! Under the bed, man. Man you gotta do something! My girl and I were in bed, getting into it, getting ready to fuck, man, and we hear this disgusting screaming!? What the fuck is this place! It's caught in two glue traps somebody put under there. A big fucking hairy ass rat, man. I thought you said it was clean. Fucking rats!? What the fuck is this! We want our money back!"

Amjad looked at me with his Bangladeshi-dark eyes and I followed him to the room. New tenants.

I heard it before we walked into the narrow fluorescent-lit room. The rat was screaming. Nothing screams like a rat. It's a high-pitched, ragged, screeching, vomit-raising sound, as if the city rat knows who he has become, knows that he has become the hated receptacle of all that is diseased in human society, and has no choice but to squirm through that for eternity.

I could tell the woman was naked under the dingy brown fake-wool blankets and the nasty bedspread she had pulled up over her head. Her bare feet stuck out, and so did the top of her stringy ash-blond hair. I smelled sex, cigarette ashes, and day-old rotting food in the trash. "It's under the bed! Oh god, Oh god!" the girl screamed. That started the rat shrieking again.

"Man," the dude said, putting his fingertips against his temples. "I'm going to throw up. What kind of fuckin' place is this? Oh man oh man!"

Amjad went to get a shovel.

I didn't say anything. I knelt down to look under. Something live was under there, humping and struggling and kicking its one free leg. The two white plastic traps were smashed onto him and that glue was not letting go no matter how much he kicked and screamed.

Amjad scooped the rat out. He was the size of a young housecat. His eyes bulged, his neck muscles strained, he bared his yellow teeth, he tried to arch his gray-furred back, which had a couple pink pimples or sores on it, but his throat, belly, tail and three legs were stuck. He jerked himself, and almost succeeded in tipping over out of the shovel. He kicked and scratched his one free leg wildly and it suddenly snapped up into the glue with the rest of him. He screeched, and shit and piss squirted out.

"What you gonna do with him?" I asked Amjad as we went out into the hall and the guy slammed the room door. They were stuck here at least for the night. And I knew they'd probably end up staying. That was the way it was in Hotel Hell. After the first few nights, you got used to it. "You need to knock him over the head or something."

"Man, this place is as bad as Bangladesh. I think that's why they hire us." In the lobby he went out the first glass door. "Hold the door for me so it don't close." I placed my body in the way, holding it open with my shoulder. He opened the outside glass doors. A gust of cold wet air blew in. He tossed the rat into the street, glue traps and all, and came back in. He shook a shudder out of himself. "Fucking disgusting, man!" he said.

I went out onto the landing, rain mist blowing into my face, letting the glass doors close behind me. A cab sped by, missing the rat by inches. The rat screamed and shrieked, gurgling at the top of his lungs, struggling against the glue traps. I hung back on the step under the narrow awning. Another car heading down Central Park West passed, tires hissing on the slick pavement. Across the street, building-sized glaciated rocks loomed in the dark woods, overgrown in scraggly trees whose roots were crawling down into cracks and over their faces.

The rat's shrieks filled the space between the hotel and the dark park. Another yellow cab came, heading downtown, and this time smashed the rat, ripping part of a glue trap from his body and sending it skidding. Whitish-yellow guts and reddish organs smeared. Silence returned — just the rain falling into the dark North Woods of Central Park across the street.

I struggled to find product. I was losing money each week. I'd left everything in Colorado, my house, belongings, even my car in the long-term parking at Stapleton Airport in Denver, everything, and come back here to grow my money. Instead, the account was draining, and I couldn't stop it, get it right. My working relationship with Camron grew strained, began disintegrating. He got very pissed at me when I couldn't produce. Sometimes we had to be a no-show, because product was scarce. And my wires were way up, because I knew dealers all over town were desperate for product, and when people get desperate, they get stupid.

Hotel Hell also seemed to be physically collapsing, and it seemed to have a domino effect on its tenants. The filthy toilets flooded shit water out into the hallways. Bloodstains appeared on the stair landings, and stayed there, growing darker. Maintenance — who the fuck knew where they were. People shot up in the back. One guy's window just fell out and crashed down into the airshaft. Day and night I could hear rats tumbling down inside the walls. I opened the cabinet under my little sink and a huge rat jumped out and bounced around my room, scratching and screaming in terror, sending me bouncing away from it until I managed to get my door open. He bolted out, running for hell down the hallway, where he skidded around the corner in the shit water into the bathroom, and jumped for the ragged pipe hole in the wall beneath the sink.

Sitting on a toilet on the top floor, my head in my hands, the toilet seat wet from hydrogen peroxide, clapping against my ass as it dried, I knew I was stuck. If only you had stayed in Pueblo. You coulda stuck it out. Think how beautiful and calm it was out there. The blue sky. The bike trail. The dry prairie and western mountains. But you got greedy, restless, hateful. Now you losing everything, and you stuck. You had $20,000 to your goddamn name, free and clear, and could have set yourself up nicely. Built shit up from there, methodically and carefully. Everything you ever wanted. You made a very big mistake. Why can't you ever fucking learn?

Out of the blue, an image appeared of this dead man I'd seen a few years ago, this brother sitting up against the wall at a street corner, and the cop lazily throwing a white sheet over him.

When I explained the situation to Lahumba, she seemed like she was exasperated, as if she'd been for a long time. She said: "Jihad, you have got to have a plan!"

When another rat jumped out, chasing me around my room, I decided to listen to Lahumba. She'd said something groundbreaking: "Why don't you just get an apartment, a share, like a normal person? And make a plan — that you can follow — to move back out West when you are ready?"

It was hard to accept, but I was here now. And in too deep.

CHAPTER TWENTY-SIX

Scarred Face

Bloodstained floors… sticky carpets… sweaty, soot-grimed face, t-shirt drenched against my back between skin and backpack, wearing my trademark armpit-holstered knife blade hidden beneath my shirt, bicycle legs pumping… NYC heaving early into a very hot summer, 1995. Wild crazed overheated looks in the eyes of more than a few I pass by. Everybody wants something, some relief… it's like crack almost…

Me, I was desperate for product, trying to hold the line. Reinvesting, but not making my money back.

After midnight on a Friday night. Getting down to Sound Factory Bar late. It didn't matter — we didn't have enough of anything to last us more than an hour. I threaded my way through the perspiring mass of people dancing to Frankie Knuckle's style of house music, trying not to touch anybody. It was Friday night, White night, and many of them had their shirts off, and the place was so crowded they couldn't avoid crushing into each other. Wet, raspy shaved chests occasionally scraped against my arm.

I found the security guards; palmed them their $400. Like pulling teeth for me. Couldn't sustain this. Was fuckin' stuck. Rock and a hard place. In the shadows, lit by those club-red dim lights, I could see the look in both their eyes. They knew we were struggling.

"You cool?" Rick, one of the security guys, asked, eyeing me from beneath his baseball cap.

"What," I said, hardening my face.

Back at our corner, Camron turned to me. "Jihad, I need more! You're not doing your job! I already ran out!" I noticed a couple little queens, some of his groupies, standing near to the side, staring at us. His eyes glared beneath his cap. "Look!" He nodded over at our main rival, Victor, and his two workers. They were surrounded by customers. They were making bank.

I leaned in close so I could hear and be heard over the speakers. "Give me the money," I said. "I'ma take care of it."

"No! You wait till we get back to my crib."

I flared, and forced myself to stay still, gritting my teeth. "I said, I'll take care of it. You get your share! I'm goin' uptown and reinvesting all of it. Yours and mines."

"NO!"

Momentarily I tilted my head back, maintaining control, eyes fixing on the ceiling and the air vents streaming refrigerated air. The old thought, *Where the hell are you?* came and went. I knew exactly where I was. And how I'd gotten here. I looked at Camron. "This is it, then. Come on, let's go. We're out of here." Some muscle-queen party-boy came over to Camron, tapped him on the shoulder, offered up his closed fist, right side up. A small pile of white powder was on the web of his thumb. "Hey Camron!" he said, "Want a bump?"

Camron looked at me, then the guy, but didn't move. I grabbed him by the back of the arm and he shoved me off. "Come on," he said, shaking his head overdramatically at the whole fucked up situation. "Let's go."

I sat sweating on the edge of the dirty, stained, bedspread, in my sticky room in Hotel Hell. I folded the newspaper and threw it to the floor. The Arctic National Wildlife Refuge was under attack again. The Newt Gingrich/104th Congress was making a plan to drill for oil in the Refuge's Coastal Plain, 125 miles of the purest, wildest grassland left in the Western Hemisphere. My only Safe Place left in the world. I got up, began walking around in circles, not big circles but little five-foot circles because that's all the room I had. If I could've I would've bounced off the walls. Shit out in the world was hitting the fan and splattering everything, and here too. I yanked up the end of my damp shirt and swiped at my grimy Hotel Hell face. I sat down hard on the bed, burying my head in my hands. *Why are you here in New York? What are you missing? Why did you come back, risk everything?* I jumped up, grabbed my bike and gear, and bolted out the room.

Riding a bike is the closest a man or woman can come to flying…

The blocks whizzed past me, brown and red and gray square buildings all blurring into each other, shapes of people, color splashes of their clothing…

I had made my delivery, another big ball of coke, the shit I said I would never deal. I was free for the rest of the day. Dodging cars, my ears functioning as my usual second pair of eyes as the constantly shifting horde of mad, tooth-grilled cars roared up behind and just barely past me. I continually claimed my space, maintaining my push and play on the streets of Manhattan. The only language known in traffic is aggression. If you show a moment's weakness or hesitation, you are overtaken. Either pull back or — tough — get knocked out of the way. And I was not gonna have anybody take my space. Having been outside for most of my life, I was keenly aware of how my body acted like a sensing mechanism to constantly shifting stimuli as I snapped forward. Temperature differences, hot or cooler, from hot chrome sparking off a car, the heat-softened asphalt, between pavement and a manhole cover (slightly hotter), a small park (cooler oasis breath), a brick wall; even a single tree planted in the sidewalk gave off a very slight but noticeable cooling effect.

And the parks — big Central Park, and linear Riverside Park running up alongside the Hudson River on Manhattan's west edge from 59th to 125th Streets — drew deep green cool breaths, sucking me in. Riverside Drive was the most peaceful stretch of Manhattan pavement to ride, even if it was a little hilly and everybody's car had an alarm with a pre-alert sensor that I set off click-click click-click as I flew past. Central Park and Riverside Park were my territory; I knew nearly every square foot and secret about them, just like I had grown to know over the years nearly every square foot of Manhattan's streets, and a lot of BK and South Boogie Down, too.

I pulled up to the water railing in Riverside Park and sat back on my bike saddle. Always came down to the water's edge in the evening. Physical and free, calmer, at last, if momentarily. The Hudson pushed its swells relentlessly southward toward the harbor and the ocean. I gulped in the breaths of open green space and light from a Sun riding out over a far West that I knew but couldn't see, far past the cliffs of New Jersey. I knew what I had here, something almost wild — the seawall rocks, the areas where the grass grew unmowed, and where the path turned into a single dirt track six inches wide as I got north into the Harlem reaches running hard up against the river. Hawks, ducks, sea birds, and other kinds of animals also knew this part of the park. And so did some people, though not many, and when I saw this scar-faced dude materialize onto my overgrown path, heading my way, I thought: "Who is this blatino muthafucker walking like a thug, shirt off, coming into my path; in my park?"

He came right up to me and dapped my hand like he'd known me for a year. "What's up," he said. "Louis." I assumed he said "Luis." He was my height, not as built as me, head shaved, jeans a little tighter than the 'relaxed fit' ones we all wore, which made him look off, like something wasn't right. Yellow skin shiny with New York mid-summer evening humidity. A silver hoop earring the size of a quarter. Diagonally down the side of his face was a jagged Frankenstein scar with stitch-marks as if it had been hand sewed. He smiled; nice smile. Something jogged inside my stomach.

"What the fuck happened to your face. Bet everybody ask you that," I said. I could hear birds singing, and gentle river water lapping, big contrast to the violence apparent right before me.

Another clue, I vaguely realized. Skin will always tell — into harder drugs than that cigarette he's smoking. Skin a little puffy or stretched, pores open, often one or two stubborn, purplish, pimple-like bumps under the skin on the cheekbone or temple. I listened to him tell me how somebody had slashed him, and I found myself wondering how much of the story he was changing or leaving out. "...and he jumped out the car and next thing I knew, my whole face was split open. It was not too far from here, neither. I could've stuck my finger inside my face and out through my eyehole," he said.

"What you do, sew that up yourself?"

"Nahh, stupid," he said, and laughed. "I'm from Parkchester. We're middle class, not ghetto. But I took the stitches out myself." He didn't explain further. Still, I had a feeling he'd gone to a "local" doctor, and for a reason he wasn't saying. A slight breeze came in off the moving river, temporarily lifting the sticky air. He unconsciously turned into it, and I saw he had a paperback copy of Moby Dick in his back pocket. I wrinkled my eyebrows. I had never read it. For some reason I again had an abrupt flashback to those wild dolphins surging out of the surf off Baja, Mexico.

"You love that bike, huh," he said. "Huh?"

"Yup. But you don't know nothin' about that."

He put his hands on my handlebars and I instantly recoiled, resisting the protective urge to yank me and my bike backward. Nobody touched my bike. "I bet you love it because it's your freedom. It's not just your bike." He left his hands there on top, and it seemed defiant and challenging, his fingers curled loosely over and down, his body in my space like that. His fingernails were clean and cut, and I could smell a slight hint of Cool Water or some similar kind of cologne. "It's like when I come down here," he said. "I feel like I'm out here in Nature, and I can be all alone with my thoughts. I have a personal relationship with God. Not too many people know there are hawks here. Red-tailed hawks, and they had a nest this spring. You know, they had a nest!"

I looked down at my black Specialized bike shoes, at the red S on top of the vegan leather, trying to think for a second. I put my foot down and pulled back, pulled my bike out from under his hands, looking him straight in the eye. "Ok, Scarface," I said.

"You wanna get some juice later? 100%. I only drink 100%. I'll meet you later. We can go hang out in the Park and talk." He meant Central. "If you want, man." He smiled, smiling in a way he knew worked with people.

In my room's cramped little nook where the sink was, I bent over to wash my face, thinking of Scarface... Luis. I was starting to ache — neck, shoulders, chest, back, arms, all over — like some inside wall was being torn open against my will, and I knew a bottomless pit plummeted on the other side. I couldn't handle that empty pit.

You know something ain't right with him, dawg. Trouble there...

But something is there, I thought. Just couldn't put into words. We shared something. Street-scarred, tough, but what was that beneath all that...

Loneliness. Raging, bottomless pit of inconsolable emptiness.

I couldn't deal with that pit; the thought of it made me jumpy and claustrophobic. But we wouldn't have to. We could be there for each other.

I scrubbed my face harder, ears subconsciously registering the muted background noise of all the other tenants whose rooms faced the airshaft. The water didn't smell right, but then it never did. Turning off what passed for hot, I splashed cold water on my face, and it felt good enough. Rubbing my hands all over my face and throat and back of my neck, I stood back up, reaching for the towel hanging off the nail. I heard a gurgling noise and instinctively jumped out of the way just as a three-foot high stream of brown piss-smelling water shot upwards out of the drain and arced onto the floor like the sink itself was pissing. It began puddling on the dirty blue carpet. I grabbed for the cabinet door to see if there was a stopper or anything, and a rat flew out and in my sick imagination it seemed to come flying out with all four claws spread wide ready to clamp onto me like a rat devil. He bounced into the wall, shrieking like only rats do, rebounding around the room with me jerking out of the way until he got under the bed.

I yanked open the door, grabbed my wallet and keys and stormed downstairs, towel around my fucking neck. This was it.

Two rooms, with hardwood floors, all to my own, on 104th between Columbus and Amsterdam, in the back where it was quiet, had a view of real sky, in a share with Big Jewish Mama, a massage therapist who lived in the two front rooms with her tiger-marked cat Sid. Her name was Shere, and she instantly began calling me "Glossie" because she saw me as healthy and fit and without any problems. Just an athlete and personal trainer who, though we'd never met before, was part of the larger NYC fitness community that she lived and worked in. I'd posted a flyer on the glass wall of the bus station in front of the big Korean deli on Broadway and 110th. Said I was a fitness professional looking for someplace clean, healthy and decent to live.

The 6th floor apartment was still in Crack Valley just a few blocks from Hotel Hell, but to me a world away and a huge step up. Drugs, and some hallway disturbance shit sometimes went on in this building also, but I could not believe how nice it was, compared to everything else I'd had. I even had my own phone. What a weird feeling! For the first time in years I didn't have to go out to find a working payphone every time I needed to make a call. I could literally just pick up a phone right in my room and call somebody. It had never even occurred to me to get an apartment until Lahumba had scolded me, had finally knocked some sense into me when I told her of the latest incident at Hotel Hell, and she again told me I had to have a plan. I'd already had to fly back out to Denver to get my car because Stapleton Airport was closing, replaced by the massive new Denver International Airport out on the plains east of the city. Left my car down in Pueblo with my Vietnamese friend, the owner of Kozy Motel. And I'd asked Jack, the landlord of my little house, to sublet it so I wouldn't have to pay the $250 per month anymore.

Lahumba said: Get stabilized first, then go back West when everything is set, when I had enough money and everything in order. Here, I was only paying a hundred dollars more than Hotel Hell. And by comparison it was paradise, even though I knew in the back of my mind it was temporary. I began taking supplements and herbs for my stomach — acidophilus, papaya enzymes, slippery elm, licorice root tea. I chewed slices of raw ginger. I religiously went down to the juice bar on 96th and Broadway for raw organic carrot, beet, celery, spinach, collard and ginger juice, and 2 oz. wheatgrass shots with fresh squeezed ginger. I began to feel the best inside ever. Though I knew I still had a long way to go.

The shiny blond maple floors in the apartment — I could feel the trees that they used to be. Getting home for the night, exhausted, I'd lie on my back in my second room, just breathing there on the bare floor, soaking in the cleanliness. Kept the rooms as bare and spare as I could. Just a futon mattress on the floor in the one, a table and foam couch and desk in the other. Sid the cat took an interest. I'd catch him peering around the doorframe at me. His thing was to try to sneak up without me noticing. As soon as I did, he'd bolt down the hallway, claws scrambling, as if willing me to chase him.

Scarface and I sat on the concrete bench just outside Central Park in the gathering dusk. The unopened Crazy Horse malt liquor 40 waited patiently on the concrete bricks at his feet, the glass bottle perspiring between us. Arms spread out across the bench top, he let his head fall back, looking up through the voluptuous green branches at the darkening sky. A cigarette was tucked behind his ear. Casual, and cool, I looked up too, privately wondering what he saw. I knew what I saw.

"I'd like to move to Maine," he said. "Everything's so green up there. Just get away from all this."

I smirked, thinking how weird this shit was. But I had to front: "Man, I'm straight about the City. Stayin' right here. Least fo' now."

"What about out West?" He grinned hard at my face.

"Too many rednecks," I mumbled, trying to put it all out my mind, closing my eyes tightly for a second as I struggled to push away that other jagged, bottomless pit that urgently pulled me there v.s. the one that kept me here.

Quiet filled the space between us, buffering the outside world.

He plugged the cigarette into his mouth and lit it, puffing out that first pungent cloud of tobacco smoke. I waved the smoke out of my face. "I hate that shit," I said.

He reached down for the 40 and cracked it open, swallowing a gulp. Something flashed behind his eyes, or I thought it did, and for some reason I imagined his pores enlarging. He got up and walked off quickly without saying anything, back square.

"What the fuck," I said. But he was hurrying down the street and didn't hear me.

I made a delivery to Angel, being my kind of bike messenger. He lived in the lower west 50s and during the day wore thick cotton sweatpants with no drawers. His bathtub faucet ran full blast and he couldn't shut it off, so it went like that 24 hours a day. He said he'd gotten used to it. The landlord wouldn't fix it, he said. He agreed with me that it was a big waste of water. Angel was from Colombia, and worked in the club-kid kind of clubs, the trendy places Camron and I never went to.

Afterward, I headed over and down to the 20s, west of Fifth. I glided down the street till I found the address I was looking for; got buzzed up to a working loft.

A handful of white guys sat around a table, smoking cigarettes, drinking beers. One of them had a gun next to his beer; Techno dance music was playing low out of the speakers. I stood my bike up against the wall and sat down. Introductions. One of them took a line of some white powder on the table. Offered me a hit or a beer. I shook my head to both.

"You know things are getting tight out there," Adam, my contact, said.

"What can you do?" I said. "I need it by Friday."

"That's not gonna happen. We have links on one shipment coming in from Switzerland, and they don't expect that for two more weeks, from this Friday. The delay is it's not in a packagable form yet. That's the best anybody can do. And we need a down payment up front."

I squeezed my fists in my bike gloves, sitting back. "That's not gonna do. I need by Friday. We have — " I stopped myself. I didn't want to talk about the who, what, where of my business.

"We know Camron works for you, and you work at Sound Factory Bar, just down the street. But anybody you see out there selling, they're either selling fake or pumped up shit, or they have a stash laid up. It's what I would've done if I were you. Stashed up. Anybody who sells fake or pumped up shit is gonna lose real quick."

"Why didn't y'all save up a big stash? You big wholesalers are supposed to be prepared to weather the ups and downs. Now everybody's scrambling, and you seem to be the only cat who can get."

"I did. I sold it out. To Victor. To everybody. We sell to everybody."

I burned. Victor… our main competitor. "Why the fuck. You know we need."

"Sorry, man. You were the Family. You weren't ours. Everybody else was a regular. So you're last on the list. Now you have to come to us because we're the only ones right now. We got people in New Jersey who were moving 2000 retail a week. Don't think Giuliani's not killing us too."

I had only $9,000 left to my name. Inside, I twisted. Voice inside telling me *no, just walk.*

"Well it's twelve a piece, unless you buy a thousand, then I can give it to you for eleven. And everybody is paying up front now. You can be here five minutes after they get here, we can arrange that for you, put you on the schedule, you'll all come in one at a time, but that's the way we're doing this now. Until we can get this shit rolling again. That's the way it is."

I shook my head. "Some 'down payment.' I need to see it on the table in front of me before I pay."

"Well you can sell flowers for the Korean deli then." They all laughed.

I looked at them hard.

Eleven thousand dollars to get a thousand. It was the quantity I needed, to get enough profit, get back on top. But I didn't even own that much money anymore. Shit was never this expensive. I used to get it for so much less because I could move it and, as a regular, my quantity over time was factored in, so I got in at the lowest price.

I forced myself to think clearly. 300 would gross $7500. Profit would be $3100, after this week and next's rent at the club totaling $800. Though we would have to forfeit this Friday. Camron and I would both have to give up our profit the first week or two. But, if it could be steady after that, we could build it back up. It'd be a tightrope, it was a gamble, but—

"Ok," I got up. "I'll take three, if you can promise a three minimum every week after that." I reached over my hand, and looked at him very seriously as he shook it. I said, "When you shake my hand, that is bond. That's how I operate. And I need them before Friday night of that week. I don't want them if you can't." This meant I would have to pay two weeks of rent, $800, with only a little blow and K to sell. And Camron, it was like pulling out his teeth to get him to go in there without E. He had always pressed me about K and coke, but ecstasy was still the mainstay and always had been.

We made arrangements. I paid up, practically pulling my own teeth to do so, but I had no choice. I was now down to $4,100, already subtracting the $400 I'd have to give up Friday night just to keep our spot in the club. We could add maybe a thousand from the rest of the services we still had. It was hard to believe that at one time I had been able to count out $40,000 in cash on my dirty carpet floor.

Riding past a deli store window, my eyes caught sight of a Marlboro poster. It showed a stupid cowboy model in a cloud of dust rounding up a bunch of cattle on an overgrazed landscape that ads like this employed to make people think was the "real" West. I twinged with the rise I felt about that, remembering the real reality, the important thing. At the same time, though, that reality — the work I needed to do — seemed far away. Couldn't believe the mess I'd gotten myself caught up in. Not too long ago I had been set and home free. Now I was on thin ice, when I knew I needed to get out West urgently. But I was stuck. Had to make my money back. And...

I checked my feelings. *What was it? Something else?* I thought of Scarface.

It was late August, 1995. I'd been back almost a year. Completely tangled up.

"It's Louis. Not L-U-I-S. You got a pen?" he asked. I was staring at the crack pipe that he'd pulled out of his pocket. He was sitting on my bed. He reached over to the desk, picked up a Bic, pulled out the ink head and tube, and with the top of the plastic casing began scraping the residue down inside the pipe. "You can use the pen casing too, you know, but I keep my own glass pipe. I don't like to inhale the plastic. It melts a little."

I hadn't spooked *this* shit. Or had I, when I'd looked him in the face that first evening we'd met? And just ignored it?

"Not in my house," I said.

He had started gritting and grinding his teeth. Big drops of sweat were oozing out of his facial pores. I realized he'd already been high once today. The chemicals were still in him.

"Uh uh, man, not in my house, man. You gots to go." I stood up and moved in on him, making him stand. For some reason I was a little nervous, wires up, on alert.

"It's just another drug," he'd said. "Come on."

I tried to adjust my thinking, but couldn't. I knew crack was a demon. The kind of shit that made guys go home to their mama's house and unplug the tv she was watching right in the middle of her programs and take it down to the corner to sell it for a three dollar rock.

"Out the fuckin' door, dawg," I said, forcing him up and down the hall. He protested, but I didn't even look at him. I closed the door in his face, and threw the bolt lock.

But I couldn't stop thinking about him. He called me. Wanted to hang out. When he was down from the Bronx he stayed in a basement apartment with a bunch of other people on 91st St., between Broadway and West End. I went in once; saw it was a crackhouse. Didn't like the smell and left, as they all started getting high. How could they act like it was just a party drug, like a joint to be passed around? I wanted nothing to do with the notorious Crack Cocaine.

Again on the bench across Central Park West, by the rock wall that bordered the Park. Just the two of us. Funny… certain moments uptown, especially right after rush hour drops off and it's near dark, when the city suddenly feels almost empty, quiet, buffered. He said his parents were ok, family was fine, everything was normal except for the secret fact that he sometimes messed around with dudes, which messed with him. Did a couple years for robbery. Got hooked on the shit up there. Said he hated it, couldn't help it. How it sometimes just overtook him. "I'm warning you in advance," he said, even as he showed me his private Central Park hangout place, this little boulder inside a small clearing a couple hundred feet in from the West 72nd St. entrance. Hidden by a green overgrown jumble of branches and vines, people walking into the park didn't even know it was there.

We talked about my experiences out West, and how I couldn't wait to get back out to the high and dry country for good. He said his parents had taken him to Germany when he was little, but he didn't remember much. He really wanted to go to Maine. "I've never been there," he said. "But I've seen pictures, and it's cool and got all these green trees, and the ocean there too. It's clean. And I can just chill." He always talked about going to Maine.

He turned to me and suddenly said, "You know, I used to hustle. Not in the way we hustlas now, regular street-surviving hustlas, but …

"I know what you mean."

He got up and stood in front of me.

"What? Get away," I said.

"You never tell me anything about you." He put his hand on my knee and leaned his face in close to mine, then stepped back. "Tell me the truth. What, you used to turn tricks too?"

I didn't say anything, just shook my head at him, drinking from my bottle of water.

"Hah! You the same as me! Hah! Mr. Vegetarian Bike Rider Homeboy. I knew it!" He got up on the bench and sat on its back. "I been meaning to ask you. You ever go up to LFC?"

He meant Latino Fan Club, the big blatino porn enterprise housed in the big old castle on 116th and 1st Ave. It was owned by a bunch of fat old Russians who actually cooked borscht soup or something like that, and it had so many rooms you could get lost. It had rooms for young cats off the street to come hang out, shoot pool, or whatever, as well as film production facilities, and rooms where old men would go to turn with young guys, sometimes just paying $20 to jerk off while looking at the young dude with his clothes off. A full-size original set of knight's armor complete with helmet stood in the hallway like a hollow metal security guard. I'd been there once.

I nodded.

"I admit it," he said. "Sometimes I still go up there, every couple months or so. I'm 28, and they still pay me just to look at me. I go when I ain't got nothing else, and I need to get high right away. Sometimes it's ok to go and just hang out, too. I was thinkin' maybe you'd want to come with me sometime."

"Need to cut that shit out," I said.

The way he looked at me he knew I meant all of it.

"Man, I know. Don't you worry bout me and my business. I'ma go to school." His eyes focused on something, nothing, in the distance, then drifted down. He stared for a moment, as if suddenly concentrating, and I followed his gaze. On the bench I'd set the three dollars and change I had left over from buying the bottle of water. He reached down and took the money and walked off quickly before I could react. "J, I'm just goin' to get me some 100% juice, man. I'll be back." He said it over his shoulder, without looking at me. My anger rose, but I let him go.

As experienced and lived in as I considered myself, I was having a hard time figuring out where Louis ended and Crackhead began. I knew I was totally going against my instincts even hanging out with him. The thing with crack is, the minute a crackhead starts entering the second stage, which is the moment he starts thinking about getting high again, even if he's still at that moment completely straight, he's just as dangerous as when in the grips of a full-blown high. In fact, he's more dangerous because the monster is still hidden inside, beneath the surface.

But when Louis and I hung out, and it was just Louis, I began to imagine that it was him and me against the world. Upstairs one night, lying on the bare floor, talking, door closed, shirts off, jeans still on, we fell asleep like that, face to face, me on top of him, one of his arms around my back, my face in his neck. It was the first non-violent human physical contact I'd had in years and years. The masculine scent of our bodies together and sporty-thug cologne mingled in the hot, humid, still air, and was lifted just barely by the tabletop fan whispering a breeze as it turned its wire-grid face left to right and right to left. Still, a sweat built and trickled down between our chests. I could hear the crack and smoke damage rattling inside his body, and it unnerved me. This was not what I wanted; we were not the same, like he insisted. Like I wanted to believe. I knew full well the only thing he could really care about was the pipe. I was the vegetarian clean-living super athlete now. I wasn't new. I knew what time it was, and that I was treading in dangerous waters.

So? How sure are you that you're that different?

At the same time I couldn't resist the contact as it was, as it came. Pressure, and need for man-to-man contact that meant something, whatever that was, radiated out from my groin into my stomach and chest, taking over my whole body. Couldn't take it, couldn't quench it. I dozed off, face in his neck, knowing the moment would ride itself out soon.

Julie's voice on the phone. Julie, Camron's friend, the curvy, pretty Puerto Rican girl who always wore those big sexy sweaters in the wintertime, frantic: "Jihad, you know nobody has anything except what they saved from before. Camron acted the stupid and almost got himself real close to killed, trying to squeeze something from nothing."

I shifted my feet in agitation, knowing that this pair of pay phones on 106th and Central Park West wasn't secure. But she was so frantic. Some homeless guy was on the other phone.

"...Anton was involved," she said. She sounded scared, angry, very upset, exasperated. "Everybody. And they were, believe me, they were already on their way.... were going to kill him. Had him in the car and everything, taking him to Greenpoint. What was he thinking? Oh my god! If I hadn't happened to call Anton — he's got one of those new phones, the cellular kind, and I begged and begged him. I was hysterical when I found out. I was almost too late. Camron had $26,000 in that bag. They weren't going to sell him anything! How stupid is he? They were just going to put a bullet in his brain when they got there and dump him out. How fucking stupid is he, Jihad? I want you to stop working with him. Next time, I know he — and you — won't be so lucky!"

"Whose money was it?"

"What? I thought it was your money. Oh my God. Who else is he working with?"

I stared at the green park across the street, not even seeing. I tried to imagine Camron getting into a car with $26,000 in somebody else's cash, on loan, with four big dudes who didn't play, to "go make a deal".

"So Julie, there never was anything?" I asked.

"No, Jihad. You know there isn't right now. You know — "

WHOOP-WHOOP! I jumped, dropping the phone, and backed up quickly to the brick wall as a police car popped its siren twice and jumped onto the curb aiming for me. The car braked and both officers, one male and one female, ran at me and the homeless guy talking on the other payphone.

"Drop everything! Hands on your head! DON'T MOVE!"

The female cop went for the other guy, who looked like a homeless or a drunk. The other cop, coming at me. said, "STAY WHERE YOU ARE!" He edged up to me, and began searching me. I watched the phone swinging at the end of its cord. The cop reached in, grabbed it, and said, "Who is this!"

I imagined I heard a click. The cop slammed the phone down, and began patting me down, searching me. "Do you have any drugs, needles or weapons on you?" he asked.

"I found just this, George," the female cop said, pulling out a half-drank pint bottle of whiskey from inside the other man's pants.

A small crowd was gathering, mostly females, Riqueñas and Blacks — including a lot of grandmothers with cans of Budweisers (wrapped in paper napkins) and baby strollers, and a couple round-the-way thugs.

My cop tugged at my pants, pulled them down part way. Reached down. Tap. Felt under my balls. Up the crack of my ass. Tap. Patted my legs all the way down.

He got up, looked at his partner, nodded.

"Somebody said you had a gun," he said, nodding back at the bank of apartments. "We had to make sure."

Yeah sure they did, I thought.

Their radio crackled, calling them. They got in their car and pulled out, the seen-better-years blue-and-white NYC cop sedan falling hard back onto the street, leaving the homeless guy and me with our pants partway down.

I sped down toward my Friday noon appointment, wanting to be there when the FedEx guy came. Been waiting for this for two and a half weeks. We lost two whole Fridays.

On instinct, I decided to do a buzz-by, first. I rode down the avenue past the street, discreetly looking to the side.

Nothing.

I had arrived a little after 12. Isn't that what the dude had said?

I circled, one block north and south of the street. Thinking. Wires coming up, (why?) and tiny tendrils of nervousness slipping into my stomach. Coming up on the outer pass I saw a car speeding off. Didn't recognize anybody in it. Maybe not related?

Wait. Maybe a DT? Plainclothes? My wires really shot up.

Naaah... These dudes been in it for a long time; we were all professionals. They had their checks and balances. They couldn't have messed up.

Suddenly a cop car raced past me, silently, siren off. My stomach shot acid.

Feeling at a loss, but having to look purposeful, I kept my pace riding. I decided to ride down to Union Square, where I knew there'd be a secure payphone. Everything would be fine. Had to be. I needed to stop tripping myself out.

But I couldn't stop my nervousness. I dialed my voice mail. Entered my passcode. "You have one new message, 18 saved messages. Press 1 to hear the first message." That computerized lady had spoken so many times into my ear canal that her sultry pro-tech coo was stuck in my brain.

I pressed 1. Listened. My stomach dropped, heart racing. That panicky feeling in your gut like you're suddenly gonna have to take a shit even when you don't came on, that I'd really fucked up. I'd lost my money. Cop bust. Now what. Shit! I pressed 1 again. Only half heard. "...FedEx delivered to the wrong floor. The people downstairs called the cops. The FBI. We're out."

I called two others to verify, just to be sure nothing was getting thrown. One dude, the dude with the gun, had already been arrested, and Alice was closing in on the others.

I hung up and took off, the panicky feeling fueling my momentum.

I tried hard to remember that evening on the dry concrete curb in front of my Pueblo house a year ago. I remembered the fortune cookie: "Everything will now come your way."

Everything was now in ruins.

Taking way too big a risk, I rode up 6th Ave., doing my best to look like just a casual ciclista riding uptown, and hoping the cops hadn't seen me stop or slow or circle earlier coming down 5th. In the split second that I passed the street, without turning my head I glanced out the corners of my eyes, knowing I should not be doing this. A couple marked and unmarked cars were bristling in front of the building where my product and my last chance to get a last step up had come in. I got another jolt of panic when I suddenly wondered if my fingertips had touched anything. But aside from the money — and I knew that was difficult to lift off of — I didn't think I had. I dug hard into my pedals and shot uptown. Somebody had fucked up big time.

Who did? You, maybe?

I had dodged a bullet — but lost nearly everything. Unable to make any immediate decisive action, I treaded water, watching a couple weeks pass in New York City.

Scarface said: "And when I had the board set solid on the railing, I'd ride up it as fast I could and shoot over the lake and jump off and let my momentum take me as far as I could before falling into the lake. I had the bike tied to a rope, and I just hauled it back in after I swam back to shore. That was when I was a teenager though. Didn't do the best for the chain and the gear."

"Whatever. I don't believe you. Remember, you're a crackhead."

"Fine. You don't have to. I have a personal relationship with God."

"So you say. It still don't change anything. I ain't here to compete with you. Because you'll lose."

I wondered why I had a moment's hesitation when I said that. I looked at the Central Park lake reflecting the early evening sky and the voluptuous trees across the way. Its surface was mirror-still. The little wooden bridges arching over parts of the lake seemed to leap and dive over deceptively deep waters. Across, on the more populated side, a few people were out on the lake in boats, dipping their oars, breaking its surface.

He began pacing. I sat on the picnic table that was painted Central Park green, my bike up against me. I bent down to refasten the Velcro straps on my bike shoes. He came and stood next to me. I knew that meant he wanted to talk.

"What," I said, play-fucking around with him like I didn't want to be bothered.

"You ever kill somebody?" he suddenly asked me.

I eyed him directly, and for a moment everything else was gone, and I saw what I had wanted to see in his eyes. Over the years, I had noticed numerous people involuntarily reacting when seeing my eyes. But at this moment, he was in my eyes, we were seeing inside each other, and he couldn't hide his feelings, and it gave both of us a pulse. He quickly looked away, breaking the connection, and it was gone, but he stepped closer.

"Fo' real. You need to tell me. You can tell me."

"Kill somebody?" I paused. "Naah, man. Even though I should've. Many of them deserved it."

"You sure? You know, there's no statute of limitations on murder," he said.

"Why you keep askin,' man? Sounds like there's mo' to this, just like that scar on your face."

"Well, whoever you killed, you're still liable. For the rest of your life."

He sat down next to me, and put his hands again on my bike. "Can I ride?" He nodded his head at my bike. I had just washed and waxed it, and put that new White

Lightning lube that everybody was raving about on its chain. Kept the chain lubed and clean, and your leg clean too.

I put my foot over and through its main frame. "Nobody ride my bike. Only me. I don't even like nobody to touch it. Especially you. Get away."

He turned his face, close, looked at me.

"What," I said. I stopped playing around.

He said: "I once shot this guy so hard I could see his thoughts; the whole top of his head flew off. He just pissed me off. I killed two others, too. Got away with murder, huh. It felt good at the moment. But after, I felt nothing. And I couldn't even remember really why I'd wanted to kill them. I told myself they deserved it. I mean I remember hating them at the moment, but it was nothing deep, just an impulse. But the third one, I just killed him because I wanted to get high. And because he reminded me of everybody I hated. At least that's what I told myself. So I just shot him. And all he had on his ass was four fucking dollars."

I listened, watching every pore of his face tell me the truth, his round nostrils flaring.

"I hate like that all the time," I said, quietly. "Or used to." I was thinking of ranchers and politicians mostly. Anybody who was The Oppressor. Cops too. Anybody who ever got over. "But my shit wasn't random like that. It was very specific."

"Sometimes," he said, "I think hate just becomes itself, feeds off itself, and how or who you hate becomes secondary. Does that make sense? You just hate. You know what I'm sayin'?"

I didn't say anything. I realized it was almost dark now. Inadvertently, our voices had lowered with the sky. I watched a few fireflies make erratic journeys into space, a few feet up off the ground anyway, and fall back to Earth.

He said, "They say you hurt the ones you love, but I really didn't know any of them. The last one was a complete stranger."

"You don't feel bad for none of that, huh?"

He looked down, as if trying to figure that out himself. One of his hands was still on my bike.

"Man," I continued. "Shit like that would have me sure of something coming right back at me. You know, what go around come around. At least if they didn't do nothin' to you. If I learned one thing in this life, it's that: You reap what you sow. Every dawg get his day. What go around come around."

I got on my bike and raced up the little bellied slope we were hanging out in, half hidden by trees, popping around to shoot down the dirt track and catch air. I swung around at the top of the slope and jumped, lifting the bike, landing back to ground evenly on both tires and slowing to a dust-up turn to go back up the slope and do it again. He lit a cigarette, its ember burning in the almost-dark. Behind him, a firefly glowed lemon yellow, a wavering neon strike rising in the lower level of air, then traveling in a drunken horizontal line as if he wasn't sure himself where he wanted to go. He winked out. Soon, I thought, the fireflies would all be over with. Again. Another year. But right now, it was September, and still summer. And I was treading water. I couldn't think about anything right now.

"Yeah," he said, jamming his thumbs into his jean pockets.

On the bike, my heart rate got up, and I began to feel a little better.

"I bet there's millions more of fireflies in Maine than we got here in NYC," he said. He squashed out his cigarette and tossed it.

"Whyn't you pick that up. I thought you said you loved Nature."

"Can I ride? Let me try. I got more tricks than you."

"You think."

"Let me show you." He got up and blocked me. Put one leg over my bike frame, while I was still on it, his back to me. He turned around to look at me. He was too close. "Well?"

I looked at him. "Get the fuck 'way from me," I said. I looked at him again, straight in the eyes.

I shook my head, and pulled off the bike. "Here. But just for one shot."

He stood up on the bike and rode up the little hill, turning around. He leapt, but not as high as me, and crashed down hard, one tire wobbling out, squishing dust, before he got it under control. "Top that," he said, grinning.

"I already did." I got up and moved toward him. "Aiight, that was it."

He geared down on the pedals, picking up speed again. "Here. Lemme get just one more."

He flew past me, popped up the hill, and kept going, heading down the trail. I stood, watching blankly, my bike-gloved hands hanging at my sides.

I burst forward, racing up, following, not believing what was happening, thinking at first he'd just gone to get more backup speed for the jump. But he turned toward the street. I ran as hard as I could, spit and my heart flying out of the corners of my mouth, but running in those stiff bike shoes felt like what a woman must feel trying to run at top speed in pumps. I watched the little stick figure on the little stick mountain bike — my thousand-dollar mountain bike, my freedom and health and ability to fly — ride out of the Park and cross Central Park West, disappear down the street.

Days passed as I morphed into a twisted, writhing, hating monster. The apartment's empty L-shaped entrance corner, ten feet in where I kept my bike, mocked me. Over and over in my head I repeated the Mobb Deep rap: *There's a war goin' on outside no man is safe from; you can't run.* I couldn't eat or hardly sleep. I hunted that mutherfucker down, my knife strapped and holstered under my shirt. I hid in the bushes down off 91st across West End, for hours at night, knowing that he sometimes crashed at the basement apartment there, waiting for him to make a mistake. But I was on my feet, and he had my bike, so my wings were clipped. Just going anywhere seemed so slow and tedious. And he was nowhere to be found, seen or heard of in our uptown area.

He obviously knew I was looking for him. I thought back over everything. He had deliberately stolen my freedom, my soul, for no reason other than to just do it, inflict damage, just like a crackhead. It wasn't the bike. He knew the bike wasn't a physical object. It was my fucking freedom and personal relationship with everything. Scarface crackhead deliberately did to me the worst thing he could do.

Sid the cat and his Big Jewish Mama stayed away from me.

Seven days passed, and suddenly he called me, from a payphone.

"You gonna come get your bike? I'm tired of riding this shit around. I'll be at the rock in 20 minutes."

"What the fuck! Where you— "

He hung up.

I strapped my knife on under my shirt, adrenaline *burning* in my body. Yanked on a pair of loose jeans and boots. Jammed my bike gloves into my back pocket. I would get my bike back. My freedom back. My bike was only minutes away.

I nearly ran to the train at 103rd and CPW, hopping down the stairs three at a time. I lucked out in catching a train just blowing into the station as I forced my token into the turnstile. Surfing the swaying train, feet planted as it hurtled downtown, narrowing the distance between me, my bike and him, I averted my eyes from the few passengers sharing my subway car. Needed to remain anonymous.

As soon as the doors opened at 72nd I popped out and hauled up the stairs. It was still daylight, a few hours left to the humid warm evening. Cars streaming up and down Central Park West seemed to be going unusually fast and loud, their colors too bright. I crossed CPW like an animal hurrying to get to green-tangled growth on the other side.

Central Park opened its arms to me as I stalked in from 72nd. I moved my feet silently. I reached inside my shirt and undid the velcro strap around the knife so it hung open from the black canvas sheath, ready.

Totally aware of my surroundings. Didn't think I'd raised any suspicions. Good. At the turn off into the bushes and tangles, I veered quickly and ducked in, then stalked fast, noiselessly up the winding path.

I approached the rock, peering through the leafy branches.

The black frame of my bike was visible. There it was, my prize freedom, so close again to my body, its wheels, handlebars, frame, right in front of me through this last tangle. Scarface sat on the rock drinking a 20 ounce clear bottle of cheap malt liquor that looked like foamy amber piss. His back was to me.

He hadn't seen me yet. Though he had to know I would be coming from this way. He was just sitting there, drinking the beer. Is something up?

I wanted him to see me. I wanted him to look me in the face, and see my hate for him manifest itself, just before he got what he gives.

I stepped into the clearing, to the side in front of him.

His head swiveled casually to the side to look at me, pores sweating a little, a post crack-high cold sweat, like the glass bottle he was holding in his hand. He raised his eyebrows at me, and smiled. His silver hoop earring shined. "What's up," he said softly. I stared him straight in the eyes, breathed deep in through my nostrils, reaching up under my shirt for my knife. This was it. Bitch gon get it fo' real. In one quick, final moment, I took another deep breath, laughing inwardly that he couldn't see yet, didn't know, and I — I —

I lunged forward and cut him across his right cheek, opening a big bloody gash bigger than the one on his left side. A splat of blood went flying, slapping onto a green leaf hanging over him. "AUUGH SHIT!" he screamed, dropping the bottle and it rolled, spilling foamy beer into the leaf-moldering soil. He jumped up holding his face, made a step toward me, and I side-kicked him in his knee. I thought I heard something snap. He fell down on that knee, then forced himself up again. Blood was draining out of his face in sheets, soaking his white t-shirt. I could smell it. That dank spilt blood smell.

"What go around come around," I said through my teeth. He flashed his eyes into mine. I lunged again and drove the blade into his chest, where I was sure his heart would be. He spat up blood and collapsed, convulsing like a fish. I heard the sound of his head crack against the rock as he fell backward —

I fell backwards myself, the soft damp dirt and rotting forest duff cushioning my fall. I could see parts of the cloudy sky through the green tops of the trees, and those parts looked like puzzle pieces. I sat up, crossing my arms around my knees, holding the knife. It was still clean and shiny. Sitting on the rock, he smiled down at me and nodded, drinking from his beer.

"Why don't you just fucking go to Maine," I exhaled, shaking my head. "Get out. For good. I don't even want to see or touch or even breathe the same air as you." I hung my head. I wanted to sleep for a thousand years.

He drank from his beer again.

"You can't kill anymore, huh," he said.

Silence.

"Remember, there's no statute of limitations." He got on my bike, and before I knew it, rode off again, disappeared for good.

Aaaaaaaaaauuuuuuugh........

I allowed myself to fall back again — thump — dirt and twigs sticking into my back through the t-shirt. Spreading my arms out wide, still gripping the knife in my right hand, I stared at the puzzled sky. Something inch-long, wormy, squiggled against the back of my neck, uncomfortable in the position I had put him in between me and the soil. I gripped the rubberized knife handle so hard it hurt. I relaxed my fingers. It lay loosely on my open palm.

"*Have you finally had enough?*" I heard God say. Then: silence.

The leaves on all the branches seemed shiny, like they do on sticky, overcast, late-summer afternoons in the humid East, as if it had just briefly rained, though it hadn't.

"I'm through. Sir. Yes." Exhaustion steamed out of me like a thousand tiny souls rising, like erratic lit-up fireflies, my belly lifting and falling with each breath. "Everything is hate. Jagged. Disjointed. Can't do it no more. Tired of everything bein' hate. I can't base everything in my life on hate no more. That's it. I'm through."

I gulped a deep breath and exhaled. The worm beneath the back of my neck squirmed for something, anything more comfortable. I slightly lifted my head so he could move. He stayed where he was, stuck to me. I let my head flop back down. "I'm ready to heal," I croaked. "I really am."

"Bout time," I swore I heard God say.

I narrowed my eyebrows up at the sky. God had left, and it was up to me.

I closed my eyelids, tried to relax my body, lay there, just breathing. I called out. Was it a sound in my throat, in the woods, and did anybody hear it? "But that don't mean I'm still not going to fight back or stand strong where needed! I'm just gonna flip the script — for the rest of my life I hereby swear I wont let anybody, including myself, ever pull me down again to that ugly vicious-circle of hate. I've made it this far. I will battle where needed; but out of deep love for Earth, not out of hate for people."

You mean like your hate for yourself?

I shook my head vehemently from side to side. *I reject all that is hateful, ugly and life-destructive in the Universe. I am part of All that is vital healthy sacred and Life Prairie Ocean powerful in the Universe. Thank you, Dear God and Mother Earth, for letting me learn, for letting me survive, for letting me be healthy. Thank you for my life. I am in Your service.*

Lying there. Stomach rising and falling.

O.K. Now what?

Adrián 2006

CHAPTER TWENTY-SEVEN

Refuge

Picture the Earth… and your place within her.

Picture the Earth….

Cloud and shadow… space and sky.

I lowered to my knees, eyes peeling over the immense view, my breath always overtaken by the size of these animals. So close, in the silence, a bull buffalo, his head lifted, black Viking horns glinting. Three females from his harem hugged close to his side, all heading in the same direction. A tawny pronghorn antelope buck stood to the left, staring in my direction, three does near him. At their feet, a prairie dog was popping his head out of a burrow. Behind, the southeastern Wyoming bluffs and late summer grasses stretched out for miles and miles, and the herd of buffalo was equally endless, merging into the cloud shadows, flowing like a stream down a small canyon, continuing around the mesa, disappearing out of sight. I could almost smell the dry, crackly buffalo grass, prickly pear cactus, and blue grama grass in the foreground, ripe for a lightning strike… The afternoon… I knew it was dry, very clear, air as pure as the Universe itself, puffy cumulus clouds bright against blue sky. Out there, prairie dogs would bark, a meadowlark would warble his Plains song….

I closed my eyes, bowed my head. *Picture the Earth, and your place within her…*

I heard the clicking of shoe heels on the shiny marble floor, opened my eyes to cast a slitted sidelong glance. Big shoes, sharply polished.

A giant's fingers touched my right shoulder.

"Son," a bass voice said quietly, as if not to disturb the preserved silence. "You all right?" A large gold band on the ring finger glinted in contrast to shiny dark, almost coal-black skin. The stiff cuffs of his navy-blue uniform jacket hung just past his wrist.

I looked up, orienting myself. In the darkened hall, light from the museum diorama reflected from his glistening face and the shroud of dark-stained mahogany walls behind him. He had creases in the skin folds beneath each eye.

I looked back into the Plains, the frozen, stuffed, High Plains, created in 1934. Mounted animals on real dirt and preserved grass in front of a seamless painted background. I could see my face faintly reflected in the glass. The last half hour before closing time, there was never anybody in here, the American Museum of Natural History, on Central Park West and 81ˢᵗ. I could have the dark halls to myself. Get lost in the portals to my other world.

I nodded and got up. The giant in the security uniform returned the nod, fading back.

I heard a small commotion around the corner, as if a few last stragglers were trying to be quiet. I faded back.

A Puerto Rican schoolgirl with frilly curls, maybe 5 or 6 years old, moved up to the plate glass in front of the buffaloes, followed by her mother. She wore a yellow rainslicker and a checkered Catholic schoolgirl's skirt, with a little backpack over her shoulders. They stood silhouetted in front of the outback.

"That's how big they were?" she whispered in a voice like small bells.

"There used to be thousands like that," her mama whispered. "All the way across."

The little girl spread her palms on the glass and peered. "How come they had to kill so many?"

* * *

Somehow, Sid the cat knew. No matter how silently I tiptoed up the six flights, making sure not to make the slightest noise, he would be there sitting, right behind the door, waiting. I tried everything, even not putting the key in the lock. I'd crouch down near the bottom outside the door, and very quietly mouth the first sound of "S" as in "Sid." Yup, sure enough, he was there, instantly rolling that little gurgle of his. He was sitting right there. I couldn't figure out how he knew I was coming.

I'd never liked cats. "Dumb Cat," I called him, even as I bought him tuna and spirulina and he became strong and muscular, his coat thick and lustrous. He loved drinking from the bathroom sink faucet, head turned sideways, raspy tongue darting out, fangs bared, every few minutes shaking off droplets from his whiskers. When he shook his head it sounded like the *brrrrt* of a hummingbird's wings.

When I would come in from work or the gym or Central Park and lie flat on my back on the bare maple floors, letting my body rest, feeling through my back the trees that were now polished wood strips beneath me, their lives through days of sun and rain reaching up into me, their great arms stretching into the sky over time, their solid roots holding dear and digging deeper, he'd climb onto my chest and lay there. Rising and falling with my breath. At night when I was in bed he'd scratch on my door if I'd closed it, and yowl if I wouldn't open it. On my chest, his chin right under mine, he'd adjust his breathing in sync with mine, rising and falling, his purrs buzzing like a deep chest cavity engine, vibrating into my own chest and down through the maple hardwoods and the walls of the building rooted in Manhattan Island soil hundreds of thousands of years old.

During the afternoons, if I was off, and reading newspapers or old American West books, or writing in my journal in my front room, I'd suddenly look up to see one eye peeking around the corner of the open door, staring. The instant our eyes met he'd make that little gurgle — he had this way of rolling a little high-pitched two note gurgle in his throat when he knew he'd been caught — and, unable to resist, I'd bolt up knowing it's what he wanted me to do, and chase him down the long narrow hallway, his claws clattering on the wood floor as he raced to turn the corner and leap onto his mother's sofa, flipping around to crouch there, pupils dilated and excited, sides and ideas pulsing. It became his game.

Crack Valley didn't get any worse or better. The corners of 107th and 108th at Manhattan, and 105th and Columbus, were as they'd always been, especially at night. A child in a stroller got shot in a crossfire, and the flowers and candles and cards lasted a week before they melted with the weather and the ongoing rush of New York. Street crews took away what was left and the sidewalk was again as if nothing at all had happened. The last sticky days of summer passed. Autumn blew in; the days began to get cooler and shorter, drier, with spurts of rain that clumped the falling leaves to the pavement till winds from New York Harbor and the Catskill Mountains blew-dry them again.

Shere, my roommate, was a little too boisterous for my quiet ass, but she was a nice lady with a good heart, and we got along fine. We didn't see each other that much. She smoked cigarettes, even though she was in the fitness industry, and had some substance issues going on as well.

She was always having drama with her worthless Argentinian boyfriend, who I couldn't stand. And not just because he'd leave the water running and was so wasteful about everything. One time Shere threw all his shit out the 6th floor window. She was sort of thick-bodied, strong-boned, and when she sat in the bathtub, with her eye makeup running a bit, she looked like a Jewish version of one of those earnest 1920s Hollywood starlets who never really made it. When her boyfriend wasn't around, sometimes we hung out; she always needed to talk, so I listened. Sometimes we would eat fresh bagels and tofu cream cheese from the deli on Broadway, and have fresh carrot juice and blueberries — my favorite. I learned how to be a pretty good roommate.

I rarely went past the old hotel anymore unless I was going on up into Harlem, because my Central Park entrance was on 103rd St, and Hotel Hell was between 106th and 107th. Central Park and Riverside Park down by the Hudson River were the two places I spent most of my free time now.

Camron had completely severed our relationship when he found out I was serious, that the shit was through, that I wouldn't be getting any more, even if and when it became available again. I was through. He couldn't believe it, and never called again.

I sat in the swing-set in a deserted section of Riverside Park. A gust of wind blew through; dry oak and sycamore leaves raced a potpourri of dirt into the corners of the stone wall and spun around. Now what?

I thought about a quote I'd read from New York Times columnist Frank Rich: "Much of life is about career, love and loss."

I had my little job down at the health food store on 7th Ave. and 12th St. Took my vitamins, herbs and supplements religiously, chewed fresh-cut slices of raw ginger root daily till there was nothing but pulp left, building up my core, healing my insides, getting better and stronger. *Nothing but pulp left inside, huh.*

I kept to myself, concentrating on work and being healthy. Sometimes I would notice, after the fact, that somebody had been trying to talk to me in a cool, non-obvious way, but most of the time I was so caught up on thinking about mission and movement stuff it didn't occur to me till it was too late. Lahumba would sometimes meet me down at the gym, and she would always smile and give me one of them world-class hugs, and that would make me feel better. She'd make me get on the floor and do abs with her, which was cool because I could do a thousand crunch twists without a prob.

I knew things were ending. But not just yet. There was something. Just once in my life, I needed, wanted to experience —

The old thought came again — but now mellowed with time: *Where the — Where are you? Right now?*

As I went to the gym, as I rode my new mountain bike (which I'd struggled to pay for), as I made organic vegetable juices for customer after customer, as I mopped the floor at 10 o'clock at night after everybody had long gone, listening to Hot 97's top dj Funkmaster Flex, I looked at myself in the reflection in the window. Squeezing out dirty gray water in the chute of the big yellow bucket, I thought to myself: "You're basically a normal guy now." *So what's the problem, dawg?*

The New York Times said the Gingrich 104th Congress was in full swing, and they were clamoring to cut out the heart of the Arctic National Wildlife Refuge for oil, and that would be the end of the 125 mile-long Arctic Refuge Coastal Plain. The industrial, end-of-the-world metal monster had made it to the edge of my million-year old Safe Place and Refuge. As long as the Arctic Refuge was still alive, as long as there was one completely whole place left on Earth, there was hope. The Arctic Refuge circle of life, the great migrations, the human-animal cultural understanding, the soar of pristine wild open country, clean and undefiled, sacred, silent except for all the bird and bug voices, calls of the pregnant caribou, and the lapping of the Arctic Ocean waves, bursting with abundance and vitality, was everything the Great Plains once was.

The destroyers figured they'd found a surefire way in. The Clinton administration was trying to balance the budget, and the Republicans were insisting on drilling the Refuge as part of their negotiations.

I read all the arguments and statements from people trying to save it. Except for the rare quote that made it into the news from Gwich'in Indian people who lived there and whose culture was inextricably intertwined with the great caribou herd, much like the former relationships between Plains Indians and buffalo, people were missing the point. People with good intentions were comparing the Refuge to man-made places like the Sistine Chapel, or they rattled off statistics. The Refuge was created by God and Earth. It wasn't an artifact; it wasn't a cathedral. As valued as those are, this was a critical, living, breathing homeland, birthing ground, and Safe Place, a Refuge upon whose survival millions of animals and an entire culture of people depended. It didn't seem like anybody was speaking about what really mattered. They were tripping over themselves about statistics, all of which were important. But I didn't think any movement could be built and won on statistics.

The passion and life and vitality were not being communicated in a personal way. The public did not seem to know about this Coastal Plain Refuge. Somehow, I had to help others discover what it means in terms of life, soul, Earth, and future. Gwich'in people had lived within and alongside it for 20,000 years in balance with immense migrating herds of caribou, wolves, bears, birds, wild rivers, and much more. Gwich'in people called the Coastal Plain "the sacred place where life begins." The Arctic Refuge

Coastal Plain, cooled by summer Arctic Ocean winds, was a nursery and the wildest grassland left in the Western Hemisphere. Not just caribou, but wild birds from every continent on Earth including Antarctica migrated thousands of miles up to the Coastal Plain each summer to give birth in a place as wild, pristine and primeval as it was a hundred thousand years ago. People needed to stand up and protect this Refuge because if we couldn't at least save this last place all the way up at the edge of the Earth then, in my opinion, human "civilization" had no meaning, morals or values.

I got consumed. I found myself down in the basement of the Wetlands Nightclub, on Hudson down in Tribeca, where I knew from the Earth First! Journal there was an activist hangout. To my surprise, James, one of the guys who worked down there and was in charge of activist campaigns like battling Mitsubishi over rainforest destruction, went and talked to the owners and managers. They said I could use their phones and fax. I wanted to make a show of national support for permanently protecting the entire Arctic Refuge as wilderness. I wanted to generate a thousand petition signatures from each state, as an awareness-raising tool, and then stage a candle light vigil/demonstration in front of the White House on the seventh anniversary of the Exxon Valdez oil spill March 24 of next year. And on the bottom of each petition was GREAT PLAINS RESTORATION COUNCIL, with a Pine Ridge Indian Reservation address, where a friend was picking up the mail, and a temporary NYC address set up for this campaign. It was a group in name only. But it sounded official!

I had to change how I was. I had hardly ever talked in my life, and now I had to call strangers up, people in each state who might be able to help, or might know some volunteers, and I had to get them interested in why this was so important. My head threatened all the time to shut down, but I managed by sheer will, and by slipping out, when it was absolutely necessary, to a back stairwell in complete darkness for five minutes. I met a lot of good, interesting people over the phone. None of the big national environmental groups would help me at first, and I felt it was mainly because they had a patronizing and dismissive preconception about what little knots of people could accomplish. But lots of small grassroots groups, like Free the Planet!, Student Environmental Action Coalition, and People of Color Caucus helped spread the word nationally.

I just started calling up people, explaining what the Arctic Refuge meant, and they got on board and recommended others who could help, and it spread like that. Soon volunteers were showing up at Wetlands, offering their time.

Over the phone, I became friends with this cool, passionate, quiet-spoken girl named Turtle, who worked at the Earth First! Journal offices in Tucson. She helped me out a lot in disseminating the campaign, and we talked nearly every day. She had a nice, soft laugh that reminded me of a small, perfect bubble popping. I could tell there was hurt and fierceness behind that. She told me how she loved to swim. In the winter it was great, but in the summer she sweated too much, so she tried to go early or late. Sweating while swimming, I thought, thinking back to the warm almost hot Gulf of Mexico waters.

Ambika, an East Indian-American girl from Kentucky who hung out at Wetlands wanting to get active, offered to assist in anything, and she became a right-hand woman in the effort to save the Refuge.

Sean, this guy with short dreads from 108th Street whose neighbor's Petey-eyed pit bull had committed suicide by jumping off the apartment roof, helped me table in front of Barnes and Noble on 82nd and Broadway. It was my first time dealing face to face with the public like that, but I found a lot of people were friendly. A few were hateful, including one middle-aged man who wanted the Refuge destroyed, felt there was way too much wilderness already (even though we have more land in pavement than in wilderness), that it's only value was its oil, and that the world was solely put here to be used by mankind. When he saw he couldn't win the argument, he said: "Well, at least it keeps you off the street." Sean shook his head, motioned for me to be cool, that people like that weren't worth the energy.

Tracey, from Westchester, black brassy-skinned and soft-spoken, with the prettiest smile, normally worked on rain forest issues, but regularly came to help me out too.

I'd sometimes put in 20 hours. Go in early, 7 a.m., then to the juice bar job, then back down to Wetlands and stay till one or three in the morning to work some more. We continued to get closer to our goal of 50,000 signatures — at least 1,000 from each state. At the far end of the day, exhausted, walking through the western reaches of a city murmured by deep night, I found that after dealing with people all those hours I was still alone. Outside, just glad to be in outdoor air, exhausted but feeling better with each step, I might bypass my 25-minute wait for the subway train and keep walking, nearly seven miles uptown. I thrust myself toward Central Park; it might be four in the morning by the time I got there, where concrete ended and grass and soil and trees began, and I dove into its reverence.

The last time I worked at Sound Factory Bar, I had met this guy Allan who lived in Harlem, just a few blocks from me, up on 111th Street. He wasn't no thug or anything, but he seemed cool, nice gym body, nice lips, big smooth hands, very nice looking. He was more R&B than hip hop, but he loved Biggie Smalls' flow, as did everybody who was into East Coast. I finally called him; went over to his crib. We listened to music, ended up having sex. Afterward, I lay there as he fell asleep, the B.I.G. beat still in my head, a sinking mood creeping in.

I looked up into the large silver-framed photo print he had on his wall. Three dolphins stretched out in mid-flight above the ocean, their bodies and the seawater almost black in the angle of the late afternoon light, the low Sun behind them glowing yellow over an infinite horizon, glinting off the water's hard surface and their wet backs. I could feel their power, their freedom, their raw, vital selves purified by water and motion, at one with their ocean world. I remembered again the wild dolphins that had startled me as they burst out of the surf off the beach in Mexico. In Allan's poster, for such power, the image was quiet, nothing at all like those two dolphins I'd seen.

These dolphins had hardly broken the surface upon their entrance into the sky, and appeared to be flying perfectly horizontal a few feet above the water.

I felt even emptier than before. I looked at Allan dozing off, one of his arms draped over me. He wouldn't understand the real me even if I tried to explain. He'd never understand. He was cool, nice looking, not a punk, he felt good, but the shit had just been, had just felt… like my heart wasn't really in it. *Maybe it's you, not him.* I remembered something somebody had said once: "Every time you have sex with somebody you give up a little piece of your soul."

I rolled over and quietly got up, needing something to mean something. I again looked up at the dolphins. Craved for my back to be wet like theirs, craved to be with them out there in that ocean prairie, leaping and diving, flying through clean infinity like that. But I couldn't. I was stuck here. And I couldn't connect with anybody. I needed to leave the city; I was just wasting time.

I slipped out of his apartment and walked back to my own. Ran up the six flights and quietly grabbed my bike, stepping around Dumb Cat (who of course was right there at the threshold, waiting) as I opened the door. Meow gurgle whine rub chin and back of ear against my leg, arch back.

Riding — my second-choice soul purifier and chance to connect — catching air and motion, I flew down to the Hudson River and the north-south path at river's edge. Checking the speed on the little handlebar computer, I bore down on the pedals till I was flying along at 22 mph and kept my pace there, heart and bloodstream pumping, fighting the north wind on the way up, sailing even faster on the way down with the wind at my back. I rode up and down the miles-long path along the Hudson River, dark night waves whipping little whitecaps in cold windy air. They looked like little animal faces rising out of the water and baring their teeth before slipping back under.

Standing in the doorframe to my sparse bedroom with only the yellow corner candle on the floor for light, I wrapped my wrists in boxer's tape and clasped the overhead metal bar in an underhand grip. It was late at night, after three a.m. I had the window cracked open; a cool dry breeze slipped in and licked the candle's flame in its tall glass tube. Crossing my legs at the ankles, half-cut shorts hanging off my pelvic bone, I let my body hang to open the spine, then squeezed off a round of 15 pull-ups, isolating my biceps as I pulled up over the bar, then slowly lowered.

Sid was down the hall, crouched in the shadows against the floorboards, watching me. That good, familiar, puffy-swollen feeling was beginning to spread into my upper arms. I rested for one minute, drinking from my bottle of water, then wrapped my fingers around the doorframe's edge and stretched out one arm. I opened it up all the way into my chest, rotating my shoulder drop backward, turning my body away, at full stretch wiggling my fingers for blood flow and making sure not to twist or torque my anterior deltoids. I did the other arm.

I pulled off another set. It's true being fit like this was a new addiction. I couldn't get enough of this feeling. I'd finally gotten healthy and very in shape. Though I liked to look good, it was not just for physical appearances or vanity. The surge of health and sense of freedom, wellness — of having broken through into a new being — was electrifying. To live inside an extremely healthy, clean, well-functioning body, able to handle so much more now, became the best thing. And from that, I could at last go forward and do what I needed to do in this life.

I didn't want to wake Shere up. This was my silent time, my time to be all alone — well, except for Sid — in the darkness. I did 5 sets of 15, with only one minute rests in between, till the burning sang into all those pressure points, so many sensations going off at once, quivering in my body. I imagined it was what great sex would feel like.

The corner of the room was my shrine. Near the candle I had some buffalo wool, a dried coyote paw I had found, and a few other items from out West. I had a black-and-white photo I'd cut out of the New York Times taped to the wall near the floor where I did my pushups. It was an in-your-face close-up of a Chechen grandmother in front of bombed-out war-torn rubble that used to be Grozny, the capital of Chechnya. She was an innocent bad-ass old survivor lady just trying to live her own life, disgusted with being caught between Muslim rebels and the Russian government, the latter having basically destroyed the secessionist capital with breathtaking brutality. She had on a head scarf, her crunched-up, wrinkled, survivalist face thrust into the camera, missing teeth, looking wild and crazed by sanity, able to handle anything because she already had. I kept her right at eye level in front of where I had my metal pushup bars so whenever I didn't think I could do anymore, I looked her right in the missing teeth, and knew I could do more. On impulse I went over and pushed out three sets, even though I wasn't planning to do chest until tomorrow, when I could hopefully get to the gym. I was a member of Body Strength now, walking distance at 110th and Broadway, but it only stayed open till 10.

Still not sleepy. It was a warm night for November. Pulled on a hooded sweatshirt, adjusted my knife, capped my head with a skully, and popped my bike onto my shoulder. Tiptoeing in my stiff riding shoes, I quietly left the apartment, making sure not to let the heavy door slam or make any noise. Taking the stairs down two at a time, I went out the front door and zapped over into Central Park, picking up the outer 6.2 mile loop just past the creek and the bridge over the lake they call The Pool. A barn owl, a couple raccoons, and me had the entire Park to ourselves. 843 acres of woods, lakes, creeks, gorges and meadows, smack in the middle of Manhattan, impressive to me each and every single time. I squeezed out two laps, making it 12.4, not counting approach and return. On the northern approach, down into the gorge of the North Woods up in the Harlem end, there is a life-size sculpture of a mountain lion coming out of the forest, overlooking the road. His face is pulled back in a fangs-bared scream.

Courage of my convictions, I thought to myself, under the pale orange street-light, pulling my hood up over my head. My breathing fell back to normal as I sat on the bench under the stairs they call Stranger's Gate, which led up to the Great Hill that was on top of some of the giant glaciated boulders. I rested my bike up against me, arms out across the top of the bench. I was right in the threshold between the Park and the city, not yet ready to cross back over. I lingered, relaxed, chilled, hung out, breathed.

Hotel Hell was just up the way, one block, across Central Park West. I thought of how many times I had gone in and out of those double glass doors. I could see the little yellow-lit buzzer to the right.

A cab drove past, heading uptown, then braked a half block ahead. The passenger side rear door opened, two long legs in heels poked out as the occupant paid the fare.

She got out as I scrunched up my face, wondering who was stopping to be let off on this side of CPW, in the middle of nowhere, into the North Woods.

I recognized her, Tiffany, one of the drag queen hookers from Hotel Hell. She stalked over to me, her heels wobbling a little on the cobblestoned walk.

"You look tired," I said.

"How come I can't have a boyfriend like you?" she said. Her lipstick looked like she had just put on a fresh layer.

I nodded at her. "How you doing?"

"Scoot over," she said, plopping down on the bench. "Fine. Thanks for asking. I'm tired." She flung her hand. "Tired of all those Wyoming truckers. I hate cowboys. Ugh."

I couldn't help but break a smile.

"What is it they got for sisters? Probably because they don't have any out there." She huddled into her soft beige coat, crossing her legs at the thigh, causing her skirt and the flap of her coat to ride up. "Aren't you cold?" she asked. It was getting a little chilly.

"Naah. I been riding. I'm still warm from that. And anyways, I don't mind. Just bein' in the outside air is enough for me." I turned my head to look directly at her. I could see the little electrolysis bumps where a few remaining stubborn whiskers had recently been attacked.

"You just said that because you think I'll think it makes you different."

I looked at her, thinking about that. "Alright, I guess. But it's true in a way. I'd be glad to be outside till the day I die and beyond. And I'm an activist. An environmental activist."

"What do you act for? I mean, where do you start? The world's gone to hell. People made it like this."

"And they got names and addresses," I said, crossing my arms homeboy-tough and lifting my chin. I broke out of my pose, almost laughing, which startled me. "Naah, I'm kidding. I'm working on the Arctic National Wildlife Refuge. You ever hear of it?"

"Uh-uh, sweety."

I checked her facial expression. She seemed like she was interested and paying attention.

"Well, it's this big open place, this great big prairie 125 miles long at the top of the world, that's as pristine and wild and full of thundering life as it's been for thousands and thousands of years. And these Indian people, they're called the Gwich'in Nation; they've lived up there in health and balance for 20,000 years. Right alongside, following hundreds of thousands of wild caribou that migrate up and over these mountains to reach this big Coastal Plain to give birth in the spring. These animals have done that journey for hundreds of thousands of years. They migrate back out in the fall." I paused, checking her face. She was still listening. "Well, it's a long journey. It's this great big absolutely pristine, untouched place, right up against the Arctic Ocean, cooled by ocean winds in the summer. The wind blows away the bugs while they have their babies. There's no mechanical noise, no roads, no nothing. It's that remote. It's a paradise, it's quiet, and it is the last place like it left. But the destroyers want to drill it for oil, bringing in their trucks, bulldozers, pipelines, poisonous chemicals, burning smokestacks and everything else."

I cleared my throat, still watching her face, wondering if I was talking too much. I remembered mentioning to Turtle one afternoon that actually I rarely talked at all, and hadn't for most of my life. She'd said: "I find that hard to believe." What could I say?

"Wow," Tiffany said, uncrossing her legs and putting her knees together, smoothing out her skirt, like a secretary. "How come I haven't heard about this?"

"They don't want people to know. They figure we're all too busy with our own lives, just trying to make it through each day, and that's exactly where they want us to stay. Cause then they can go in and do whatever they want. They might poison your water today and put cancer in your air tomorrow, and they'll laugh all the way to the bank because you too kept down and unaware to do anything but allow yourself to be their victim." I felt my throat overheating. "They laughing all the way to the bank, destroying and raping everything they can, ruining the present and damning the future and, by us not being aware and not standing in their way, by not doing anything or helping other people find out what's going on or at least doing something, we become like willing partners. Just by accident."

She was looking down at her high-heeled feet, and her forward leaning was making the tops of her breasts push out a little from her dress. I had to give it to her. She looked nice. Considering.

"So, how can I help this Refuge place? I'm serious."

I pulled out of my right back pocket a couple folded, crinkled petitions. "We're doing this petition drive getting people all across the country to educate others about this, and demand to protect the Refuge, then send the petitions back, then we're gonna have a big demonstration in front of the White House next March."

"Who thought up this?"

"I did."

"You? For real? I would've never thought that, looking at you."

I nodded. "I live on the Great Plains. I'm not really from here. I live way out there." I pointed over the buildings, over the river, out West. "When you see me here, I'm just here temporarily. For work. And the Refuge is like how the Great Plains used to be 150 years ago, full of life and health and vitality, when it had the massive herds of buffalo, and Native people and all that. Now, the Plains have been so damaged, there's been so much killing, it's mostly a wasteland. Just struggling to stay alive. We can't let them do that to the Refuge."

"Huh. I've heard about the Buffalo Soldiers," she said.

"I think the US Army after the Civil War found itself with a bunch of enlisted black men with guns, and sent them out to do the dirty work of killing the Indians. Pit the two most oppressed against each other. For role models I'd rather look at York, who was Lewis and Clark's slave, who did so much of the work on their trip out there, or Esteban, the Morrocan slave who washed ashore in Texas with his conquistador-masters and was able to help smooth the way with the Indians because he was a person of color. Shit, the Chinese built the railroad. With their damn hats, those straw pointed hats. People of color were part of the whole scenario from the get-go. It wasn't just Little House on the Prairie, and it wasn't — and didn't have to be — just war."

I knew I was off on a tangent so I just stopped speaking. I imagined those Chinese guys out there in the Nebraska wilderness, working under the hot sun. There had to have been moments where these big ol' buffaloes or little prairie dogs came up to the Chinamen workers, and they both stared at each other, eyes meeting, wondering about each other. At that exact moment, looking at each other, what were they both thinking?

"Wow," Tiffany said, breaking into our thoughts. She was huddling into her coat now, arms crossed over her knees, holding her elbows. She was getting cold. "They sure don't tell about any of that in the history books; they sure make sure about that. I'm sayin'." She shivered. "You know. I don't think I've ever had a conversation like this before. All people ever want to talk about is who looks fiercer, or who cut who with a razor, or, well, you know."

"Wanna take a petition and get some your friends to fill it out?" I lifted my eyebrows.

She reached over and took both copies. For a second, the orange streetlight flashed in her polished fingernails.

"I'll take both of them." She stood up and smiled. "And I'll meet you back here at this bench, same time, next week. I'm serious."

"Cool," I said, a little amazed. "Thank you."

I got on my bike and rode the empty streets for another forty minutes, warming my bloodstream back up, but I didn't go back into the park. I was already on this side. And fine with people tonight.

I thought about all the people up in their apartments, snuggled up in their beds, with somebody they cared about, sleeping soundly in each other's arms, breathing in the good smells of each other's warm good skin.

One of these days I'm gonna crack in half and die of loneliness, I thought to myself, finally heading home.

As I pedaled up 106th toward Manhattan Ave. to make a left back down to 104th, a red maroon car with its lights off sped through the intersection. A guy clung to the driver's side window frame like an insect for dear life, holding his legs up only inches from a rushing pavement that would tear him to bloody pieces should he slip. There was no way he was going to be able to maintain his hold for long. At that moment, and at that speed, he was the most alone he'd ever been in his life. And this was his moment.

I faxed petitions and updates, and got people to chain-fax them and call their friends, and ask their friends to call their friends, and so on. At the same time everybody was asking everybody to call their representatives and senators as well as President Clinton. People were bombarding Washington with phone calls. We had a 50 state grassroots campaign going. Some kid from Missouri called up and said he had put the petition and alert up on the Internet. I asked him what the Internet was, and when I still didn't understand, he said "It's basically a bunch of computers all connected to each other." Pretty soon people we'd never heard of from places we'd never thought of were calling us, including women from a Garden Club in Long Island, to Earth First!ers in North Dakota (who would've thought!) to an elderly couple in a nursing home in Amarillo. Even people from the big nationals started calling, people who had ignored me at the start. And Tiffany, good ol' Tiffany, met me exactly like she'd said she would late that night in front of Stranger's Gate, and handed me two fully filled out petitions, 24 names.

She said: "I took it because I thought about how you said that place was so quiet. I got all my girls, and those Arab guys at the deli where we have lunch at night, and some people on my floor to sign it," she said. "Maybe some them did it just to humor me. But I tried to explain."

I said: "You know, the whole world used to be like that. Silent and full of life like that. All this — " I nodded my head around us — "is all very recent."

"Well, honey, good luck. We should save at least one spot." She bent over and kissed me on the cheek, leaving a perfect pucker of lipstick rose.

"The hotel still the same?" I asked as she clattered off, obviously anxious to get home, get to sleep.

"Still nasty as hell," she said, with a swoop of her hand out to the side.

A few nights after Christmas, late, I lay on my futon on the shiny maple floor, a candle burning, my Chechen grandmother's face glaring in the candlelight. Sid scratched at the closed door, yowled, whined, but I just lay there. He kept crying; he eventually went back to his radiator.

I had worked out at the gym till my fingertips were shaking, till they shut the place down at 10. Then I rode for a couple hours, flinging up and down Manhattan's far western and deserted avenues like a rubberband shot from one end to the other.

I took a hot shower, then a cold shower, then hot again.

Still, I'd been unable to get rid of this feeling, that I was going to implode and explode at the exact same moment, and nothing would be left but a charred POOF in mid-air. I needed… something. I gripped my arms around myself as hard as I could, but nothing helped, nothing permeated, nothing quelched the blowtorch inside. For a moment I thought about taking care of myself but I knew that wouldn't do anything. The shit wasn't down there, it was throughout my whole body, on fire in every cell and molecule, tearing at my soul. An involuntary yelp or whimper squeezed out of my throat; I turned over and dug my face into the pillow.

Without getting up or raising my head I reached over and pressed PLAY on the boom box, turning the volume down low. At last I relaxed, and Mary J. Blige (*Not gon cry*) sang me to sleep.

And January, 1996. On Hot97, DJ Angie Martinez said: "Hip hop is at a zenith right now."

I thought to myself: And so am I. In this new year, there's no way I'm gonna waste that. If you want something to change, you gotta change some yourself too.

Shere got me a job at Advanced Medical Rehabilitation, down on 53rd and Madison, where I instructed injured patients and walked them through the exercise therapy the two doctors prescribed. Seeing that most people were very disconnected from their bodies, I was able to use my experience and awareness to produce profound results in those who needed and wanted help, especially women, and I was proud of this.

Some of the patients were truly hurt, others were just there so they could collect on pending lawsuits. There was a whole room of billing employees, but only two of us "exercise physiologists," plus a chiropractor. I only had to work Mondays, Wednesdays and Thursdays, and I got $15 an hour, so it was perfect.

My patients took to me, especially women who had a real need to heal. I actually spent time with them, instead of just putting them through a rote circuit of machines, as some others before me did. I helped them learn about their own body, how to listen to it, helped them rebuild, and gave them as much spiritual and emotional support as I could. Nearly all my patients were black, or non-English speaking Hispanic from Puerto Rico or the Dominican Republic. One patient, Mrs. Larkin, maybe four and half feet tall and 80 pounds including the Naomi wig she wore, was on dialysis, and always came in with her upper arms twisted with purple bruises. I always had the feeling that she was about to pass right then and there; she was very tired of life. I couldn't blame her. She had to rely on a machine to eliminate wastes and it was very hard on her body. I got her on spirulina, did what I could to get her bloodstream flowing, get her rejuvenating as best she could, and she began coming regularly. The others did too. They passed compliments on to the front desk. I built up a record patient attendance rate. Rosa, a sort of hairy, blushing, 30-ish Dominicana, was one of them. She never said a word of English and spoke with a heavy accent about how none of the life here in NYC was like on TV. I told her I wasn't sure that was true, until I found out all she watched were the afternoon and evening novelas.

God, everybody was so broken from life. Others came in with older or more minor injuries, but digging those out often brought up the most pain or the most protest. I responded, "You ever see that bumpersticker 'May All Beings Be Free of Suffering'? It should read '…Be Free of Human-Induced Suffering.' Getting through natural life struggles is how people evolve, become stronger. Push — give me two more reps. *Respire, p'afuera p'adentro.* Breathe out breathe in. Come on, push, it'll make your muscles stronger, your bones denser, and you'll feel even better than before your accident. C'mon — push. Breathe. Relax your face. There you go. Good."

Public pressure for the Refuge only continued to build. President Clinton had vetoed the budget bill, with all its War on the Environment riders, and the federal government was shut down except for the most essential operations. The Arctic Refuge drilling provision was cited as a major factor. It was a standoff.

A few days later a giant 100-year blizzard piled feet of snow onto the city, freezing the Hudson River, shutting down the West Side Highway, the Brooklyn-Queens Expressway, all the streets, everything. The city was muffled in after-storm silence and sprinkled with the laughter of playing children rolling down 9-foot snow hills. People cross-country skied down Fifth Avenue, and just as I've always been a little bemused by how many people have guns when New Year's Eve rolls around, I was wide-eyed at how many people had cross-country skis. I had never seen anybody in the city skiing before, or even with ski racks. For a day, Manhattan Island was a different village.

In his January 11th news conference on the impasse over the budget, President Clinton said: "I don't see why we should cloud this budget agreement with controversial items like whether we should drill in the Arctic National Wildlife Refuge. Those things are not necessary to balance the budget." The previous president George Bush had slobbered at the prospect of drilling for oil, saying: "The caribou love the pipeline. They rub up against it and have babies." What a difference. We felt a tipping point. We might win this. We didn't know if our little national grassroots campaign had helped with this, but with all the petitions, calls, letters to the editors, and increasing signs of support, we felt we certainly had been ground troops shoring up the back, filling in the gaps; we felt part of a movement, part of being on the right side of history. And on one of the petitions, the signature of Newt Gingrich's lesbian sister Candace had come in, putting smiles on everybody's face.

As the temps warmed, the Hudson River broke up. Large jagged ice floes surged downriver in a steaming, grinding, popping crush of slush and flat blocks of hard ice. In Riverside Park, a frosty late morning mist hung low in the air. A red-tailed hawk huddled in the wet-black branches of the trees. The snow was gradually melting, and it sounded like the whole world was trickling away in little streams. Huddling into my big black bubble coat, my skin a little damp, everything feeling a little clammy in the changing air, I expected to have the whole park to myself, at least this far-uptown part of it. I tensed when I saw a human figure, engulfed in mist and steam rising off the river, leaning over the railing and staring at the grinding ice.

I got a shock as I realized it was Scarface. I could tell by the shape of his round, shaved head, and the way he held his body upright. At the same moment, he happened to turn and see me approaching.

I didn't feel like killing anybody today. I didn't even feel like talking to anybody. Yet, truth be told, I'd wanted this moment, a second chance, for months. Even though I'd said I was through, I still had moments of anger where I'd fantasized about a moment like this, running into him down here by the deserted river, faking like I gotta tie my shoe and grabbing his legs and flipping him over the railing. He'd probably drown. There was no hold on the concrete seawall below the railing. He'd have to make it all the way upstream, to the rocks, against the current, in the ice cold water. Not likely.

I hurriedly tried to dredge up my old hate and anger as I came up on him, boots squishing in the slush on the asphalt path, but I couldn't. I tried again, thinking of what he'd done.

He smiled as I approached, his high-yellow cheeks a little reddened from the cool, damp air, his jagged Frankenstein scar stretching like a purple leather lip up the left side of his face.

I stopped in front of him. My eyes glanced at the wooden top of the steel railing, where young people over the years had blue-inked their love and hate for each other.

"So I guess I don't get a hug," he said, breath vapor coming out of his mouth, looking at me and cracking a smile again. He stopped smiling and looked down, then sideways at me again, serious. "Well, anyway, you look good."

I leaned on the railing, looking at the moving ice, then at him.

"Better than you ever will," I said. "What the fuck you do with my bike. You... how the fuck you gon tell me you got a personal relationship with God, when all you care about is ruining shit for everybody you come in contact with?"

His face seemed to recoil.

"You know," I said, "Not too many muthafuckas I let in. I could easily kill you. I just ain't gonna let you bring me down to your level. I got too much going on to mess with somebody who got nothing."

"I wish you would," he said. Was it a challenge, or an ask? "Why don't you, right now? Come on! They's nobody here. I've been thinking about how quiet it is down there at the bottom of the river, below all that ice. Sometimes I wish I was down there."

Ice cracked and heaved on the moving river, grinding slowly southward. Again he'd thrown me off.

"So what you say, J, my main man? Help me go find out, for both us. I've been here for the last hour, and I know it's your spot too. I wasn't even surprised to see you. If anybody was gonna come down here today, I knew it'd be you." He lit a Newport, and his breath vapor mingled with blue cigarette smoke. "I knew I'd eventually run into you down here, if I came back. Funny, I just got back. I knew you'd be looking for me for real after I took your bike for real the last time. I went out of state — Connecticut. Cause I'm sure you went to Parkchester too, looking for me."

Lifting the corner of my lip into a sneer, I spat, "So where's my bike."

"I took off those damn prize handlebars of yours and rode it around for about a week till I got tired of having to drag it around with me all the time. Then I just left it."

I was shaking my head. "Can you even hear how that sounds? That is so fucked up." I looked upriver to the gray skeletal span of the George Washington Bridge, barely visible in the mist. "I'd be happy just watching you suffer and die."

He flushed a little, as if not used to being disrespected like that. He turned toward me, looking me in the eyes. "Ok. I deserve it. I admit it — you are the bigger person for even talking to me. Man — I am sorry. But I can't help what's done. And I knew it was your soul, the freedom that bike gave you. I just couldn't help it. You're the bigger person, and I appreciate that."

I slitted my eyes, watching the chunking, grinding ice floes moving downriver. (What was he doing?)

I knelt down to tie my yellow-corded bootlace, my face *this* close to his leg. I stalled for time, trying to get to that red hot, for my heart rate to increase, for my scalp to burn. All I had to do was grab and heave, and he'd be in the river, only minutes from death, with no way out. I strained to find my anger, make it swell and explode. But — no dice. I felt like the morning inside, neutral, damp, and mist-cooled. I tried imagining the satisfying, icy-cold, hypothermia-inducing splash, and his blubbers for help as he choked down frigid water, jagged ice floes grinding into his face and neck, cutting him up.

Nothing.

Sometimes I hate you, I said to myself. I finished retying my boot.

He looked down at me.

"Anytime, nigga." He blew smoke.

Finally I stood up.

"Did you see that red-tailed hawk back there?" he asked. " I think she's the same one had babies last summer. She looks so cold and wet up there. I feel bad for her."

I shoved him, sending him stumbling. His hand jerked up, as if a long splinter had jabbed into it off the wooden railing.

"Shut the fuck up, already," I said, turning and walking away.

Mail poured in from all over the country. Petitions piled up, signifying the tens of thousands of people in support of the Refuge. Handwritten notes of support, passion, vision, spirit. For the March 24th event, some groups across the country were planning to stage simultaneous gatherings for the Refuge in concert with our main candle-light vigil in D.C., which was now officially sponsored by Great Plains Restoration Council, Free the Planet!, Alaska Coalition, and even National Audubon Society, one of the big nationals. Since I had headed this up, I was supposed to be one of the closing speakers. I was so busy working toward the culmination of the campaign that I didn't have time to think about the fact that this would be my first time in front of people, and the fact that if I wasn't by then completely exhausted, I'd probably be nervous and fuck my speech up.

We pushed forward. Susan Alexander from the renowned Public Media Center in San Francisco offered excellent public relations advice. Everything was going great. In a few months I had talked more than I had my whole life, and the overall experience had been so unusual I felt like something had changed inside my body, and I was... somewhere else.

Walking home one night, passing up through the West Village, I saw a MISSING flyer on a telephone pole with Angel's picture on it, the drug dealer I'd used to supply wholesale. The message from his brother sounded forlorn. The pic had Angel in some club-kid kind of gear. I had never known him like that. He was just a Colombian homeboy to me.

D.C. is a Southern city, I realized, upon seeing it for the first time. And the White House is a plantation mansion. I was exhausted and wired as I scanned the hundreds of people gathering in Lafayette Park in the last of the afternoon light, waiting for dusk and our candlelight vigil. Snipers walked back and forth across the White House roof. Our multiracial crowd grew in front of the big iron gates, holding all kinds of posters and signs. A giant banner behind the main speaking area yelled ENVIRONMENTAL RIGHTS NOW! FREE THE PLANET! NO DRILLING THE REFUGE! Volunteers passed out thin white candles skirted with little paper drip disks. I had driven down with Tracey, the brassy-skinned girl from Westchester, who'd helped out a lot.

I went off by myself and sat on a park bench, my work done for the moment. I looked up at the bare branches of the hardwood trees that were just beginning to bud in the park. Some had baby leaves. A chill wind passed, and was gone, and for a moment I sensed ocean. Somewhere near. Atlantic.

This was it. All I had left to do was speak. The petitions were being delivered tomorrow, Monday. My stomach was unsettled as I tried not to be nervous about speaking in front of all these people. It was Sunday, March 24th, 1996, the seven year anniversary of the Exxon Valdez catastrophe. Here I was in Washington, D.C., in my green and black windbreaker, black nylon sweatpants, sneakers and a ballcap, with my typewritten speech folded in my pocket. I started to think back to where I was when the Valdez spilled seven years ago, and didn't have the energy. I didn't even want to think about a year ago. This, all this, *where I was now*, is what I needed to be thinking about.

An unshaven guy with long, stringy dirty blond hair and smelling of drink rolled up on me, sticking his chest out. "Man, you got a pencil!" he yelled.

I shook my head no, trying to keep my train of thought.

"I said, you got a pencil!"

I looked him straight in the eye, to let him know I wasn't playing. "No, I ain't got no pencil. I'm trying to—"

"Oh, so you think you can fight, huh? You wanna fight! Come on, motherfucker, come on, motherfucker." He said it in a Southern twangy voice. He was already standing over me, a few feet away, and he made as if to take a step at me.

"God-damn," I blurted, shaking my head. "It never ends, huh?" I got to my feet, exhaustion spilling out of me like a burst spleen. "I said I don't play." I made a step toward him. "I said, if you don't give me back my pencil" — realizing how insane I was sounding —"I'ma cut you."

The guy looked at me confused, and took a step back, then puffed himself up like a rooster.

Rick, from Free the Planet!, coming to get me, heard me and grabbed my arm. "Manos! Come on!" he scolded sternly and pulled me away. "Man, what the fuck are you doing? Keep your cool. We have a big event. This is it!"

I shook my head and walked with him, my back tingling from turning away from the dude.

"Man, it never ends," I said. "No matter who it is, they see somebody getting their shit together, they try to pull you back down to their level."

"So you gonna knife somebody about that? That's real good."

"Man, please," I said, trying out a grin that came out cockeyed on a face so unused to smiling, and probably looked like a half deranged sneer. I patted my left chest to show the clothes were flat. "You think I'd really bring a blade to something like this? Please."

As the last of the Eastern spring light faded from the sky, I moved into the crowd. Candles were being lit from one to the other, casting soft glows on beautiful faces, on people who found in their lives the ability to care, to get involved. They began gathering in front of the big banner, in front of the White House, in the capital of the United States of America, pooling like light itself.

Rick Taketa, Brock Evans, and a Jewish woman representing the Inter-Faith religious community spoke first. I was second to last, to be followed by a young Gwich'in guy who would culminate the event. He was the next generation, and he would represent the continuity of his nation's 20,000-year-old ancestral caretaking of — and belonging to — the Refuge.

I paced and paced in the background as it came near my time to speak. Listening to the others make their smooth deliveries, I tried to open up my tightening throat. Finally, I focused on what I had been blessed with beforehand. Sarah James, from Arctic Village, legendary spokeswoman for the Gwich'in determination to protect the Refuge, had called me out of the blue to say thanks for the work and offer encouragement. In her clipped accent from the roadless top of the world, she offered her suggestions to my comments about being nervous to speak, each word delayed by a second and sounding hollowed over the shaky satellite transmissions,

"Pray," was all she said. "I say a little prayer, to Creator, right before I go up to speak."

"I thought you were only supposed to pray for the really big things."

"Nooo, it's ok. If you pray, you will be fine. Okay."

And then it was my turn. A light shined on me. I couldn't see people's faces, just the shapes of their heads. All eyes on me… My gut dropped; my throat constricted. I gulped for air, then said a quick little prayer — not for me, but for the world — and —

Clutching my sheet of paper, I began:

"The calendar said it officially turned Spring the other day. But as the non-humans of the world know, this event we call Spring has been building in the blood for weeks now. Birds are coming back. Trees are waking up. As Earth's northern hemisphere lifts its face to the Sun, the great warmth migrates northward, spreading a living green, until it reaches this place at the edge of the world, this place we call the Arctic National Wildlife Refuge. The reason all of us are here today.

"Refuge. Spring. Migration. These words ring with significance. Maybe we forget that this place we care so much about is a Refuge. We're always repeating the mantra that the Arctic National Wildlife Refuge is our nation's last great Wilderness. But we must pay attention to what these words mean to the great cycle of life that bursts out of the Arctic Refuge.

"Life is very tough if you are not a member of the human race. We humans have changed the world unbelievably over the last couple hundred years. The non-human races put up with all of our discord, all our pavement, pollution, noise et cetera not because they want to but because they have no choice. They do so because the will to survive is very strong in all living things. Birds from every continent on Earth travel thousands of treacherous miles every Spring to get to the Arctic Refuge. Imagine yourself being a wild bird from Africa or Antarctica. Like the salmon swirling out of the deep Pacific to spawn all the way up some inches-deep Idaho mountain stream, as a migrating bird only you would have possible clues to the great mysterious pull that led you there. Imagine after flying all that way, the great sense of relief and gladness that comes as you crest over the Brooks Range and the sacred Coastal Plain comes in sight. Incredibly lucky that you made it there alive at all, as you lower down onto the great grassy Plain, you know you can at last find Refuge from the roar of the Industrial Era. Here you suddenly drop back to the Pleistocene. Here the cycle of life has not changed for the last 20,000 years. Blink and half expect to see a Woolly Mammoth stomping through the tussocks. Here you are in the land of the Big Wild. Here there are no roads, no pipelines, no smokestacks, no power lines, no belch and roar of internal combustion engines. This is the point. Up here, the largest sounds you will hear will be the thundering hoofbeats of the great wild herds migrating, or the click of your mate's beak in your ear. As a wild bird having flown all the way in from, say South America, exhausted from a trip across a planetary industrial zone, you can now finally get down into this last great grassy Wilderness. Cooled by Arctic Ocean winds, with the mountains at your back, you can now find Refuge from the outside world, and join the ancient primitive dance of wild things.

"Some of us humans can share in this sense of exhaustion and desire. The Earth convulses under our weight, strapped to the relentless economic machine. And unease gnaws at our souls. I have never been to the Arctic Refuge, and I don't need to go. As long as I can go to sleep with the knowledge of its continuing vitality, free of industrial filth and clamor, that assurance provides Refuge to my exhausted soul, and excitement in my gut. It gives me hope for the Future.

"Again, this is the point. The point is NOT how much minimum output in caribou numbers can be produced inside a Big Oil industrial zone ("as they rub up against it and have babies"); the point is this is supposed to be a Refuge.

"I live on the Great Plains, and out there, we have lost everything. There are no migrating herds of buffalo, no wild freedoms, everything has been raped and ravaged, there is no Refuge. Indigenous people, and native wildlife struggle tooth and nail to survive through each day.

"Up in the Arctic Refuge, there is a chance to save and cherish what has been lost elsewhere all over the world. The hateful small-minded men and women in Industry and Congress who seek to destroy this last great Wilderness do not represent the interests of the common people. This strongly-worded petition that I initiated sought to demonstrate that. I was not planning on starting my group Great Plains Restoration Council for at least another year, but because the Arctic Refuge was once again coming under attack, I could no longer sit still. (Mobil Oil doesn't know that it is breeding revolution with its endless dump of drill-crazy ads on the Op-Ed page of the New York Times.) So with $500 out of my own pocket and starting off from scratch, I hit the ground running. Thanks to the help and use of office space, phone and fax from Wetlands Environmental Center and Nightclub in New York, I was able to just start talking to people, try to spread a good idea, a vision. I think that's what we ultimately need to do. Not just say what's wrong, but offer an alternative vision. Talk to people. Share your feelings of hope and inclusiveness; why we and the Arctic Refuge are connected, why we even care. These are our family values. Put into terms like this, few people can not relate.

"In this manner, even though the "issue" had to be explained nearly every time for every signature, a tiny handful of people across the country managed to go out and gather tens of thousands of signatures in a short matter of a couple months, with no budget, representing all 50 states. A lot of this was targeted at rural areas. Be assured that there are people in all these areas who are frustrated with their state or region's negative, backwards reputation. Promote a shining alternative, and watch how many people you will attract. The hateful, unreconstructed bigots who hate all life other than their own can and will be marginalized."

A few flashbulbs popped, disorienting me.

"So… in this time of global crisis, with ecological collapse threatening all over the world, I believe the Arctic Refuge is metaphor for all battles for ecological justice everywhere. This candlelight vigil marks not only our day of solidarity with the Gwich'in people and the caribou of the Arctic Refuge Coastal Plain, but also the starting gun of the New Conservation Movement. We see and know that all our struggles are connected. The niches are filling up; the front solidifying. Our diversity, unity, and seriousness strengthen us."

My voice began to break, croak, years welling up behind it. Fire and exhaustion…

I pushed on. "The selfish overgrown children who run both the multinational corporations and the government and who seek to block our path to a healthy and vital, wide-open Future should be aware. With this day and forward, we demand a dif-

ferent definition of what it means to be alive on Earth. We demand a different definition of the Future itself; we demand that our human race reach a state of maturity and
responsibility; we seek the achievement at last of tenancy, of dignity here on Earth, we
demand that our intellectual evolution catch up with our technological; that we at last
learn to live with and alongside a healthy, prospering and wild Earth.

"On this day of action, this day of renewed determination, of anger and even
private moments of silence for what's already been hopelessly lost, we say we embrace
a Future measured in the true prosperity of Earth's health and vitality and in our sincere connections with each other and all life; and we say we REFUSE the only option
being presently decided for us — an existence ruled by an imperial few who seek only
their bulging pockets at the cost of our utter, abject and final poverty, a brown, barren,
polluted and lifeless Earth.

"For us, protecting the Arctic National Wildlife Refuge, the Coastal Plain, the
sacred place where life begins, is just the beginning."

Clapping erupted, people swelled around me. I faded back, sucked backwards
by the need to get out of the spotlight. Tracey came up to me, handed me a bottle
of water. I put my arm around her shoulder. A flashbulb went off. A picture of a
moment, and at that moment, I was right here, right now. I knew where I was.

The young Gwich'in guy, wearing a striped sweater, moved into the spotlight, to
complete the event, the evening, and the campaign. In a soft voice he began to speak
of his homeland, his culture's relationship with the land, the animals, the Coastal
Plain, the sacred place where life begins.

As we packed up, people came up to me to talk, congratulate, thank. I thanked
them instead for all their help and for caring about the Refuge. A man from Alaska
Public Radio came to interview me; I told him it was now time for me to go back to
my Great Plains, which once had everything the Arctic Refuge Coastal Plain has, but
now has nothing. I told him I wished Alaskans could see how important and priceless
what they still have is. On the Great Plains, we have to rebuild everything, up from
the ashes.

SECTION EIGHT

"We need another and a wiser and perhaps a more mythical concept of animals... They are not brothers, they are not underlings, they are other nations, caught with ourselves in the net of life and time, fellow prisoners of the splendor and travail of the Earth."

— Henry Beston, *The Outermost House* 1928)

"There is genius out there ... but what's missing is that warrior spirit. There's a whole different spirituality that goes with the warrior spirit that [people] died for."

— Nas

CHAPTER TWENTY-EIGHT

Things Surely Turn to Autumn

I opened my eyes, seeping upward out of a perfect night of deep sleep. Thankful. Every muscle loose in my body, I lay flat on my back, stretched out in a straight line under the sky-blue cotton sheet, the futon mattress beneath me evenly supporting my length.

This was the most perfect feeling. Every muscle, every joint, every organ in place, not hurting, not resisting.

I held on for a few seconds more, letting my eyelids close again. Then my waking heart rate began to rise and it all came tumbling down together and it was just me again, along with all my aches, injuries and the background hum of pain that I could only manage with constant physical activity. I grimaced and opened my eyes to look out the open window. Sort of cloudy looking. Warm. That was good. Still humid. It had been a cool, almost absent summer. Now it too was passing. I heard Shere banging around in the kitchen, always late or in a hurry, looking for something, cursing if the pots and pans fell on the floor cause she'd overstacked them on the dish drainer last night. I guessed she'd be heading out the door soon, so I decided to chill in my room until then.

My thoughts drifted, focusing on nothing. I suddenly remembered what I'd heard a while back on the street about Angel. He'd been hit over the head with a hammer, then injected with Drano; then, after he'd started to rot in the bathtub, they'd cut him in half and dumped him into the Hudson River. I'd heard his legs had washed up on Long Island. To make it worse, it was two overgrown club "kids" who'd killed him. That's about as disrespectful a way of going out as it gets. The cops hadn't done nothing. And nobody on the street or in the clubs cared, either. To everybody out there, he was just a gay Colombian drug dealer.

September already... The year, the summer, had gone just like that. Work my four-day physical therapy job toward my three-day weekend, then ride Friday through Sunday, then do it all over again. I only had to talk when I was at work and had patients. The rest of the time I was mostly silent.

Lahumba crossed my mind. Though she was in the city, I didn't hardly see or talk with her anymore. I guessed she was off doing her own thing, trying to impress her new man. I missed her. I suddenly doubted I would see her again. Best of luck, Sistawoman, I thought, sending it out with good intentions. Goodbye.

I remembered how back in January I'd promised that this year would be different. I'd told myself I'd meet somebody real; somebody I wouldn't have to "settle" for. I wouldn't have to wake up alone anymore.

Most mornings I felt skinned alive, but hid those feelings inside. That was the problem with being hard as hell on the outside, but really a big baby on the inside.

I knew time was ticking; I knew I was biding time. Why was I still clinging to the city?

I had survived my own life. I had to get back to battle. What else was there for me to do but give back? But… here I was, still hesitating. And now it was already September. September 1996 already. I kept putting off the moment when I would give my notice to Shere.

Yeah I was basically just a normal, well-adjusted guy now. But with that there was room inside me. An emptiness had opened up a pit I couldn't close or fill. It's true I felt good most of the time, my stomach was better, I had my hair cut in a stylish Caesar-fade, my t-shirts fit, I wanted to help others out as much as I could, I felt clean and great. I was the healthiest I'd ever been.

But nothing could calm that inner agitation, console that emptiness. My strong arms and chest needed something stronger around them. After almost driving myself crazy over the world's problems, after almost losing my mind to militancy, rage and despair, to where nothing else mattered, I wanted to experience at least one part — the most important part — of normal young life.

You need to leave the city as soon as possible. Then you don't have to deal with it. Fuck this personal shit. Nothing else but the battle matters. And that always made things simpler.

Just go. Your West is waiting. Go! Follow the Sun. Just go into the Sun. Out into the prairie. God and Earth. Follow your path. Leave. There is nothing left. You're not meant for the human world. Accept it. And anyway, anything else, anybody you might meet here, would just hold you back.

I had missed out on the young life most people have.

I'll never meet somebody, be able to just chill, just hang out undistracted, just have fun. Let alone fall in love.

It'll never be me. Accept it. It's over.

You need to stop your complaining. The Great Plains prairie is out there.

I imagined myself down in the open space by the Hudson River, along the tar path where I'd been hundreds of times. My back bristled with buildings, but before me, past the river, out over New Jersey and Pennsylvania, past the cut-forest and plowed-prairie Midwest, I felt her western edge leading across a high plain all the way to the Rocky Mountains. Over the curvature of the Earth. Damaged as she was, she shimmered like the ocean. Prairie and ocean — sisters. Beneath the *Sun*. God. Blazing God. God and Earth. They were all that mattered.

You need to leave out as soon as possible. Forever.

But —

But what!

Stop talking to yourself like you're a separate person.

I'm human. You're still a — I'm still a young man. For a while longer. I'm here. Right now. I'm here right now. I know where the hell I am, at this moment in time, on Earth, in the crack between two worlds.

I curled my toes.

Well yeah, you definitely missed out on a lot. I mean, *I* missed out on a lot. But that's all your fault.

Lying in bed, wrapping my arms around my shoulders, I listened for distant city sounds. I pretended I was down by the Hudson River, and imagined close water sounds, little wavelets lapping. A muted siren all the way across in New Jersey. A bird on a rock.

I rolled onto my side. I'm gonna crack in half and die of loneliness.

Stepping out to the sidewalk with my bike over my shoulders, I picked up the green scents of Central Park two and a half blocks down to my left. The Sun was coming out. Finally, some warm days. I pulled on my black padded Izumi gloves, fastened the velcro straps on my Ground Control riding shoes, and adjusted the little computer mounted on the bike stem back to 00.00 for MXS, AVS, CLK and DST. Everything but ODO. I'd ridden over 4000 miles in ten months, just in the city and outer boroughs alone. Last fall, I had ripped part of the right side of my face off under the eye when the sleeve of my hoodie, which was wedged between my back and backpack, had slipped out and into the front brakes and catapulted me head over wheels into the sidewalk path crossing the North Meadow of Central Park. Skin on pavement burns black, like rubber tire skid marks. I was amazed at how quickly the scar under my eye was disappearing. Good immune system.

The endorphins kicked in. I rode down through Manhattan, slinging traffic lights over my shoulders, and out through Brooklyn to Gateway National Recreation Area on the Atlantic Ocean. Twenty five miles exactly from door to sand. The beach was practically empty.

I dove into the ocean, swam out, turned over onto my back, letting my body float. Salt water trailed out of my mouth. Swells lapped in my ear canals as the Atlantic gently pushed me up and down. I sensed my vulnerability, large things moving beneath me, unknown depths. Woman Water. The ocean is a prairie with its life underground, and a perfect sky above.

A strong wind began to blow in off the open expanse, churning the surface of the water, soon making it unswimmable, and I pushed my reluctant ass onto shore. The wind blew the beach clean of footprints. The late summer light shimmered, the coastal dunes grew wild green grass; all up and down the park the concession stands were closed for the year. I shivered, nipping out, skin goose-bumping as I waited for the wind to dry me off. I noticed there were only three people left on the beach. The afternoon was slipping. About a quarter mile down an older Rasta man squatted by his ten-speed in a meditative pose, staring at the ocean. Up the beach, a fat white woman sat in the wet smooth sand that puckered bubbles at the water's edge, staring at the ocean. Both seemed held over here, in a last day's contemplation of the world and another passing year. And then there was me, staring at the ocean too. I'd gone as far East as I could. I could still feel the wave motion inside my bloodstream and my ears. For the last time I turned my back to the eastern ocean.

With the ocean wind behind me, I began flying back at top speed. The evening Sun shined over Manhattan 20 miles away in an unusually clear blue sky. As I rose up over the giant hoop of the Marine Parkway bridge, the dark Atlantic water sparkling below me, I again marveled at how you could see the World Trade Center and the Empire State Building looming over Manhattan Island from this distance. I had often imagined, as I streamed down into Central Park from Harlem's North Woods and out into the large open space of the North Meadow, the Twin Monoliths anchoring a futuristic "Cloud City." People working high up in the World Trade Center said they sometimes watched storms below them. Camron and I had gone to the top once, in an "express elevator," which was like a smoother express subway train into the sky. From the top, the sprawling metropolis was sensory overload; definitely looked like something was "really going on down there." We only knew the city from its underbelly streets, looking up. I knew nearly every square foot of its Manhattan Island streets, and a lot of BK and the Bronx, but as I crossed over the bridge, with the city like a mini-model of itself in sharp relief in the distance, I knew I'd never know if it'd be that Cloud City.

Back uptown, sitting cross-legged in my corner shrine on the bare wood floor, next to my push-up bars, lit yellow candle and Chechen grandmother, I pulled from my folder of clippings an article from the Times, from the autumnal Equinox in 1993. I re-read the passages I had underlined, Sid trying to squirm under my arm and onto my lap, purring like a Mack truck. The article was about a convent nun, Sister Miriam Therese MacGillis, in rural New Jersey leading a celebration of the fall Equinox. She said:

> "The seasonal cycles of death and rebirth should remind us not to be afraid of the darker side of our own lives, but to have the wisdom to face our fears and grow spiritually. Our technology has given us electric lights, climate control, food on the supermarket shelves — the illusion that we can control our world. But we are hungry for something that connects us with the power and the mystery of what is happening in the natural world."

I punched my wrapped, gloved fist into the hanging Ringside heavy bag, straight right, left jab, stepping on my toes around the swinging bag as it came back at me and I hit it again. Upper cut, left/right hook. Liver shots. Head blows. Sweat trickled down my temples. Forty-five minutes of this took the edge off my aggression. And (*admit it*) loneliness and emptiness.

Drinking a bottle of water, I went down to the gym to work my chest and tri's a little, drying my face off with paper towels.

Benching two 45s on either side, plus the bar made it 225 pounds. A lot for me, but I could finally do it. I grunted with the exertion, and squeezed out four reps.

I smelled fresh cologne. A figure came standing over me, and lightly placed his hands palms up under the bar, waiting for my go-ahead. "Come on, playboy. Gimme three more."

Straining, I nodded, and with his help was able to squeeze out three extra reps. The most ever so far at this weight.

I'd seen him before, baseball cap, medium-skinned dude, one of those omelet-black muthafuckas who you couldn't really tell what he was. Not that I should talk, since nobody could ever figure me out either and just assumed boricua.

I sat up, stretching my chest and arms out on the bench posts.

"Thanks."

"Saw you. Thought you might need a little extra."

"Cool. I did. Tryin' to get up there." I looked up at him, remembering now. I'd thought I'd noticed something the last time, but just ignored it. Probably mistaken.

"Just finishing off a few squats," he said. "I been here an hour and a half already. Need to get back to my girl before she get mad." He looked at me.

'Yup," I said, and walked over to the tricep rope pushdown. "Guess I been in my own world. Thanks for the spot."

"Can tell by the way you work out you ain't no joke." He held out his hand. "Thomas."

I shook it. "Sup. I'm J. Don't worry," I said, sensing some kind of good energy off him and suddenly feeling defiant and bold, like everything in life was coming to a head and I didn't care. "Actually, I'm so sensitive sometimes I think I'm gonna implode and explode at the exact same moment and there won't be anything left." I got back to my tricep pushdowns, concentrating on maxing out the stack at 150 pounds x 12 reps, then forcing another three reps after 5 secs rest. Then I halved the stack and supersetted 18 reps going for 20 till my arms burned so bad I couldn't get the grip halfway down the last two. He gave me a spot, helping the last two to completion.

He nodded. "I can tell," he said. "What you take for all that energy?"

I thought about his vibe. He didn't seem like he was a loud, outspoken person. It was cool, and comfortable, whatever was coming off him.

"Man, it's called vegetarianism," I said, calming my breath. "Also, I hit that spirulina, both in tabs and powder in my rice milk shakes, and bee pollen, ginseng all that."

"Yeah, I heard about some of that. But a lot of people wouldn't know where to start really taking care of their health."

"You here in New York. It's easy here. There's juice bars and shit on almost every corner; we even got botanica spots, right on Columbus in Crack Valley. Man, you should see it out West. Lot harder out there. I go out West a lot." I didn't want to tell him that for me it was the other way around, that I lived out there, and came East a lot. "It's much harder." I was thinking about everything, not just health spots. "Even in the big cities, which aren't big by comparison, and are few and far between."

"I stay right here in New York. I ain't living anywhere but right here. I'll go to D.C., Florida, the islands. I'd even go to Europe. But those states out there? Hell no. Won't ever go." He sat down on the brick windowsill next to a big potted plant, leaning on his thighs.

"Yeah, I know, man," I said quietly, wanting to change the subject.

"But as far as health though, I think actively taking care of your own health is the most radical thing you can do," I said. "There are so many problems in this world, with the environment, health, our young people, and it's like a vicious circle of always being kept down. If people were healthier, they'd be more alert, and able to challenge what's always coming at us."

He was quiet over there by the big green plant.

"I read that our bodies have the same percentage of water as the Earth. What you think about that?"

"Yeah, I know," he said.

I took a gulp of air, realizing I was getting on my soapbox. "That should tell you something. But we trash ourselves, and we trash the Earth. We don't even pay attention, or care. And just as bad, we allow others who have a lot more power to trash everything, including ourselves and our bodies. People of color especially act this way. If people think about it at all, we think we're way too disconnected and shit don't have anything to do with us to care. When actually it's the other way around. All things are connected. I for damn sure ain't gonna be nobody's victim. And I'm gonna keep getting healthier and stronger, smarter and more alert, each day and every chance I get. Cause I might need to get in their face one day."

He sat there watching me, almost staring, not saying anything. I resisted the urge to crack a smile, able to tell my words had had some impact. I stretched my tri by grasping the overhead bar on the cable pulley machine and stepping forward, creating a light pull all the way down my arm into the insertion *teres minor* where it met the shoulder. Then I did the other.

He was still staring and it made me uncomfortable.

"What," I said.

He shook his head as if clearing his sights. "Nothing, black. I wasn't staring at you. I was just thinking. People just don't talk about shit like that."

I didn't say anything. I sat on the edge of the bench and polished off 50 jacknife abs, keeping my stomach tight against my spine.

"I got a pair of skates," he said. "Sometimes I like to go blading. Not too many homeboys do that. Everybody walks around with a look on their face like they want to fight. You too. I thought that when I first saw you. Until we started talking. And I realized you were different."

"It's cool," I said. I had nothing else to say.

"Alright, J, man." He shook my hand. "I'ma get out of here. I'll see you around. Peace."

I watched him as he walked out, then I hit another set. I stayed at the gym until 10, when it closed. Carol, the woman with the long cornrow braids who worked here, often played the sole CD from The Braxtons last thing at night. Usually by that time, it was just Carol, the Braxtons and me, in the top floors of the southeast corner of Broadway and 110th, closing down another day at Body Strength, the last song "The Boss" vaguely sounding like a cover of an unknockable diva's dance song from the clubs long ago.

I gave my notice to Shere, who had no idea I had this alternate life out West or any thoughts of moving. When I told her, I didn't go into details. I just told her I was moving to Colorado, but I didn't mention that I'd already had a place out there for the last two years. She had simply assumed her "Glossie" was this boricua dude from the city.

I had a couple weeks left. At last it was warm, in the 70s. Most of the summer of '96 had been so cool and rainy, with only a few warm spikes in between, that it hardly even seemed a summer. Our warmest days had been in September and October. I knew any day now the weather would change for the long cold ahead.

I tried to think about my impending, permanent life change. I didn't have a plan, I was just going; I'd figure it out from there like I always did. What mattered was to get settled, and start GPRC up for good this time. I left out of the apartment with my bike to get some air.

Lying on my back, by my old friend the black walnut tree at the north end of the North Meadow, I watched a large fox squirrel climb onto a branch directly over me, a walnut in his mouth, his big, glossy tail flicking excitedly.

And suddenly, I was amazed by long ago trace memories of my childhood filtering in, things I hadn't thought about in a lifetime. By the lake near the Ohio prairie meadows and inside the back hardwood forests, there had been a couple of black walnut trees and I'd considered them so important. Important because I knew the giant luna moths, the rarest of the rare silk moths, unreachable apparitions, luminescent green and seven inches long from tip to tail, loved black walnut tree leaves when they were caterpillars, and spent their winter transformations in cocoons beneath them.

I began remembering the unbelievably frigid winters and boiling hot humid summers. The Midwestern thunderstorms making afternoons dark with low, lake-green light. Big butterflies and big flowers, tall grasses, old fields. Lots of rain, green growth, black soil. Extraordinary-looking butterflies with names like tiger swallowtail, red-spotted purple, zebra swallowtail, orange fritillary. Blue and green dragonflies divebombing ponds and streams. Thick fragrant stands of goldenrods, prairie roses, milkweeds, blazing stars, black-eyed susans, lilies and orchids — the milk of tattered remnants of a fertile Prairie Earth hidden in places I knew intimately. Second-growth trees growing right through hand-made farm implements, returning exposed hills to forest, blending with tatters of original old growth. I hadn't thought about that for years. Lying on my back next to my bike, I stared up at the squirrel.

City and suburb people have this image that rural life is serene and idyllic. They probably get this idea because they see it only from the roadside, from a drive in the country. They have no idea the brutality, what lies beneath…

I cringed, trying to stop the other memories from flooding into my head. I couldn't believe I had actually been a trapper for a year or so. I had actually trapped and clubbed to death a raccoon, possum, rabbits, squirrels, drowned a muskrat, to sell their fur for a pathetic couple dollars each. You were supposed to kill them that way to save the fur. I had thought I was living off the land. Going back to the wilderness. I remembered their faces, their convulsing bodies, unconscious but blowing blood bubbles out of their nostrils, still refusing to die, their trapped hands shredded to the bone by the steel jaws, bones often broken. All for somebody's fur coat somewhere.

I remembered the biggest largemouth bass I had ever seen, suddenly materializing out of the greenish-black depths of the lake and attacking my topwater chugger. Had never caught anything on such a big lure, and never expected to. Was just mindlessly casting it out and popping it back in because I'd had nothing else better to do. He broke the carelessly tied, way-too-light monofilament in a second. A month later I found him washed up skinny and dead on the earthen dam, his formerly fat green-gold belly shrunken in against his ribs, my lure's razor-sharp treble hooks lodged in his throat. My stupidity and carelessness had tortured and starved him to death, had wasted his magnificent life, after he had lived so many years hidden from humans down in those black sweetwater depths.

Hunt, fish, trap, it was what people in the rural Midwest did, whatever your ethnicity was. My father had picked it up with a passion. I remembered being told to hurry and filet fish even if they were still alive after knocking them over the head. I remembered fillets of white fish flesh without any skin or attachment to any other body part, just a hump of meat, still jerking its muscles on the cleaning table. In Texas I remembered brilliantly-lit ocean fish caught for mere sport and clubbed down to death. Wounded ducks and egrets gasping with pain and misery in the salt marsh flats off Aransas Pass, shotgun-strafed, the hunters long gone. Horrifying crimes that were and are a part of rural life.

In Ohio, I remembered a squirrel, just like the one above me, getting accidentally caught in one of my leghold traps. The steel jaws had partially clamped on his body, and he was sitting up, swooning in pain, too gravely injured to do anything else. The only thing I could do was put him out of his misery. With trembling hands I raised a heavy branch over my head, not knowing what else to do. And he clasped his own hands over his head and cowered in the last second before the blow rained down, something that horrified me so much I'd forgotten it until this day.

Yet, even with these crimes, I'd always deeply loved the woods and prairies and the natural environment, and worried about its destruction. I killed even while I loved.

I shook my head, lying there beneath the young black walnut tree. One or two tears burned out of my eyes, and I tightened my face, cutting it off. I rolled onto my side in the dirt. I've deserved everything I got, I told myself.

Something hit me in the side of the face. I rolled back onto my back and looked up. Another chip of a nut shell nailed me in the forehead. I narrowed my eyes. The squirrel's wet black eyes were glistening right into mine, even as his busy paws and jaws worked at shucking the walnut. Just to see, I moved a few inches over to the side. The squirrel adjusted his position directly over me again, and dropped another chip, smacking me again. His eyes sparkled.

I tried to smile and bout bust out crying. I slammed my bike-gloved fists into my eyes until I got control. The squirrel began busily eating away at his walnut, cheeks and jowls working overtime.

"I'm sorry," I whispered up to him. "I don't want your forgiveness, but I do want you to hear I'm sorry."

The squirrel chomped away at his prize, dropping crumbs and chaff on my face, his beautiful eyes and lustrous fox-colored fur shining.

I thought about it as I got up and began walking my bike out of the Park, after taking off my glove and ritually palming the rough bark of the black walnut's trunk like I always did. Dirt and chaff stuck in my shirt and short bristled hair and I didn't care. Since then I had erased all memories and thoughts of all of that long-ago back there. It was all death in one way or another anyways. I had birthed and lived my own life since then.

Other trace memories slipped in... The muddy dirt street where I stabbed the shoulder of the big Polish kid who was always harassing me, always saying I was dirty in my handmade or Goodwill clothes. I'd probably been eight or nine years old. Of course he ended up beating the shit out of me. What did I think was gon happen? And how I'd wished I'd nailed him in his throat, tore open his neck, killed him. Shoulda killed him. I remembered all the old men who'd stalked and harassed and tried to molest me since I was three years old, hundreds of them since then, and it was never-ending. If I'd taken a shotgun and blasted their asses like I wanted to and should have, they'd still have won, because my ass would be locked up for good, I'd have irrevocably fucked up my own life. The constant, rattling, burning hate and anger and the contradictory numbness... The cheap places I'd robbed of cheap worthless shit... I remembered that old vice-principal, that walking cadaver...

And so here I was, an inner-city urban tattooed muscled ex-drug dealer homeboy thug hyper-sensitive vegetarian animist homosexual ciclista rural outback plainsman who could sleep on a subway train while keeping his outer "Watchman" self on alert who also knew the curls of buffalo grass and the smell of an active prairie dog burrow from ten feet away and was able to return cross-country through the blackest night eight miles back to the nearest road. Hah. People would never know.

I sat again cross-legged on the wood floor by my shrine, facing into the corner, my palm over my face, breathing in and out. I'd let Sid in and closed the door, and he'd climbed into my lap. I tried to concentrate on just one thing, just my breathing, sitting perfectly upright, chest out, shoulders back, stomach in, hips square on the floor. Next I concentrated on my heartbeat, willing it to slow, relaxing every last molecule in my body, slowing things down till I felt the cool flow move through my veins, in perfect rhythm with my low breathing.

I sat like that for ten minutes until my body raised its temperature and rhythm back up, refreshed.

I looked at the purring little Mack truck in my lap; gently lifted him off and sat him on the floor. I grabbed my journal and opened it to a new page. Sid peered his head in.

"Friday, Oct. 18th (!) 1996. Been in the 70's last few days. 2 1/2 weeks left forever to my life in NYC. THE COUNTDOWN"

I noticed Sid's wide green eyes concentrating hard on the pen tip's contact with the paper, a look of intense forward amazement. I smoothed my hand over his head and ears and he arched into it at the same time he crouched lower, still staring at the page. I tried to explain. "It's called writing," I said. "I'm sending communication, only to myself sometime in the future. Communication. You know, like when you meow at me. I'm putting mine down on this piece of paper inside this book. It's like a letter; you put your meows down and send them off to a different place for somebody else to hear...." My voice trailed off as I realized how strange this concept was. He lashed his tail, still crouching, still staring close at the page. I continued to write.

"I'm so desperately lonely, and I don't know what to do about it. Stuck. Just want once — one time — before I leave, to feel loved and comforted by somebody strong, cool... I have had such a difficult time in finding somebody who I could relate to as at last my spiritual equal — at the same time physically and intellectually evolved. This guy Thomas I met at the gym... there's still a lot of <u>unanswereds</u>....."

"I want just one night, one perfect moment before I leave.

"The last few weeks riding around, living, working out, compelled to seek... something... some feeling, some experience, some final cap, catharsis to all the struggle, violence, hurt, sadness, loneliness, anguish, intensity, despair, desire that has been NYC, my adopted city, for me. Seeking some feeling. Last week I became aware that what I was/am seeking is this one perfect, <u>defining</u> moment where all these emotions crystallize for me into a something I can get a handle on. A looping aurora borealis of emotions around me. I want I need to pull all of these into me, wrap my arms around them and funnel them into *and through my body and spirit. It's a physical as well as a spiritual thing. Every last nerve ending wide open and tingling. I have so much love now, it feels pure at the same time good, hard and masculine. I want to give this, not just to Earth, who I am forever in her service, that's a whole different level and above all else, but this is different, on the human tip, just once want to be fully human, to feel this solid connection. The most intense thing.*

"I know my life will change radically once I depart... this is the final capping of my youth and all that the hard-edged city represented for me. Despues, I go off to be an adult, fully a man, with lots of political work to do — so many changes coming — know I must take a leadership role out there.

"So many changes coming. I really need to at least cap this moment in time as a young street-wise NYC homosexual man. There. I admit it. If I can only have just one perfect moment."

I drew out a calendar of my last October/November days left:

18 19
20 21 22 23 24 25 26
27 28 29 30 31 1 2
3 4 5

Bicep seated preacher curls. 35 on each side, plus the bar. Focusing, eyes half closed. I knew it was getting late because Carol, the gym and I were into the second Braxtons song, "*Slow Flow.*" I strained to get the weight up and hold strict posture, keeping my stomach tight against my spine like a natural weight belt. It was too much weight tonight. I was tired. I closed my eyes.

"Come on, bro! Keep it up; come on give me a full rep. Two more."

I smelled sporty cologne as I felt a little assistance at the gravity belly of the repetition, the hardest part.

I opened my eyes. Thomas was standing in front of me, his palm under the easy curl bar giving me a good spot, taking off just the bare minimum of what I couldn't do, still making me do all the work, following my lead rather than leading and having me follow. That's the difference between a good spot and a bad spot. I pulled up two more with his help, gasping, arching my head back, trying to stay in form, trying not to squirm on the seat with pain.

"I'm bout to drop it," I croaked on the second negative, which made that set 11. With both hands he lifted the bar out of my hands and placed it in the rack.

"Looks good, man. Sup with you?" He walked over to the bench press and lay down, fixing his hands on the grips.

I got up and went over to spot him. I saw his hands were a little unequal on the bar and I knocked at them outwards, getting him to move them half an inch equally past the etched-in ring on the bar. "Let's go," I said, helping him with the lift-off.

He pumped out ten, then began to weaken. His neck strained as he grimaced.

"Breathe, man. Relax your body. Keep it loose but supported. C'mon. Give me two more. Breathe! Exhale with the push, and on the return fill your diaphragm with air."

He sat up, rolling his head from side to side, trying to loosen up, like he needed a massage. He glanced around the small gym. There was only one other person in here, a perky girl with a blonde ponytail and fast moving elbows on one of the treads in front of the bank of windows facing out onto the nighttime street. Outside, the Body Strength banner lifted and fell back in a breeze.

He turned to look at me. "Man, sometimes my work keeps me so late, by the time I get here I'm worn out or it's too late. Tomorrow I'ma get off in time so I can least get here early, by 7 or so. We do the construction for the displays in the department stores. The parts you don't see. What you got left to do?"

"I'm through. I'll do one lightweight burnout set, that's it. I been overtraining a little. Not a good thing, especially this late. Last time I did that wasn't able to sleep. On top of all the other shit. But I'm done for the night. Maybe I'll go run down by the river for a mile or two to cool out everything."

Carol poked her head into the main gym floor and shouted over the smooth R&B of her Braxtons. "Gym closes in half an hour. Last call!" She always liked to say something like that. She was a big girl with a big smile.

"So what else you do besides work out?" he asked me.

I decided to tell him. "In two weeks I'm leaving for Pueblo." My heart raced a little as I said it. "I'm moving there." There. By saying it, it was done. A done deal.

His face furrowed with surprise as he thought for a second. "Pueblo, Colorado?"

"Yeah. I'm through with it here. I'm starting a whole new phase of my life."

He looked like he was a little in shock. "When?"

My throat was tight. "Today's the 22nd, right? Tuesday? Two weeks from today. Election day. I'm just ridin' it out till Clinton wins again, figure it'd be a good day to head out."

"Man, the only thing I know about Pueblo, Colorado is from those late-night commercials where you order something like a blender or a greatest hits CD and the place to send a check or money order to is in Pueblo, Colorado."

"I don't watch tv," I said quietly. I looked down, but forced myself to look back up, that hollow hurting feeling in my chest slipping up into my throat again. "Anyway… uh… no big deal but, say man, you wanna hang out before I leave. Go chill or some shit?" My voice dropped off. "It's cool. Whatever. It's cool." I didn't look at the way his nice upper arms creased into his t-shirted chest.

"Sure. Yeah, man. That'd be cool. You know what's different about you? You don't need to talk much. You can have comfortable silence. That's straight. And I can still understand where you comin' from."

I nodded. "Cool. That's real cool," I said.

He smiled. "Maybe it's cause you so sensitive. Bet not too many peeps know that though, huh."

I shook my head, thinking that I could really like this muthafucka. "People who talk too much give me a headache," I said, picking up my water bottle. "So, uh, when? I'm gone on November 5th. For good."

"I'll meet you here Friday night, 7:30. They close at 8 on Fridays. We'll figure it out from there."

I raised my head, nodding at him once, ready to head out. "Cool," I said, dapping his hand. "Peace."

Later, I couldn't sleep, thinking about it, gripping my pillow, too hunger-filled for human contact. I was gonna tell him about me. I needed to tell him about me, and I wanted to know about him, just get him alone where we could really open up to each other. I knew he had his girl; he knew I was moving. I knew we both knew what was up, even though we hadn't talked about it directly, it was all on the low, it was cool, it was just between us. He was mos def his own person; I thought if it came to it, I might even let him enter me. I'd never done that before, or was even sure I'd know how. But I didn't care. I needed to be completely consumed in a good way just once, inside somebody else's arms who I felt was worth it, who I could relate to, as an equal, where it would feel completely right, just once.

Friday evening. Sid gurgled from behind the door before I put the key in. I pushed in, bike over my shoulder, opening the door slowly so he would back up out of the way as usual. He came forward as I got inside, standing up on his hind legs for a second and arching into my leg. "Excuse me, Sid," I said, stepping around him. "I got to get ready."

"GLOSSIE IS THAT YOU?" Shere yelled in her loud New York Jewish accent from her far side of the apartment, like she always did when she was in.

"No, it's the postman," I said. "Coming for you for real this time. Can't hold myself off you any longer."

I showered, shaved, sprayed some CK cologne on. Had bought a bottle up on 116th St. Pulled on a close-fitting white t-shirt, some relaxed-fit blue jeans, and my Timbs, lacing them loosely. My pant legs bunched up against the tops of my boots. Put my thin silver chain back around my neck, pulled on a navy blue hooded cotton sweatshirt over that, slicked my hair down and headed out.

Carol was bending down behind the desk doing something as I reached the top of the stairs, so I just walked back into the leg machines area on the main floor. Not dressed for it, but I can do a little something while I wait, I figured. I pulled off my sweatshirt and put it on the brick ledge between the plants where Thomas had sat. Looking past Broadway up over the tops of the apartment buildings I could see the last of the dark blue in the sky. A lot of the leaves had already fallen. Time goes so fast, I thought.

There was hardly anybody in here. Friday nights are always the slowest gym night anywhere. I sat on the leg extension, popping out a set, sitting there, trying to let my mind drift. I did another set. My stomach was acidy and I felt tense. Don't know why you — I'm — so tense; ain't nothing to be nervous about.

I just need everything to be perfect, I thought to myself.

Probably just about 7:30 now. I'm cool. I don't sweat nobody or nothing. I'm just gonna be back here chilling, getting a little workout on, when he comes. I moved over to the hamstring curl, laid face down on the bench, gripped the black foam-padded handgrips. Squeezed out a set, focusing on getting the work all the way up the backs of my hamstrings into my glutes, then rested up on my elbows, heart rate increased just a little bit.

Carol put on some Biggie Smalls, the Notorious B.I.G., who was next to Nas the best of the best NYC rap. It was a change for her.

I glanced backwards, around the gym.

Laid back down, did another set. Rested. Breathing. Not thinking about anything. Trying not to.

Did another set and sat up, looked around. Went over to the cable pulleys. I didn't want to start sweating. I decided to just do range of motion, very light weight. Twenty pounds, maybe a hundred single-arm tricep handle grip pushdowns each arm. I realized I forgot my watch.

I saw my reflection in the black window between the plants. I was frowning.

I finished off both arms. My throat felt tight. My pulse was beating, as if nervous about some shit. The gym was empty.

The back of my throat got tighter. Time kept passing. I sat down on one of the benches, put my head in my hands. I swallowed, closing my eyes. I thought if I split in half right now, I would clatter to the floor, pieces of a hollowed out shell. I dug the heels of my hands into my eyes.

The ceiling fans whirred above me silently, feathering the cool-to-the-touch silver chain lying over the back of my neck. Outside, Friday night traffic going up and down Broadway increased, its volume muffled by the big plate glass windows.

I finally looked up at the clock. It was 7:50.

Grabbing my sweatshirt, I headed out.

As I got around to the front, Carol looked up at me from her logbook in surprise, her ink pen held in mid-entry. My throat was so tight I didn't want to talk to her or anybody.

"When did you get here?" she asked. "I didn't know you were here. That guy Thomas came by looking for you."

"What?" I croaked, staring at her. "What?"

"Yeah, baby. I didn't know you were here. That was like twenty minutes ago."

I pulled my hood up over my head and clumped down the stairs to the street.

My last few days in the city sped by. I had this feeling I was slowly falling off a cliff, my stomach in my throat. I pictured my city; it'd become the only place I had a chance for human interaction. So many missed opportunities. My head had been too clouded. With clear hindsight, I remembered times other quality dudes on the street or wherever had been trying to discreetly talk to me, check a situation out, and I'd been so preoccupied I was clueless, had totally dissed.

Man, I'd been caught-up, first with immediate survival, then with survival of the Earth. Everything was always immediate and to the extreme. I'd never learned how to adjust or balance myself within human life until it was too late. I thought of the chances I might have had to develop deep, meaningful human connections. I thought of all the mistakes I had made in all areas of life, and how it was so hard to learn before making the same mistakes again because too much personal shit was always getting in the way.

I resigned myself to my fate. That kind of deep personal interaction had not been meant for me. It was for other people. I accepted it. The only thing that mattered now was Earth. I was in her service. I began packing up what little I had, discarding most.

I didn't see Thomas in the gym until Thursday. He said we should try again Monday night after work. He had to work in Queens that day, but we could at least try to hook up, since it was going to be my last night here.

Sean, from 108th, who had helped me out with the Refuge and was about to marry a blonde woman from New Zealand, wanted to take me out Friday night with a couple of his homeboys from New Jersey. We went to Joel's, this little spot up in Washington Heights off 190th St. The place was crowded with thugged-out black and Latino men in ballcaps, baggy jeans, Timberlands. Hip hop boomed on the speakers; the feeling was warm and comfortable, like family, a rare place for mugs to get away from the streets and from having to be straight, if only for a few hours. Still I hung back by the front wall, just listening to the music, drinking my club soda with lime, standing next to Sean. His friends were off in the crowd. People passed by, nodding at me. I nodded back tightly and looked away.

Sean had said he'd be moving to New Zealand in about eight months, a month or so after his girl had the baby. A tall black drag queen got up on the little podium along the side of the wall and clamored for people's attention, but this crowd didn't feature drag queens, because we always just wanted each other. We used to say, "If I want a woman, I'll get me a real one." When the crowd continued to ignore her she pulled a gun out of her wig and started talking ghetto shit and trash. The dj let her have a few minutes, people laughed with her good-naturedly, then the music came back on and Sean looked at me. "Come on, man. All these dudes out here? You ain't find yourself interested in any of them?"

I shrugged, not feeling like talking much. "Just too late," I mumbled.

A guy came up to me, maple syrup smooth skin, soulful Chinese-lookin' eyes; looked me straight in the eye. He smiled a nice shy but masculine smile, unable to hide desire, shook my hand like he already knew me and thug-hugged me one-armed over-the-shoulder. The sudden closeness gave my body involuntary shivers. "What's up," he said warmly, nice white teeth showing.

"I'm moving to Colorado on Tuesday," I said. "To go help save the prairie dogs."

"It's only Friday," he said, not missing a beat.

I nodded, meaning nothing, saying nothing. He stood there, till he got uncomfortable, looked to the side, thought about it, and walked off.

Sean punched me in the shoulder, shaking his head. "Come on. Let's leave."

I don't know how the deer got into Manhattan. Young button buck. Only thing I could figure out is, seeing the long green huddle of Riverside Park from New Jersey, he'd swam all the way across the Hudson River, quite a feat in itself. He hadn't expected the West Side Highway that greeted him as he dragged himself onto the bank and leapt. He had managed to make it to this side of the Highway, mortally wounded by some very surprised driver, and laid down to die on his side in the autumn-ripened grasses and fallen leaves. His brown fur skin had shrunken and slipped back, revealing his white buck teeth and edges of his white skull. His mouth was open. He was in an area difficult to climb down into. I doubted that anybody else would ever notice him here. As I waited for a lull in the traffic to allow us a second of privacy, I pulled the red apple from my pocket and polished it with my shirt. When that momentary breather came, I stepped out from between the trees, kneeled down, and placed it in front of his open mouth.

At the lower tip of Manhattan there is a stone sundial in front of the Museum of the American Indian, inlaid with green and blue tile, showing a bird's eye view above this part of the Earth upon which New York City was built. The Earth curves out into the lands leading west, and to the ocean waters swelling east, with the starry sky above. Everything is clean. The waters are blue, the lands are green and laced with Indian and game trails and no roads, nothing else. Bright pointed stars are visible in the outer stretches of the fading-to-black Universe. It is a whole-life picture, an unbroken hoop of absolute purity and silence. A moment in time, before choices were made. It's a picture of wind, water and land, and green living things that were more than things. On it I could see the tip of the island they called Mannahatta, right where I stood now, on my last day here, in my city near harbor waves rolling below a blustery-cool, clear November afternoon.

Picture the Earth, and your place within her.

I went to the gym anyway, though I had no expectations. When Carol came to get me, said I had a call, I wasn't surprised.

At the front desk, I ducked my head, trying to keep the conversation private.

"Man, I'm stuck out here in Queens. Gonna be here late. We're still on this shit here, and I don't know when we'll get off. They always do this to me. I won't be able to make it."

"Cool," I said. Silence.

"Anyway, I'm sorry we never got a chance to hang out. Good luck out there. You're a strong, good-looking brother, aiight? Keep yo' head up!"

"Cool," I said. I cleared my throat and cupped the phone, turning away. Carol was busy with her own thing back there, so it didn't matter. I cleared my throat again. "Well, I just wanted to say that... in another lifetime... I don't know. Maybe you mighta been the friend I been looking for. Maybe you're the coolest bro I ever met."

There was silence except for Carol's music on my end, and the street noise on his. I pictured him at the payphone standing there with his baseball cap pulled down, Tommy backpack over one shoulder.

It sounded like he smiled, as he said, "Thanks, man. Thanks. You too. Good luck alright?"

"Yup, you too. Peace."

And at last my life in New York City was whittled down to a bare wood floor in an empty room. I didn't even get to say goodbye to Lahumba. I sat cross-legged in the shrine's abandoned corner. The candle was out, all my shit was packed and shipped, even my Chechen grandmother was gone. Sid, crouching outside the emptied room, stared at me one-eyed around the doorframe as if stricken. Dumb Cat always thought I didn't see him peeking in. When I had tried to pet him earlier, he'd cried and moved out from under my hand. The lightbulb in the ceiling seemed too bright. I lay myself face down, flat on the floor on what roots and limbs and green leaves had made a long time ago, and just breathed.

CHAPTER TWENTY-NINE

Unconditional Love, Straight Up

Face down in the hot plains grass, hidden in the ravine, I breathed in the roots of blue grama and buffalo grass, the legions of buffalo hooves that thundered in the past, the million-year old civilization of the prairie dogs. For about half a second.

Rifle shots whined through the air over our heads or to the side, followed by loud booms. Lauren was running about five yards behind me, each footstep kicking up dust in the dry plain, when I'd dropped face down heart racing to say the quickest of prayers for the prairie animals and for our own little team right before we'd break into view. I jumped up and with Lauren, joined Nicole and this guy Scott, who I didn't know, and we bunched up at the lip of the ravine, then burst onto the flat into the middle of the prairie dog town.

Exploded prairie dogs lay all around us — shreds of bloody flesh, torn limbs, flung entrails like obscene noodles. The Red Mist Society and Varmint Militia members were just up the rise, maybe a hundred yards, elbows dug into their shooting tables, expensive rifles shouldered, barrels pointing right at us. Another shot rang out. A shooter jumped up, gaping, as we rushed right into their line of fire and hurried to twist and lock the chain around all of our necks together. We threaded our arms into each other's at the elbows and clamped down tight. One of the killers lifted his rifle again, the other put his hand on it and pushed it down. Another jumped up and ran to his monster pickup truck, blasting off to find a ranch house with a phone, his big ugly monster tires tearing up whitish-brown clouds of sod and dust behind him. The other killers sat back, putting their rifles down, and stared. A red keg of beer stood behind them.

Scott and I had agreed to put the two women on the inside, so he was on one end and I was on the other. He began shouting "What do we want! ANIMAL RIGHTS! When do we want it? NOW!" Chanting wasn't my thing but hey, whatever, each his own. I kept quiet as we waited, knowing for sure that we'd be going to jail in a few minutes. The dry, hot summer sun seared down into our necks. Streaks of dirt and sweat ran down the sides of our faces. My head kept getting turned to the side, drawn out into the prairie.

The surviving prairie dogs had disappeared underground. This championship killing contest was shut down for now.

Law enforcement appeared in marked and unmarked cars. Khaki-uniformed cops with pistols holstered on their hips and black coil-corded radios in their shirt pockets ran toward us, pulling out their handcuffs.

We held on strong as they tried to yank our arms apart. They got rough, and with them piling on us, were finally able to jerk our arms behind our backs, where we were cuffed. The metal cut into my wrists and I twisted into them to find a position that would release some of that pressure. They only cut deeper. My sunglasses started to slip down my hot face. I motioned to Nicole; with her mouth she helped me get them right again. The sun heated the thick, locked chain around our necks.

"We're gonna need a van," one of the cops said to another. He called for it on his radio.

Up on the hill, the sheriff appeared in a big shiny black sedan. He stepped out. Suit, badge, big belly, aviator sunglasses. We were way out in eastern Colorado, Kit Karson Kounty, just before the Kansas state line. Not a tree in sight as far as the eye could see.

They hauled us in one chained-together, cuffed mass up the rise to the shooting area, where they dumped us onto the ground.

A guy with big bolt cutters arrived and used the hard steel beak to bite the chain off our necks. He did it with speed to show us he didn't care if he accidentally snagged part our skin — or throats.

I said, "Y'all are the same as people who stick firecrackers up cats' assholes! Supposedly grown-ass "men", and you're out here blowing up prairie dogs for sport."

The sheriff began ticking off the charges, as one of his underlings took notes. "Criminal trespass, resisting arrest, interfering with a lawful right to hunt, conspiracy…"

We went limp as they tried to drag us. When that didn't work, they ganged up, and heaved each of us into the van. All I saw was Lauren's pale legs, socks and hiking boots wheeling in the sky.

As the van lurched down the long dirt road to the highway that would take us to the county seat and the county jail, I felt a rush of pressure break inside me, and was suddenly delirious. I leaned forward, handcuffed hands behind my back going numb. "I'll take a Days Inn, if you got it. You got a Days Inn in town? Or how bout one them Red Roof Inns. I like to stay in style."

The cops in front kept strangely silent, which was very un-cop like. My longtime experience of them had been that they blew up at the smallest real or perceived challenge from me. Maybe it was because we were in a group. The cops actually ignored me.

Nicole, sitting next to me, said under her breath, "It's not for me to tell an activist how to be, but maybe we should be strictly serious, just to let them know how serious this issue is to us."

Getting my senses, I nodded and sat back.

We decided to go peacefully into the police department. As we were led inside single-file, eyes adjusting from the blinding High Plains high noon light to the subdued artificial indoors, I glanced out to the end of town where the prairie opened up again, promising silently that I would be back out to her as soon as I could. This action was important, and if we could leverage this into getting killing contests shut down in Colorado, we would do whatever it took. I consciously recorded the last whisper of prairie air on my neck as the door closed behind me.

A line of sheriff's deputies in khaki short-sleeve shirts and brown uniform pants stood at the bottom of the stairs leading up to booking, as if they were a cruise ship welcoming party. Unblinking, I stared them each in the face as I passed. I suddenly gaydar'd one of them, who was sort of pudgy and red-faced and watching me, and I 'bout bust out laughing but I held it in. As I neared I stared him down with slitted eyes, head cocked upwards a little to the side; then just as I passed I mooned my face right at him. He squirmed and fidgeted and looked down.

It was a long holiday weekend, Independence Day for the United States of America. It was around 1 p.m. on Thursday, and the judge was gone until Monday or Tuesday, which was the earliest we could get arraigned and begin the long process of preparing for trial. The girls were temporarily put in a cell close to ours, and we could talk through the bars for a couple hours before they were moved to some other part of the county jail.

Our cell was one big cage set inside a rectangular room painted light blue a long time ago, bars set a couple feet in on all sides from the walls. Two small rectangular windows were at the very top of the back wall. The cage held four freestanding sets of stainless steel bunk beds, each with a foam pad and a sheet. There were other inmates, all Mexican. The toilet was inside a notch in the wall, right in front of everybody, offering no privacy except for the little fly-swatter of a hinged quarter-door, and filthy with piss and shit. We were issued the standard orange or blue jumpsuits, socks and black plastic sandals, a Styrofoam cup, a three-inch pencil, and a three-inch toothbrush.

We'd had no intentions of posting bail, even if we could've afforded it. Nor did we plan on eating at any time while we were in here, even if there'd been something we'd want to touch. We were on hunger strike.

When the guards were gone, I climbed the cage like a monkey. Getting up as high as possible, and twisting my head to the side, I could just barely see out the window. I could see the top of the American flag down there flying in front of the courthouse. It let me know which way the prairie winds were blowing. I climbed and roamed around the cage, pacing, thinking. Scott slept, and we didn't talk for the rest of the weekend. I didn't know him.

Some of the Mexican guys came up and wanted to know what I was in for. They had a hard time understanding when I told them it was for the *perritos* of the *pradera*. They were all in for drugs and piled-up traffic violations and weapons shit, regular knucklehead shit. One guy'd been in this same cell over a year. My bunk was at the end of the room; it was available because it was the farthest from the TV.

I took the top bunk; the one below was empty. The only reason there were even this many people here in this High Plains county outpost was because I-70 ran past town on its way east into Kansas and beyond.

Pretty soon everybody noticed I wasn't being sociable. They all stayed bunched up at the other end in front of the tv, or playing cards on the table. I didn't see how people could eat three meals a day, starting at 5 in the morning, then go right back to sleep and do nothing, no exercise, no nothing, with the last meal at 4. I'd fill with shit and die if I did that.

I fasted, drank the nasty tap water, and withdrew into myself, climbing the cage every once in a while day or night to look out the window. My energy began to sap from lack of food, but it was nothing I hadn't handled before. The guards and deputies refused to give me anything to clean the toilet when I asked them, and taunted me with stupid jokes about how they were going to make me eat, and that my lunch would be prairie dogs. Soon I didn't even hear them. It was an ongoing accumulation of hours. This was what I was doing, right now. This was where I was, right now.

I thought about my new friend Paula, who was very voluptuous. She wore black capri pants and these dainty little jeweled, thong sandals that showed off her painted toenails. Since I'd been back out West I'd been helping Paula hand-rescue prairie dogs who were in imminent danger of poison gas attack or bulldozing. We'd quickly become friends in a fast-moving new movement for change on the prairie. She'd shown me things I didn't know about prairie dogs, like how they speak an actual, documented, complex language. And how their underground apartments had separate living quarters, bedrooms, bathrooms, even landings. Prairie dogs had been around for a million years, and had developed a culture and civilization that works. I'd do anything for those little dudes. I'd seen a guy — from the Varmint Militia or Red Mist Society — wearing a t-shirt that had a full color painting of a prairie dog with his head exploding in a gusher of blood, and the words "This is your brain on hollow points" written on it. It had been all I could do to hold myself back. She'd told me it wasn't worth it — even though she was the type to lean out the passenger window while I was driving and yell at and flip off passing drivers of cattle hauler trucks, her large boobs in her little v-necked shirt I'm sure causing the trucker all kind of confusion.

But Nicole, who was fierce and militant and different in her own way, and never met a jail cell she wouldn't go to if necessary, took me aside one day and told me a parable. She told me the story of a woman walking along a river one day, only to be shocked and horrified to see a live baby floating down with the current, waving its arms and wailing. The woman jumps in to save the baby, and drags herself and the baby dripping onto the shore, where she is thrilled to have saved it. No sooner has she done so when she sees another baby coming down the river, so she jumps back in, catches the baby and, coughing and sputtering, hair tangling in her face, claws herself one-armed back up onto the muddy riverbank. Saved another one! Catching her breath, she is thrilled that she's been able to save both babies, who are now crawling and wallowing around and wiggling their butts and all that, like little animals on the grassy bank. As she wipes her face with the bottom of her wet t-shirt, only to realize that won't do any good because her shirt is wet too, the woman lets her shirt back down and sees yet another baby coming down the river.

Agitated now, she jumps in and saves that one too. But again, as she gets up onto the bank, she sees another, and another, and soon they are coming down in a regular stream of crying, drowning babies. She clutches at her hair and her face, and feels certain that the world must be ending. How could such a horrible thing be happening?

She is horrified that she is ultimately so helpless. She can't keep jumping in and saving each of these babies! More and more babies pour down the river. Still, she snags as many as she can, wrenching herself apart inside for all the ones she is letting pass by, to ultimately die.

Finally, half-drowned, bedraggled, worn out and horrified with the world, she suddenly gets an idea. She storms upstream, traveling miles and miles, tearing her body through rose bushes and sunflowers and burrs, following its winding course, trying to stay focused on where she's headed even as dozens of babies splash by in the water, wailing and crying. At last, in sight, she sees her mark. A group of people is standing at water's edge, throwing all the town's babies into the river. She resists the urge to charge into them, rushes to the town, going door to door to get help, and forms a crew that streams down and stops the evil people from throwing in the babies.

Well, Nicole didn't tell it exactly like that, I thought to myself, sitting cross-legged on the metal bunk. But you get the point. The point was — is — we can drive ourselves crazy trying to save as many individuals as we can. Working to save the individual will always be very important and honorable. But some of us have to storm upstream and work to stop the problem at its source.

I lay back on the hard bed, folding my hands behind my head. The tv and lights were shut off at 10 p.m., leaving only little night lights that cast the jail cell in a dim yellow glow.

And I felt like I was a cell myself, a different kind of cell, a living tiny cell within the body of Earth, staying alive by learning, growing, adapting.

On the third or fourth night, late, everybody asleep, I sat upright cross-legged, keeping my bare back very straight, breathing deeply, quietly, in and out, flushing my organs with oxygenated blood, wearing only my prison blues, the cord loosely tied around my waist. Time passed. Something was building outside.

The old building began to creak. I could just barely hear it, but I couldn't yet *feel* it. I needed to feel it. Winds outside, strong, getting stronger, pushing into the old prairie limestone edifice... A High Plains thunderstorm was developing. Winds howled and whistled. They pushed harder, and soon, finally, I swore I felt the building move, ever so slightly.

Alert like a wild animal, through slitted eyes, I looked around the cage. Everybody else was deep asleep. Thunder suddenly cracked, right overhead, cracking the silent universe. One of the Mexican dudes, the tall one, leaned up on one elbow, sheet still half over his shoulder, unable to keep his eyes open. "Yeah I'll be there!" he said, blinking, looking around the room, sleep drool all up in his mouth. "I said I'll be there!" He plopped back down and slipped all the way under his sheet, head disappearing.

Again I looked around the cage. Nobody stirred.

Lengthening my spine upwards, squaring my hips, closing my eyes, I placed my hand over my face, and listened as intently as I could. I began to feel the wind's push against the outer walls of the building, feel it pushing into cracks and crevices and weak spots. The building shook. I heard humming and a sharp scissor-like sound, and I realized that the wind had snagged under the edges of the roof, was girdling around it.

Lift…. *up, lift up, lift… UP.* Thunder again cracked, a primal boom that causes faces to uplift into a splitting sky. Finally, the drop came, and the rain and hail began pounding furiously into the windows and roof.

And I knew then that all the animals I thought had died, had been killed, were still here. The herds of buffalo, tens of millions of them, were back, streaming up out of their Shadow World portal. The billions of prairie dogs were back, jumping up and yipping as the first flare of sunlight flashes across the curve of the morning plain. Millions of antelope, elk, bighorn sheep, lions, wolves, eagles, coyotes, ferrets, butterflies and lek-dancing prairie chickens… Endless flocks of storm-and freedom-tossed cranes, ducks, geese, swans, quail and songbirds… Boat-sized fishes roiling in the warm, flooding river waters. Snakes mating in writhing coils under the hot Sun. Badgers and tiny swift foxes digging their dens. Insects scurrying at the grass roots, buzzing in the skies, singing up to the stars at night. Nighthawks and burrowing owls wheeling through the air; jaguars returning to lush prairies as thick with floral life as tropical rainforests. And yellow grizzly bears, massive in size, guard hairs bleached yellow by the intense light of the prairie sun, rolling over on their backs in the yellow grasses, batting their dumb cubs with fleshy paws the size of swinging saloon doors.

Breathing upward from my diaphragm, hand over my face, I knew that this time of bloodshed, suffering and sorrow that had gripped this land for so long would be over. Not now, I understood, but within our lifetimes. My life as a single cell on Earth — what I was now, what I had learned after so many mistakes, wrong turns, and missteps — perhaps could split into two, create new living cells, better cells, and they in turn could help create others, all living, all truly, fully alive within themselves and on Earth. And so on. No matter how few in number, it would be real, and it would make a difference. I knew I wouldn't bother breathing another day without the promise of a time 30 or 40 years from now when great cities and small hamlets alike are run entirely with energy from the Sun, when "minority" is a meaningless word, people can again kneel and drink directly from the lakes and streams, and there is equal opportunity, wellness, community and beauty for everyone, including the mighty buffalo survivors, whose brethren and grandchildren will again blacken the yellow grass plains, and smart-mouthed prairie dogs again stretch their million-year old civilization across hundreds of miles of freedom and vitality.

I heard the hard hail stop, then the wind and rains taper off. I could almost feel the old building shudder back into place, dripping.

Without moving a molecule of the cell that was my body, I lifted out and climbed the cage one last time. Funny I didn't even have to hold on. I could see through the black window into the night, and the summer monsoon, that great big glowing cloud out there, sailed off to sea across the plain like a towering spirit, dropping fierce rain and thunder, new life to the ground, to Earth, on all that it passed.

R.I.P. the PASSENGER PIGEON
EXTINCT: September 1st, 1914
1:00 P.M.

Adrián   2006

BREAKING thru GRIEF...
Rejecting all that is HATEFUL and Ugly,
embracing HEALTH and VITALITY.

— The Struggle Continues —

Buffalo Commons
(The American West as Afghanistan)

"What went ye out into the Wilderness to see?"
— Jesus speaking to John the Baptist; Matthew 11:7

"…deliver us from evil."
— The Lord's Prayer

"The West is an interrupted dream. Different groups of people that have come to the West have interrupted the natural evolution of the groups that they found there. And so we have a constant meeting in the West, a constant migration and meeting of groups, and their real story lies in how I think those groups affect each other."
— Rudolfo Anaya

"The worshippers of the All-Merciful are they who tread gently upon the Earth."
— the Qu'ran 25:63

August 2009

It's been over twelve and a half years since I left Crack Valley for the last time and returned West once and for all.

We all know how life leads us to unexpected places.

I lasted about a year in Pueblo, moved down to Albuquerque for two years — where I learned a lot from Animal Protection of New Mexico about running and managing an organization — then moved up to Denver to grow Great Plains Restoration Council into an official non-profit. Finally, in 2001, I came home to Texas for good. I never stopped missing Texas — her subtropical Prairie Earth, heat-twisted oak savannahs, Gulf of Mexico beaches and coastal prairies, and sky-stretching yellow grass Llano Estacado. Now, as I prepare to spend more time in Houston, where we are expanding, I am bringing my own long journey to completion, back to the Texas coast where it all began, where the prairie meets the sea. I cannot wait for what is next.

GPRC got its federal non-profit status in October 1999, after morphing out of direct action rescues of prairie dogs in imminent danger of poison gas attack or shooting. We've become a leader in the emerging Ecological Health movement. Ecological Health is defined as "the interdependent health of humans, animals and ecosystems". Since 2002 we've been developing and honing practices and principles to improve personal health through hands-on prairie restoration projects. Check out our website www.gprc.org for GPRC's trademarked Life Wheel, which is the founding diagram of our work.

When I founded Great Plains Restoration Council, I knew it needed to become a different kind of environmental organization. I wanted a cultural and social movement that thrived like a living art project of renewal, creativity, and work outdoors that improved the physical, mental, emotional and spiritual health of people every step of the way. "The environment" had become separate from our lives, to the great peril of all life, including us.

I also noticed that many environmentalists interacted mainly amongst themselves and often did not share their work, lives, passions and dreams with "the general public", and that there were few people of color involved. There was almost no outreach to communities of color, and a lot of the work seemed to be endless paper battles and litigation sitting behind computer screens.

I needed something different. I mean, we're talking about our living, breathing, gasping Earth and the health and future of all young people! I needed to get people outside and richly into work.

Great Plains Restoration Council is headquartered in Fort Worth, TX. The kids in GPRC's Plains Youth InterACTION, our long-term-tracking youth leadership development program, all face serious challenges and many have great holes in their lives, but through their outdoor work to help themselves and our prairies at the same time, they not only learn new technical skills but also introspection, stamina, value of work, faith in work, faith in self through work, altruism, conflict resolution, tools for cleaner diets and healthier lives, and the "ripple effect" – consequences good or bad of any action.

It's a dug-in process, and no miraculous change occurs overnight, but partnering with them through place-based education, service learning, and skills-training in a trust and motivational environment, all in service of the ecosystems which give us life, allows them to improve their life outcomes, develop into leaders in life rather than bystanders or helpless victims, and have fun too. This is the 'Body and Earth, Soul and Soil' approach to prairie restoration. True Ecological Health. Damaged lives are healed through healing damaged prairies.

GPRC's motto is "Serving our Youth, Protecting our Prairie Earth." Our kids have developed their own unofficial motto: "By taking care of others, we take care of ourselves." Youth InterACTION has won a "Friend of the EPA Award" from the Environmental Protection Agency.

We've got a committed, diverse Board of Directors, all highly respected professionals.

GPRC has protected two preserves, the 4,600 acre Oglala Prairie Preserve with 6.5 miles frontage directly adjacent to Badlands National Park in South Dakota (created in partnership with Wildlands Restoration Corporation, a private philanthropy trust), and the Fort Worth Prairie Park, a rare tallgrass prairie southwest of Fort Worth.

From 2002 to July 2009, GPRC Oglala Lakota members operated a satellite office and Plains Youth InterACTION program up on Pine Ridge Indian Reservation in South Dakota. The last two years PYIA was jointly run with Thunder Valley Community Development Corporation, a youth-based, Indian-run non-profit based on Pine Ridge. In summer 2008, the Oglala kids came down to Fort Worth to join their Black counterparts for a successful 5 day Plains Youth InterACTION summit. Thunder Valley is now able to take over all South Dakota operations, and from here on out, GPRC will only be working on the Southern Plains. (Aside from helping provide public support for the boundary expansion of Badlands National Park to include our new 4,600-acre Oglala Prairie Preserve).

Now, at the end of summer 2009, we're completing an organization-wide restructuring that allows GPRC to concentrate on a few tightly streamlined goals.

Inside this Great Recession that has throttled the world during the last year, two main 'perfect storm' factors brought us to this point. Even we underestimated how deeply endangered some of our remaining native Southern prairies are, especially tallgrass, and we also became aware that young people need more sustained critical attention and education support. Their challenges are so deep, painful and tangled that even kids who've made it 90% can fall through a crack without sustained, 'bridging' support. With financial resources scarcer all over, we needed to hone into the work areas of greatest need — the Southern Plains and Youth.

So, with our new, streamlined focus, all ecological work is to be engendered through social work. It's our niche and specialty, and GPRC is expanding into Houston with our brand-new Restoration Not Incarceration™ initiative.

In getting this organization up and running, the going was rough, mainly because a.) we had no money, b.) I had no professional training or contacts, c.) I was feeling my way through the dark, and d.) I was still battling my transition from a very introverted person into someone who had to speak out and communicate clear thoughts that pushed the envelope and brought people together. What followed were years and years of 60-80 hour work weeks. Even though the conscious life is one where you may feel endlessly under siege, especially as an activist, I have no regrets.

Committing to *stand* vs. accepting to *fail* shows you how much stronger you really are. For example, in June 2005 I rode my mountain bike solo from Fort Worth to Denver, 1040 miles in 12 days, as both a fundraiser and show of commitment for our youth program. There were times I was so tired pedaling late at night or in the middle of the hot afternoon that the road looked like a pillow. But I've committed my life to success, where failure is not an option, and applied that to Great Plains Restoration Council. I may make deliberate adjustments as life goes along, but *work* gets you to your overarching goals.

In founding GPRC, I had to really be serious about changing the way I was around people. I not only had to invert my introversion, but had to always be on guard that I didn't revert to the old anger anytime I was in public. I needed to deeply commit to my newfound faith in people. I'll say one thing: I never realized what I was missing in not building relationships with people.

I work with all kinds of people, from progressive activists to single mothers to corporate Republican businessmen to grandmas to laborers to the devoutly religious, and everybody in between. Believe it or not, GPRC even has a few ranchers as members. Admittedly, I've found myself surprised.

This journey upwards has been one of faith and stamina. Faith in God and Earth, a gradually increasing faith in self, and finally, a faith in people. I'd be lying if I said that this newfound faith and trust in people hasn't been shaken at times.

Overall though, it's been a positive, challenging experience. I accept all challenges as a personal test of spirit and will. God gives you nothing you can't handle. Spirit is the ultimate wilderness.

Become a seeker, don't be afraid of your journey: A culture of atrocity has become the norm for us. Wherever we look — if we take the time to look — we can see colossal suffering, destruction, waste and killing done if not by our own hands then in our name, yet we're numb and move on. The violence we do to the Earth mirrors the violence we do to each other and often accept into ourselves. Pathological violence has become Perfectly Acceptable Behavior.

Protecting the Earth and our children's health and future are one and the same. That is our crucible and sacrament. It may be a severe scorching test, but it is something holy. By healing the Earth, we heal ourselves.

We need to become a nation of workers again, and involve youth in every way. This is a call for people to come to battle now to fight to protect our children and planet, fight for safe places, work to rebuild our civilization here on Earth.

I've looked at this planet, spinning blue and green in the blackness of space and time, and my soul has echoed with wonder. I've looked at the intensity, intricacy and perfection of life on Earth, and realized I'm beholding an indescribable miracle, largely laid to waste.

We have no evidence of any place like Earth, yet we have smashed ourselves on top of all creation as if we were the only ones here, only to find that same misery and death now catching up to us in the end. Call it the ripple effect, karma, the Muir Web, or simple ecology — the interconnectedness of all life — our health and vitality, or disease and decay, are caught up with everyone else's.

Through practical, hands-on restoration work, we must fiercely demand protection, renewal and rebirth. We cannot stand by or stand still when immediate action is being called for.

One way we can do this is by using prairie restoration to help fight climate change.

Healing the Earth — Healing Ourselves: With climate change a certainty, added to burgeoning ecological collapse, possible "multi-system failure", and the impending 6th mass extinction, we humans are about to be tested like never before. The question is: will we thwart the worst of it by acting now? Nothing short of a global public effort, involving every aspect of our lives, like the American World War II effort on steroids, will make a difference. This is even more critical if we're going to prevent the worldwide melting of Arctic Circle permafrost, which would release billions of tons of highly potent methane, a "time bomb" that will then set off a very dangerous "out gassing" feedback loop more than doubling the amount of carbon in the atmosphere. As a recent Newsweek article states: "… [O]ur fate may be riding on an obscure contest between plants and permafrost."

One thing we can do is restore great swaths of prairies as brand new carbon sinks. To our knowledge, nobody has ever calculated how many billions of tons of carbon were released when the prairies were destroyed.

But recent science is now showing that restoring our damaged native prairies helps fight global warming by soaking up carbon from the atmosphere and storing it in the soil for thousands of years. *And new jobs for people can be provided doing that.*

Without major emission reductions, no carbon sequestration will help mitigate the planetary global warming crisis, but … "Using prairie [restoration projects on already damaged land] … "even when grown on infertile soils" … "would lead to the long-term removal and storage of from 1.2 to 1.8 U.S. tons of carbon dioxide per acre per year. This net removal of atmospheric carbon dioxide could continue for about 100 years, the researchers estimate." (National Science Foundation report, 7 December 2006.) What an opportunity for new green jobs development not to mention great human healing.

Rebuilding large expanses of healthy wild grasslands will be tools in our work belt that jumpstarts a new culture of work and caring, providing multiple benefits simultaneously. Beyond soaking up atmospheric carbon, beyond preventing desertification, these benefits include: refuge for threatened native wildlife and plants already facing the extinction spiral and who now must also deal with climate changes; flood control and renewed water tables; improved river and stream quality; meaningful open space;

greatly enhanced public health; a new exhilaration for what is possible in a time of crisis; and ultimately, a massive expansion of skills-training, educational opportunities, treatment programs, and new green jobs for tens of thousands of young people.

Eventually, the nation could decide to rewild millions of grassland acres straight up the middle of the country, if we're going to get serious about *climate change resilience* — for both people and animals. Native prairies and their indigenous wildlife are particularly suited to withstand severe climate and weather upheavals — but only if given enough room, and relief from human pressure. Avoiding extinction of biodiversity and saving ourselves go hand in hand.

Great Plains Restoration Council is set up to help.

The Plainsman/Plainswoman's Journey: For most of his life, Malcolm X was a divisive, angry leader. Later in life he became introspective and a seeker of knowledge. If he were still alive, he'd be an elder statesman now. His journey ultimately led toward humanity and away from hatred. He understood that his backlash hatred made him little different from his oppressors. The fiery radical plainsman from Nebraska had come of age, and it filled him with earned humility and pride.

Everybody has a deeper story. We can all learn. We can all go on our own journey of introspection, knowledge, consequence, and responsibility.

In the coming years, the uncertainty of our long-term survival — our children's very health and future — will hit the mainstream. As the general public realizes that our basic life support system is dying, and that all our civilization's great works, immense struggles and legendary stories, our music, languages and ability to deeply love another human being may have been for naught, many more people will begin struggling with the grief and depression that I knew for so long. Optimism against multi-system failure comes from dedicated action now. Faith and work. I do it every day. It's not easy, and I still struggle, but we're all stronger than we think we are.

It's up to all of us to create – through practical restoration works involving youth in every step of the way – the new settlement of Planet Earth, the newly defined real Progress and real Enlightenment. Our civilization a hundred years from now, while solemnly honoring the grief and loss of the past but renewed by actions begun today, will be marked by compassion, sensitivity and the *desire to cause less pain*.

In *Reason for Hope*, Jane Goodall wrote, "So here we are, the human ape, half sinner, half saint, with two opposing tendencies inherited from our ancient past pulling us now toward violence, now toward compassion and love."

You've come at last upon your two roads, diverging in the yellow plain.

Like the great blue flocks of passenger pigeons who once thundered up the continent from the Texas prairies to virgin Ohio country so they could give birth in their once safe, sacred groves, like Sethe in Toni Morrison's *Beloved* who struggled barefoot through the wilderness to get across the Ohio River to freedom, we must now all strain to get across the river, into the future, to create safe places, no matter how tired and torn we get. It's not too late. *We can do this!* If we act now.

Lastly, when you go on your journey, please don't be afraid to speak for what is sacred. And please make sure to fill your life with passion, integrity, action and excitement; go home with muddy hands, tired feet and clear eyes.

* * *

Writing this book was difficult because, in order for the reader to experience the journey as if in "real time", I had to relive it. I'm very glad I used to keep a journal; otherwise I might not have been able to go that far down, especially into that murky world of backlash hate and anger that used to consume me. I was so angry I didn't see anything else. Forget about embarrassment at youthful indiscretions; in writing this I found myself dumbfounded at my earlier inability to see, think and process things clearly.

These days, I often feel like I haven't been brave enough, that I could do more.

My heart is not very pure, I still sometimes hate back, sometimes I'm still angry, and I'm *still* tormented and harassed by big men in big gleaming vehicles who think they own the world. I walk a lot because I have a lot of injuries and physical pain from a lifetime of bangs and breaks etc., and walking helps. Some just want to run you down, some (cops) just want to harass, humiliate, search and dominate, while others *still* think I'm just fresh trade out on the street. Sometimes I get very angry and have to cork it down, bottle it up. I'm amazed at their boldness; of course they're always emboldened inside their big metal machines. I'm amazed because I truly do not look like somebody to be fucked with. But I guess when you own everybody and everything, and you got your car or SUV doors locked and your fast gas pedal or gun ready in case anything goes down, you can do whatever you want.

When I'm riding my mountain bike or blading, and people try to curb me or run me off the road, I admit I sometimes wouldn't mind putting a bullet through their head as they speed off laughing. Blam — all over the inside windshield. But I don't carry a piece. I hardly even carry a knife anymore. And me without a knife is like a suburbanite without an SUV.

When it is time for me to die, I will welcome the rest with gladness. One thing: I expressly forbid any autopsy or embalming or any molesting of my body at all. I would regard such a violation of my physical self as worse than rape; it is a forced entry into my body against my will, and my soul would never forgive the person or persons who attacked me like that. I don't subscribe to the common religious thought, which holds the body separate from the spirit. The spirit inhabits my flesh as much as it inhabits the soil. Soul, flesh and soil are all part of each other. I'm to be wrapped in a blanket and taken way out into the prairie, absolutely hidden, facing west, and left for the coyotes and mice (and hopefully wolves, if we've allowed them back by then).

These days, I still go into the Shadow World, though not as often. Most of the time it's just a sense of floating and silence, and temperatures and colors, washes of green, blue and liquid yellow … sometimes just a diaphanous whiteness all around. But sometimes I do go somewhere specific, and it is an incredible, greatly enhanced shadow of something I knew in *this* world, boosted up into future-primeval wildness. Moving air and silence, green plant life streaming in the wind, absolute purity, always leading, always pulling out into open, distant grassland I can see or sense in the distance, even if I'm standing inside the leafy edge of a dark, old-growth forest thick with tree trunks, shining orchids and billowing under story, where 2009 is ancient times. Vein-plumped leaves waxy and green beneath afternoon pre-storm skies darkening, creeks and rivers rushing, the air wild with an undercurrent of something alive, happening. The world pulls your heart out of your chest, the world so clean and connected, so wild and healthy you can drink the water, and walk a thousand miles.

Sometimes I'm floating on my back out in the ocean, off the coast, up and down, weightless, water washing over me but never over my eyes, the Shadow World sun bearing down. Heat is lushly twisting me inside out, and a brown pelican lands nearby with that big splash they always make. He turns his head with that big beak and says something. But when I come back, I can never remember what it was he said.

And sometimes I've made it to the top of a giant hill on my bike to find a stomach-dropping descent below me, and the sky is swirling, drooping in giant reddish-blue clouds and electric mist that lights the evening from horizon to horizon as if a rain has just passed. And I'm so awed and humbled I'm unable to look up; I bow my head, duck my shoulders, eyes watering from the pressure.

Coming back from the Shadow World, of course it takes me a few hours or more to get over the lamenting that immediately sets in.

* * *

As far as the personal life, shit, I still ain't found nobody to kick it with. I dated a few dudes, but they ended up in jail or tried to cut me open when I wanted to split. (Why mf's always tryin' to cut my stomach?)

I've tried to change the pattern, and I'm still hoping I can find somebody that's a good match. I'll say one thing: So much of modern life is profane. Finding somebody who you can share serious, quiet intimacy, deep caring, understanding, and private refuge in each other is difficult. I know I'm picky, but I don't want what my friend, Christopher Brown, in L.A. calls "fake love" where you just convince yourself you've got this tight relate. Another friend thinks the soldier strain of work, of me having my face in the fire for so long, has burnt up all my emotional ability to be able to love another person intimately. It's not true at all.

I feel life would be much easier if I were straight. I've caught flak for saying I wish I were. But I'm just being honest. I am a really imperfect person. Being not straight just represents one more obstacle in life. I know I have to come to a place of self-acceptance, and I'll get there, if for no other reason than I need to be able to help younger people struggling with this same issue.

I have a militant child-protective instinct. I've also been a father for almost a decade now. Years ago a woman asked me to adopt her infant black/ Rican son Kaiden as my own. He's never seen his biological father. While I'd always planned on having my own child, life has a way of telling you things, and he is most definitely my own and I am his. I love him like crazy.

At some point, another child is in my future and Kaiden will get to be a big brother, but for now, with all my responsibilities, he's my priority.

I'm such a family man I'm a fool for it. Kaiden is now eleven, he's already learning martial arts, has been accepted into a magnet school, the girls can't keep away from him, he loves to climb rocks and swim in the Gulf, and do all kinds of active things like his daddy. The days I've spent with my son in Galveston, on that coastal prairie island lit in yellow and blue light, exploring barefoot the remaining natural areas on its east and west ends, swimming in those fertile warm Gulf waters, and just hanging out (or running — Kaiden is a runner and good at spontaneously triggering me to chase him, sort of like how Sid the cat used to do back in the day) on the beach, have been the best experiences in my life. I try hard not to imagine the coming day when the seas rise and drown Galveston Island permanently, most of which is only 3 feet above sea level.

I'm also making sure Kaiden is learning all he needs to know about gangs and drugs and everything else, and while I'm usually the good cop to Karla's "I'll whup your ass!" bad cop, he knows what he'll get from me if he ever even thinks about rolling with a set. We're not worried.

It's nice to be healthy, have family and friends, and enjoy people. I'm on my eleventh life already. I can't imagine even being alive if I weren't vegan. Becoming vegan has allowed me the most explosive athletic and personal power, and an ability to handle huge stress that might otherwise crush a person. You can have the most exhilarating life by getting healthy and giving back. Also, the personal evolution, this new life of sensory awareness, that sets in after being vegan for a while — is almost like a sixth sense of hyper consciousness, sensual experience, and performance.

Regardless of any challenges, you won't ever hear me complain. Daily I see people who have had it much, much worse. And I could be in Darfur or Somalia or Baghdad or a thousand other places. So I count myself very blessed. Walking down the street sometimes feels like a ghetto version of a Coke commercial, with people stepping onto their broke-down porch or stoop to say hi, kids riding their bikes, Chow dogs grumbling and never smiling, their big orange-furry heads resting on their paws, just chilling, watching the whole scene, and pretty Southern black females smiling, waving and calling out "You cookin' for two tonight?" I smile back, even though smiling still makes my face hurt. What a big shift from the wretched old days.

And there are times when, coming in from the backcountry, the juxtaposition still throws me. It's like the ocean waves still pulsing in your bloodstream a day after swimming in the water. I'll be driving or walking somewhere — cleaned up, shaved, fresh haircut and Adidas cologne — and something will catch my eye: the sunset at the western edge of the city, or a remnant savannah of wild grass and Texas live oak trees at dusk, or the edge of a quiet park or green space welling in darkness, and my head gets turned, attention pulled, nostrils flaring …

And everyday, I still automatically shake my boots or shoes out before I put them on. Never know what might have crawled in there, you know?

But hey, reader, I'd like to thank you for coming on this journey with me. I certainly think I live in one of the most amazing, beautiful regions on Earth, which is, I know, odd, because it's been so devastated. I guess it's mainly because of our light and sky, so unbelievably swooning, like no place on Earth. And because of the surety that our Prairie Earth used to match that power above. She will again.

God gives us each day, and then it's gone. Day by day we watch our lives pass, letting clutter and noise blot out the quiet unease or subterranean panic that there could have been something more, or something we could've done better with this day. Something that might've illuminated more of a personal sense of purpose, or a glimpse of God's meaning for us, like sun suddenly sparking through wet. We need to be so incredibly thankful for each day, never be wasteful, and make sure we trade each day for something valued. I want you to have the most meaningful life through personal action.

And I also want you to use me to your highest advantage while I am alive and vital. If all that I've learned goes with me to the grave, that will be a waste. I know that, at my best, I help broken people recover from hurt and despair. Use me while you can.

I hope you will come out to the Great Plains, and see and feel our prairie ocean for the struggling sea she is. Believe in her universal sense and self, not as a patch of fenced-in ground. It's the whole experience, from the thunderstorms and lightning to the ants and buffalo grass roots to the blizzards and windstorms and golden eagles racing through the sky. From the flash of first light across the plain to the hushed blue rose twilight and billion-chorus of otherworldly crickets, to the antelope and prairie dogs and buffaloes and meadowlarks still trying to make it, to the Sun setting in a cloud bank with an underbelly fluff of lemon-white-and-orange ripping out to the swinging north-to-south winds, to the cold-white gauze of stars washed across the black winter sky, to the 20-mile whine of 2 a.m. coyotes across a sudden dead calm. Come experience our world of open country. Life is still here. Getting stronger.

See you at the crossroads …

* * *

Eight miles out on the treeless plain, in the western outback of Pine Ridge Indian Reservation, South Dakota, far from roads and even farther from civilization, I laid out my bedroll on a natural cushion of buffalo grass. In the midst of the largest prairie dog colony left in the United States, all around me the Oglala grassland was alive like few have seen it: prairie dogs barking and talking to each other while obsessively making improvements to their great city, golden eagles soaring, big black and yellow tiger salamanders scratching in the dirt, rabbits, coyotes, swift foxes, burrowing owls, rare migratory song birds nesting and calling softly, antelopes prancing and trying to get downwind of me, trying to figure out what this thing walking on two legs was …

Whole families of prairie dogs stood upright, tawny and sleek like African Meerkats on white earth mounds. A mother prairie dog had her house about five feet from my sprawled-out, tired feet. After the first day she got used to me, and went about sunbathing, grazing in the monsoon-green grass, landscaping her burrow mound or grooming her glistening fur, only occasionally keeping an eye on me.

Nighttime in the prairie outback is never easy, even in the Northern Plains late spring or early summer when total no-glow-on-the-horizon darkness lasts only five hours. Cold comfort from galactic mysteries above does little to quench the oversized feelings of animals and birds and me in the blackness — our sense of aloneness even in each other's company. We are of the Plains, so we are helplessly children of the Sun.

A few birds and animals couldn't control themselves. Because they are beyond human, their moods and expressions are always like uncontrollable symphonies. In the middle of the night, some cried out, or warbled, or squeaked, or murmured. Predawn set a gathering restlessness; the ensuing eastern horizon a rising crescendo glow, and soon everybody was pulling, pulling for the planet to turn until, in that final moment, and gloriously, the Sun flashed across the plain, instantly bathing everybody in bright new light. Prairie dogs threw up their arms and "jump-yipped," their soft belly fur flashing the gold back. Birds flipped in the air, singing, diving, and spinning. A doe antelope turned in the distance and I imagined the wetness of her black eye blazing.

After five weeks of work on the reservation, I'd headed into the primitive back-country of the western part of the rez. The American Indian and the African Arab of going out alone into the dry country, to fast and pray for days and nights at a time, hopefully to return stronger, share a tradition. In Lakota, it's called "*hemblecha*;" in Arabic it is "*Ehtekaf*." It was my time.

In the distance: BANG. Then again. Sound travels far in dry air. My belly clamped cold inside. Nahh, I told myself. Not out here, all the way out in the most remote part of Pine Ridge Rez. I conjured explanations other than my fear. Maybe a military gunnery range that I didn't know about?

I continued my day in denial as the jarring BANGS continued. I was in the middle of what was supposed to be the largest remaining road less area on the Great Plains. This was Indian Country. The killers wouldn't dare come out here, tearing up the road less grassland with their shiny new pickup trucks, blowing up prairie dogs with their elephant rifles. I knew the Oglala Lakota *tocalas* (warrior societies) wouldn't let them.

The BANGS finally stopped. The dry air grew hot and silent. Sweat in dry, sunny country feels different, clean, tiny clear creeks trickling down your dusted ribs and evaporating.

Lightheaded, halfway through my four-day fast, I walked a few miles, exploring. Fasting always makes my senses super-alert, and also brings me closer to the Shadow World; where part of me knows it is OK to die, to slip quietly over the edge, rest.

The Prairies and Plains always have stories to tell, revealed only in person at the last moment, at each step. As I climbed up into the Cedar Bluffs I passed sea animals and petrified trees millions of years old.

The BANGS started again. From on top the rocky table, I scanned the horizon, looking for glinting chrome.

Down below on the other side, half a mile out, I walked up on a week-old shoot. Scores of gut-exploded prairie dogs — pups, adults, yearlings — as well as shot native birds. Bodies slumped or thrown back by the impact, entrails and viscera blown out backs or bellies. Again, not a single scavenger animal had touched any of these exploded bodies. In the hot dry sun and wind, they'd all turned to rigor-mortified gore and fur cardboard. Truck tire tracks gouged the supposed-to-be-road less prairie grassland. I had walked on foot all these miles to get here, and they'd driven with abandon.

The Red Mist Society. The Varmint Militia. High-powered rifles. Thousands of dollars spent on killing equipment, including special shooting tables, spotting scopes, ear guards, elbow pads, goggles and more. They even have their own magazine and websites. These were the people with the big new trucks who drive off-road onto the prairie, set up for the day and blow up prairie dogs for "IVG" — "Instant Visual Gratification" — and "Red Mist" until their rifle barrels get too hot or they run out of 4 inch bullets.

I kept hearing the BANGS. My spiritual quest was (once again) turning into something else. But I was too far away to do anything about the shooting. I only heard the BANGS. Loud echoing BANGS. *This is what it must have been like back in the 1870s to hear those constant gun bangs as the buffalo were rapidly shot down.*

Finally, halfway through my fast, at evening, using my natural three-mile stare, I spotted some killers within range about three or four miles away. They had driven out here over the road less prairie in their giant new pickup truck, believing they were completely alone.

I knew that for survival I'd have to monitor my remaining energy reserves. I still had an eight-mile cross-country trek back to civilization on Friday morning. This was only Tuesday night.

Not yet knowing exactly what I was going to do, unarmed except for a 2 inch pocket knife against their elephant rifles, and resisting my strong hemblecha/ehtekaf need not to be seen by or talk to anyone, especially an enemy, I stalked the terrorists up a dry creek bed. Its overhangs were leafy green from late spring rains. Luscious wild sunflowers, roses and sand plums offered cover.

They didn't see me coming in from the side, a brown ghost in the grass. Peering out at them, almost on top of them now, adrenaline surging through my fasting body, in a split-second I took in the evening light, the blue of the sky, the position of their shooting tables and rifles, a breath, my choice of running into danger, my uncontrolled love for the plains. I cased out the way they were sitting sideways to me 50 yards away, aiming into the colony, facing east and west, padded elbows on their tables, backs to each other. I remembered the times I'd nearly lost my life from "men" like these.

My survival instinct warned me to be careful. It said, "Muthafucka, life is triage. You have your group — that's worth something. Think of the big picture. You're getting good work done now. These dudes could easily blast you — and gladly would. Way out here nobody would ever know."

My justice instinct and sense of self-worth considered how I would feel if I backed down, knowing that within the next few seconds I could save lives.

I stood up and began walking quickly but not running at them, intent on stopping the very next trigger pull. The killers still didn't see me. I waved my arms, not wanting to startle them and make them act like Denver cops in Police District 2. "Sneeze and they'll shoot," we used to say.

"Hey!" I croaked. No sound came out. I hadn't talked for a couple days, not since my drop-off out by the dirt road to Red Shirt Table. "HEY!" It finally came out, scratchy, hoarse.

Both their heads whipped around. Two men in freshly washed long sleeve khaki shirts, one with a big cowboy hat and chinstrap and big red curly beard. The beardless dude put down his rifle and stood up, pushing his clear rubber goggles onto his forehead, staring at me with disbelief, and something else. I eyed the other, who held his rifle in both hands.

I didn't even want to look at them. "This area is closed to shooting," I croaked. My rusty voice made me sound like I was thirteen.

The guy in front of me grew red in the face. "We have permission from the rancher," he said. He had rubber welt marks around his face from the shooting goggles.

I swept my hand back at the bluffs and hills behind me. "I come in peace, but all back there people are fasting and praying. There are plenty of public lands for you to do this on," I said, kicking myself for even making that suggestion. It's interesting what the mind will suddenly and shamelessly sacrifice to get an immediate opening, finding itself stuck with a mortal body that has gotten into a dangerously tight spot. "This area is closed."

"But, we came all the way out here, and we've been planning on this trip for —"

"I said this area is closed." I pushed the words out of my throat so my voice would have more weight.

The two stared at me across the short space and tense silence. A distant meadowlark's voice floated through the air like a liquid butterfly. I noticed my hands were not itchy nor my fingertips trembling, like they sometimes did in confrontation. It was something I hated and distrusted about myself that percentage of fear, which I think is worthless, coupled with the anger the adrenaline, the aggression, which I used to have no control over.

I was actually peaceful. I was standing within a few feet of the ugliest kind of people on Earth, bathed in the most unbearably beautiful light on Earth. I realized that this contradictory moment represents exactly the modern American Great Plains.

"O.K.," the guy in front of me said, eyeing me hard. "I guess we'll pack up and leave ..." He stepped backward to his pickup, facing me.

The armed bearded guy and me looked at him in amazement.

The guy made it to the truck turned and began packing it in, keeping me in side view. His bearded friend shook his head angrily and followed.

I walked west into the grass about 100 yards and sat down, watching to make sure they did leave, and so they would not know where I might be camped.

With my arms loosely folded over my knees, the late sunlight clear and yellow in the spring-green prairie grass, I cringed as their big truck tires crushed new tracks through the virgin grass as they headed north, going up a slow rise. The sun reflected off the truck's shiny new silver sides. It disappeared over the hill. On the prairie dog mounds all around lay freshly exploded pieces of prairie dogs and red sprays.

I thought about how I have made a lifetime practice of seeing people before they see me. I'm good at it, and it has made the difference many times. As I began walking back toward my hidden spot out on the prairie, I realized they'd been so focused on their killing I could easily have snuck up on them and taken their guns — first one, and then the other at gunpoint — and shot up their truck.

Or even —

Nobody would ever know.

But I didn't. I'd actually said something like, "I come in peace."

Diplomacy, not war. Internal and external. Wiser older women I know across North America confide intimately about the darkness before the dawn. They warn to be careful of whose energies we get pulled into.

I have a small family now. I'd much rather work hard for the world's future than worry for it.

Years ago, a gorgeous inner city mural of twisting vines and toiling brown and black bodies proclaimed Earth's survival revolution: *¡La lucha Continua! Al nidal mustamir!* The Struggle Continues!

Far out on a tattered remnant of the once-great North American prairie, on a pastel-lit, late spring evening, the air aching with the clean, sweet smell of Earth's raw vitality measured in grass, something made me stop and turn. I immediately dropped to the ground. The big shiny silver truck had reappeared, and was heading this way.

A plainsman or plainswoman is ultimately somebody who embarks on a physical and/or spiritual journey through challenges, treachery, potential danger and uncertain outcome. At journey's end, one hopefully is wiser, stronger-hearted, changed. Different. This kind of journey has its roots in the most ancient lore of humankind.

Perhaps most people won't become seekers, won't take their journey under the Sun, due to fear of solemn personal responsibilities that might reveal themselves. But God and Earth have always offered each person everything needed to privately seek and understand wisdom on the deepest personal level, and continuously grow. I see the quest for truth, healing, community, and *action now* as the only hope for modern humankind.

The best of the future has nothing to do with hatred and killing, but simply people reconnecting with themselves, each other, and our sacred, shattered Earth.

* * *

"The Old Ones tell the stories
of the time when words were like magic,
and the People and Animals talked.
They mean, *to each other*.
Can you Imagine that?"

— Susan Ring, *Ravenous*

The End

GREAT PLAINS RESTORATION COUNCIL'S 12 COMPONENTS OF ECOLOGICAL HEALTH

— **Create Safe Places for people and wildlife.** Work to protect, restore and connect wildlands.

— **Protect, teach and serve young people.** Ensure that youth interact with nature, and that they learn nature is not made up of objects but is a community of living beings and interwoven relationships that includes us.

— **Understand consequences of actions.** Accept personal responsibility.

— **Strive to cause less pain to others,** whether it is to people, animals, yourself or Earth.

— **Embrace vitality.** Eat clean and low on the food chain (preferably plant-based). Reject factory farming, reduce your carbon footprint, exercise daily, and drink at least half a gallon of pure water each day.

— **Embrace earned confidence and humility.** Reject arrogance, waste, violence, hatred and ugliness.

— **Live like a watershed.** Become an ecosystem participant wherever you live. We all live downstream.

— **Embrace physical work; fear no mental challenge.** Becoming unbreakable — building stamina that leads to resilience — is perhaps the most important foundation you can build for yourself and the new millennium. *"We're all stronger than we think we are."*

— **Fight Environmental Injustice pollution** as the act of violence it is.

— **Seek peace and health-based solutions** over endless conflict; claim the same over endless despair.

— **Give thanks; get outdoors** with our living, breathing Earth.

— **Seek silence, wisdom, deeper thought and personal growth** for the rest of your life.

BIBLIOGRAPHY

Beston, Henry. <u>The Outermost House.</u> New York: Penguin Books, 1928.

Black Elk and Neihardt, John. <u>Black Elk Speaks: The Story of a Holy Man of the Oglala Sioux</u>. Lincoln: University of Nebraska Press, 1932.

Breitman, George, ed. <u>Malcolm X Speaks</u>. New York: Grove Press, 1965.

Brown, Dee. <u>Bury My Heart at Wounded Knee</u>. New York: Holt, Rinehart and Winston, 1970.

Frank, Anne. <u>The Diary of Anne Frank</u>. New York: Contact Press, 1952.

Gibran, Khalil. <u>The Prophet</u>. New York: Alfred A. Knopf, 1923.

Gold, Julie R. "From A Distance." Perf. by Bette Midler. Some People's Lives. Atlantic, 1990.

Goodall, Jane. <u>Reason for Hope: A Spiritual Journey</u>. New York: Warner Books, 1999.

Guterl, Fred. "It's Too Late to Stop Global Warming." <u>Newsweek</u>. August 24–31, 2009.

Izzard, Bob. <u>Adobe Walls Wars</u>. Amarillo: Tangleaire Press, 1993.

McClung, Robert M. <u>Lost Wild America: The Story of Our Extinct and Vanishing Wildlife</u>. New York: William Morrow, 1969.

McLuhan, T.C., comp. <u>Touch the Earth</u>. New York: Pocket Books, 1972.

"Nas: The mature voice of hip-hop." Associated Press Interview, 4 January, 2005.

"This is What Peace Looks Like: Watts, Los Angeles. The Satya Interview with Aqeela Sherrills." Satya, November 2002.

Sheldrake, Rupert. The Rebirth of Nature: The Greening of Science and God. London: Century, 1990.

Smiley, Tavis. Doing What's Right: How to Fight for What You Believe — And Make a Difference. New York: Anchor Books, 2000.

Smith, Sherry L. The View From Officer's Row: Army Perceptions of Western Indians. Tucson: University of Arizona Press, 1990.

Photography credits for visual tour in the back of *Ghetto Plainsman*:
   – Bison close up; Dan Licht, Pronghorn Productions
   – Prairie dog pups; Sandy Nervig
   – Buffalo hanging, Yellowstone National Park; Mike Mease/Buffalo Field Campaign
   – Prairie dog blasted, SD; J. Manos
   – Magpie hanging; J. Manos
   – 7 Coyotes aerial-gunned, 2 more up the road, Rita Blanca National Grassland, TX; J. Manos
   – Mule deer doe hanging; J. Manos
   – Prairie dog killers and truck on road less area; J. Manos
   – Texas Jaguar hanging (photo at Laguna Atascosa National Wildlife Refuge Visitor Center); J. Manos
   – Texas buffalo survivor confined to 330 acres, Caprock Canyons State Park; J. Manos
   – Ana holding Malaya who was blinded in poison gas attack; J. Manos
   – Youth summit, nature (at Fort Worth Nature Refuge); Lisa Callamaro
   – Plains Youth InterACTION prairie restoration crew, Fort Worth Prairie Park before spring green-up, March 2009; GPRC
   – Canadian River swoon, northeastern New Mexico plains; J. Manos
   – Cyrene Inman and the coyote scramble; J. Manos
   – Tallgrass Spring 2007, Fort Worth Prairie Park; J. Manos
   – Doris and GPRC Grass Creek restoration crew, Pine Ridge Indian Reservation, SD; GPRC
   – Youth summit, dancing; Lisa Callamaro
   – Paula and Walking Stick; J. Manos
   – First buffalo in the grass in 150 years, Fort Worth Prairie Park; J. Manos
   – GPRC youth workers and chaperone in Texas, Plains Youth InterACTION Summit, Summer 2003; Jean Belille
   For clarity, we added the word "Texas" to the bottom of the hanging jaguar photo because the Rio Grande runs through multiple U.S and Mexican states.
   Jim Brandenburg photographs inspired the prairie dog illustration by Adrian Torres.
   Adrian Torres, illustrator for *Ghetto Plainsman*, lives in Conil de la Frontera, on the Southern coast of Spain, and can see Africa from the beach. His excellent artwork, and contact information, can be viewed at http://www.adriantorresart.com.

The American West
They Don't Tell You About

Yellowstone buffalo

Prairie dog

Magpie

The American West
They Don't Tell You About

Coyotes

Mule deer doe

Jaguars once roamed the area along with mountain lions as recently as the late 1940s. The cat in this photograph was killed near San Benito in January, 1946. It was the last documented jaguar killed in the Rio Grande Valley, Texas.

Jaguar

Prairie dog killers

Great Plains Restoration Council's American West

Great Plains Restoration Council's

American West

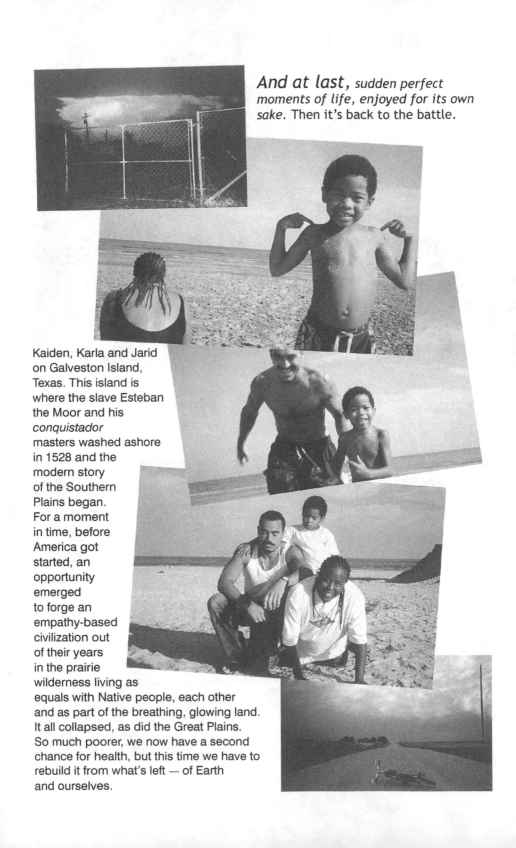

And at last, *sudden perfect moments of life, enjoyed for its own sake.* Then it's back to the battle.

Kaiden, Karla and Jarid on Galveston Island, Texas. This island is where the slave Esteban the Moor and his *conquistador* masters washed ashore in 1528 and the modern story of the Southern Plains began. For a moment in time, before America got started, an opportunity emerged to forge an empathy-based civilization out of their years in the prairie wilderness living as equals with Native people, each other and as part of the breathing, glowing land. It all collapsed, as did the Great Plains. So much poorer, we now have a second chance for health, but this time we have to rebuild it from what's left — of Earth and ourselves.

About the Author

Jarid Manos is an American writer and activist. He is Founder and Chief Executive Officer of Great Plains Restoration Council, a non-profit organization based in Fort Worth and Houston, Texas. GPRC's three main programs are Plains Youth InterACTION™, Restoration Not Incarceration™, and Your Health Outdoors™. Manos has been published or featured in media across the U.S. and several other countries. He is a featured guest speaker at universities, conferences, organizations, churches (and other places of faith), jails, events, businesses, schools and other places nationwide.